Funding of Political Parties
and Election Campaigns

A Handbook on Political Finance

Funding of Political Parties and Election Campaigns

A Handbook on Political Finance

Editors:
Elin Falguera
Samuel Jones
Magnus Ohman

Contributors:
Julie Ballington
Elin Falguera
Muriel Kahane
Juan Fernando Londoño
Karl-Heinz Nassmacher
Magnus Ohman
Daniela R. Piccio
Fredrik Sjöberg
Daniel Smilov
Andreas Ufen
Daniel Zovatto

Political Parties, Participation and Representation

© International Institute for Democracy and Electoral Assistance 2014
Reprinted 2015

International IDEA
Strömsborg, SE-103 34, STOCKHOLM, SWEDEN
Tel: +46 8 698 37 00, fax: +46 8 20 24 22
E-mail: info@idea.int, website: www.idea.int

International IDEA publications are independent of specific national or political interests. Views expressed in this publication do not necessarily represent the views of International IDEA, its Board or its Council members.

Graphic design by: Turbo Design, Ramallah
Cover illustration: © Ellen Isaacs
Printed in Sweden
ISBN: 978-91-87729-24-9

Foreword

Over the course of my career, I have witnessed the negative impact of money on politics and governance. There is increasing evidence that corruption and unregulated donations are exercising undue influence on politics and undermining the integrity of elections. In some countries, money from organized crime has infiltrated politics to gain control over elected officials and public institutions. These threats to democratic politics help explain why large numbers of people around the world are losing faith in politicians and democratic processes. For example, recent research shows that more than two-thirds of Americans trust government less because of the influence of big donors.[1]

The need to regulate uncontrolled, undisclosed and opaque political finance was identified by the Global Commission on Elections, Democracy and Security[2] as a major challenge to the integrity of elections in emerging and mature democracies alike. The Global Commission argued that poorly regulated political finance can diminish political equality, provide opportunities for organized crime to purchase political influence, and undermine public confidence in elections. Indeed, a failure to regulate political finance threatens to hollow out democracy and rob it of its unique strengths.

Citizens all over the world want political parties and governments to represent their views and be responsive to their needs. However, all too often parties are disproportionately representative of the interests of the donors who have largely financed them. If large corporations and rich individuals are able to buy greater influence through large campaign donations, then citizens can lose faith in, or be marginalized from, the political process. This is compounded by a lack of citizen participation in political parties, which further adds to people's alienation from politics.

Although the funding of electoral campaigns and political parties has an important role in the functioning of democracy, unregulated money in politics means that the political playing field is not level. The explosive growth in campaign expenditures fuels the perception that wealth buys political

---

[1] Brennan Center for Justice Research referred to in the report of the Global Commission on Democracy, Elections and Security (2012, p. 34).

[2] The Global Commission on Elections, Democracy and Security was established as a joint initiative of the Kofi Annan Foundation and the International Institute for Democracy and Electoral Assistance (International IDEA). The Commission's 2012 report, *Deepening Democracy: A Strategy for Improving the Integrity of Elections Worldwide*, can be downloaded at http://www.global-commission.org/report

influence and threatens political equality. The abuse of state resources by the ruling party to put itself in an advantageous position also remains a problem in many countries. This lack of a level playing field prohibits the equal participation and representation of all citizens in democratic political processes.

Recent years have seen a growing penetration of transnational organized crime and illicit funds into politics. In Latin America, West Africa and in many other parts of the world, opaque electoral finance and lack of transparency and oversight are providing opportunities for organized crime to gain influence over elected officials by financing their campaigns. This not only undermines democracy, good governance and the rule of law, but also has negative consequences for economic development and the alleviation of poverty.

There is clearly an urgent need to better control political finance. Governments should regulate political donations and expenditures effectively. This will require full transparency and disclosure of donations, with penalties for non-compliance. Effective monitoring and enforcement of regulations are also crucial.

This new publication from International IDEA on political finance around the world is a timely and much-needed contribution to the field of democracy support. It builds on International IDEA's previous work and provides a better understanding of the current state of political finance regulation. It also offers recommendations on reforms for a range of stakeholders and provides concrete suggestions for future research. Through sharing global practices in the field of political finance, this handbook is an important step in safeguarding the integrity of elections and of democratic politics.

Kofi A. Annan

Chair, Global Commission on Elections, Democracy and Security

Preface

Democracy is a system in which the government is controlled by the people, and in which people are considered equals in the exercise of that control. However, unequal access to political finance contributes to an uneven political playing field. The rapid growth of campaign expenditure in many countries has exacerbated this problem. The huge amounts of money involved in some election campaigns makes it impossible for those without access to large private funds to compete on the same level as those who are well funded.

There is no doubt that political parties need access to funds in order to play their part in the political process. At the same time, the role of money in politics is arguably the biggest threat to democracy worldwide today. This threat is clear across all continents—from huge corporate campaign donations in the United States and drug money seeping into politics in Latin America, to corruption scandals throughout Asia and Europe. Evidence shows that large portions of the electorate around the world are left with the perception that their politicians are more concerned about money than about representing citizens' interests.

Recognizing the many challenges of money in politics and the gap in comparative knowledge, International IDEA has been focusing on the topic for over a decade and has worked on a broad range of activities, including stimulating national debates on legal reforms, building institutional capacity and producing global comparative knowledge. This handbook builds on the 2003 International IDEA handbook *Funding of Political Parties and Election Campaigns* and is unique in its global scope. By offering an overview of political finance around the world, its aim is to advance the debate and stimulate action to improve the role of money in politics.

There are a myriad of problems related to money in politics: financial scandals, the abuse of public funds, drug cartels' supply of illicit money to parties, and private corporations funnelling vast sums to party figures in order to garner favours.

Women candidates in particular suffer disproportionately from lack of access to campaign finance. In many countries, unfair allocation of public funds distorts the playing field in favour of ruling parties. This abuse of state resources is particularly problematic in former Soviet countries and Africa.

It is common for money in politics to operate behind closed doors and involve shadowy practices. The exact amounts and origins of donations to political parties or candidates are often unknown. This creates a system that is open to abuse by big business or organized crime, which contributes money in return for influence. Donations seen as an investment by corporate interests have been reported from virtually all regions, not least the older democracies of

North America and Europe. The penetration of illicit funds into politics poses a particular danger to democracy and its institutions on all continents. This is especially so along the Latin American drug-trafficking corridor stretching from the Andean region to Mexico, where drugs money has infiltrated political life and elections.

In all regions of the world there is a deeply worrying trend of money in politics drowning out the voices of ordinary citizens. For a democracy to be healthy, it must revolve, first and foremost, around the citizen. And for a democracy to be sustainable, it requires transparent, accountable and inclusive political parties that can channel the demands of the people and truly represent them.

Attempts to tackle these challenges through political finance laws and regulations are often undermined by a lack of political will or capacity, as well as poorly designed and enforced measures.

This handbook addresses these and other problems of money in politics by analysing political finance regulations around the world and providing guidance for reform. The chapters are divided by region; each assesses the current state of regulations and challenges and offers a series of recommendations to tackle the identified shortcomings. This geographical approach has the benefit of revealing regional trends and patterns, and offers insights into what has (and has not) worked in different contexts. An additional chapter focuses on gender, reflecting the reality that women remain grossly under-represented in politics around the world, while the increasing influence of money in politics perpetuates this inequality. While context is a crucial component of any discussion on political finance, some general recommendations and messages are identified.

An important basis for this work has been International IDEA's Database on Political Finance[3] which received a major revision and update in 2012. We hope that this database, which has become the leading and most exhaustive source on political finance regulation worldwide, will, together with this handbook, provide tools that will be useful to those actors and stakeholders in a position to undertake reforms that will address the numerous challenges of money in politics.

Yves Leterme

Secretary General, International IDEA

---

[3] See http://www.idea.int/political-finance

Acknowledgements

The production of this handbook would not have been possible without the kind support, contributions and expertise of a number of individuals.

First, we would like gratefully to acknowledge the contributions of the authors: Julie Ballington, Elin Falguera, Muriel Kahane, Juan Fernando Londoño, Karl-Heinz Nassmacher, Magnus Ohman, Daniela Piccio, Fredrik Sjöberg, Daniel Smilov, Andreas Ufen and Daniel Zovatto. We also thank Elin Falguera, Samuel Jones and Magnus Ohman for their overall coordination and editing of the handbook.

Our sincere thanks to UN Women for contributing the valuable chapter on 'Women in Politics: Financing for Gender Equality'.

We would also like to thank the following people, who have generously given their time, ideas and insights during the development of this book: Adhy Aman, Raul Avila, Elin Bjarnegård, Andrew Bradley, Catalina Uribe Burcher, Elaine Byrnes, Andrew Ellis, Judith February, Alfonso Ferufino, Harold Jansen, Barbara Jouan, Norm Kelly, Lisa Klein, Michael Koss, Laura Sanz Levia, Paul Lewis, Susan Markham, Percy Medina, Graeme Orr, Rafael Roncagliolo, Delia Ferreira Rubio, Kristen Sample, Victor Shale, Pilar Tello, Wondwosen Teshome, Dirk Tromsa, Alejandro Urízar, Sandra C. Urquiza, Jorge Valladares, Sam van der Staak, Vasil Vashchanka and Lotta Westerberg.

Thanks also go to International IDEA colleagues Millad Matin, Andrea Milla and Nadia Handal Zander. We would also like to express our gratitude to Kelley Friel and Eve Johansson for their highly professional editing of this book. Finally, we would like to extend our thanks and appreciation to International IDEA's Member States.

Contents

Acronyms and abbreviations

AEC	Australian Electoral Commission
ALL	Albanian lek (ALL)
ALP	Australian Labor Party
ANC	African National Congress (South Africa)
ANFREL	Asian Network for Free Elections
APRC	Alliance for Patriotic Reorientation and Construction (the Gambia)
ASEAN	Association of Southeast Asian Nations
AUD	Australian dollar
BDT	Bangladesh taka
BJP	Bharatiya Janata Party (India)
BQ	Bloc Québécois (Canada)
BRL	Brazilian Real
BTN	Bhutanese ngultrum
CAD	Canadian dollar
CAPF	Coalition for Accountable Political Financing (Kenya)
CEDAW	Convention on the Elimination of All Forms of Discrimination against Women
CGP	Clean Government Party (Japan)
CNCCFP	Commission Nationale des Comptes de Campagne et des Financements Politiques
CNE	National Electoral Council (Consejo Nacional Electoral)
CNRT	Conselho Nacional de Reconstrução de Timor (National Congress for Timorese Reconstruction) (Timor-Leste)
CoE	Council of Europe
COP	Colombian peso
COWAN	Country Women's Association of Nigeria
CPC	Conservative Party of Canada
CPP	Cambodian People's Party
CSO	civil society organization
DPJ	Democratic Party of Japan
ECNZ	Electoral Commission in New Zealand
ECUK	Electoral Commission in the UK
EISA	Electoral Institute for Sustainable Democracy in Africa
EMB	electoral management body
EMILY	Early Money Is Like Yeast
EP	European Parliament
EU	European Union
EUR	euro
FEC	Federal Election Commission (USA)
FYROM	Former Yugoslav Republic of Macedonia

GBP	pound sterling
GDP	gross domestic product
GEL	Georgian lari
GRECO	Group of States against Corruption
HUF	Hungarian forint
I$	international dollar
IDASA	Institute for Democracy in Africa
IDR	Indonesian rupiah
IFE	Instituto Federal Electoral (Federal Electoral Institute) (Mexico)
IFES	International Foundation for Electoral Systems
INR	Indian rupee
JPY	Japanese yen
KES	Kenyan shilling
KMT	Kuomintang
KRW	South Korean won
LDP	Liberal Democratic Party (Japan)
MAD	Moroccan dirham
MDC	Movement for Democratic Change (Zimbabwe)
MEP	member of the European Parliament
MP	member of parliament
MPLA	Movimento Popular de Liberaço de Angola (Popular Movement for the Liberation of Angola)
MVR	Maldives rufiyaa
MXN	Mexican peso
MYR	Malaysian ringgit
NDI	National Democratic Institute (USA)
NGN	Nigerian naira
NGO	non-governmental organizations
NOK	Norwegian krones
NPP	New Patriotic Party (Ghana)
NZD	New Zealand dollar
OAS	Organization of American States
ODIHR	Office for Democratic Institutions and Human Rights (OSCE)
OECD	Organisation for Economic Co-operation and Development
OSCE	Organization for Security and Co-operation in Europe
PAC	Political Action Committee (USA)
PAP	People's Action Party (Singapore)
PC	Progressive Conservative Party (Canada)
PEERA	Political Parties, Elections and Referendums Act

PKR	Pakistani rupee
PPEA	Political Parties and Elections Act (UK)
PPP	purchasing power parity
PvdA	Partij van de Arbeid (the Netherlands)
SADC	Southern African Development Community
SGP	Staatkundig-Gereformeerde Partij (the Netherlands)
THB	Thai baht
TI	Transparency International
TRT	Thai Rak Thai (Thailand)
UAH	Ukrainian hryvnia
UK	United Kingdom
UMNO	United Malays National Organization
UMP	Union pour un Mouvement Populaire (Union for a Popular Movement) (France)
UNCAC	United Nations Convention against Corruption
USA	United States of America
USD	US dollar
WIN WIN	Women in the World, International Network (Japan)
WISH	Women in the Senate and House
ZANU-PF	Zimbabwe African National Union – Patriotic Front
ZAR	South African rand

CHAPTER 1

CHAPTER 1

Introduction to Political Finance

Magnus Ohman

Why is political finance important?

In the last few decades there has been a transformation of political rhetoric worldwide. Only a small number of regimes claim to adhere to an ideology of governance other than democracy. Regular elections between competing political parties and movements have become the dominant method of selecting governments. In this process, political parties and candidates need access to money in order to reach out to the electorate and explain their goals and policies, and receive input from the people about their views. Dynamic election campaigns can engage citizens in the electoral process, and active political parties can involve people in the democratic dialogue between elections. Thus political finance has a positive role to play in democracies: it can help strengthen political parties and candidates, and provide opportunities to compete on more equal terms. Indeed, sufficient access to funding that is provided with no strings attached is crucial to the overall vibrancy of an electoral and democratic system—which helps citizens believe in (and trust) politics and politicians.[1]

Unfortunately, under the surface political systems often work rather differently from the ideals of inclusiveness and fair play on which the idea of the democratic process is based. In extreme cases, elections become a mere sham, offering no real choice to the electorate. Such extremes can be caused by many factors, including elite dominance, electoral fraud and the threat (or use) of violence. One of the main factors preventing the political process in many countries from attaining democratic ideals is the influence of money. While money is necessary for democratic politics, it can also be a tool for some to unduly influence the political process by buying votes or influencing policy decisions. For example, interest groups may buy access to the corridors of power or issue outright bribes to decision makers. Foreign interests and criminal groups use money to manipulate politics in their favour, while government parties use state resources to maintain their grip on power.

The flows of money through the political sphere can threaten key democratic values. Politicians become less responsive and accountable to voters if they are too closely tied to financiers, and the equality of political competition is skewed if access to funds becomes a determining factor. The desire of various actors to hide how they raise and spend money on political activities can seriously hurt the transparency of the political process. Around the world, awareness has gradually been building that organizing well-administered elections does nothing for democracy if the outcome is decided by the banknote rather than the ballot.

The open and transparent funding of parties and candidates is crucial in the fight against corruption and to gain and maintain citizens' trust in politics. Among other things, transparency helps level the playing field by exposing and punishing undue influence over politicians, protects against the infiltration of illicit money into politics, and encourages parties and candidates to adhere to the rules. This need for transparency in the role of money in politics has been recognised internationally through the United Nations Convention against Corruption (UNCAC), which states that countries should 'consider taking appropriate legislative and administrative measures… to enhance transparency in the funding of candidatures for elected public office and, where applicable, the funding of political parties'.[2]

In general terms, *political finance* refers to all money in the political process. While many interconnected areas relate to money in politics, it is beyond the scope of this handbook to cover them all. This publication focuses on the subjects most closely related to the process of electoral democracy. We therefore define political finance as the (legal and illegal) financing of ongoing political party activities and electoral campaigns (in particular, campaigns by candidates and political parties, but also by third parties).

Political finance around the world currently poses many challenges. In an attempt to address these challenges, all countries now have at least some regulations concerning political finance. In many cases, however, effectively enforcing these regulations has proved to be a major challenge. Many problems—ranging from the penetration of illicit funds and criminal networks into politics to the high costs of electoral politics and the undue influence of business interests—are exacerbated by badly designed regulations and poor enforcement. The internal behaviour of political parties toward money is also key to tackling the myriad challenges. A lack of grass-roots financial support from the party, the abuse of state resources, a lack of political will to make the necessary changes and the design of political finance regulations are all closely related to internal party finance behaviour. An analysis of the relationship between gender and political finance reveals further challenges, not least women's unequal access to funds.

Political finance regulations

Various attempts have been made around the world to manage political finance, with varying degrees of success. While some countries have grappled with how to control money in politics for centuries, in most places this issue has only come to the attention of legislators during the last few decades. The International IDEA Database on Political Finance (Political Finance Database) shows that all of the 180 countries included use at least some form of regulation of the role of money in politics,[3] such as bans on donations from certain sources, limits on spending and provisions for public funding. Regulations of this kind are now an integral part of political transitions: barely six months after declaring its independence, South Sudan passed a Political Party Law with various political finance provisions, while new legislation in this field was approved by the Libyan National Transitional Council less than five months after the overthrow of the Gaddafi regime.[4]

The goal of such regulations is to prevent certain types of behaviour while creating transparency in how money is raised and spent. Regulations are also needed to provide for the effective enforcement of rules and to sanction those who violate them. No set of rules will work the same way in two different countries or regions—an issue that will be discussed at length in the different regional chapters of this handbook.

The International IDEA Political Finance Database offers free access to data for 180 countries and over 7,000 answers on the nature of their regulations. As a brief introduction, Table 1.1. shows that the level of political finance regulation varies significantly between the different regions discussed in this handbook. The table shows an (admittedly crude) categorization based on the share of regulations in the Political Finance Database that is used in each country. A high level of regulation does not necessarily mean that the rules are stricter than in a country with a low level of regulation, although the regional chapters in this publication bear out the main impressions from the table.

Table 1.1. Levels of political finance regulation per country, by region[5]

Level of regulation in each country[6]	Africa	Americas	Asia	Eastern, Central & South-eastern Europe and Central Asia	Western Europe	Anglophone	Global
Low	22%	11%	55%	0%	38%	17%	22%
Medium	53%	28%	5%	28%	33%	33%	38%
High	24%	61%	40%	72%	29%	50%	40%

Note: The percentages refer to the proportion of positive answers in a region to the 26 yes/no questions in the International IDEA Political Finance Database.

A higher level of regulation does not necessarily mean that the role of money in politics is more transparent, or that rich competitors have fewer advantages. Indeed, as is discussed in the next chapter, a high level of regulation may not be desirable in all situations, depending on the social-political context and the objectives of regulation in a particular country. It is worth noting that there is considerable variation in the level of political finance regulation that countries in different regions have found to be the most suitable.

Enforcement

Formal rules alone cannot have a significant impact; dedicated work by numerous stakeholders is required to manage the role of money in politics. Reformers must emphasize how political finance regulations can be effectively implemented.

With the increase in political finance regulations around the world, the problem in many countries is how these rules are (or are not) enforced. The institution most often tasked with enforcement is a country's electoral management body, although other bodies, such as government ministries or specific auditing institutions, are also common. International experiences do not indicate that any one of these types of institutions is necessarily better than others. How the institution is organized and its relationship to stakeholders can, however, be of crucial importance, as is discussed under the section 'Enforcing political finance regulations' in the next chapter.

As shown in the regional chapters of this handbook, political parties and candidates often violate regulations with complete impunity, and in some cases political finance sanctions are used as a tool to punish those who oppose the incumbent regime.

This is not to say that the imposition of sanctions is the goal of effective political finance oversight. Whenever possible, it is better for monitoring and enforcement agencies to emphasize positive engagement with stakeholders to encourage them to abide by the rules and increase transparency about where their money comes from and how it is used.

However, failure to punish blatant violations undermines public confidence in the oversight system and makes political competitors less willing to respect the regulations. The issue of enforcement is crucial, and is discussed further below and in the regional chapters.

Internal party finance behaviour

Even if suitable formal regulations are combined with strong enforcement mechanisms, transparent political finance is unlikely to follow unless key political actors are willing to play along; indeed, no democracy can survive unless its main players agree to follow the law (both the spirit and the letter).

Political parties' internal handling of their access to and use of money is the foundation on which the rest of the political finance edifice is built.

Since it is normally the elected representatives of parties who ultimately design and adopt new legislation, how parties and election campaigns manage funds sets the tone for how citizens take part in elections and politics, and how political finance laws and regulations are designed and enforced. Parties' behaviour also affects women's access to funds and ability to campaign on an equal footing with their male counterparts. In short, responsible and well-organized party finances form the cornerstone of the debate on political finance.

Political parties' income often comes from donations, public finance and membership fees.[7] Each of these three categories is usually of a different magnitude and thus requires a different fundraising approach, internal controls and reporting requirements. For instance, attracting private donations requires a combination of fundraising capacities, whereas membership contributions are more connected to building a broad-based grass-roots organization with which citizens are willing to engage; public finance does not require fundraising. Controlling each of these types of fundraising requires different approaches. Public funding is normally easy to monitor, as it tends to arrive in bulk payments from the state. With membership contributions, the risk of money going astray rather than ending up in the party coffers needs to be controlled. The internal control challenge is, however, the greatest regarding medium-sized and large donations. Apart from the risk of the outright theft of such funds, party members may be tempted to withhold such donations from the party accountants in order to support their own political campaigns, or to hide prohibited donations.

The way in which political parties handle their internal finances depends on both their capacity and their political willingness. Parties, especially in young democracies, often struggle to establish a transparent and well-functioning control framework for income and expenditure due to a lack of financial management capacity. Diversified fundraising and strong accounting require professional organizations with trained (often expensive) staff and established support networks. Internal checks and balances that include regular financial accountability to party members are crucial to maintain the trustworthiness that all parties require. In reality, though, political parties are typically underfunded, understaffed organizations that rely on volunteer support and political enthusiasm rather than well-oiled organizational machineries. Parties may also be factionalized and the picture further complicated if party funds are controlled by numerous internal actors, or if party leaders are contributing their own sizeable private funds. Party leaders may even obstruct transparent finances if they perceive such transparency as a threat to their control or influence.

Moreover, and often even more importantly, parties too often cross the line of political integrity out of political opportunism or even fear of criminal retribution. Major funders or criminal networks can form tempting or threatening levers for party leaders wanting to win elections. Withstanding such pressures under circumstances of intense political competition requires both integrity and courage.

These omnipresent challenges, and the difficulty of combating them, have often made political parties the weakest link in the debate on how to control the role of money in politics. Introducing stronger laws is often not enough, if only because laws normally require the support of the political parties themselves. Therefore, no discussion of strengthening political finance structures should overlook the capacity and willingness of the political parties to improve their internal financial control.

About the handbook

Ten years after the launch of the first International IDEA handbook on political finance, this book analyses political finance frameworks around the world today: whether they have improved, what their strengths and weaknesses are by region, and what lessons can be drawn to overcome the weaknesses. Regarding formal regulations, the different chapters draw significantly on the International IDEA Political Finance Database, and unless another source is presented regarding a formal regulation, the information is taken from the Database. The book also compares countries' formal rules (as presented in the International IDEA Political Finance Database) with the reality on the ground: do they work, and if not, why not? The impact of political finance shortcomings on parties, candidates and the overall democratic landscape is also considered.

While it has inherent value as a global overview of political finance, this handbook is particularly targeted toward policy makers, enforcement bodies, political parties, civil society groups and media actors with a stake in political finance issues. The goal is that such stakeholders will be able to draw on the content of this publication to better understand political finance as it relates to them, and to offer suggestions for reform. The overall objective is that this, in turn, will contribute to improving political competition and the democratic process. Each chapter is written by a different author; the book reflects their collected views.

Chapter 2 discusses different types of political finance regulations and presents practical information and advice to those interested in reforming political finance in a particular country. Chapters 3 to 7 constitute regional studies of political finance and review both the regulatory framework and the political reality in Africa; Asia; Latin America; Eastern, Central and South-eastern Europe, and Central Asia; and Northern, Western and Southern Europe. Chapter 8 takes a slightly different approach and analyses six anglophone democracies, whose particular similarities (and differences) allow for valuable comparisons. In each chapter, particular attention is given to the challenges of enforcing the formal rules in each country and region. Other areas assessed include the sources of income of (and spending by) parties and candidates, the enforcement of political finance regulations, and the role of civil society and the media.

While all the regional chapters deal with gender aspects of political finance, Chapter 9 focuses exclusively on the hitherto largely neglected relationship between money in the political process and gender equality in political participation, and analyses worldwide political finance through a gender lens. Discussions of the political participation of women and men often highlight insufficient access to money as a major hindrance for women wishing to run for elected office, but the conclusions drawn from this fact are often limited. Conversely, discussions about political finance seldom take into account the gender impact of different regulations and the behaviour of political stakeholders. Chapter 9 assesses the various financial challenges faced by women running for office, what regulations can be used to improve the situation, and other initiatives women and men can engage in to better level the political playing field. It examines the increasing use of gender-targeted political finance regulations, the impact of regulations that are gender-neutral in their formulation, and the role of political parties in increasing access to funding for female candidates and closing the gender gap.

Each chapter ends by offering recommendations to key stakeholders—especially policy makers, enforcing institutions, political parties, civil society groups and the media—about reforming the role of political finance in the particular region. These recommendations are discussed at a global level in the conclusions in Chapter 10.

Naturally, no publication can deal with all issues regarding money in politics in all countries, and certain delimitations had to be made. For example, the focus is on national-level politics; sub-national regulations and behaviour (which play a central role in federal countries, in particular) are not generally discussed. Also, no direct distinction is made between different types of elections. The dynamics of money in politics is likely to vary between presidential, parliamentary and local elections. The variation may be less about *how much* money is used than *how* money flows—from whom and to whom.

Finally, some countries in the Caribbean, Middle East and Oceania are not covered in the handbook. These are all very interesting countries (not least given the current political changes in the Middle East and the micro-state nature of many countries in the Caribbean and Oceania). However, the rapid changes currently taking place in the Middle East, as well as the practical challenges of including micro-states, have made it difficult to collect sufficient and reliable information on them or to identify trends that appear sufficiently sustainable for the near future. We hope these countries will be covered in forthcoming International IDEA publications on political finance.

Introduction to the regional chapters

Most countries in the world are covered in the regional chapters. The chapter on *Africa* covers all 54 countries on the African continent. That on *Latin America* includes the 20 mainland countries south of the United States. The chapter on *Asia* covers 20 countries from Afghanistan to Indonesia. There are two chapters that cover parts of *Europe*: Chapter 7 on Northern, Western and Southern Europe deals with 24 countries from Portugal in the west to Finland and Greece in the east. The European countries formerly behind the Iron Curtain are covered in Chapter 6 on Eastern, Central and South-eastern Europe and Central Asia, as well as Turkey and former communist states as far east as Kazakhstan (29 countries in total). Chapter 8 on the established anglophone democracies includes Australia, Canada, Ireland, New Zealand, the United Kingdom and the United States.[8]

The Africa chapter shows that although all African countries have regulations on how money is allowed to flow in and out of politics, these formal regulations play a very limited role in how politics function. Apart from limits on donations and spending, this also relates to public funding, which is used in more than two-thirds of African countries, but which almost universally has no more than a symbolic meaning. With some exceptions, African electoral campaigns are largely funded through candidates rather than political parties, and are frequently influenced by clientelistic networks.

The chapter on Asia shows that there is wide variation in how money functions in politics in a region that encompasses countries from Afghanistan to Indonesia to Japan. In many Asian countries, however, there has been a commercialization of politics that has strengthened ties between the political sector and business interests. Reliance on public funding has generally been low, although it is increasing in parts of Asia. Enhanced enforcement of existing political finance regulations is emphasized as crucial for increased transparency in the region.

In Latin America, enforcing regulations is a major problem in many countries. There are also concerns about increasing spending on electoral campaigns in several countries in the region, combined with often-strong ties between the political sector and illicit funding, including from the drug trade. Other countries in the region display an increasing reliance on public funding, and a subsequent fiscal laziness on the part of political parties.

The chapter on Eastern, Central and South-eastern Europe and Central Asia shows how most of these countries have come to regulate political finance in more detail than any other region. The reasons for this phenomenon are many and complex, but one factor is the communist legacy that many countries in the region share, which left behind both a mistrust of political actors and a tradition of state involvement. Problems remain despite (or sometimes because of) these extensive regulations, and abuse of state resources is highlighted as one of the most common challenges.

Northern, Western and Southern Europe are covered in a chapter that shows how these countries are fairly modest in the regulation of political finance. Focus is less on donation and spending bans or limits, and more on provisions to enhance transparency in how money is raised and spent. Of significant concern is a trend of increasing reliance on public funding that goes beyond the balanced approach recommended by regional actors (an average of two-thirds of party funding now comes from public funds, with parties in many countries receiving 70–85 per cent of their income from public means).

Finally, the experience of political finance in established anglophone countries shows that, while there may not be a Westminster model of political finance, there are certain commonalities. These include an unwillingness to have political parties rely on public funding (relative public funding levels are significantly lower than in surrounding countries), and in some cases a reluctance to regulate the activities of political parties and election campaigns in much detail. There are certainly problems in the funding of politics in these countries, including an over-reliance on corporate and trade union funding and the sometimes unregulated involvement of third parties.

The chapter on gender and political finance reviews the role of money in politics from a gender angle in all regions. The concluding chapter draws together the lessons learned from the regional studies, identifies common challenges and offers recommendations to address them.

Before turning to a regional perspective of political finance, the following chapter looks at the wider political context in which reform takes place, as well as the different ways to regulate money in politics and enforce these regulations.

References

Global Commission on Elections, Democracy and Security (2012), *Deepening Democracy: A Strategy for Improving the Integrity of Elections Worldwide*. Stockholm/Geneva: International IDEA and Kofi Annan Foundation.

United Nations Office on Drugs and Crime (UNODC) (2005), *United Nations Convention against Corruption*, available at http://www.unodc.org/unodc/en/ treaties/CAC/, accessed 4 February 2014.

Notes

[1] Global Commission on Elections, Democracy and Security 2012, p. 33.

[2] UNODC 2005, Article 7.3. The UNCAC has 170 state parties as of early 2014.

[3] The International IDEA Political Finance Database is available at http://www.idea.int/ political-finance

[4] South Sudan Political Parties Act 2012 and Libya Electoral Act 2012.

5   The percentages do not add up to 100 per cent in all cases due to rounding.

6   These levels are calculated from the answers to the 26 yes/no questions in the International IDEA Political Finance Database. 'Low' means less than 33 per cent of valid positive answers, 'medium' 34–66 per cent valid positive answers and 'high' above 66 per cent valid positive answers.

7   Other sources of income—such as party-owned business activities, party leaders' private funds and salary deductions of elected party officials—are discussed in the regional chapters in this handbook.

8   The UK and Ireland are covered in Chapter 8 on the anglophone democracies as well as Chapter 7 on Northern, Western and Southern Europe, for two reasons. First, they serve as useful comparisons with other countries in both regional groupings and their omission in one region would therefore leave a gap. Second, since some readers may only read one of the chapters, it makes sense to include them in both.

CHAPTER 2

CHAPTER 2

Getting the Political Finance System Right

Magnus Ohman

Introduction

What is the best way to regulate political finance? What set of regulations can make sure that money is available to political actors in sufficient quantities for them to fulfil their necessary roles in democratic politics, while ensuring that the sources of that money (and how it is used) do not damage the democratic process? Importantly, how can regulations be designed in a way that allows them to be implemented effectively? This chapter takes an overall view of political finance regulations by providing a framework for those interested in political finance reform, while the concluding chapter draws together the lessons learned from the regional studies.

Policy makers and legislators can use this chapter as part of a 'preparatory' exercise to better understand how to control the role of money in politics before beginning a process of law drafting/reform. Different regulatory options are discussed, as well as issues that need to be considered in their application. The factors highlighted here—for example political context, challenges faced and political goals—should all be borne in mind when reading the subsequent regional chapters. Likewise, the outline of different ways to regulate political finance presented in this chapter serves as an introduction to the discussion on regulations in the following chapters.

The best way to reform political finance regulations

A basic understanding of the respective challenges and legal situation in each country, together with a reflection on what the regulations should ultimately aim to achieve, will give policy makers a greater understanding of the regulations that need to be put in place or reformed in their country. In the handbook, this discussion is built on three concepts: political goals, context and current regulations.

Figure 2.1. Building blocks for political finance reform

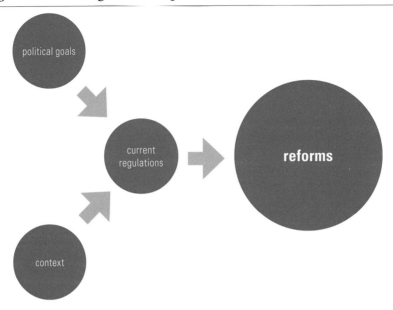

Any reform-minded person must start by considering how they would like democratic politics to be organized, what political system should exist and what form of democratic process is desired. Too often, political finance regulations are the result of reactive measures to crisis situations, and reform discussions start with whether a particular regulation should be used rather than a more holistic consideration of broader issues such as the view/role of political parties and election candidates (and the role of the state in controlling these actors).

These issues form a central part of what is referred to here as the *political goals* (see below for further explanation of this term) which should guide the type of regulations to be put in place. Since the view of what is politically desirable varies significantly between countries, political finance regulations should vary accordingly, even between countries that are otherwise similar. An historical example of this is the regulatory system in Sweden, where a nearly total absence of limitations on the financial behaviour of parties resulted not from negligence, but rather from a political belief that the central role of political parties in Swedish democracy meant that they must be left free from government regulation. As the political culture in Sweden has gradually changed, support for this approach collapsed and, after much debate, new legislation has been developed.

Second, the *context* of each country must be taken into account. Regulations are not created in a vacuum, but in real-world situations with often-formidable challenges. These challenges can affect the desired set of regulations in different ways.

Two aspects are included here under the notion of context. The first is the *political system* as a whole. This includes structural and institutional factors that must be taken into account, as they often have a significant impact on the suitability and effectiveness of different political finance regulations. Examples of important structures are the electoral system and presidentialism versus parliamentarism. The other aspect is the particular set of *challenges* faced by each country relating to money in politics, including a strong influence from wealthy interests, an uneven playing field, a lack of political will to instigate reform and the existence of criminal networks. Such challenges can lead well-intended reforms to have unintended effects, make other reforms ineffective and, in certain cases, prevent reforms from even being initiated.

Some of the most important challenges faced in each region are presented in the regional chapters, and they are elaborated on throughout the discussions about how political finance works in different countries.

After considering the desired goals and the existing political system and regulatory challenges, reform-minded individuals need to look at the existing, or proposed, regulations. A thorough understanding of the current regulatory system is necessary for any well-considered reform effort. The International IDEA Political Finance Database includes detailed information about the regulatory situation in 180 countries. Reform-minded individuals can use this information to compare the regulatory situation in their own countries with those of surrounding countries and further afield. Based on their political goals and understanding of the context, decisions can be made about making necessary and relevant reforms of the current regulations.

In some cases the required reforms may be limited (or non-existent). If, for example, the independence of political parties and candidates is considered the prime concern, then a country that already has limited regulations may already be where (or close to where) it needs to be.

In other cases, significant changes may be needed. If people in a country with very limited regulations feel that a low level of trust in political parties and candidates demands strict political finance regulations, an entirely new set of rules may need to be introduced (and consideration must be given to what may hinder the effective enforcement of such rules).

Political finance reform does not mean piling new regulations on top of existing ones. Some may feel that a particular country that already has a high level of regulation is stifling political competition and that the regulatory system needs to be scaled back to lessen the burden on political parties. Others may feel that instead of a highly regulated but poorly enforced system, it may be better to adopt a system focused on transparency with fewer limitations.[1]

Reform does not always have to involve the legal system. In many cases, the most relevant reforms may involve ways to strengthen the capacity, independence and/or political support of the enforcing institution, so that it can better implement existing legal provisions.

Each of the concepts of political goals, context and regulatory situation will now be considered in turn.

Political goals

It is not possible to determine the most suitable political finance regulations without taking into account the political goals and view of politics (in particular of political parties) in each country. The way that political finance should be regulated needs to be the result of a country's political goals: how the people consider politics in their democratic system as a whole, and in particular how political parties and election campaigns should be organized.

Political traditions and culture vary between countries, and it should not be assumed that what is considered the ideal solution in one country would even be acceptable in another. To put it differently, since there is no form of democratic governance that is preferred everywhere, there is no ultimate method of regulating political finance.

This does not mean that the advantages and disadvantages of different forms of political finance regulations cannot be discussed. To assist the discussion, various dimensions can be considered that impact how political parties and election campaigns, and subsequently political finance, should be viewed (see Figure 2.2.).

Some important dimensions involved are the view of political parties and election campaigns (candidates) as private or public entities on the one hand, and the role of the state/administration on the other. Regarding the former, a view from one end of the spectrum would be that political parties are seen as voluntary grass-roots organizations that organize and support political participation. According to this view, parties should be protected from undue outside interference; excessive rules limiting their freedom would do more harm than good. Their finances should accordingly be considered as primarily their private concern.

At the other end of this spectrum is the view that, notwithstanding their traditional and crucial stand-alone position in the separation of governance powers, the roles of political parties and election campaigns are closer to those of government bodies, similar to election management bodies or courts. According to this view, it is reasonable that party behaviour is more regulated to maximize their utility in the democratic process. This can be done, for example, through levelling the playing field by using spending limits and public funding (what some would consider *manufactured equality*).

Figure 2.2. Examples of considerations for political goals

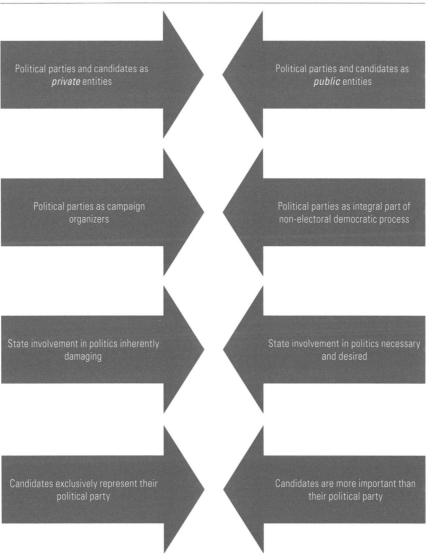

The view of political parties in non-electoral aspects of the democratic process is also important. Particularly in some parts of Europe, it is considered crucial for democracy that political parties are grass-roots-based and active in the democratic debate between elections. In other regions (particularly in the United States), many observers consider political parties as less relevant actors in non-campaign years. Perceptions of this issue are crucial for assessing political finance regulations that support the organizational development of political parties.[2] Of course, some hold that political parties are much less important to democracy than individual candidates; with such a view political finance regulations should encourage independent candidates (for example by giving public funding directly to candidates rather than to political parties).

Another dimension relates to the role of the state (also called administration or government in some countries) in democratic politics.[3] At one end of the scale is the view that any significant state involvement in the functioning of political parties is likely to be detrimental to democracy. Therefore the state should not control how money is raised and spent in politics.[4] With this view, regulations can be used that increase transparency in the sense of providing information to the electorate (for example, requiring political parties and candidates to publish their financial accounts). At the other end of this dimension is the view that the state has an important role in ensuring fairness between political parties and citizens. An example of this is whether donation limits imposed by the state should be viewed as unacceptable limitations on freedom of speech or as part of the state's responsibility to create a level playing field and counteract undue influence from wealthy interests. There are possible overlaps between the dimensions relating to the view of political parties being independent and the view of the state as having an important role. Someone with a positive view of state involvement (but who still sees political parties as predominantly private entities) may be in favour of detailed financial reporting to a state agency, but against these reports being made publicly available. In either case, discussions about what political finance regulations to use should start with a consideration of the political values and goals that are most important.

Context

Two further crucial areas should be considered when discussing political finance regulations: (1) the country's political system and technical factors and (2) the challenges of regulating money in politics.

Political system and financial and technical factors

A number of structural factors in every country significantly impact on the political process. One is the electoral system. In proportional representation systems with closed lists, candidates play a minor role in campaigning, and some countries exclude them from campaign financing altogether (by banning them from receiving or spending any funds in relation to election campaigns). In contrast, in some countries that have majoritarian electoral systems and single-member districts, the focus is almost exclusively on the candidates,[5] yet it must be kept in mind that political parties can be used to exploit loopholes regarding limits and disclosure rules.

Another factor is the governmental structure, in particular presidentialism (not to be confused with a country that is a republic) versus parliamentarism. Political parties are generally weaker in presidential systems and play a more central role in parliamentary systems, which is significant for the regulation of political finance.[6] The overall regime type can also be of particular importance. Whether a country has mainly experienced a one-party system, dominant party, two-party or multiparty system is also a major factor in how politics functions.

Technical aspects may also play a role, such as the penetration of the banking system and information technology in a country. Where all citizens have bank accounts and Internet banking facilities, it can be a good idea to demand that all donations are made electronically to facilitate monitoring. Yet in countries with no banks outside major cities, it would be an unreasonable burden to require candidates to deposit all donations into a designated bank account.

Challenges

More often than not, real life gets in the way of good intentions; this also applies to the field of money in politics. In contrast to the political system factors discussed above (which are not necessarily problematic for political finance control), the challenges discussed here make the role of money in politics problematic from a democratic perspective. Two overall categories of challenges can be distinguished. The first refers to challenges that negatively impact on the role of money in politics in a broader sense, by harming the democratic process. This can include an influx of illicit funds into the political process, widespread vote buying or a particularly uneven electoral playing field. These can be called *political system challenges*.

The other category is more directly connected to the possibility of effectively monitoring political finance; these can be called *political finance control challenges*. A consensus among elite groups not to address political finance issues can block effective reform. In addition, if the state machinery is not independent of the governing party, this can hamper enforcement (abuse of state resources can thereby be both a political finance control challenge and a political system challenge). In particular, a lack of capacity or political support for those responsible for enforcing the political finance regulations is a problem in many countries.

Box 2.1. Common challenges in political finance

Political system challenges

- Unequal access to funding for different political actors
- Ability of wealthy interests to unduly influence politics
- Influx of illicit funding into politics
- Co-optation of politics by business interests
- Abuse of state resources
- Widespread vote buying

Political finance control challenges

- Unsuitable legislation (ambiguous or overly ambitious legislation or rules not suitable for the context)
- Lack of political will to control money in politics
- Popular acceptance of vote buying
- Lack of independence of enforcing institutions
- Biased enforcement of political finance regulations
- Lack of resources for enforcing regulations

The regional chapters will discuss the challenges that are of particular importance in each region (of course there is very large variation in challenges between countries in the same region). Some of the most frequently mentioned challenges are shown in Box 2.1.

It is essential to consider each country's particular challenges when evaluating which political finance regulations are the most suitable. Political system challenges can mean that regulations that would otherwise be considered undesirable may be necessary. For example, even if it is felt that political parties and candidates should be allowed to raise and spend money freely, a particularly unlevel playing field may necessitate spending limits.[7] In other countries, strict disclosure and auditing requirements may be required to counteract the influence of illicit funding in the political sphere.

Political finance control challenges may mean that otherwise-desirable regulations are unsuitable because they would not work or may prove counterproductive. The level of political openness or authoritarianism must therefore also be taken into account. For example, even if strict regulations are desired, a blurring of lines between the government party and the state could mean that giving a theoretically independent state agency a powerful enforcement mandate may lead to the harassment of opposition political parties and candidates. Alternatively, ambitious donation and spending limits may be of no use if there is no independent and capable institution to enforce such regulations. Taken together, the political finance control challenges often lead to a lack of enforcement of regulations.

Ways of regulating political finance

While all countries use at least some form of regulation of the role of money in politics, how they do so varies significantly throughout the world. Information on the regulations used in different countries can be found in the comparative tables in the annexes, with more information in the International IDEA Political Finance Database. Taking into account the political goals and context discussed above, reform-minded individuals can draw conclusions about how political finance should be regulated. This section discusses the main regulatory options that are used in different countries.

Donation bans and limits

In the same way that in most countries the right to vote is limited to adult citizens of the country in question, regulations are often imposed on who has the right to make financial contributions to political parties and candidates. The purpose of donation bans is to completely stop contributions that are seen as particularly damaging to the democratic process. Table 2.1. discusses the rationale behind different types of donation bans.[8]

Table 2.1. The rationale behind different types of donation bans

Type of donation ban	Rationale
Foreign entities	To prevent external/foreign influence; principle of self-determination.
Corporations	To limit influence on financing from vested interests; ensure independence of candidates/parties from special interests.
Public and semi-public entities	To avoid use of public funds for political purposes.
Trade unions (sometimes all forms of legal entities)	To avoid improper influence from organized interest associations, a ban on trade union donations is sometimes used to balance a ban on corporate donations in systems where some parties depend on corporate contacts and others are close to the trade union movement.
Corporations with government contracts	To reduce the risk of quid pro quo donations (i.e., companies make donations in the hope of being awarded government contracts).
Anonymous sources	To ensure transparency of party funding and a greater chance to monitor compliance with political finance regulations.
Indirect donations	To make control of other bans easier to monitor, some countries explicitly ban donations given through another person or entity.

The most common ban is against donations from public institutions to particular political parties and candidates. Such bans target the abuse of state resources (though often not successfully). Foreign donations are also banned in most countries, as are anonymous donations (if anonymous donations are allowed, it becomes very difficult to enforce other forms of donation bans, though some countries allow small anonymous donations to protect the privacy of ordinary donors). Around one in five countries bans corporate donations, and banning donations from trade unions is slightly more common. Direct bans on donations of illicit origin are only used in a handful of countries.

Banning private donations altogether is exceptionally rare (although Tunisia did so in the 2011 National Constituent Assembly elections, forcing candidates to rely on public funding and 'own funds'). Such bans are not usually desired, as they de-link parties from their support base in society, and encourage hidden donations. However, over 40 per cent of the countries analysed use some form of limit on how much eligible donors are allowed to contribute. Unlike donation bans, donation limits do not directly target particular types of interests. Instead, the focus is on limiting the influence that any one donor may have on a political party or candidate, and subsequently on the political process as a whole. Thirty-eight per cent of the countries in the sample limit donations to political parties (as an annual limit and/or in relation to election campaigns), while 30 per cent limit donations to candidates.

The real-life impact of donation limits varies based on their level; if the limit is very high it will have no impact, since it will not reduce donations in practice, while if the limit is very low, donors, political parties and candidates will find ways to get around it. A donation limit that everyone ignores risks undermining confidence in the entire political finance regulatory system. The correct level of donation limits depends on the political goals that the regulation is attempting to achieve and on how able political parties and candidates are to raise sufficient funds from sources other than large donations. Donation limits are notoriously difficult to control, since it is often easy to channel money through other people (sometimes referred to as 'straw donors').

Public funding

A complementary approach to regulating private donations is to give political parties (less frequently candidates) access to money from public sources. If it is done right, the provision of public funding can have a significant positive impact on the role of money in the political process.

Sometimes the purpose of providing public funding is to ensure that all relevant political forces have access to enough resources to reach the electorate, thereby encouraging pluralism and providing the electorate with a wider choice of politicians and policies. Another goal can be to limit the advantage of competitors with access to significant resources by giving everyone access to funds for campaigning. This second idea is unlikely to work unless public funding is combined with limits on donations and/or spending, since the relative gap will not be changed by providing money to both rich and poor. There is a third potential advantage of providing public funding: the threat to withhold it if political parties (or candidates) fail to follow other rules such as spending limits or reporting requirements can prove a highly effective incentive to obey the rules. This will only work if the amount provided is high enough that recipients will adhere to the rules to avoid the risk of losing it.

Public funding can be either direct or indirect; providing money or free or subsidized goods or services. Two issues must be addressed when discussing public funding: (1) who should have a right to receive it (eligibility threshold); and (2) how it should be distributed among those who are eligible (allocation criteria).

Figure 2.3. The provision of direct public funding for political parties

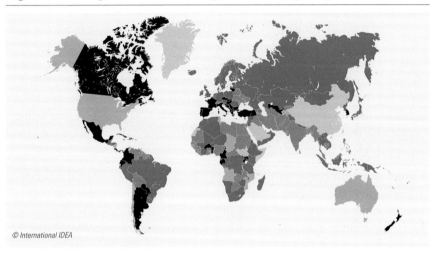

© International IDEA

■ **Yes, regularly provided funding**
■ **Yes, in relation to campaign**
■ **Both**
■ **No**
■ **No data**

Source: International IDEA. This map is based on data collected up to February 2014. Data are continuously updated on the International IDEA Political Finance Database. See http://www.idea.int/political-finance/question.cfm?field=286&region=-1

It may seem fair to decide that all political parties and candidates should have access to public funds; in some countries, all registered political parties receive public funding. However, such an approach creates the risk that people will form parties or run for office simply to get state funding, and it may also be a significant waste of public resources to support parties and candidates that have no support among the electorate. Most countries therefore use a threshold of support that a party must have to gain access to public funding—normally a certain share of the vote in an election or of seats won. Enacting a very high threshold (e.g., 10 per cent of the vote in Bhutan and Malawi) can mean that new political forces find it difficult to establish themselves. The type of eligibility criteria to be used also partly depends on the timing of the distribution (see below). Globally, 21 per cent of countries with direct public funding use a threshold for all such funding based on votes received (on average 3.5 per cent), while 18 per cent limit funding to parties with representation in parliament, and 15 per cent use a combination of these two criteria. Very modest requirements are used in 14 per cent of countries (at most demanding that a party is registered and participates in elections), while the remaining countries use various combinations of eligibility criteria, often with different criteria for different portions of the funding.[9]

Regarding the allocation criteria, it may again seem the most democratic approach to provide all eligible political parties (or candidates) with the same amount of support. However, giving the same level of funding to parties with minimal support among the electorate as to the largest parties is arguably to disregard the views of the voters, and can easily be a waste of taxpayer money (if there are many eligible parties, a lot of money will have to be distributed to make any difference to party politics).[10] There is also the risk of political party fragmentation, as a party split could lead to additional public funds, while a merger may mean parties receive less funds. In some cases, regimes have used this approach to fragment the opposition.

A more common option is therefore to allocate all or some of the funds in proportion to the support a party has received in elections—normally its share of votes or seats. A downside of proportional allocation is that most of the public money may end up with the government party, which arguably needs it the least. Globally, only 7 per cent of the countries in the sample provide funding equally, while 41 per cent use a fully proportional allocation calculation and 29 per cent use a mix of the two.[11]

There are alternative ways to distribute public funds, such as the matching funds system used in many elections in the United States and Germany (though rarely in other countries) in which the government matches all or part of the funds raised privately by political parties or candidates. Such a system supports parties that are active in private fundraising, though critics argue that these systems risk rewarding parties that have good business contacts with additional funds from the public purse. One way to avert this could be to encourage parties and candidates to raise small donations by only matching such donations, as is the case in New York City.[12]

Most countries also provide *indirect* public funding to political parties (and sometimes to candidates). The most common form is free or subsidized access to public media for campaigning purposes, but other examples include tax relief for parties/candidates or their donors, access to public buildings for campaign events and subsidized postage. The advantage of indirect public funding over direct support is that it is easier to control how the funds are used, and there is normally less of a burden on the taxpayer. A disadvantage can be that the support given is not always useful in helping the stakeholders reach the electorate effectively.[13]

When we consider the importance of public funding provided in different countries, we must also consider the timing of the distribution (i.e., campaign assistance provided the day before polling will have little impact)[14] and the amounts provided (are they sufficient to affect political activity?). These issues will be discussed in the regional chapters.

To get the system of public funding right, lawmakers must consider how they wish politics to function in their country, and in particular the role of political parties in the political system. Table 2.2. summarizes the rationale behind the provision of direct public funding, as well as some of the key considerations to be taken into account and choices to be made. Many countries use combinations of these options, such as providing some money equally to all parties and some proportionally according to votes won.

Table 2.2. The rationale and considerations regarding direct public funding

Rationale	Comment	
Help all relevant political forces reach the electorate	The desired level of political pluralism depends on the overall view of politics (see below).	
Decrease the impact of financial differences between rich and poor parties and candidates	If public funding is not combined with donation and/or spending limits, it will not reduce the absolute difference between rich and poor actors.	
Stimulate the good behaviour of recipients	Offering access to public funding can be an effective way to make political parties submit financial reports, include female candidates, etc. May jeopardize the independence of political parties from the state.	
Consideration	**Main options**	**Comment**
Eligibility threshold (who should get access to public assistance?)	No threshold	Maximizes pluralism, but risks political fragmentation and waste of public resources.
	By share of votes won	Ensures access is limited to parties that have some proven popular support (exact level important).
	Parliamentary representation	Excludes irrelevant political parties, but makes it more difficult for new political forces to come forward.
	Number of candidates presented	Ensures that funding is limited to parties that actively participate in elections.

Allocation criteria (how should the money be distributed among those that have reached the threshold?)	All eligible parties get the same amount	Supports pluralism, but may create party fragmentation; risks waste of public funds.
	By vote or seats won	Connects financial support to electoral popularity (but may lead to largest parties getting the bulk of the money).
	Related to candidates fielded	More active parties get more funding (though fielding candidates may not be a good indicator of level of activity).
	Share of expenses reimbursed	Support private fundraising activities (but may reward parties with good business contacts).
Timing of distribution (should funding be given before or after elections, or regularly?)	Regular distribution	Can support party activity between elections, though may not function where party tradition is weak.
	Distribution before an election	Political parties get funding in advance to use in election campaign (eligibility/allocation criteria normally based on earlier electoral results, which may not match current level of popularity).
	Distribution after an election	Funding can be based on current popularity, but disadvantage is that parties have to first raise the money privately to get reimbursed later.
Level of funding (how much money should be paid out?)	What level suits the political democratic goals?	Too little money will have no impact on party/electoral politics, but too much may disconnect parties from the public (and be very unpopular with the people).
Earmarking of funds provided	Electoral or non-electoral use?	Some countries only allow public funds to be used for campaigns; others ban the use of public funds for campaigns (all dependent on the view of parties and elections).
	Connection to other goals, such as gender equality	Can serve positive goals such as enhanced gender equality, youth wings, research arms, etc. (critics argue that it limits the freedom of parties).

Spending bans and limits

While there are many examples of donation bans, few types of spending are banned around the world. Vote buying and the use of public resources for partisan purposes (excluding regulated public funding) are banned almost everywhere, but otherwise there are few examples other than a ban on TV advertising (sometimes on all advertising) used in a limited number of countries.

More common are limits on how much political parties and candidates are allowed to spend in election campaigns. Unlike limits on donations, the purpose is not to regulate the influence of individual donors but rather to reduce the advantages of political parties and candidates with access to large amounts of money. Special cases include candidates who fund their campaigns using their own money, or when party leaders provide the bulk of funding for the party they lead—two phenomena that are common in emerging and some established democracies alike. Although candidates and party leaders can arguably not unduly influence themselves, the advantage they get from their personal wealth can be limited either by extending donation limits to use of own funds or by imposing a spending limit.

Around 30 per cent of all countries limit the amounts that political parties may spend, while over 40 per cent limit candidate spending. Just as with donation limits, the effectiveness of spending limits depends both on whether the limit is set at the right level to curb the advantage of those with access to a lot of money without hindering inclusive and engaging campaigning, and (in particular) on whether they are enforced. Other factors that may have a bearing on effectiveness include the definition of spending (e.g., are staff costs included?) and the time period of any limits (i.e. does the limit cover a long enough period of time to achieve its purpose?).

Figure 2.4. Spending limits for candidates

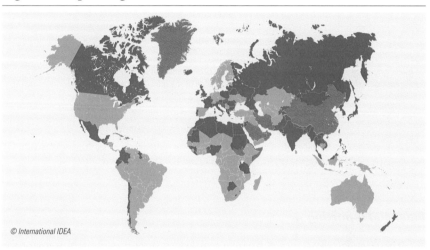

© International IDEA

■ Yes
■ No
■ No data

Source: International IDEA. This map is based on data collected up to February 2014. Data are continuously updated on the International IDEA Political Finance Database. See http://www.idea.int/political-finance/question.cfm?field=286&region=-1

A separate issue is whether limits should be put on campaign spending by actors that are neither political parties nor candidates (so-called third parties). The easiest solution may be to ban anyone who is not directly competing in elections from participating in campaigns, but such an approach would be seen as a violation of human rights in most parts of the world, in particular the freedom of speech.[15] Most countries have no regulations on third-party spending. Of those that do, some impose various limits on spending or require third parties to submit financial reports. This issue is discussed in the regional chapters, in particular Chapter 8 on the established anglophone democracies.

Table 2.3. The rationale and considerations regarding spending limits

Rationale	Comment
Reduce the advantage of candidates with significant access to money	Donation limits may better serve this purpose (if limits are set on how much of her/his private money a candidate can use). A spending limit may impose limitations for parties and candidates that are able to raise a large number of small donations, and small donations are normally considered worth encouraging.
Reduce the overall spending on election campaigns	Very high levels of electoral spending are sometimes seen as morally reprehensible in countries with widespread poverty, and may reduce public confidence in political parties and candidates.

Consideration	Main options	Comment
Calculation	Fixed sum (such as USD 1,000 per party/candidate)	Easy to understand, but does not take into account variations in the size of electoral districts.
	Amount per voter (such as USD 1 in each electoral district, for each party/candidate)	Allows for variation in spending limit where population sizes of electoral districts vary (more money is needed to reach the voters in a larger district); does not take into account variations in *geographical* size of electoral districts.
Explicit amount or inflation indexed	Explicit amount (such as USD 1,000)	Easy to understand, but inflation may quickly reduce the actual value of the limit (this can be avoided by indexing the amount to the inflation rate).
	Multiples of minimum salary	Automatically indexed to inflation, assuming that a minimum salary (or similar) is maintained.
	Multiples of average salary	Less dependent on government policy than minimum salary, but requires reliable statistical data.

Financial reporting

A cornerstone of any political finance regulatory system is the requirement for those involved in politics to submit information about how they raise and spend money. Such reporting has two main purposes. First, this information can help achieve the transparency called for in the United Nations Convention against Corruption (UNCAC), allowing voters to make informed decisions when they go to the polling station. The fear of scandals and of losing public support can serve as a better defence against misbehaviour than any legal sanctions.

The second purpose of reporting requirements is to make it easier for those responsible for enforcing donation and spending bans and limits to oversee whether these rules are being followed. While violators cannot be expected to admit to infringements in their reports, requiring them to provide financial accounts provides a paper trail that can assist further investigations.

At least some form of reporting requirements exists in nearly 90 per cent of countries, normally for both political parties and candidates. Yet some countries with fairly detailed political finance regulations do not require either parties or candidates to report on their finances.

The information required in financial reports varies considerably among countries. Often, the most controversial is whether reports must reveal the identity of donors; this is required in approximately half of the countries with reporting requirements. In some of these countries, the identity of the donor must only be disclosed when (s)he makes contributions above a certain amount.[16] Such provisions seek a balance between transparency and protecting the privacy of those making smaller donations; they also limit the administrative burden on those required to submit reports. Countries also vary regarding whether the reports submitted should be made available to the public. Around 20 per cent of countries have no requirement to make financial reports publicly available, which is against the spirit of the UNCAC provision cited above. Others provide reports that are cumbersome and difficult to access. Ideally, they should be made available online in an easily digestible and searchable format.

Table 2.4. The rationale and considerations regarding financial reporting requirements

Rationale	Comment	
Increase transparency in political finance	Financial reporting is crucial to enhance transparency in line with the UNCAC.	
Facilitate oversight	While theoretically possible, effective oversight of other regulations is very unlikely without financial reporting.	
Consideration	**Main options**	**Comment**
Frequency/timing of reporting (many countries require both the listed options)	Regular reports	In countries where parties are active between elections, their regular financing is important. Even where they are not, only requiring reports for election periods allows parties to circumvent rules by raising and spending money earlier in the process.
	Campaign reports	Where parties are only required to report annually, information about campaign spending may not be available until much later. Reporting during the campaign period can give voters valuable information, but may not be a feasible option in countries with limited human resources.
Entities required to report (most countries use a combination)	Political parties	While candidates raise and spend most of the money in many countries, information about party financing is crucial for transparency.[17]
	Candidates	Where the electoral system focuses fully on political parties, candidates are often not required to submit financial reports. This may be reasonable, but can reduce transparency and allow the circumvention of bans and limits.
	Third parties	Can provide valuable transparency and close loopholes, but it is sometimes difficult to establish what third-party spending is.

What must be reported (most countries use a combination)	Income	The sources of party and campaign funding are important for voters to judge the independence of political parties and candidates.
	Spending	Most countries require reporting on spending, which facilitates control of spending limits and lets voters judge whether parties spend money (including public funding) wisely.
	Assets and debts	Information about sizeable assets and debts is valuable in judging potential conflict of interest (and if the wealth of elected officials changes in between elections).
What information is made public	None	In some countries, financial reports are kept secret by the receiving institution. This protects privacy but does not aid transparency.
	Summaries only	Many countries only publish summaries, but these often provide little transparency.
	All received information	Provides for maximum transparency, but there may be a need to protect the privacy of those making smaller donations.

Enforcing political finance regulations

The most important lesson to learn from the regional chapters in this book, though hardly surprising for anyone with knowledge of politics in general and political finance in particular, is that even the best formal regulations come to nothing if they are not enforced. Any regulation of how political parties and candidates are allowed to raise and spend money must therefore be combined with ways of ensuring that these rules are respected.

When deciding what regulations of political party and campaign finance to use, thought should be given to the enforceability of individual regulations and steps that can facilitate this. Donation limits are notoriously difficult to monitor, since donations are often made in secret. Equally, it is easy to ban corporate donations, but making sure that funds from corporations are not given to political parties via private individuals is much more complicated. Other rules are easier to enforce. For example, to regulate spending on TV advertisements in the Philippines, a limit has been set on the number of minutes per day that any candidate can advertise.[18] Another consideration should be the level of burden that the enforcement of any regulation will place on political parties. If the benefit derived is minimal but the burden on parties is high, one should ask whether the regulation is necessary.

No regulatory framework guarantees the effective enforcement of political finance regulations. Political factors will always play a role, as discussed above and in the regional chapters. The situation is complicated by the fact that in any democratic society, laws controlling the financial behaviour of politicians must be passed by the politicians themselves. Some of them may not be particularly interested in seriously limiting their own chances of raising and spending enough money to get elected or re-elected. The willingness of political parties and other stakeholders to moderate their use of money in the political process is essential for long-term improvements in political finance.

Effective enforcement requires a public institution with a clear mandate and enough independence, resources and willingness to engage with political finance issues. The Organization for Security and Co-operation in Europe's Office for Democratic Institutions and Human Rights and the Venice Commission have argued that 'effective measures should be taken in legislation and in state practice to ensure [the enforcing institution's] independence from political pressure and commitment to impartiality'.[19]

Remarkably, the Political Finance Database shows that in nearly 25 per cent of the countries for which information is available, no institution has a legal mandate to receive financial reports or investigate violations of political finance regulations. Of the countries that do have such designated institutions, the electoral management body is most commonly given this task, though ministries, auditing institutions and bodies created specifically for this purpose are also used. There is significant regional variation in this regard, as is discussed in the regional chapters.

Figure 2.5. Is it specified that a particular institution(s) is responsible for examining financial reports and/or investigating violations?

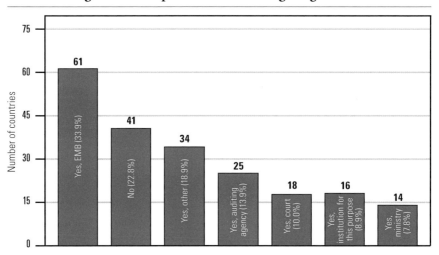

Source: International IDEA. This chart is based on data collected up to February 2014. Data are continuously updated on the International IDEA Political Finance Database. See http://www.idea.int/political-finance/question.cfm?field=294&region=-1

Note: EMB = electoral management body

Public institutions responsible for enforcing political finance regulations must have both the mandate and the capacity necessary to carry out their role effectively—and must act independently and with conviction. This does not mean that they should seek to impose strict penalties for the smallest of violations; positive engagement with political stakeholders will increase their understanding of the need for financial oversight and their willingness to comply. Proportionality and the impact on political pluralism and the democratic process should be considered when imposing any sanctions. Enforcing institutions should also follow general good regulatory practice such as transparency, consistency and accountability.

The requirements for a political finance oversight body are similar to those for institutions that manage electoral processes as a whole. To sum up, these requirements include:

- a clear and sufficient mandate that does not overlap with that of other institutions;
- an inclusive and transparent process of leadership appointments that ensures independence from political pressures and public confidence;
- secured tenure of leadership and staff to protect against undue influence;
- sufficient funding and control over the budget of the institution; and
- the adoption of an attitude within the institution that it will act impartially and transparently and engage with the regulated community to (wherever possible) encourage compliance and prevent violations.

There must also be a range of enforceable, proportional and dissuasive sanctions available to punish violations. Issuing warnings or 'naming and shaming' violators may be effective in contexts in which political parties and candidates fear popular rejection (such an approach is greatly enhanced by making financial data public, thereby allowing media and civil society actors to identify and highlight infringements). However, fines, loss of public funding and even imprisonment may be required to deter more serious legal infringements. Almost all countries have sanctions, at least on paper; fines are the most common form.

One of the most important tasks of enforcing institutions is to make sure that information about how political parties and candidates raise and spend money is made available to the public. This gives journalists the opportunity to track, for example, who provides funding to a particular political party or candidate, and whether this donor benefits from subsequent government contracts or regulations. The media have a crucial role in political finance oversight and the enforcement of the rules. Investigations by journalists have often uncovered more political finance violations than formal reviews by enforcement institutions.

Civil society as a whole also has an important function in enhancing transparency in political finance. Independent monitoring of campaign finance is becoming increasingly common in many parts of the world, and together with campaigns for raising awareness, such initiatives can provide important impetus for reforms and changed behaviour.

References

New York City Campaign Finance Board (2013) *Public Matching Funds*, available at http://www.nyccfb.info/candidates/candidates/publicmatchingfunds.aspx, accessed 20 January 2014.

Ohman, Magnus (2012) *Political Finance Regulations Around the World*. Stockholm: International IDEA.

Organization for Security and Co-operation in Europe, Office for Democratic Institutions and Human Rights (OSCE/ODIHR) and Venice Commission (2010) *Guidelines on Political Party Regulation*, CDL-AD(2010)024.

Reynolds, Andrew, Reilly, Ben and Ellis, Andrew (eds) (2005) *Electoral System Design: The New International IDEA Handbook*. Stockholm: International IDEA, available at http://www.idea.int/publications/esd/, accessed 4 February 2014.

Smilov, Daniel (2008) *Dilemmas for a Democratic Society: Comparative Regulation of Money and Politics*, DISC Working Paper 4/2008. Budapest: Central European University, Center for the Study of Imperfections in Democracy.

United Nations Office of the High Commissioner for Human Rights (UNHCHR) (1996) *The Right to Participate in Public Affairs, Voting Rights and the Right of Equal Access to Public Service*, General Comment no. 25, available at http://www.unhchr.ch/tbs/doc.nsf/0/d0b7f023e8d6d9898025651e004bc0eb, accessed 4 February 2014.

Notes

[1] For example, unreasonably low donation and spending limits are likely to reduce accuracy in financial reporting.

[2] An excellent example of this concerns the earmarking of public funding. In some countries public funds must only be used for electoral activities, whereas in others they can only be used for non-electoral activities. While these approaches are diametrically opposite, in practice the difference may turn out to be small; in the absence of effective enforcement mechanisms, political parties can often find ways to channel funds to where they are most needed.

[3] These two dimensions combined are similar to the 'ideological dimension' described by Smilov (2008, p. 1), in which he compares libertarian and egalitarian views of 'politics and legitimacy' in creating a typology for political finance regulatory systems. His second dimension is institutional, which this analysis deals with under the concept of *context*.

[4] An excellent example is the brief statement on the website of the Swedish Parliament that, while political parties receive public funding, 'the state and parliament currently do not control how the political parties use the public funding' (translation by author). Available at http://www.riksdagen.se/sv/Sa-funkar-riksdagen/Fragor--svar/Ledamoter-och-partier/?faqid=37664

[5] For more information about different electoral systems, see Reynolds, Reilly and Ellis 2005. A study based on the International IDEA Political Finance Database found that a country's electoral system affected which political finance regulations it used (see Ohman 2012).

6   Smilov 2008.

7   UNHCHR 1996 states that 'Reasonable limitations on campaign expenditure may be justified where this is necessary to ensure that the free choice of voters is not undermined or the democratic process distorted by the disproportionate expenditure on behalf of any candidate or party'.

8   This table was originally developed by Daniela Piccio.

9   Analysis of the International IDEA Political Finance Database, based on 114 countries.

10 This was the case in Nigeria after a 2010 court ruling that the same amount had to be distributed to all parties (there were over 60 at the time). The result was that direct public funding was removed in the late 2010 revisions of the Electoral Act.

11 Analysis of the International IDEA Political Finance Database, based on 110 countries. The remaining countries use various combinations of allocation criteria, which can include the number of candidates presented in an election, share of women among the candidates of a party or the number of party members.

12 New York City Campaign Finance Board 2013.

13 This can for example be the case when a large number of political parties are given equal air time on public TV. Few viewers are really going to pay attention to a large number of campaign advertisements one after another.

14 The OSCE/ODIHR and the Venice Commission (2010, Article 184) recommended that 'When developing allocation systems, careful consideration should be given to pre-election funding systems, as opposed to post-election reimbursement which can often perpetuate the inability of small, new, or poor parties to compete effectively. A post-election funding system may not provide the minimum initial funding needed to fund a political campaign. Thus, systems of allocating funds in the post-election period may negatively impact political pluralism. Further, allocation should occur early enough in the electoral process to ensure an equal opportunity throughout the period of campaigning. Delaying the distribution of public funding until late in the campaign or after election day can effectively undermine electoral campaign equality and works against less affluent political parties'.

15 Two rulings by the European Court of Human Rights in relation to the United Kingdom have established that in a European context reasonable limitations on third-party involvement in election campaigning are acceptable. See the *Bowman v. the United Kingdom* (141/1996/760/961) ruling from 1998 and the *Animal Defenders International v. the United Kingdom* (Application no. 48876/08) ruling from 2013.

16 The reporting threshold for donors' identities varies from I$10 in Liberia to I$62,000 in Italy (for donations to political parties).

17 For information about the involvement of political parties and candidates in campaign finance, see the regional studies in this handbook.

18 Admittedly, some candidates have found ways to get around this limit by paying other candidates to de facto campaign for them rather than for themselves.

19 OSCE/ODIHR and Venice Commission 2010, article 212l.

Regional Studies on Political Finance: Regulatory Frameworks and Political Realities

CHAPTER 3

CHAPTER 3

Africa

Magnus Ohman

Few observers of African politics would deny that money plays a role in its political dynamics. In fact, how political parties and candidates raise and spend money can have a more significant impact on the fairness of an electoral process than anything that happens on election day. Unfortunately, many domestic and international election observers fail to take this crucial truth into account. Much more must be understood about how political parties and election campaigns are funded on the African continent, and how these resources are spent.

Introduction to problems in African political finance

African countries face a myriad of complex issues related to political finance regulations that could (and sometimes do) fill entire books, and the situations vary in different countries and sub-regions. Therefore, this is a brief introduction to some key problems of African political finance (none of which is unique to the African continent).

Access to funds for all relevant actors

A major concern is the lack of a level playing field, with opposition parties often considerably disadvantaged by their weak financial position.[1] This often becomes a direct struggle between those who are in power and those who are not, in other words 'between all opposition parties and candidates on the one hand, and the governing party's candidates and the state on the other'.[2] These gaps can make it difficult for the opposition to convince (or even reach) the electorate with its messages. This lack of access is particularly troublesome for traditionally marginalized groups such as youth and women.

Abuse of state resources

The abuse of state resources is a key problem in the field of political finance in Africa. While all incumbent political parties use their position to increase their chance of re-election to a certain extent, directly misusing public resources for political gains can have very harmful effects and contributes to the uneven playing field discussed above. As one analysis states:

> It causes damage to democracy by creating an unlevel playing field which improves the re-election chances of incumbents. In addition, putting public assets at the incumbent party's disposal in its drive for re-election negatively influences the quality of government, since the diversion of resources incurs financial costs for the institutions involved and may reduce the quantity or quality of services provided to the public.[3]

Clientelism

Clientelism (alternatively known as neo-patrimonialism or patron-client systems) refers to a situation in which a patron (in this context, normally a politician) builds a relationship with a larger group of voters that trades its support for various favours (personal or communal). Its role in African politics is frequently debated and somewhat controversial,[4] but can be summarized as follows: 'Political authority in Africa is based on the giving and granting of favors, in an endless series of ... exchanges that go from the village level to the highest reaches of the central state'.[5]

Vote buying

Offering money instead of innovative political ideas to convince individuals to vote for a certain candidate is not unique to Africa. Even so, it is a major concern in many African countries, and is often directly connected to clientelistic relationships (and the significant poverty levels in most African countries). This form of electoral spending (which is illegal in all African countries apart from, it seems, Djibouti and Mauritania) will be discussed in more detail below.

Illicit funding

A significant problem, apparently on the rise, is the influx of illicit funding in African political processes. Funds from the illegal trade in natural resources are sometimes used to entice politicians not to investigate wrongdoing in the extractive industries. In addition, those involved in the transport of illegal drugs from Latin America via (especially West) Africa to Europe sometimes use their resources to influence African politicians and political parties.[6]

Dependency on foreign funds

Although the exact impact is difficult to assess, the dependency of many African countries on foreign financial assistance significantly affects the flow of money into and out of politics.[7] Increased dependency on foreign aid can raise the stakes of electoral competition, as politicians compete for access to aid money. However, the structural adjustment requirements that often accompany foreign aid have in some countries moved significant funds out of the public sphere. For example, political stakeholders may set up superficially independent civil society organizations in order to access international donor money. How foreign aid is structured may therefore have a significant impact on the dynamics of political finance.

The cash nature of African economies

Compared with other continents, African economies remain relatively dependent on cash transactions. This reliance negatively affects the economy as a whole and makes it more difficult to monitor the role of money in politics. The limited penetration of the banking system in many African countries makes the effective oversight of financial activities more difficult.[8] Cash transactions are more difficult to track than bank transfers, and the low levels of tax payment compliance mean that much of the funding of political parties and election campaigns leaves no paper trail.[9]

An overview of political finance regulations in Africa

All countries in Africa—apart from Chad, Equatorial Guinea, Eritrea, the Gambia, Somalia and South Sudan—have signed or ratified the 2005 United Nations Convention against Corruption (UNCAC), which states that all countries should 'consider taking appropriate legislative and administrative measures ... *to enhance transparency in the funding of candidatures for elected public office and, where applicable, the funding of political parties'.*[10]

In an African context, the overarching guidance comes from the African Union Convention on Preventing and Combating Corruption, which states in Article 10 that '[e]ach State Party shall adopt legislative and other measures to: (a) Proscribe the use of funds acquired through illegal and corrupt practices to finance political parties; and (b) Incorporate the principle of transparency into funding of political parties'. More guidance is provided by the Southern African Development Community (SADC), which has stated that electoral management bodies (EMBs) should be 'legally empowered to prohibit certain types of expenditures so as to limit the undue impact of money on the democratic process and the outcome of an election'.[11]

The Electoral Commissions Forum of the SADC countries developed the 'Principles for Election Management, Monitoring, and Observation in the SADC Region' in 2003. This document states that '[t]he use of public assets and funds for party political purposes should be regulated in order to level the playing field for political competition ... Political parties and candidates should account to the EMB for the use of such resources'.[12] As is the case in most regions except for Europe, Africa has only limited regional guidance documents regarding political finance regulations.

Sources of income for political parties and candidates

Various forms of regulations are used to control how political parties and candidates are allowed to raise income, including bans and limits and the provision of direct and indirect public funding.

Contribution bans

Some sources of income for political parties and candidates are considered so detrimental that they are banned altogether. In general, the bans relating to political parties vary little between Africa and other regions. The most common type of ban (present in 80 per cent of African countries) relates to state resources given to a particular political party (which represents efforts to avoid the abuse of state resources). Bans on foreign funding (60 per cent) and funding from anonymous sources (50 per cent) are also common. The latter aids transparency and helps the oversight body and voters determine whether other forms of donation bans are being adhered to, and can be effective in reducing illicit funding. In contrast, less than 20 per cent of African countries ban donations from corporations or trade unions.

Figure 3.1. African countries with bans on corporate donations and donations from foreign interests to political parties

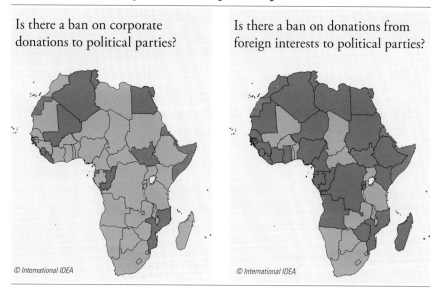

Is there a ban on corporate donations to political parties?

Is there a ban on donations from foreign interests to political parties?

© International IDEA

© International IDEA

■ Yes
■ No
■ No data

Source: International IDEA. These maps are based on data collected up to February 2014. Data are continuously updated on the International IDEA Database on Political Finance (Political Finance Database). See http://www.idea.int/political-finance/question.cfm?field=246&region=2, and http://www.idea.int/political-finance/question.cfm?field=248&region=2

Bans on certain types of donations to parties are often not accompanied by similar rules for electoral candidates. In many cases, bans are twice as common for political parties as they are for candidates. This discrepancy between bans on candidates and parties makes enforcement more difficult, since candidates often run their own campaigns, which are separate from the political party that nominated them.

Contribution limits

Very few African countries limit the amount that eligible donors are allowed to contribute: 14 per cent limit the amount that can be given to a political party annually, while only 3 per cent limit donations to parties in relation to election campaigns, and 7 per cent impose limits on donations to candidates.

Existing donation limits are often very high: the Kenyan annual donation limit is 5 per cent of the party's spending in the previous year.[13] In Mauritania, ten people can legally provide the entirety of a party's campaign funds. In Uganda the limit is almost 400 million shillings (UGX) (I$500,000), while a single donor in the Republic of the Congo can contribute the equivalent of 1,000 minimum salaries per year (ten times the level in Algeria). Nigeria has a more modest donation limit: 1 million naira (NGN) (I$14,000) to any election candidate.[14] However, since candidates are not required to submit financial reports, this limit is largely unenforceable. The annual donation limit to political parties in Morocco is around 100,000 dirham (MAD) (I$16,000).

The level of contribution limits only matters if contributions are monitored and violations penalized. Overall, contribution limits play a negligible role in the de facto regulation of political finance in Africa.

Sources of private income

Most political parties in Africa rely predominantly on funding from private sources. The different categories of private income for political parties and candidates are discussed below.

Membership dues

Arguably, relying on membership dues is the best solution for political parties from the perspective of democratic engagement and grass-roots ownership. We do not know how important membership dues are for financing African political parties, because reliable data are not available from any country on the continent. Remarkably few African political parties can even provide reliable membership lists.[15] Given the importance of clientelism discussed above, African party members should perhaps be considered recipients, rather than providers, of funds. Musambayi has noted about Kenya that 'rather than support the parties, the public expect the parties to give them handouts if politicians want their support'.[16] In Ghana, party membership 'is generally insignificant. But even where it is substantial pervasive poverty among Ghanaians limits the amount ordinary members can pay as dues to their parties'.[17]

While this may seem to be a major difference between political finance in Africa and in other parts of the world—in particular in the more established democracies in Western Europe—the contrast is not as large as it first seems. It is time to do away with the myth of membership-funded political parties as a dominant approach anywhere on the globe today. Decreasing party memberships in older democracies during the last few decades, and increases in public funding, have led to a gradual decline in membership dues as a source of party income.[18]

Given the level of poverty in most parts of Africa (an average of 46 per cent live on less than 1.25 US dollars [USD] per day), it is unlikely that membership dues will become a major source of political party income in the near future.[19]

Small donations

Alongside membership dues, small donations are often seen as particularly beneficial for democracy, since a party that relies on small donations will not be dependent on any particular financial interest, and will need to build and maintain a large support base. The problem with relying on small donations to political parties in Africa is similar to that of membership dues; high levels of poverty and clientelistic tendencies reduce the likelihood that large numbers of people can donate enough money for a political party (or election campaign) to rely on.

There are, however, cases in which political parties can use innovative ways to raise funds. While in opposition in the 1990s, the New Patriotic Party (NPP) in Ghana sold bread with the party logo on it as a combined fundraising and campaigning approach.[20] South African political parties have also started engaging in SMS-based fundraising.[21]

Large donations

Large donations (from wealthy individuals, corporations and certain types of organizations) are often seen as problematic, since there is a danger that the recipient becomes beholden to the giver, which can jeopardize both democracy and governance. Some countries try to discourage large donations by limiting the amount of contributions, though this is an uncommon practice in Africa.

Corporate donations may be motivated by a sense of public duty on the part of the company leadership, but they may also entail expectations of assistance in the future. In such cases, companies are unlikely to support political parties they perceive as having little chance of winning elections. This will normally benefit the governing party, as in the Gambia, where reports noted 'televised donations by private enterprises to the [governing] APRC [Alliance for Patriotic Reorientation and Construction]'.[22] A former African National Congress (ANC) treasurer-general in South Africa claimed that the party would receive a customary 2 million rand (ZAR) (I$350,000) gift from individual black businessmen.[23] In African countries without long-term dominant political parties, corporations sometimes decide to support all the main parties to 'hedge their bets'.[24]

Sometimes political parties and candidates make a show of complying with the rules. The electoral law in Nigeria sets a limit of NGN 1 million (I$14,000) on individual donations to a candidate. At a fundraiser in 2010, Alhaji Abdulsamad Rabiu handed over NGN 250 million (I$3.5 million) to the incumbent president, arguing that this was legal since he had collected NGN 1 million (I$14,000) from each of his 250 family members.[25]

Corporate donations are not always voluntary. In a survey of corruption in Mozambique, companies named 'involuntary donations to political parties' as one of the major problems; 21 per cent reported having been asked for contributions during the previous year.[26]

Funding from the party leadership

Another source of party funding is the private resources of the party leader or the national party leadership. In Zambia, it has been argued that 'the burden of fund raising for campaigning falls on the top leadership structures of the party'.[27]

Funding from party leaders is unlikely to play a major role for government parties or large opposition parties. Running a major political party simply costs so much that other funding sources are required.

However, party leadership funding is not necessarily seen as inappropriate by the electorate. An opinion study in Uganda found this to be the most commonly approved form of funding (21 per cent, putting it ahead of membership dues at 15 per cent).[28] This view may be related to a sentiment that politicians who are interested in political gains should use their own money to achieve these goals. On the other hand, if a political party is predominantly funded by the party leader, the prospects for internal party democracy are likely to be limited.

Funding from electoral candidates

It is traditionally assumed that when a political party nominates someone to represent it in an election, it will also provide at least some financial support to the candidate's campaign. In Africa, the presidential campaign is often funded at least in part by the nominating political party (in major political parties).[29]

For other (non-presidential) elections, however, the situation is often different. In Ghana, Sierra Leone and Kenya, for example, individuals who want to represent a political party often have to pay to even be considered as a candidate.[30] In African countries with strong political party loyalties, being nominated by the 'right' party is often more important than the election itself, since it can literally guarantee electoral success. Therefore, more money may flow during the candidate nomination process than during the electoral campaign.

Thus candidates often have to pay for their own campaigns. A 2011 report on Tanzania noted that 'smaller parties had to choose their candidates according to their financial capacity to sustain their campaign by themselves'.[31] Another study noted the 'personal risk of bankruptcy that many candidates face as they attempt to raise money for elected positions'.[32] In the 2007 elections in Kenya, '[m]any parliamentary candidates funded their own campaigns, with most of their money coming from personal resources, including family and friends' donations and pyramid schemes, and loans drawn from savings credit and cooperative societies, banks, insurance companies and personal business funds'.[33] The same report estimated that on average, only 5 per cent of candidates' spending came from the political parties that nominated them.[34]

This dependency on the funds that a candidate has (or can raise through donations or loans) benefits rich individuals and often significantly hurts the chances of those with less access to resources, including many female candidates.

Why would anyone be willing to spend such large amounts on running for office? After reviewing the possible benefits of being a member of parliament in Kenya, one study concluded that '[f]or those who spend and get into Parliament, therefore, it makes sound business sense. However, for losers, it may herald the dawn of bankruptcy'.[35]

Income from elected officials

Deducting money from the salaries of elected officials who belong to a party is, in effect, a form of indirect public funding, since the salaries of elected officials are paid from the state budget. There is nothing particularly African about such practices, as systems of this kind are used, for example, in Germany and Italy.[36] Helle claims that in Uganda 'opposition parties get a significant share of their funding from their elected officials, who contribute a portion of their salary to the party. This share is typically between 10-20% of the elected official's salary'.[37] This practice has also been reported in countries such as Botswana, Lesotho, Nigeria, South Africa and Zimbabwe.[38] This type of fundraising can generally be considered legitimate, though it has been pointed out that it 'increases the general importance of winning office: if the party loses an electoral race, it also loses a very important source of income. The party thus "loses twice"'.[39]

However, if state employees are required to share part of their salaries with a particular political party[40]—a practice known as 'macing', which exists in different parts of the world—it is highly detrimental to both democracy and effective governance, since the state and its staff should be separate from any political party.[41]

Income from commercial activities

If political parties become commercial actors, this increases the risk of conflicts of interest and blurs the line between political and commercial interests. In some African countries, such as Ethiopia and Kenya, political parties are explicitly prohibited from engaging in commercial activities. In other countries, such as Sierra Leone and Mozambique, this practice is not directly banned, but is not included among the allowed sources of income. This does not necessarily mean that parties in countries that ban parties from engaging in commercial activities do not raise funds in this manner; the government party may benefit specifically from close contacts with the business sector. Some African countries allow parties to engage in commercial activities, such as Benin and Libya (in the latter case limited to cultural and media activities).

Given the lack of funding available to many political parties, the unwillingness of many private interests to support them and the limited public resources available, it may be advisable to consider allowing political parties to engage in limited commercial activities related to their normal activities, such as printing and publishing. Certain limitations should be in place: (1) commercial activities by political parties should not be considered for public contracts, (2) the share of total income that a party can derive from such activities should be limited, and (3) transactions connected to any commercial activity should be included in the party's financial reporting requirements.

Foreign funding

A majority of African countries bans foreign funding of political parties (although only 30 per cent explicitly ban foreign funding of candidates). This does not necessarily mean that no such funding takes place, and indeed it is notoriously difficult to find reliable data on this subject. Foreign funding is often seen as a detrimental interference with the political process of the recipient country, but it is not necessarily equated with the illicit funding of political parties and election campaigns. Some African countries—such as Lesotho, Namibia and Tanzania—allow foreign funding of political parties as long as such donations are made public (though they seldom are).

Another issue is when political parties and candidates raise funds from Africans living abroad. Many larger African political parties have chapters in countries such as France, the United Kingdom and the United States, and receive (sometimes significant) funds from their expatriate supporters in the diaspora.[42] There is nothing wrong with citizens living abroad supporting political activities at home (as long as they follow the same rules as everyone else); it may help to connect expat Africans with the political process in their home countries.[43] However, foreign interests may use these financial flows to support particular political parties, and it is next to impossible for African political finance regulators to ensure that money coming from abroad does not originate from foreign sources.

Illicit funding

A particular problem in some parts of Africa is the influence of illicit funding on the political process. The drugs trade from Latin America via West Africa to Europe has an estimated value of USD 2 billion annually.[44] Several struggling states such as Guinea, Guinea-Bissau and Mali have been identified as particularly vulnerable to the influx of drugs money, to the extent that the term 'narco state' is being used.[45] However, this trade has also been said to have a corrupting effect on the political process in otherwise stable countries such as Ghana.[46] One observer has argued that:

> Democratic Politics needs money to oil its wheels: winning elections and securing power means paying for campaigns and ensuring wide networks of political patronage. While the international community

sought to transition these post-conflict and fragile states towards democracy, it neglected to acknowledge that an independent source of resources in the subregion over the last decade has been the proceeds of drug trafficking.[47]

In addition, Kupferschmidt has identified 'foreign corporations exploiting natural resources' as particular culprits in high-conflict countries in Africa.[48] One study indicated that the influx of money from recently discovered oil in São Tomé and Principe led to an increase in vote buying, and another found a link between oil bunkering and campaign funding in Nigeria.[49] Of course, natural resources are not necessarily a curse for African political and economic systems. As Throup has pointed out, 'Oil has the potential to be a force for economic good or a major source of instability.'[50]

Public funding

A clear distinction must be made between the regulated provision of direct and indirect public funding on the one hand, and the abuse of state resources on the other.

There is one African case in which public funding has been combined with a ban on private donations—meaning that electoral competitors had to rely exclusively on the public funding provided. This was the 2011 elections in Tunisia. However, political parties were still able to receive funds from private sources, and nothing prevented them from transferring these funds to their campaign accounts, which created a significant disadvantage for independent candidate lists. Candidates were also allowed to use their own resources in the campaign.[51]

Direct public funding

More and more countries in Africa offer funding to political parties from the state.[52] Today, 69 per cent of African countries provide provisions for direct public funding to political parties. When South Africa first introduced public funding of political parties, the responsible minister stated that the reform aimed to 'reduce the dependency of political parties on one or two powerful financial backers, and thereby reduce the possibility of the subversion of political parties and also the subversion of Parliament itself and of our democracy'.[53]

Countries that do not provide public funding include several that have doubtful claims to democratic governance, such as the Central African Republic and the Gambia. However, some of the more stable African democracies have resisted repeated calls for public funding, notably Botswana and Ghana. Public funding has also been discontinued in some African countries, as in Egypt and Nigeria in 2011 and 2010, respectively.[54]

Level of public funding

In some cases, no funds are provided at all, despite legal provisions. This was reported to be the case in Burundi, Guinea, Sudan and Togo in recent elections.[55] In other places the amounts provided have little impact on the overall funding of political parties. The Electoral Institute for Sustainable Democracy in Africa (EISA) reported state funding in Malawi as 'inadequate to meet the needs of the parties'.[56] In other cases, public funding of election campaigns is provided too late to help the recipients mount an effective campaign. In the 2008 Angolan elections, for example, most contestants received the funds only three weeks before polling day.[57]

In absolute terms, the African countries with the highest amounts of public funds are Morocco, South Africa and Tanzania. The 2011 elections in Morocco saw the distribution of MAD 220 million (I$32 million), while in South Africa ZAR 99 million (I$17.3 million) was distributed during 2010–11. In Tanzania a total of 17 billion shillings (TZS) (I$30 million) was dispensed in 2008–09.[58] It cannot be said with any certainty what share of political parties' total income this represents, since there are no reporting requirements regarding private funds in South Africa and no reliable reports from Morocco or Tanzania. Even so, one report about South Africa claims that '[p]ublic funding remains woefully inadequate to run election campaigns', while the amounts distributed in Tanzania in 2010 were described as 'insufficient'.[59]

Morocco, Namibia and Seychelles probably have the highest levels of public funding per capita (over I$1 per citizen), compared to around I$0.7 in Tanzania, I$0.35 in South Africa, I$0.23 in Chad, I$0.18 in Cameroon, I$0.14 in Mozambique and Rwanda, I$0.08 in Niger and a meagre I$0.03 in Ethiopia.[60]

Table 3.1. shows the amounts of public funding provided in different countries (note that funding provided for an election campaign is not directly comparable with funding provided annually).

Table 3.1. Amounts of direct public funding distributed in ten African countries

Country	Year	Amount	Amount I$	Population	I$/ citizen	Comment
Cameroon	2013	850 million XAF	I$4.0 million	21.7 million	I$.018	For parliamentary elections
Chad	2011	575 million XAF	I$2.7 million	11.5 million	I$0.23	For parliamentary elections
Ethiopia	2010	13 million ETB	I$2.7 million	84.7 million	I$0.03	For parliamentary elections

Morocco	2011	220 million MAD	I$32 million	32 million	I$1	For parliamentary elections
Mozambique	2009	50 million MZM	I$3.5 million	23.9 million	I$0.14	For presidential and parliamentary elections
Namibia	2005–06	15.2 NAD	I$2.4 million	2.3 million	I$1.04	Annual allocation
Niger	2011	350 million XAF	I$1.2 million	16 million	I$0.08	Annual allocation
Rwanda	2008	340 million RWF	I$1.5 million	10.9 million	I$0.14	For parliamentary elections
Seychelles	2011	0.5 million SCR	I$107,000	86,000	I$1.24	Annual allocation
South Africa	2010–11	99 million ZAR	I$17.3 million	50.6 million	I$0.35	Annual allocation

Note: XAF = Central African CFA franc; ETB = Ethiopian birr; MAD = Moroccan dirham; MZM = Mozambique metical; NAD = Namibian dollar; RWF = Rwandese franc; SCR = Seychelles rupee; ZAR = South African rand.

Very small parties, in Africa as elsewhere, do not qualify for public funding.[61] This matters little, since their role in politics is negligible, especially since the notion of *local political parties* that are active only in local politics is rare on the African continent.[62] The parties that depend the most on public funding tend to be those that just manage to qualify for such assistance. An example of this is South Africa, where '[s]maller parties are highly dependent on public funding while larger parties obtain the bulk of their funding from donations from the private sector and foreign governments and companies'.[63] The opposition United Democratic Front party in Namibia, which has just qualified for public funding in recent elections, estimated that 80–90 per cent of its funding comes from the state. It has been reported that the opposition 'party headquarters are often closed when state funding runs dry, only to re-open when the next batch of funds comes through'.[64] In Rwanda in 2008, apart from the government party, the 'other contenders were mainly dependent on the limited state subsidies'.[65]

The ruling ANC in South Africa received 60 million ZAR (I$11 million) in 2009, and a senior executive of the party claimed that they spent around 200 million ZAR (I$35 million) on the 2009 campaign. If we assume that most of the public funds received by the ANC that year were spent on the campaign, the public funds accounted for over one-quarter of funds spent on the campaign.[66]

Overall, the amounts provided (or the time at which they are supplied) are such that public funding makes little impact on the functioning of political parties and election campaigns in most African countries.

Problems with public funding

It is important to get the eligibility criteria for public funding right. If the criteria are too liberal, parties may be created with the sole purpose of accessing funds. At the 1990 National Conference in Gabon, delegates were invited to form political parties, which would receive financial aid from the government. More than 70 *self-declared* parties were created, and each was granted 20 million Chadian francs (around USD 35,000) and a four-wheel-drive vehicle with which to conduct the electoral campaign. Most of these parties disappeared after receiving the state funding and did not reappear.[67] This is one example of a situation seen in several African countries in which 'some parties seem to have no real permanent life, but only come into existence for the purposes of obtaining access to these funds'.[68]

However, if the threshold is too high, few political parties will be able to access these funds. In Malawi, where the threshold is 10 per cent of the vote, only three political parties qualified for funding in the 2009 elections, while the smaller political parties and the independent members of parliament (MPs)—who together hold 18 per cent of the parliamentary seats—were left without financial assistance. In Zimbabwe, political parties were previously required to win 15 seats (13 per cent) in order to qualify for public funding. Only the governing Zimbabwe African National Union–Patriotic Front (ZANU-PF) reached this threshold in the 1990 and 1995 elections, before the Supreme Court ordered that the threshold be lowered to 5 per cent of the votes. This meant that the opposition Movement for Democratic Change (MDC) qualified after the 2000 and 2005 elections, though the formation of the unity government after the 2008 elections again meant that only political parties with representation in government received public funding.[69] Only ZANU-PF and the MDC-T gained a sufficient share of the vote to qualify for funding according to the 2013 election results.

Public funding and gender equality

There is a global trend for countries to link the provision of public funding to the gender equality of a political party's candidates. Such rules can alter the incentive structure of political parties that would otherwise choose male candidates as the 'safe bet'.

A small but growing number of African countries has adopted rules of this kind.[70] In Mali and Niger, 10 per cent of the available funds are earmarked for parties with elected women officials, whereas in Burkina Faso parties that do not nominate at least 30 per cent of either gender lose half of the public funding that they would otherwise be entitled to. In Kenya, parties that have more than two-thirds of their elected officials of the same gender are not eligible for public funding at all (the same applies to parties in Cape Verde that nominate less than 25 per cent of candidates from either gender). Morocco has a specific fund to support the political representation of women.

So far, these regulations have not had a dramatic effect. The share of women in parliament is 10 per cent in Mali, 13 per cent in Niger, 16 per cent in Burkina Faso, 19 per cent in Kenya, 21 per cent in Cape Verde and 28 per cent in Ethiopia, with only Ethiopia being above the average for African parliaments.[71] It is possible that these regulations will have more effect as time goes by, but unless parties are significantly dependent on public funds, rules of this kind are likely to have a mainly symbolic impact. Complementary approaches must be sought to address the particular financial challenges faced by women wishing to enter politics.

Indirect public funding

Indirect public funding is the provision of state resources other than money to political parties or candidates. The main form is free or subsidized access to public media, but other versions include tax relief for parties or their donors, free access to public buildings for rallies or other party activities, and the provision of space for electoral advertising.

Figure 3.2. Free or subsidized access to media for political parties in Africa

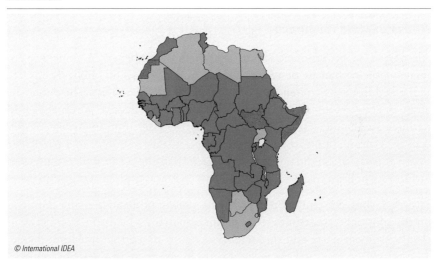

© International IDEA

■ Yes (there is free or subsidized access to media for political parties)
■ No (there is no free or subsidized access to media for political parties)
■ No data

Source: International IDEA. This map is based on data collected up to February 2014. Data are continuously updated on the International IDEA Database on Political Finance (Political Finance Database). See http://www.idea.int/political-finance/question.cfm?field=276&region=2

Indirect public funding is less common in Africa than elsewhere (55 per cent, compared to 68 per cent globally and 93 per cent in Europe). Apart from free

> African legislators should consider more ways to provide indirect assistance to political parties. It is easier in this way to control how resources are used than it is with direct public funding—which is important with the limited oversight throughout Africa.

or subsidized media access, the most common example of indirect public funding is tax subsidies for political parties.[72] In Benin, for example, political parties are exempt from taxes except for those related to commercial activities, and in Egypt and Seychelles parties pay no income tax. Other forms of indirect public funding include the provision of free space to place campaign materials in Gabon and Senegal, the provision of premises for party meetings in Cape Verde and sample ballots in Niger.

African legislators should consider more ways to provide indirect assistance to political parties. It is easier in this way to control how resources are used than it is with direct public funding—which is important with the limited oversight throughout Africa. Indirect public funding can also be less costly than direct funding, as it often utilizes existing resources (such as government buildings and broadcasting equipment).

Abuse of state resources

All parties in government try to use their incumbency in some way to increase their chances of re-election. When often-scant public funds are redirected from their intended purposes to campaign activities, however, the abuse of state resources threatens both a country's effective governance and its inclusive democracy.[73] This issue is clearly understood in Africa: 77 per cent of African countries ban the *provision* of state resources to a particular political party or candidate, and 90 per cent ban the *use* of state resources in favour of a political party or candidate.[74]

However, abuse of state resources remains a major problem in many countries on the continent, sometimes to the point of blurring the distinction between the government party and the state. One report noted that in Mozambique, '[...in theory] the state and the political party in power are two separate entities... In practice, however, there is no clear separation'.[75] The Commonwealth Observation Team to the 2011 elections in the Gambia similarly noted that the 'blurring of state and party lines was evident throughout the President's campaign. For example:

- the *Daily Observer* newspaper reported … that the Ministry of Petroleum had donated 1700 tee-shirts to the president's campaign;
- team members saw the offices of regional Governors being used as organisational centres for the APRC campaign; and
- team members saw military vehicles being used to transport APRC supporters.'[76]

Similar activities are reported from many African countries. Estimating the value of state resources used in an election is very difficult. A study of the Kenyan elections in 2007 estimated that 500 million Kenyan shillings (KES) (I$12 million) in state resources were spent in the election campaign, or around 10 per cent of the total amount spent.[77] Credit institutions reported concerns that increased budget spending ahead of the 2012 elections in Ghana could damage the country's economy.[78]

It is important to realize, however, that abuse of resources does not always involve spending money. It can also consist of the state media favourably covering the incumbent party or engaging civil servants in campaign activities while on duty. One report about Angola noted that 'the government announced extemporaneous holidays for state workers whenever the President of the Republic visited the provinces to ensure maximum impact for the MPLA [Popular Movement for the Liberation of Angola] campaign. Several opposition parties alleged that public servants were widely obliged and sometimes threatened to attend MPLA campaign activities'.[79] Another report about Tanzania noted 'excessive loyalty of certain administration officials who openly campaigned at CCM [Chama Cha Mapinduzi] rallies', while it has been argued that in Zambia '[t]he lack of clearly defined parameters between private and public resources further dissolved boundaries between legitimate use of state resources used in an official capacity and use of them to campaign'.[80]

International donors may worsen this problem by providing large amounts of funding for 'non-political activities' during pre-election periods, which allows the incumbent regime to cite new projects as evidence of its development efforts. As Speck and Fontana have pointed out, '[d]onors tend to assume an attitude of resignation towards the problem, suggesting that it is too politically sensitive for them to deal with'.[81] This attitude is unhelpful in the fight against the abuse of state resources in Africa. This is not to say that donor-assisted programmes always have a negative impact; increasing political parties' capacity to communicate with voters—and indeed helping stakeholders oversee and raise awareness about political finance—can help level the electoral playing field.

Political parties in power must refrain from abusing their position of incumbency, since, while such abuse may help secure a party's current hold on power, it will also create a political culture in which, if the party loses elections in the future, it may never be allowed to regain its position. By moderating how they use state resources, incumbent political parties help create an environment in which they can come back to (electoral) fights in the future (Ghana demonstrated this through the changes in government in the 2000 and 2008 elections, though developments in the 2012 elections, which followed the unexpected death of President John Atta Mills, present a more complicated picture).[82]

Spending by political parties and candidates

Spending limits

One way of trying to limit the amounts spent on election campaigns (and reduce the advantages of those with access to significant funds) is to impose spending limits. Such rules are fairly unusual in Africa: only 18 per cent of countries impose spending limits on political parties and 25 per cent on candidates. The limits imposed by different African countries are found in Annex I. To get a better idea of the relative size of the spending limits, we need to take into account the size of the respective electorates. Per capita figures show that presidential candidates in Mauritania and Togo are only allowed to spend I$0.06 per registered voter, while those in Liberia can spend I$2.7 and in Benin I$3—more than 50 times that of their Mauritanian and Togolese counterparts. The lowest level is arguably in Algeria, where presidential candidates are allowed to spend less than I$0.01 per registered voter (only around I$300,000 for an electorate of over 20 million).

Unless there is a reasonably functioning system of disclosure and oversight, it is unlikely that anyone will even know if spending limits are adhered to. A prime example is Nigeria, where the law limits the spending of electoral candidates, but does not require them to submit any financial reports.

It has not been possible to find any examples of a political party or candidate being sanctioned for violating a spending limit anywhere on the African continent. Given the scarcity of spending limits, and doubts about whether existing limits are enforced, it is fair to say that (as with contribution limits) this type of regulation plays no practical role in African political finance.[83]

In other regions, it is common for political parties and candidates to use nominally non-partisan institutions to channel some of their campaign spending, and thus get around spending limits. The almost complete lack of enforcement of spending limits in Africa may help explain why such so-called third-party spending seems less common on this continent than elsewhere. However, such activities do occur, perhaps due to a belief that campaigning by seemingly non-partisan actors might be more convincing than activities by political parties, in which Africans place little trust.[84] African civil society organizations (CSOs) should not involve themselves in election campaigning so as to avoid a similar decline in public trust.

Actual spending

Reliable information about levels of actual spending by African political parties and candidates is very rare indeed. A study of the 2007 elections in Kenya estimated that a total of KES 5.6 billion (I$129 million) was spent, or around I$13 per voter.[85] The estimated spending by the ANC mentioned above would amount to around I$2 per voter for the governing party alone.

It has been argued that the election campaign spending explained the 58 per cent increase in car imports just before the 2011 elections in Nigeria. In addition, the Central Bank of Nigeria expressed fears that the campaign would lead to significant inflationary pressures.[86]

Who are the (financial) beneficiaries of campaign spending in Africa? In Kenya it was found that:

> Beneficiaries included the media, fundraising officers, campaign paraphernalia manufacturers, travel and hotel companies, rally and event organizers, campaign strategy advisers and consultants, campaign coordinators and party agents, pollsters, security companies and personnel, as well as amorphous youth and women groups.[87]

In the 2007 presidential elections in Sierra Leone, then Vice-President Solomon Berewa reported having spent 17 billion leone (SLL) (I$10.4 million) on top of the SLL 440 million (I$270,000) spent by his party (I$5 per voter). Unfortunately, the All People's Congress challenger, Ernest Koroma (who is now president), failed to submit a financial report, while his party claimed to have spent SLL 910 million (I$550,000).[88]

Vote buying

A discussion about vote buying in Africa could easily fill a book on its own; in the interest of space, only a few key points can be made here. As with the abuse of state resources, there is clearly an awareness of this problem: 96 per cent of African countries have imposed a ban on vote buying, often with serious sanctions attached.

Vote buying is often considered to be a simple transaction in which a candidate hands over money in return for a vote. This has led some observers to wonder how vote buying can be an effective vote-gaining strategy, since the 'buyer' normally cannot know how the voter actually voted.[89] However, vote buying in Africa must be interpreted in a broader context. The provision of goods and services by candidates and political parties is often done to demonstrate the contestant's wealth and generosity to the electorate, with the implicit understanding that their vote will secure future largesse. This has been described as 'non-transactional' vote buying, and Mushota has argued that 'a candidate's ability to deliver the goods was a priori determined by his/her ability to meet the incessant demand for sharing in the spoils system'.[90] When Lindberg asked Ghanaian MPs how much of their spending was used for 'personalized patronage' in the 2000 election, more than half admitted to having spent at least a quarter of their funds for such purposes.[91]

One difficulty in dealing with the issue of vote buying is the often-steady supply of people who are willing to sell their votes. Bratton's study of Nigeria revealed that, while 90 per cent of average respondents in an Afrobarometer survey saw vote buying as morally despicable, less than half saw anything wrong with voters selling their votes.[92] As long as this forgiving attitude to vote selling persists, it is unlikely that electoral contestants will be able to resist the temptation to increase their electoral support base by financial means. This may also prove an enduring problem for female candidates as long as they are unable to raise as much money as male candidates to distribute to the electorate. In one case, female political aspirants in Kenya were harassed and 'the youth threatened to detain women aspirants at some points when they stopped to address them if they [the women aspirants] didn't give handouts'.[93]

Accurate estimates of money spent on vote buying are rare. One study regarding the 2007 elections in Kenya estimated that '[b]y the end of Party Nominations week almost 5 million shillings [I$115,000] was distributed to voters in each constituency and an estimated 900 million shillings [I$21 million] was distributed in 210 constituencies'.[94] A related study found that the average amount handed out per bribe during the election campaign was about KES 200 (I$2).[95]

The relation between political party and candidate spending

In comparison to some other regions, in particular in the former communist bloc, running as an independent is seldom a viable option for aspiring African politicians. With some notable exceptions, African politicians need to appear on the ballot paper as being sponsored by a major political party. However, this does not necessarily mean that the political parties control their candidates or their campaign finances. As discussed above, candidates often finance their own election campaigns, and correspondingly they also spend their money independently. In countries that have a proportional representation system (mainly in Southern and West Africa), candidates may play a less active role in fundraising and campaign spending.[96] However, in such cases it is possible to use candidates for fundraising and campaign spending as a way to get around the limits and disclosure requirements related to political parties.

> Donation bans and limits are much more common for political parties than for candidates, while several countries impose spending limits on candidates, but not on the parties they represent. This opens significant loopholes in many, if not most, African countries that can be used to bypass existing regulations.

These facts should have a significant impact on the regulatory systems in African countries. Unfortunately, donation bans and limits are much more common for political parties than for candidates, while several countries impose spending limits on candidates, but not on the parties they represent. This opens significant loopholes in many, if not most, African countries that can be used to bypass existing regulations. Regulatory reform should seek to produce transparency in the finances of political parties and candidates, and make it more difficult to hide less legitimate (or outright illegal) financial flows. Ethiopia, Tanzania and Nigeria have particular problems in this regard. However, most African countries have large enough loopholes in their regulatory systems for the political party/candidate relationship to play an important role in getting around political finance regulations.[97]

Enforcement of political finance regulations

Disclosure requirements

A key aspect of any system of political finance oversight is the requirement for stakeholders to submit financial reports to a government institution with the mandate to audit these statements. Without such reports, ensuring transparency and compliance with other regulations is effectively impossible, though the submission of such reports is of course no guarantee that these goals will be achieved (since the reports may not be true). However, even inaccurate reports are better than nothing, since they provide a starting point for the authority's investigations. The reporting requirements must be detailed enough to allow for effective analysis, but not so demanding that they are effectively impossible to comply with, which would give contestants an excuse to ignore them.[98]

All but six African countries have some sort of reporting requirements.[99] However, many countries only require financial reports from either political parties *or* candidates—not from both. Indeed, only 17 African countries have both types of reporting requirements. In some other countries, political parties' financial reports are required to include income and spending that nominated candidates incurred independently of the party. Yet few African political parties have the administrative capacity to collect and verify such information.[100] Candidate-level reporting should be a minimum requirement in presidential and parliamentary elections in countries with single-member-district electoral systems.[101]

One argument against disclosure relates to potentially negative consequences if donors' identities are made public. One report has stated that:

> The advantage of disclosing ... was to ensure that parties were not beholden to a group of financial backers rather than voters. The disadvantage was that private funders who do not want to be identified because of fear of reprisals, will no longer back parties financially and this could be particularly bad for opposition parties.[102]

One solution to this problem is to require donations above a certain limit to be reported. Such rules exist, for example, in Liberia and Lesotho. In the former case, donations under I$10 are only reported in summary form, while in the latter donations above I$44,000 must be reported to the Election Commission within seven days of receipt.[103]

Scrutiny and enforcement

In most African countries, submitted financial reports are not scrutinized, and no sanctions are imposed on violators. Reports of unsanctioned refusals to submit financial reports have been received from, for example, Ghana, Kenya, Liberia, Namibia, Nigeria, Sierra Leone and Tanzania.[104] In Kenya, 30 out of 44 political parties reportedly failed to submit their financial reports for 2009–10.[105] The resulting lack of transparency is a key problem in effective political finance oversight. One report on Mozambique notes that:

> Despite the clear requirement in the law for the disclosure of information through the official newspapers, it has never been disclosed by the supervisory bodies in this way. More significantly, to date, none of the political parties or candidates has revealed any information about sources of their income and expenditures either.[106]

Even though countries such as Liberia, Nigeria and Sierra Leone theoretically have a high level of regulation, little or no scrutiny of the reports received takes place. This highlights the weakness of the regulatory enforcement and shows that the problems with political finance control in Africa lie not with the formal rules, but with how the rules are (or are not) implemented.

One problem undermining effective scrutiny is the limited penetration of the banking system. Many transactions, including legitimate ones, are carried out using cash rather than bank transfers or cheques. Therefore there is no paper (or electronic) trail for the enforcing agency to follow.

It is often argued that providing public funding can be an effective way to enhance compliance, by withholding such support from parties that do not comply with the disclosure regulations. Helle has found this effect in Uganda (where public funding is provided by international donors), and he claims that:

> ... the presence of donor funding seem [sic] to have increased financial transparency: because the parties are required to have their finances [audited] and provide documentation of this (audited accounts) in order to qualify for the grants, the opposition parties seem to more consistently hand in their audited accounts to the Electoral Commission, something which is required by law but has been poorly implemented since 2005.[107] Therefore, assuming that the amount of public funding provided is enough to make the threat of losing it an efficient deterrent (which is not the case in much of Africa today), this is a viable approach to improving compliance.

A major concern is that the legislation in several countries (such as Lesotho, Mauritania and the Republic of the Congo) makes a particular institution responsible for receiving financial reports, but does not give it an explicit mandate to do anything with them, or to investigate reports of political finance violations.

Sanctions

There is no lack of sanctions against political finance violations in African legal documents. All African countries have some sanctions available against political finance violations, in particular fines, imprisonment and loss of public funding. Indeed, imprisonment as a potential sanction is more common in Africa than in the world as a whole (71 per cent of countries compared to 52 per cent).

Unfortunately, there are very few reports of sanctions ever being applied in relation to political finance violations. Transparency International Zimbabwe noted that in Mozambique 'no precedents of actual application have been identified by the research team. None of the political actors involved were aware of any punishment that has taken place and the general public seems to be largely ignorant on this issue'.[108] As noted above, 30 out of 44 Kenyan political parties failed to submit annual financial reports in 2009–10. These parties were threatened with de-registration, but this sanction has not been applied to any party to date.[109] Similarly, a report regarding the abuse of state resources in the Gambia noted that 'despite the clear breach of the Code, the IEC [Independent Electoral Commission] failed to take action against the APRC … or even to make any public comment', while the EMB in Ghana 'turns a blind eye to obviously inaccurate returns from the parties'.[110] The resulting impunity can be very harmful to popular confidence in the democratic process. In Liberia, '[t]he NEC's [National Election Commission's] failure to penalise the use of state resources by the ruling Unity Party (UP) in the recent campaign reinforced opposition perceptions of bias'.[111]

When political parties refuse to comply with political finance regulations (for example, by not submitting financial reports), they should automatically be issued a proportional sanction. This could range from a warning to a small fine (for failing to submit reports on time) to withholding public funding or larger fines (for continued refusal to submit reports in spite of reminders). Criminal sanctions are required to prevent and penalize violations such as vote buying and knowingly receiving large illegal donations. In countries where legislation on the subject has been ignored for a long time, it is necessary to gradually increase enforcement.

It should be recognized, however, that sanctions alone will not be sufficient to create transparency in political finance. Political finance regulatory bodies should take a long-term view and aim to increase awareness among political parties and the public about the importance of political finance regulation. Rules and regulations

> To be effective, political finance regulators need to communicate closely with political parties, candidates and other stakeholders—and carefully guard their independence. Few things are as potentially harmful to effective political finance oversight as perceived (or real) bias on the part of the institution responsible for overseeing the rules.

must be suitable for the particular situation in each country. To be effective, political finance regulators need to communicate closely with political parties, candidates and other stakeholders—and carefully guard their independence. Few things are as potentially harmful to effective political finance oversight as perceived (or real) bias on the part of the institution responsible for overseeing the rules.

The role of civil society and the media

Non-state actors also have crucial roles to play in the oversight of money in African politics. As elsewhere, government actors do not provide sufficient control. Since the early 1990s, African CSOs have monitored electoral processes in most countries on the continent. These efforts have often been longer-term and covered a wide range of issues. Unfortunately, few such projects have taken into account the role of money in the electoral process. Given the lack of reliable financial reports from political parties and candidates in Africa, it is crucial that civil society groups carefully monitor the financial flows. The cash nature of most African economies makes such monitoring more difficult, but there are many effective approaches that can be adopted. For example, the Coalition for Accountable Political Financing (CAPF) in Kenya used fieldwork and surveys to provide much-needed information about the financing of the turbulent 2007 elections.[112]

The media have an equally important role to play. Media organizations can expose funding scandals and violations by political stakeholders regarding the raising and spending of funds. Areas of particular interest are illegal donations, illicit connections between donors and political parties, vote buying and the abuse of state resources. Unfortunately, media outlets are not necessarily immune to the temptations of corruption themselves. A recent report about the Nigerian media claimed that corrupt behaviour on the part of journalists is 'unfortunately condoned by media proprietors, who sometimes encourage reporters to extort money from news sources in lieu of salaries'.[113] An observer of the Ugandan media has similarly discussed the 'curse of the brown envelope'.[114]

The media and CSOs (as well as political parties) need to base their activities in this field on a thorough understanding of the country's current regulatory system. This will allow them to identify violations and suggest areas for reform.

Conclusions

This chapter has shown that a range of political finance regulations is used on the African continent. While all African countries have at least some rules in this area, oversight and control are woefully lacking; the problem lies less with the rules than with implementation. While this situation is not unique to Africa (both Europe and North America have similar problems), African countries could indeed do better.

Political parties in many African countries face a significant shortage of funds, due to a lack of donations from party members, supporters and legal entities, and low levels of public funding from the (admittedly often cash-strapped) state coffers.

Some qualifications must be made. First, in many African countries, incumbent political parties do rather well financially. Parties' widespread abuse of state resources and holding monopolies on corporate donations are significant problems in many countries, which make it harder to achieve a level electoral playing field and threaten the quality of governance. The problem is therefore not so much a *lack* of resources as their *biased distribution*.

Second, discussions about African political finance often focus almost exclusively on political parties, while the evidence suggests that a significant portion of campaign finance is focused on individual candidates. This has several implications. First, attention must be paid to the candidate selection stage, which may involve as much vote buying and other violations as the election itself. Second, the debts that many candidates incur during election campaigns can leave them vulnerable to temptations of corruption after election to public office. Third, political parties can use their candidates to channel funds in ways that avoid political finance regulations. Therefore, campaign finance regulations that do not take the role of candidates into account risk creating vast loopholes.

Finally, we must recognize that finance is not the only facilitator of political influence. Having access to large amounts of money is no guarantee of electoral success, even in areas with a shorter experience of electoral democracy. Using data from 2000, Saffu noted that 'The gross inequality of resources between governing parties and opposition parties, shown in a ruling party's ability to outspend all the opposition parties put together by 15:1, as in Ghana, probably by a bigger margin in Kenya and by as much as 30:1 in Senegal affects the fairness or democratic quality of the elections.'[115] While this may be true, it should also be noted that since 2000, governing parties have more than once lost elections in all three of these countries.[116]

There is no doubt that reforms are needed, both of formal regulations and the way they are implemented. Change may take time, and political actors may be reluctant to introduce the necessary reforms. In South Africa, the Institute for Democracy in Africa (IDASA) decided in 2000 to discontinue its legal fight to have political parties disclose private donations, since a reform route seemed more viable and the government had promised to introduce reform quickly. Twelve years later, nothing has happened; IDASA has noted that '[t]hus far the ruling party has shown very little appetite for introducing legislation in Parliament'.[117] Similarly, in Ghana the two main parties have promised political finance reform when they have been in opposition since the 1990s, but have conveniently forgotten these promises once they have gained power.[118]

> The impunity with which African political actors can completely ignore existing political finance regulations probably does more to erode confidence in controlling the role of money in politics than any other factor. It also weakens Africans' trust in political parties.

Sometimes the question of sequencing is raised: in what order should political finance reforms be introduced? There is little sense in introducing contribution and spending bans and limits until a disclosure system has been put in place that functions at least reasonably well. The foundation of such a system entails (at a minimum): (1) legal requirements for political parties and candidates to submit financial reports; and (2) a formal oversight body with sufficient resources, know-how and political clout to audit reports, investigate potential violations and enforce penalties. While the initial focus should be on building the capacity of political actors rather than penalizing them, violations must be met with increasingly sharp sanctions that are implemented in an unbiased manner. The impunity with which African political actors can completely ignore existing political finance regulations probably does more to erode confidence in controlling the role of money in politics than any other factor. It also weakens Africans' trust in political parties.[119]

In addition to formal regulatory reform, there must be work to enhance average citizens' awareness of the importance of political finance regulations and the negative impact that violations have on people's lives. It must be explained that abusing state resources is wasting money that rightly belongs to the people,[120] and that in the longer run electing politicians who will reduce poverty will be more beneficial than accepting money for votes. Civil society groups and the mass media have crucial roles to play in this regard. Unfortunately, significant progress in this area requires changing the clientelistic relationships that often exist between politicians and voters—a difficult task indeed.

No discussion of changing the role of money in African politics is complete without addressing the responsibility of political parties and candidates. Their behaviour is responsible not only for the current situation but also for shaping future generations of politicians. To a large extent, the incentives for politicians to regulate political finance lie in broadening the political horizon to see beyond the next election and secure the party's future in the long term.[121] For example, political parties that control parliamentary majorities should strive to create political finance rules that enhance the process of political competition, in order to increase their chances of returning to power after an electoral defeat.

There is no doubt that the financial situation of many African opposition parties is often very difficult. However, they need to refrain from engaging in illegal means to raise funds, and instead focus on innovative means of finding the necessary capital. They must demonstrate that they are a credible alternative to the incumbent, and that they are taking the issue of financial transparency seriously. That will put them in a better position to oversee a clean political system once they gain power.

Reforming the role of money in African politics requires sustained efforts by all stakeholders toward long-term improvement. They should strive to make incremental improvements in the oversight of political finance in each election.

Recommendations

Policy makers[122]

1. Do not attempt to move directly from no regulations to a highly controlled system. Focus instead on the most important rules and ensure that they are implemented. Control of political finance must not lead to limitations on political competition. One area to be addressed early on is the risk of illicit funds entering the political process.[123] Also consider what regulations can effectively address the gender gap in access to funds.
2. Given the often-fluid relationship between political parties and candidates, ensure that any limits, bans and reporting requirements apply to both.
3. Require political parties and candidates to provide comprehensive reports about their finances. Ensure that the reporting requirements are sufficiently detailed to allow for auditing of the financial records, without being so strict as to unduly burden those required to comply.
4. Make the provision of public funding conditional on compliance with disclosure requirements.
5. Consider indirect public funding of political parties as a cheaper and more easily controlled complement to direct public funding.
6. Consider allowing political parties to engage in limited commercial activities in fields such as printing and publication as a way to supplement their often very limited income. Any such activities would need to be reported in detail along with the parties' regular financial reports.

Monitoring and enforcement agencies

1. Issue at least a minor sanction when political finance stakeholders refuse to report on their finances in violation of the law.
2. Set up a ten-year plan to build awareness among political parties and the public about political finance issues, and gradually replace capacity-building exercises (aimed at helping political parties comply with the

regulations) with increasingly strict sanctions against those that refuse to comply.
3. Communicate closely with the stakeholders to ensure that the rules are in line with their experiences on the ground. Maintain transparency in the enforcement of political finance regulations.
4. Forcefully reject any attempts to influence the regulatory body's behaviour.

Ruling parties

1. Refrain from abusing state resources; if this becomes standard political practice and you lose an election, you will never be able to regain power.
2. Work to establish political finance rules that will make it possible for your party to return to power through competitive elections if it loses power in the future (such as generous state funding of the opposition and effective bans on abuse of state resources). Act in accordance with such principles even before they become law.

Opposition parties

1. Whatever promises you make about reforming the political finance system oversight, remember them once you gain power.
2. Seek innovative ways to raise legal funds, rather than become resigned about a shortage of funds. The key is to explain to the people and key stakeholders why your policies are the best for the country.
3. Refrain from illegal fundraising activities. Help make the political process as clean as possible so that you can take over a functioning political system once you gain power through elections.
4. Make sure you understand the existing legal framework of political party and campaign funding. This can help you raise funds legally, identify violations by your opponents and make suggestions for legal reforms.

Civil society

1. Never take your eyes off the financial flows through the political arena, for therein lies the key to understanding the dynamics of the political process.
2. Monitor the behaviour of political parties and candidates during elections, and present your findings in a way that is understandable to average citizens.
3. Build public awareness about the electorate's role in building transparent and fair political finance by rejecting vote buying, excessive campaign spending and abuse of state resources.
4. Do not let political actors persuade your civil society group to become involved in partisan activities aimed at circumventing the letter (or the spirit) of the political finance regulations.

Media actors

1. Strive to expose violations by any political stakeholders regarding the raising and spending of funds—in particular accepting illegal donations, illicit connections between donors and political parties, vote buying and the abuse of state resources. Make clear to average citizens how such abuses affect them.
2. Do not accept money from political stakeholders to report in a biased manner. Independent and fearless media are crucial for a functioning democracy.

International actors

1. Understand that the way money is raised and spent during an election campaign is often a better indicator of the fairness and competitiveness of the electoral process than what happens on election day.
2. International election observer groups that ignore the issue of political finance must accept that their conclusions will only provide a partial picture, at best. Note that effective monitoring of political finance requires a presence on the ground for longer than most international observation efforts.[124]
3. Consider whether announcing or launching a large-scale aid project during the pre-election period will upset the campaign playing field. Take into account whether the incumbent regime can take advantage of the announcement, especially if the project has a direct impact on voters' lives, such as road construction or building hospitals, schools or power plants. However, if done right (and with a long-term focus), external aid can help level the political playing field.

References

African Media Barometer (2011) *Nigeria 2011*. Windhoek: Friedrich Ebert Stiftung.

Allafrica (2010) 'Tanzania: Opposition Parties Trail CCM in Campaign Funding', 1 November, available at http://allafrica.com/stories/201011030504.html

Allafrica (2011a) 'Kenya: Audit Office Puts Political Parties On Notice', 30 June, available at http://allafrica.com/stories/201107010004.html

Allafrica (2011b) 'Liberia: Political Parties Evade Accountability Law, LDI Says', 1 February, available at http://allafrica.com/stories/201102040950.html

Arthur, John A. (2010) *African Diaspora Identities: Negotiating Culture in Transnational Migration*. Lanham, MD: Lexington Books.

Austin, Reginald and Tjernström, Maja (eds) (2003) *Funding of Political Parties and Election Campaigns*. Stockholm: International IDEA.

Ayee, Joseph R.A., Anebo, Felix K.G. and Debrah, Emmanuel (2008) *Financing Political Parties in Ghana*. Dakar: The Consortium for Development Partnerships.

Beck, Thorsten, Fuchs, Michael and Uy, Marilou (2009) *Finance in Africa: Achievements and Challenges*, Policy Research Working Paper 5020. The World Bank, Africa Region.

Boer, Martin (2004) *The Life of the Party: the Hidden Role of Money in Namibian Politics*, Occasional Paper No. 5. Namibia: Hans Seidel Foundation.

Booysen, S. and Masterson, G. (2009) 'Chapter 11: South Africa', in Denis Kadima and Susan Booysen (eds), *Compendium of Elections in Southern Africa 1989–2009: 20 Years of Multiparty Democracy*. Johannesburg: Electoral Institute for the Sustainability of Democracy in Africa.

Bratton, Michael (2008) *Vote Buying and Violence in Nigerian Election Campaigns*, Working Paper No. 99. Afrobarometer.

Bryan, Shari and Baer, Denise (eds) (2005) *Money in Politics: A Study of Party Financing Practices in 22 Countries*. Washington, D.C.: National Democratic Institute for International Affairs.

Butler, Anthony (2010) 'Conclusion: The Opportunity and Challenge of Party Finance Reform in South Africa', in Anthony Butler (ed.), *Paying for Politics: Party Funding and Political Change in South Africa and the Global South*. Auckland Park: Jacana Media.

Centre for Multiparty Democracy in Malawi (CMD) and Netherlands Institute for Multiparty Democracy (NIMD) (2008) *The Functioning and Management of Political Parties in East and Southern Africa Revisited*. CMD and NIMD.

Chikuhwa, Jacob Wilson (2004) *A Crisis of Governance: Zimbabwe*. New York: Algora Publishing.

Coalition for Accountable Political Financing (CAPF) (2007) *Election 2007 Interim Report on National Voter Bribery Survey*. Nairobi: CAPF.

Coalition for Accountable Political Financing (CAPF) (2008) *The Money Factor in Poll Race, a Monitoring Report of the 2007 General Election*. Nairobi: CAPF.

Commonwealth Expert Team (2011) *The Gambia Presidential Election, 24 November 2011*. London: Commonwealth Expert Team.

Commonwealth Expert Team (2013) Cameroon Legislative and Municial Elections, 20 September 2013. London: Commonwealth Expert Team.

Council of Europe (2003) *Recommendation Rec(2003)4 of the Committee of Ministers to Member states on common rules against corruption in the funding of political parties and electoral campaigns*, available at https://wcd.coe.int/ViewDoc.jsp?id=2183

Democracy International (2011) *Ghana Democracy and Governance Assessment, Final Report*. Accra: US Agency for International Development.

Economist, The (2013) 'Ghana, Get a Grip', 21 December.

Electoral Institute for Sustainable Democracy in Africa (EISA) (2005) *Namibia Presidential and National Assembly Elections, 15–16 November 2004*, EISA Election Observer Mission Report No. 18. Johannesburg: EISA.

Electoral Institute for Sustainable Democracy in Africa (EISA) (2006a) *Tanzania Presidential, National Assembly and Local Government Elections, 14 December 2005*, EISA Election Observer Mission Report No. 20. Johannesburg: EISA.

Electoral Institute for Sustainable Democracy in Africa (EISA) (2006b) 'Malawi: Party Funding'. Johannesburg: EISA. Available at http://www.eisa.org.za/WEP/malparties3.htm

Electoral Institute for Sustainable Democracy in Africa (EISA) (2006c) 'Zambia: Party Funding'. Johannesburg: EISA. Available at http://www.eisa.org.za/WEP/zamparties2.htm

Electoral Institute for Sustainable Democracy in Africa (EISA) (2007) 'Comparative Data: Funding of Political Parties'. Johannesburg: EISA. Available at http://www.eisa.org.za/WEP/comparties.htm

Electoral Institute for Sustainable Democracy in Africa (EISA) (2011a) 'South Africa: Party Funding'. Johannesburg: EISA. Available at http://www.eisa.org.za/WEP/souparties2.htm

Electoral Institute for Sustainable Democracy in Africa (EISA) (2011b) EISA *Technical Assessment Team Report, the 2011 Seychelles Presidential Elections 19–21 May 2011*, EISA Observer Mission Report No. 40. Johannesburg: EISA.

European Union Election Observation Mission (EU EOM) (2007) *Togo, Rapport Final, Election législatives, 14 October 2007*. Brussels: EU EOM.

European Union Election Observation Mission (EU EOM) (2008a) *Angola: Final Report Parliamentary Elections, September 2008*. Brussels: EU EOM.

European Union Election Observation Mission (EU EOM) (2008b) *Rwanda: Legislative Elections to the Chamber of Deputies, 15–18 September 2008*. Brussels: EU EOM.

European Union Election Observation Mission (EU EOM) (2009) *Mozambique: Presidential, Legislative and Provincial Assembly Elections, October 2009, Final Report*. Brussels: EU EOM.

European Union Election Observation Mission (EU EOM) (2010a) *Tanzania Final Report: General Elections October 2010*. Brussels: EU EOM.

European Union Election Observation Mission (EU EOM) (2010b) *Burundi, Rapport Final, Elections Communales, Présidentielle, Législatives, Sénatoriales et Collinaires 2010* [Burundi, Final Report on Communal, Presidential, Legislative, Senatorial and Cantonal elections]. Brussels: EU EOM.

European Union Election Observation Mission (EU EOM) (2010d) *Rapport Final, Mission d'Observation Électorale en République de Guinée, Élection Présidentielle de 2010* [Final Report, Election Observation Mission in the Republic of Guinea, Presidential Election, 2010]. Brussels: EU EOM.

European Union Election Observation Mission (EU EOM) (2010e) *Sudan: Final Report on the Executive and Legislative Elections, 2010.* Brussels: EU EOM.

European Union Election Observation Mission (EU EOM) (2011a) *Zambia: Final Report on the General Elections, 2011.* Brussels: EU EOM.

European Union Election Observation Mission (EU EOM) (2011b) *Tanzania: Final Report, General Elections, April 2011.* Brussels: EU EOM.

European Union Election Observation Mission (EU EOM) (2011c) *Nigeria: Final Report, General Elections, April 2011.* Brussels: EU EOM.

European Union Election Observation Mission (EU EOM) (2011d) *Rapport Final sur les Élections Législatives du 13 Février 2011* [Final Report on the Parliamentary Elections of 13 February 2011]. Brussels: EU EOM.

European Union Election Observation Mission (EU EOM) (2011e) *Niger: Rapport Final–Élections Législatives et Présidentielle 2011* [Niger: Final Report, Parliamentary and Presidential Elections 2011]. Brussels: EU EOM.

European Union Election Observation Mission (EU EOM) (2011f) *Uganda: Final Report on the Uganda General Elections, 2011.* Brussels: EU EOM.

February, Judith (2012) *Political Party Funding: Legislation Should Regulate Donations*, available at http://www.ngopulse.org/article/political-party-funding-legislation-should-regulate-donations

Friedrich Ebert Stiftung (2011) *African Media Barometer, Nigeria 2011.* Windhoek: FES.

Ghana News Link (2011) 'NDC is Unable to Submit Financial Report to EC', 13 September, available at http://www.ghananewslink.com/?id=16561

Global Financial Integrity (2010) *Illicit Financial Flows from Africa; Hidden Resources for Development.* Washington, D.C.: Global Financial Integrity.

Helle, Svein-Erik (2011) *Breaking the 'Vicious Cycle': Financial Challenges for the Opposition Parties in Uganda and the Role of the International Community.* Bergen: Chr. Michelsen Institute.

Hopwood, Graham (2005) 'Trapped in the Past: The State of the Opposition', in Justine Hunter (ed.), *Spot the Difference: Namibia's Political Parties Compared.* Windhoek: Namibia Institute for Democracy.

Independent Electoral Commission (IEC) (2011) *Represented Political Parties' Fund Annual Report 2010/2011*. Centurion: IEC.

Independent National Electoral Commission (INEC) (2011) *Political Party Financial Reporting Manual*. Abuja: INEC.

Institute for Democracy in Africa (IDASA) (2005) *Party Funding Court Case Briefing*. Johannesburg: IDASA.

International Crisis Group (ICG) (2012) *Liberia: Time for Much-Delayed Reconciliation and Reform*, Africa Briefing No. 88. Dakar/Brussels: ICG.

International IDEA, Political Finance Database, available at http://www.idea.int/ political-finance

International Monetary Fund (IMF) (2005) *World Economic Outlook, September 2005: Building Institutions, Issue 2*. Washington, D.C.: IMF.

Jouan, Barbara (2012) *Assessment of the Legal Framework and Practices Related to Campaign Finance during the National Constituent Assembly elections*. Tunis: International Foundation for Electoral Systems.

Kaniki, Sheshangai (2008) *The Private Sector and Cash Transfers in Africa*, Working Paper Number 80. Cape Town: Economic Policy Research Institute.

Karume, Shumbana (ed.) (2004) *Dilemmas of Political Transition: Towards Institutionalisation of Multiparty Democracy in Tanzania*. Johannesburg: Electoral Institute for Sustainable Democracy in Africa.

Kupferschmidt, David (2009) *Illicit Political Finance and State Capture*. Stockholm: International IDEA.

Lavallée, Emmanuelle, Razafindrakoto, Mireille and Roubaud, François (2008) *Corruption and Trust in Political Institutions in Subsaharan Africa*, Working Paper No. 102. Afrobarometer.

Leadership (2012) 'Financial Audit Report Indicts PDP, ACN, CPC, Others', 2 April, available at http://www.leadership.ng/nga/articles/20975/2012/04/02/ financial_audit_report_indicts_pdp_acn_cpc_others.html

Libyan High National Elections Commission (2012) *Regulation on Campaigning, Political Entity and Candidate Finances, and Financial Disclosure Reporting for the General National Congress Election*. Unpublished.

Lindberg, Staffan I. (2003) 'It's Our Time to "Chop": Do Elections in Africa Feed Neo-Patrimonialism rather than Counteract It?', *Democratization*, 10(2).

Lindberg, Staffan I. (2010) 'What Accountability Pressures do MPs in Africa Face and How Do They Respond? Evidence from Ghana', *Journal of Modern African Studies*, 48(1).

Liviga, Athumani J. and John, William (2012) *Political Party Financing and Why it Matters*. Paper presented at the Africa Regional Conference on Legal Frameworks Governing Political Parties: The Case of Party Financing, Dar es Salaam, 10–12 July.

Local, The (2012) 'Left Party Caps MP Pay with New "Party Tax"', 9 January, available at http://www.thelocal.se/38392/20120109/

Mail and Guardian (2009) 'ANC Spends R200-million on Election Campaign', 17 April, available at http://mg.co.za/article/2009-04-17-anc-spends-r200million-on-election-campaign

Maiyo, Josh (2008) *Political Parties and Intra-Party Democracy in East Africa – From Representative to Participatory Democracy*. Master's Thesis, Leiden University.

Matlosa, Khabele (ed.) (2007) *Political Parties in Southern Africa: The State of Parties and their Role in Democratization*. Stockholm: International IDEA.

Matlosa, Khabele and Sello, Caleb (2005) *Political Parties and Democratization in Lesotho*. Johannesburg: Electoral Institute for Sustainable Democracy in Africa.

Mayiga, John Bosco (2011) 'The Scourge of the Brown Envelope in Ugandan Journalism: Some Theoretical Reflections', *Uganda Media Review*, November.

McLean, Joan E. (2003) 'Campaign Strategy', in Susan J. Carroll (ed.), *Women and American Politics: New Questions, New Directions*. Oxford: Oxford University Press.

Musambayi, Katumanga (2006) *Kenya: Country Report based on Research and Dialogue with Political Parties*. Stockholm: International IDEA.

Nam-Katoti, Wilbert, Doku, James, Abor, Joshua and Quartey, Peter (2011) 'Financing Political Parties in Ghana', *Journal of Applied Business and Economics*, 12(4).

Nassmacher, Karl-Heinz (2003) 'Party Funding in Continental Western Europe', in Reginald Austin and Maja Tjernström (eds), *Funding of Political Parties and Election Campaigns*. Stockholm: International IDEA.

Nassmacher, Karl-Heinz (2009) *The Funding of Party Competition: Political Finance in 25 Democracies*. Baden-Baden: Nomos.

National Democratic Institute for International Affairs (NDI) (2011) *Final Report on the 2011 Moroccan Parliamentary Elections*. Washington, D.C.: NDI.

National Elections Commission (Republic of Liberia) *Campaign Finance Regulations for Political Parties and Candidates (2011)*. Approved by the Board of Commissioners on 16 June 2011.

Ndeta, John Harrington (2013) 'Party Primaries Robbed Women of Leadership Chance', *Kenyan Woman*, issue 34.

Netherlands Institute for Multiparty Democracy (NIMD) (2007) *Kenya: New Bill on Political Party Funding.* The Hague: NIMD.

Nigerian News Service (2010) 'Election Spending: CBN Retains 6.26% Interest Rate', 24 November, available at http://www.nigeriannewsservice.com/nns-news-archive/headlines/election-spending-cbn-retains-626-interest-rate

Ninsin, Kwame A. (2006) *Political Parties and Political Participation in Ghana.* Berlin: Konrad Adenauer Foundation.

Obasi, Nnamdi K. (2011) 'Organised Crime and Illicit Bunkering: Only Nigeria's Problem?', in Michael Roll and Sebastian Sperling (eds), *Fuelling the World – Failing the Region? Oil Governance and Development in Africa's Gulf of Guinea.* Abuja: Friedrich Ebert Stiftung.

Ohman, Magnus (1999) *Public Funding of Political Parties in Africa.* Washington, D.C.: International Foundation for Electoral Systems.

Ohman, Magnus (2004) *The Heart and Soul of the Party: Candidate Selection in Ghana and Africa.* Uppsala: Uppsala University.

Ohman, Magnus (2010) *Including Political Finance in International Election Observation Missions.* The Carter Center and the International Foundation for Electoral Systems.

Organization for Security and Co-operation in Europe, Office for Democratic Institutions and Human Rights and Venice Commission (2010) *Guidelines for Political Party Regulation*, available at http://www.stf.jus.br/repositorio/cms/portalStfInternacional/portalStfCooperacao_en_us/anexo/CDLAD2010024.pdf

Pocit (2012) '10 Major Political Parties Using Cellphone Fundraising', available at https://www.pocit.co.za/static/press/2009_jan/10%20major%20political%20parties.pdf

Punch (2012) 'PDP Holdings: Altering Formula of Party Funding', 24 June, available at http://www.punchng.com/politics/pdp-holdings-altering-formula-of-party-funding/

Reuters (2012) 'Fitch: Pre-election Spending Could Weaken Ghana's Credit Outlook', 27 July, available at http://www.reuters.com/article/2012/07/27/idUSWNA212320120727

Reuters Africa (2011) 'Election Campaign Spending Boosts Nigeria Car Imports', 31 March, available at http://af.reuters.com/article/topNews/idAFJOE72U0YT20110331

Robinson, Vicki and Brümmer, Stefaans (2006) *SA Democracy Incorporated: Corporate Fronts and Political Party Funding.* Paper No. 129. Pretoria: Institute for Security Studies.

Saffu, Yaw (2003) 'The *Funding of Political Parties and Election Campaigns* in Africa', in Reginald Austin and Maja Tjernström (eds), Funding of Political Parties and Election Campaigns. Stockholm: International IDEA.

Salih, Mohamed (2007) *African Political Parties: Challenges for Sustained Multiparty Politics.* International Conference on Sustaining Africa's Democratic Momentum, Johannesburg, 5–7 March.

Schaffer, Frederic Charles (2002) *What is Vote Buying?* Prepared for Trading Political Rights: The Comparative Politics of Vote Buying Conference, Center for International Studies, Massachusetts Institute of Technology, Cambridge, MA, 26–27 August.

Shaw, Mark (2012) *Leadership Required: Drug Trafficking and the Crisis of Statehood in West Africa*, Policy Brief No. 37. Institute for Security Studies.

Somolekae, Gloria (2006) *Botswana: Country Report based on Research and Dialogue with Political Parties.* Stockholm: International IDEA.

Southern African Development Community (SADC) (2001) SADC *Parliamentary Forum Norms and Standards for Elections in the Region.* Windhoek, Namibia: SADC.

Southern African Development Community (SADC) (2003) *The Principles for Election Management, Monitoring and Observation in the SADC Region.* Windhoek, Namibia: SADC.

Speck, Bruno and Fontana, Alessandra (2011) '"Milking the System"; Fighting the Abuse of Public Resources for Re-election', *U4 Issue*, 7.

Spector, Bertram I., Schloss, Miguel and Green, Sammi (2005) *Corruption Assessment: Mozambique, Final Report.* Washington, D.C.: US Agency for International Development.

Ssenkumba, John (2006) *Political Party Financing in Uganda.* Abuja: Friedrich Ebert Stiftung.

Tax Justice Network (2012) *Tax in Developing Countries: Increasing Resources for Development.* Written evidence submitted by the International Secretariat of the Tax Justice Network to the International Development Committee of the UK Parliament.

Teshome, Wondwosen (2009a) 'Opposition Parties and the Politics of Opposition in Africa: A Critical Analysis', *International Journal of Human and Social Sciences*, 4(5).

Teshome, Wondwosen (2009b) 'Political Finance in Africa: Ethiopia as a Case Study', *International Journal of Humanities and Social Sciences*, 3/2.

Think Africa Press (2012) 'The MDC is Funded by Zimbabweans not Foreigners', 8 February, available at http://thinkafricapress.com/zimbabwe/mdc-funded-zimbabweans-not-foreigners

This Day Live (2010) 'Why I'm Running for 2011 Presidency, by Jonathan',
    30 October, available at http://www.thisdaylive.com/articles/why-i-m-running-
    for-2011-presidency-by-jonathan/75369/

Throup, David W. (2011) *Ghana: Assessing Risks to Stability*. Washington, D.C.:
    Center for Strategic and International Studies.

Tonchi, Victor L. and Shifotoka, Albertina N. (2006) *Namibia: Country Report
    based on Research and Dialogue with Political Parties*. Stockholm: International
    IDEA.

Transparency International Zimbabwe (TIZ) (2010) *Nuru: Promoting Transparency
    in Political Finance in Southern Africa*. Harare: TIZ.

United Nations Convention Against Corruption (UNCAC) (2005).

Van de Walle, Nicolas (2001) *African Economies and the Politics of Permanent Crisis,
    1979–1999*. New York: Cambridge University Press.

Vicente, Pedro C. (2010) 'Does Oil Corrupt? Evidence from a Natural Experiment
    in West Africa', *Journal of Development Economics*, 92(1).

Vicente, Pedro C. (2012) *Is Vote-buying Effective? Evidence from a Field Experiment
    in West Africa*. Working Paper.

Wiafe-Akenten, Charles (2004) *Ghana: Country Report based on Research and
    Dialogue with Political Parties*. Stockholm: International IDEA.

Women's Environment and Development Organization (2007) *Women Candidates
    and Campaign Finance*. New York: Women's Environment and Development
    Organization.

Young, Daniel J. (2009) *Is Clientelism at Work in African Elections? A Study of
    Voting Behavior in Kenya and Zambia*, Working Paper No. 99. Afrobarometer.

Notes

[1] Teshome 2009a, p. 293.

[2] Saffu 2003, p. 27.

[3] Speck and Fontana 2011, p. v.

[4] Some argue that the discussion about clientelism presents a simplified or unduly
    pessimistic view of African politics. For a criticism of clientelism in Africa, see Young
    2009.

[5] Van de Walle 2001, p. 51.

[6] See, for example, Kupferschmidt 2009.

[7] The International Monetary Fund (IMF) predictions for 2015 suggest that foreign aid
    will represent more than half of government spending in 70 per cent of the 37 countries
    studied. Calculated from IMF 2005, p. 148.

[8] One study concludes that less than 20 per cent of African households have access to a
    bank account, which is less than half of that in many other developing regions. Beck,
    Fuchs and Uy 2009, p. 4. See also Kaniki 2008.

9   The Tax Justice Network (2012) has estimated that tax avoidance in Africa amounts to nearly $80 billion per year, which is equivalent to the continent's total expenditures on healthcare.

10   UNCAC 2005, Article 7(3). Emphasis added.

11   SADC 2001, Article 6. This document also states that 'The electoral law should prohibit the Government to aid or to abet any party gaining unfair advantage', para. 3.i.

12   SADC 2003.

13   Note that the limits in Kenya have yet to be tested in a general election.

14   Throughout this handbook, international dollars (I$) are presented alongside amounts in national currencies. The international dollar is a hypothetical currency that takes into account purchasing power parity and is therefore suitable for comparisons between countries. For countries in which the power purchasing power parity varies significantly from the United States (which is used as the baseline for the comparison), the I$ exchange rate may be considerably different from the nominal exchange rate. No conversions are given for US dollars (as this is by default the same amount as the I$) or for those instances where the original currency is unknown and a secondary currency such as the euro has been cited instead. For further information, see Annex V.

15   Hopwood's data indicate that the opposition parties in Namibia have less than 1,000 paid-up members (2005, p. 135). Boer (2004, p. 7) notes that one of the smaller opposition parties, the Democratic Turnhalle Alliance, reported in 2004 that it received the equivalent of I$1,500 per year in membership fees.

16   Musambayi 2006. p. 11. Similarly, Salih (2007, p. 15) has stressed that 'most African political parties lack membership lists, let alone the expectation that membership fees are regularly paid', and Matlosa (2007, p. 44) agrees that in Southern Africa, '[m]embership dues do not amount to enough to sustain parties' operations'.

17   Ninsin 2006, p. 18. See also NIMD 2007. A recent study suggests that Ghanaian parties receive around 15 per cent of their income from membership fees. Nam-Katoti et al. 2011, p. 96.

18   Nassmacher (2009, p. 211) has noted that '[o]nly a minority of the countries in continental Western Europe display an important contribution of party members towards the funding of headquarters' activity'.

19   The poverty figures (using purchasing power parity) are calculated from the UN Development Programme's Human Development Index 2011.

20   Author's observation. In some African countries, parties are banned from engaging in commercial activities.

21   Pocit 2012.

22   Commonwealth Expert Team 2011, p. 19. The report notes that corporate donations are legal in the Gambia, but that such donations were seldom forthcoming to the opposition parties.

23   Tom Lodge, cited in Robinson and Brümmer 2006, p. 10. As a consequence of these donations, the ANC reportedly acted as 'facilitators for black business in the country', thereby rendering itself vulnerable to accusations that it directed public policy for partisan benefit.

24   See Democracy International 2011, p. 7. Only Liberia, Mali, Mozambique, the Republic of the Congo and Sierra Leone ban contributions from domestic corporations to political parties.

25   This Day Live 2010.

26   Spector, Schloss and Green 2005, p. 12.

27   EISA 2006c.

28 Ssenkumba 2006, pp. 7ff.

29 For small political parties, the distinction may become blurred if the presidential candidate is also the party leader and main party funder.

30 Maiyo 2008, p. 61; Wiafe-Akenten 2004, p. 10.

31 EU EOM 2011b, p. 24.

32 Bryan and Baer 2005, p. 1. Data from other regions suggest that fear of bankruptcy may be a particular concern for female candidates, and may serve as a serious deterrent for women considering running in elections. See McLean 2003, p. 63, and Women's Environment and Development Organization 2007, p. 4.

33 Coalition for Accountable Political Financing 2008, p. 22. For a discussion of the same issue in Ghana, see Ohman 2004, pp. 144ff.

34 Coalition for Accountable Political Financing 2008, p. 36.

35 Ibid., p. 59.

36 Nassmacher 2003, p. 120. The Left Party in Sweden has capped the income of its elected officials and requires them to pay amounts in excess of the cap to the party. Local 2012.

37 Helle 2011, p. 6.

38 Bryan and Baer 2005, p. 124, Punch 2012, Somolekae 2006, pp. 8ff, Think Africa Press 2012, Matlosa and Sello 2005, p. 47.

39 Helle 2011, p. 6.

40 See, for example, Bryan and Baer 2005, p. 141 regarding Zambia.

41 Austin and Tjernström 2003, p. xiv.

42 Teshome 2009b, p. 407.

43 Arthur 2010, p. 2

44 Throup 2011, p. 11.

45 Kupferschmidt 2009, p. 17 and Shaw 2012, p. 2.

46 Throup 2011, p. 11.

47 Shaw 2012, p. 2.

48 Kupferschmidt 2009, p. 15. Illicit funds do not exclusively come from the outside world to Africa, however. One report has estimated that the flow of illicit funds from Africa between 1970 and 2008 may amount to as much as USD 1.8 trillion. Global Financial Integrity 2010, p. 1.

49 Vicente 2010, Obasi 2011, p. 59.

50 Throup 2011, p. 11.

51 Jouan 2012.

52 Early examples of legal provisions for direct public funding include Nigeria (1977), Benin and Cameroon (1990), Guinea (1991), Angola, Tanzania and Zimbabwe (1992), and South Africa (1993). Note that in some of these countries no funding has ever been distributed, while in others public funding has since been abolished. Ohman 1999.

53 IDASA 2005, p. 3.

54 Uganda, Tanzania and Mozambique have at times allowed international donors to provide funds that were distributed to eligible political parties. In Botswana and South Africa, private actors have sometimes set up similar mechanisms themselves.

55 EU EOM 2010b, p. 33, 2007, p. 36, 2010d, p. 33 and 2010e, p. 28. Similar occurrences were reported in Cameroon and Côte d'Ivoire during the 1990s. Note that Guinea and Sudan have provisions that political parties *may* receive public funding, but it is not guaranteed.

56 EU EOM 2010a, p. 24, EISA 2006b. Equal amounts were provided to all the political parties taking part in the 2002 elections in Lesotho; each received the equivalent of I$4,000. Matlosa and Sello 2005, pp. 46ff.

57 EU EOM 2008a, p. 7.

58 IEC 2011, p. 10. See also Booysen and Masterson 2009, and Butler 2010.

59 TIZ 2010, p. 29, EU EOM 2010a, p. 24.

60 Calculated from Hopwood 2005, p. 138; IEC 2011, p. 10; EU EOM 2008b, p. 27, 2009, p. 20, 2011d, p. 20, 2010d, p. 18, and 2011e, p. 15; EISA 2011b, p. 8, Liviga and John 2012, p. 18; Commonwealth Expert Team 2013, p. 17; and NDI 2011, p. 18. See also EISA 2005, p. 15.

61 There are some exceptions, such as in Lesotho and Madagascar where all registered political parties are eligible for at least some public funding.

62 In fact, many African countries ban local political parties by demanding that all parties have a national presence.

63 EISA 2011a

64 Hopwood 2005, pp. 135, 139. See also Tonchi and Shifotoka 2006, p. 12.

65 EU EOM 2008b, p. 28.

66 *Mail and Guardian* 2009. Admittedly, South African political parties must close their accounting books 21 days before an election and not use public funds immediately before the elections. There is, however, no direct ban on using public funds for campaign purposes. As long as they use public funds before that cut-off date and private funds afterwards, there should be no problem for them using public funds for campaigns.

67 Ohman 1999, p. 10.

68 EISA 2006a, p. 22.

69 EISA 2007, Chikuhwa 2004, pp. 42ff. The MDC, which first made an appearance in the 2000 elections, would also have qualified for public funding under the previous rules.

70 Provisions also exist in Ethiopia and in the Democratic Republic of the Congo, but the rules in the former are vague; in the latter, parties must consider the gender balance among their candidates but no threshold is defined.

71 Current as of November 2013, according to the Inter-Parliamentary Union: see http://www.ipu.org/wmn-e/classif.htm

72 The limited effectiveness of the tax collection systems in many African countries may, however, limit the value of this benefit.

73 Speck and Fontana 2011, p. 5.

74 The same figures for all countries are 86 per cent and 93 per cent, respectively.

75 Speck and Fontana 2011, p. 18.

76 Commonwealth Expert Team 2011, p. 18.

77 CAPF 2008, p. 22.

78 Reuters 2012.

79 EU EOM 2008a, p. 21. MPLA stands for Movimento Popular de Libertação de Angola (Partido do Trabalho), the governing party of Angola.

80 EU EOM 2011b, p. 23, 2011a, p. 14. Similarly, it was claimed that during the 2011 elections in Nigeria, 'the incumbent President and State Governors frequently merged their official duties with campaign activities', EU EOM 2011c, p. 27.

81 Speck and Fontana 2011, p. 12.

82 See the reported concerns above from Ghanaian credit institutions regarding election-related spending in 2012. In addition, *The Economist* has warned that the increasing

budget deficit is 'partly due to a splurge in spending by the government in the run-up to the presidential and general elections of December 2012'. *The Economist* 2013.

83   Some of the countries that use spending limits, such as Guinea, Mauritania and the Sudan, have a somewhat chequered electoral past.

84   The author noted a significant level of third-party campaigning during the 2011 elections in Nigeria. This included large billboards, claiming to be paid for by non-governmental organizations, which called for people to vote for particular candidates.

85   CAPF 2008, p. 22.

86   Reuters Africa 2011, Nigerian News Service 2010.

87   CAPF 2008, p. 23.

88   Calculated from scans of submitted financial reports in the author's possession.

89   See, for example, Vicente 2012, p. 12.

90   Mushota, quoted in Ohman 2010, p. 9. See also Schaffer 2002.

91   Lindberg 2003, p. 131. As Lindberg points out, personalized patronage is not synonymous with vote buying, but he claims that the traditional process of giving small gifts was 'exploited, or aggravated' during the democratization process in the 1990s. In another article from 2010, Lindberg reported a view among Ghanaian MPs that their spending on personalized benefits to voters had increased significantly in recent elections, with average cash handouts to individual urban voters increasing by a factor of 10–20. Calculated from Lindberg 2010, p. 124.

92   Bratton 2008, p. 3.

93   Ndeta 2013, p. 2.

94   CAPF 2007. Interestingly, the same study estimated that two-thirds of the money intended for vote buying was actually stolen by the agents who were meant to distribute it.

95   CAPF 2008, p. 50.

96   In such systems, the candidate nomination process may be particularly prone to vote buying and similar methods.

97   The EU observation mission to the 2011 elections in Uganda noted, for example, 'that the bulk of funding flowed directly to candidates, whose campaign finance remains unregulated'. EU EOM 2011f, p. 25.

98   For example, political parties in Nigeria are required to report on every single donation and expense, no matter how insignificant. INEC 2011. One interesting approach is the requirement in Libya that political competitors should submit summary reports 15 days after the announcement of election results and detailed reports 45 days after the results are announced. Libyan High National Elections Commission 2012, section 4.2.

99   The ones without are mainly in Southern Africa: the Gambia, Malawi, Namibia, Swaziland, Zambia and Zimbabwe.

100 The author had first-hand experience of this when working with the Political Parties Registration Commission in Sierra Leone in 2007–08.

101 The African countries with such electoral systems but without reporting requirements for parties are Côte d'Ivoire, Djibouti, Ethiopia, Gabon, the Gambia, Kenya, Madagascar, Malawi, Mali, the Republic of the Congo, Swaziland, Tanzania, Zambia and Zimbabwe.

102 CMD and NIMD 2008, p. 11.

103 National Elections Commission (Republic of Liberia) 2011, Article 14.2.

104 Karume 2004, Hopwood 2005, p. 137, Ghana News Link 2011, Allafrica 2011b, Leadership 2012.

105 Allafrica 2011a.

[106] TIZ 2010, p. 22.

[107] Helle 2011, p. 14.

[108] TIZ 2010, p. 22. The author knows from personal experience that no federal-level sanctions have been applied in Liberia, Sierra Leone or Nigeria.

[109] Allafrica 2011a.

[110] Commonwealth Expert Team 2011, p. 18, Ayee, Anebo and Debrah 2008, p. 10. No sanctions have yet been applied in Nigeria against the parties that failed to submit their annual financial reports for 2010. Leadership 2012.

[111] ICG 2012, p. 1. See also Allafrica 2011b.

[112] See CAPF 2007, 2008.

[113] Friedrich Ebert Stiftung 2011, p 5.

[114] African Media Barometer 2011, p. 5, Mayiga 2011, pp. 9ff.

[115] Saffu 2003, p. 29. Saffu used data by Mouhamet Fall.

[116] Senegal in 2000 and 2012, Kenya in 2002 and partially in 2007, and Ghana in 2000 and 2008.

[117] February 2012, p. 2.

[118] Ohman 2004, p. 107. In this regard, the National Democratic Congress (NDC) and NPP of Ghana resemble the parliamentary political parties in Sweden. Similarly, the Kenyan Campaign Finance Bill 2011 was debated by the Kenyan Parliament for over two years before it was passed in December 2013, which meant that the bill was not in force for the 2013 elections.

[119] Lavallée, Razafindrakoto and Roubaud 2008, p. 5.

[120] For example, when road construction is determined by the electoral cycle rather than in accordance with a long-term infrastructure development plan, resources will be used inefficiently.

[121] Admittedly, this does not apply to all political parties. Those that cling to power by abusing state resources have little to gain from reforming political finance, and must be forced to do so through political pressure.

[122] Policy makers are defined as those involved in drafting, amending and adopting political finance policies, either from the executive or from the legislative arm of government. The focus is therefore on the role policy makers play rather than a particular institution.

[123] While illicit funding is particularly difficult to address, one observer has noted that a first step is an 'effective mechanism to ensure that where drug money is being used by politicians they can be "named and shamed"'. Shaw 2012, p. 5.

[124] See further in Ohman 2010.

CHAPTER 4

CHAPTER 4

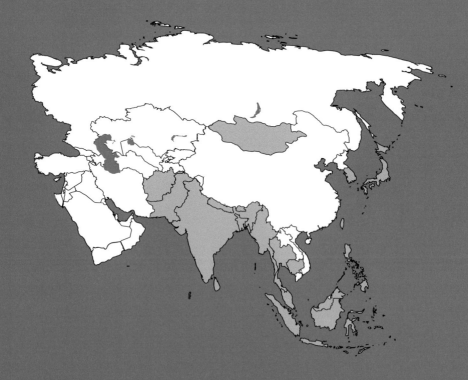

Asia

Andreas Ufen

Introduction

Financing is at the core of party and candidate activities. The way funding is organized has a huge impact on internal party structures, on the shape of party systems and on political systems at large. A transparent, rule-based financing of political actors is a facilitating factor for transitions to democracy and democratic consolidation.[1]

The 20 countries and territories analysed in this chapter[2] are located in an area marked by vast political and cultural diversity. Thus it is only possible to hint at some similarities and to stress some noticeable particularities of these countries in tackling the issue of money in politics. The diversity of the countries in the region is well illustrated in terms of economic performance. The sample ranges from highly-developed and high-performing economies such as Japan, the Republic of China (Taiwan), the Republic of Korea (South Korea) and Singapore to countries with high poverty rates such as Cambodia, Laos and Myanmar/Burma. The selection of countries used to illustrate particular points should not be taken to imply that such characteristics would also apply to other countries or contexts, or that the point applies to all (or even most) countries in this diverse region.

Another important distinction refers to each country's political system and the extent of their democratic development. The region has in the last decade taken important steps to establish more democratic institutions and ensure greater political pluralism. With this comes a steady increase in levels of political rights and civil liberties.[3] The fact that the region is the home of the world's least free country, the Democratic People's Republic of Korea (North Korea, which will not be discussed in this paper), as well as young and ambitious democracies like Taiwan, Mongolia and Indonesia, demonstrates its complexity and diversity.

In this often fast-changing and unpredictable political environment, constitutions and legal frameworks are often either redrafted or under construction. This also applies to the development of political finance laws, which makes it difficult to describe any clear patterns in terms of regulations that apply across the region.

In addition, political parties in a variety of Asian countries do not fulfil their 'classic' functions such as the articulation and aggregation of social interests, the development of political programmes, the political socialization of citizens and the organization of an effective opposition. On the contrary, the role of parties in Asia is too often to serve as clientelistic machines that generate money, jobs and licences for their candidates and supporters. In the Philippines, for example, many parties are seen as clientelistic networks that serve as vehicles for presidential candidates. They merge and split, and usually do not establish permanent structures. In Thailand, parties are poorly institutionalized, which means that factions are more important than the parties that comprise them.

The highly complex dynamics behind political finance have to be interpreted in the context of a commercialization of politics in most Asian countries. Although difficult to establish exactly due to simultaneous population growth, this translates into a sense of rising overall costs for campaigning. This development has been accompanied by a 'professionalization' of politics in which pollsters as well as marketing and campaign advisors ('spin doctors') are becoming increasingly influential.[4]

In general, parties and candidates in Asia are facing political finance challenges. State funding is often marginal (or even non-existent) and candidates without sufficient resources at their disposal find it hard to compete, since their parties often do not finance their candidates' campaigns. As a consequence, private donations (often from corporations) play an important role in financing political actors.

Today there is, however, an increased awareness in the region of the threats posed by the influence of big business and the commercialization of politics, and there are strong forces within Asian societies demanding reforms. Especially in the wake of political scandals, calls for stricter regulations on donations and expenditures and for public accountability are widespread. The international discourse, usually transmitted by national and transnational non-governmental organizations (NGOs) and national activists who focus on fighting corruption and promoting good governance, has also contributed to these rising demands.

Problems in Asian political finance

Corruption, clientelism and clans

In many Asian polities, clientelistic networks connect politicians with voters through an exchange of gifts or benefits for political support.[5] Clientelistic relations like these not only undermine the institutionalization of political parties and hinder the establishment of horizontal links based on common political interests; they also encourage rent-seeking strategies.[6] Moreover, clientelism usually disadvantages female candidates, because they do not have equal access to personal networks or large financial resources that they can distribute to garner support.[7] A peculiarity connected to clientelism in Asia is the major impact of dynasties and wealthy businessmen. In the Philippines, major parties are controlled by 'clans' of a few dozen families.[8] In Thailand, the Thai Rak Thai (TRT), the ruling party before the military coup in 2006, was financed almost exclusively by billionaire Thaksin Shinawatra. The governing party at the time of writing, a successor of the TRT, is led by his younger sister Yingluck, who also succeeded him as prime minister.

Examples of dynasties in South Asia are the Gandhis in India, the Bhuttos in Pakistan, and the families of Sheikh Hasina and Khaleda Zia in Bangladesh.[9] These types of dynastic rule disadvantage politicians from poorer or unknown families, but sometimes enhance the role of female candidates from the leading families.

In Japan, around one-third of parliamentary seats 'stay within the family'. There, around 40 per cent of Liberal Democratic Party (LDP) and around 20 per cent of Democratic Party of Japan (DPJ) lawmakers are descendants of lawmakers, and six of the seven past prime ministers have been sons or grandsons of members of parliament (MPs).[10] The combination of clientelism and family rule often exacerbates problems of bad governance, weak oversight and sanctioning, and corruption. It also has a fundamental impact on the role of money in politics, as political allegiances in a clientelistic system are generally bought or inherited rather than earned through convincing policies or governance.

Linkages between political parties, voters and business

A general comparison of the relationship between political parties, the state and private business highlights three different formations. First, in many Western democracies political parties and party systems were institutionalized early on and were largely separated from the public administration. This process resulted in the establishment of well-institutionalized parties linked to voters via programmatic, rather than clientelistic, ties. Usually, parties did not capture the state apparatus and were not captured by oligarchs or dynasties.[11]

Second, in Mediterranean Europe (and most of South and South-east Asia), financially poor and weak central states were forced to rely on regional brokers such as the *mafiosi* in Italy, *caciques* in Spain or *comatarhis* in Greece to mediate between the centre and the periphery.[12] The equivalent in Thailand, for example, is the linkage between politicians and voters that is provided by informal, local political cliques (*phuak, phakphuak*) consisting of headmen, members of the local administration and councillors via vote canvassers (*hua khanaen*).[13] These local political-bureaucratic and business alliances gained importance in the 1980s and 1990s in the wake of a fundamental socio-economic restructuring.[14] Business is intertwined with politics, which significantly affects how political parties raise and spend money. In these systems, business interests tend to dominate political processes.

A third variant is the North-east Asian 'developmental state' type, in which a strong administrative centre did not need these brokers; instead, parties were established or controlled by an authoritarian state apparatus, leaving much room for state capture by dominant parties even after democratization.[15] The most successful developmental states are those in North-east Asia (Japan, Taiwan, South Korea).[16] They have exported the model to other states such as Malaysia and Singapore and, to a lesser extent, Indonesia and Thailand, and also increasingly to South Asia, including India (which has experienced economic deregulation and privatization since 1991).

> This symbiosis between politicians, bureaucrats and entrepreneurs/ managers has blurred the distinction between public and private domains and laid the foundation for illicit practices of political finance.

This symbiosis between politicians, bureaucrats and entrepreneurs/ managers has blurred the distinction between public and private domains and laid the foundation for illicit practices of political finance, especially where political elites use the state apparatus for their own economic purposes.

These three different formations have a lasting impact on the opportunities for (and shape of) corruption, and the intensity and breadth of clientelism is connected to them. The reality of political finance today is thus often determined by political processes that started decades ago.

Ineffective implementation

In many cases, regulations are not effectively implemented due to weak supervisory mechanisms (which are often related to the enforcement agency's lack of mandate or resources). In India and the Philippines, for example, the informality of the political system makes it hard to supervise party financing and election campaigns. Regulatory frameworks often exist only on paper.

Another issue related to effective oversight is independence. In Malaysia, the Election Commission falls under the direct purview of the prime minister's department and is government controlled. It is therefore not willing to check party and campaign financing closely.[17]

In addition, legal measures do not always have the desired effect. Sanctions do not always deter as they were designed to. In South Korea, where election laws strictly regulate political contributions, many violations of the political funds law occur, but 'the heavy penalties … seem to have had only limited effect on the actual behavior of politicians'.[18]

In India, the 'introduction of tax deductibility for political donations since 2003 has had only a very limited effect on the general practice of unreported donations in black money in return for governmental favors or to buy party goodwill'.[19] These examples elucidate the complexity of regulating political finance.

Illicit funding

Although accurate figures are very hard to come by, illicit donations play an important role in Asian political life. Although the level and impact of illicit funding vary significantly across the continent, there are examples of it having seriously penetrated the economy. In Afghanistan, it is estimated that in 2012 net opium exports made up some 10 per cent of licit gross domestic product (GDP).[20] In other countries, the criminalization of politics is indicated by the sheer number of lawsuits. According to the election watchdog the National Election Watch, 162 of 543 members of the Lok Sabha, the national parliament in India, face criminal charges.[21] There are some parallels in Indonesia, where, according to the Home Affairs Ministry, about half of the approximately 500 district heads and mayors either are suspects or defendants in graft cases, or have been convicted in such.[22]

Lack of resources for opposition parties and female candidates

In many Asian countries, particularly those with authoritarian regimes, there is not a level playing field between political parties. This is especially true for opposition parties that are disadvantaged by a lack of resources and for female candidates who face different forms of discrimination because of their weaker financial resources.[23] In Asia, opposition parties in authoritarian regimes are often seen as more or less illegitimate. In addition, membership dues are often insignificant sources of income, and entrepreneurs or private donors tend to shy away from supporting these parties because they could face sanctions by the government when applying for contracts, credits or licences. Another reason for the relative weakness of opposition parties is the entrenched power of governing parties that often has developed over a long time. This weakness also pertains to young democracies in which the old regime parties have persisted with the ramified party infrastructure.

Abuse of state resources

The abuse of state resources is a common problem, particularly in authoritarian states or systems with dominant parties. Incumbent parties or candidates in a significant number of Asian countries use government resources or public money ahead of elections. In some countries, the ruling party is closely intertwined with the state apparatus and is regarded by the public as part of the state. In Thailand, for instance, it is desirable to be a candidate for the governing party, as the government provides valuable campaign funds. After the tsunami in 2004, controversies arose when the Thai government, only a few weeks before the elections, distributed bags of rice marked with the ruling party's name in the affected areas.[24]

Vote buying

The boundaries between gift giving and exchanging money for votes are often difficult to establish. It is generally assumed that poorer countries are more prone to vote buying than countries with high per capita incomes. This is not always the case, however, and factors such as legacies or cultural patterns play an important role in determining how common this practice is. Taiwan is an example of an industrialized country where this illegal form of voter mobilization is still often practised. The issue of vote buying will be further discussed below.

Regional initiatives to regulate political finance

Political finance regulations are generally becoming more widespread and comprehensive across the region. Since the 1990s, this intensification has come in the wake of democratization or democratic deepening. As in many other regions (except Europe), there are no comprehensive regional standards of political finance regulations, nor is there any intensive, official exchange of information on such regulations.

However, current political finance norms are influenced by the international discourse and international and national actors, and there have been some steps toward standardization. Activists and reform-minded politicians are continually learning about best practices within a community that is increasingly internationalized. One result of intensified cooperation is the Vision of a Blueprint for ASEAN Democracy Free and Fair Elections from 2009 by the Asian Network for Free Elections (ANFREL).[25] The Blueprint is a predecessor of the 2012 Bangkok Declaration on Free and Fair Elections, which includes an article on Oversight for Campaign Finance that demands strong scrutiny and enforcement based on 'a rigorous legal framework that fairly regulates political donations and campaign expenditures and allows for transparency of donations and expenditures'.[26] NGOs and NGO alliances from most of the Asian countries analysed in this chapter, such as the National Election Observation Committee of Nepal and the Committee for Free and

Fair Elections in Cambodia, endorsed the Declaration. Endorsement has also come from electoral management bodies (EMBs) such as the Indonesian Elections Supervisory Committee, the National Election Commission of Timor-Leste, the Indonesian National Election Commission, the Commission on Elections of the Philippines and the Technical Secretariat for Election Administration of Timor-Leste. The Declaration signals a growing awareness among stakeholders of the importance of electoral integrity.

The most important regional organizations—such as the South Asian Association for Regional Cooperation (SAARC),[27] the Association of Southeast Asian Nations (ASEAN)[28] and ASEAN+3 (the ten ASEAN members plus Japan, China and South Korea)—do not directly address electoral reforms and political finance, but usually focus instead on issues such as economic cooperation and security. Nevertheless, the ASEAN Political and Security Blueprint (2009) that serves as a road map for the ASEAN Political and Security Community until 2015 refers to democracy and governance in broader terms.

Moreover, the Declaration of Global Principles for Nonpartisan Election Observation and Monitoring by Citizen Organizations,[29] the Charter of the Southeast Asian Nations and the terms of reference of the ASEAN Intergovernmental Commission on Human Rights are relevant to non-partisan election observation and monitoring by citizen organizations.

Sources of income for political parties and candidates

The mix and balance of sources of income differ between the countries analysed, depending on the regulatory framework, the degree of commercialization of politics and campaigning, and the institutionalization of political parties (with reference, for example, to membership and member commitment). Yet one common trait is that most party funds are mobilized in the run-up to elections and are spent on campaigns.[30] The funding of parties and candidates is also not regulated to the same extent, especially the levels of allowed donations.

Contribution bans

Allowing large private donations usually benefits parties and candidates with close linkages to business, yet outright bans or very low limits on donations may encourage politicians to accept illegal funding.

In all the countries analysed (except Sri Lanka and Malaysia, where contributions are hardly regulated), foreign donations to political parties are banned, yet they are permitted to political candidates in eight of these 20 countries. In candidate-centred systems in which candidates raise and spend money independently, such a legal loophole can be especially dangerous.

Corporate donations to political parties are illegal in seven countries, and limits on such donations apply in four countries.[31] In Japan, 'since there are more limited restrictions on contributions to the party branch from corporations, the party branch can serve as an indirect path to financing individual politicians with corporate contributions from corporations and unions'.[32] Corporate donations to candidates are illegal in six of the countries studied.

Donations to political parties and candidates from corporations that have government contracts or are partially owned by the government are generally forbidden in the region, with the exception of Bangladesh, Cambodia, Malaysia, Myanmar, Singapore and Sri Lanka. In Indonesia, only donations from fully state-owned companies are banned. In Pakistan, Taiwan, Thailand and Timor-Leste, this ban applies to political parties but not to candidates.

Eight countries ban donations from trade unions to political parties, but only six ban donations from trade unions to candidates. In Cambodia (though the regulations there are not entirely clear), Indonesia, Pakistan and Timor-Leste, the ban applies only to political parties, while in Japan and Mongolia the ban applies only to candidates.

The only countries in the region that allow anonymous donations are Afghanistan, Cambodia and Sri Lanka. In authoritarian regimes, the opposition often supports legalizing anonymous donations in order to protect their donors. In Singapore, for example, Low Thia Khiang of the Workers' Party criticized the ban because it would discourage even legitimate donors who do not want to be named for fear of reprisals from the regime.[33]

It is generally prohibited for political parties or candidates to use state resources (excluding regulated public funding). There are no data for some countries, including Malaysia and Singapore, where the use (or abuse) of state resources can be considered common practice (see the sub-section of this chapter on abuse of state resources).

Other types of donations or funders are banned, sometimes with very specific regulations. In Cambodia, the donation ban applies to NGOs and other associations; in Timor-Leste philanthropic and religious bodies, as well as employers' associations and foundations, cannot donate; and in Mongolia stateless and under-age individuals, religious organizations and entities that are less than one year old, bankrupt or in debt are prohibited from donating. In the Philippines, donations are also banned from financial institutions, educational institutions that receive state support, officials and employees in the civil service and members of the armed forces. In Pakistan, only donations from individuals are allowed. In Japan, companies that have incurred a deficit in the last three years are not allowed to contribute to political parties.

In some cases, the wording in the law leaves much room for interpretation. In Indonesia, for example, 'donations have to be honest, fair, transparent and respect the sovereignty and independence of political parties',[34] whereas in Thailand donations cannot be accepted from anyone aiming at 'subverting the security of the Kingdom, the Throne, the national economy or the affairs of State, or disturbing or threatening public order or good morals, or destroying national natural resources'.[35]

Contribution limits

Limits are generally established for one of two time frames: in four of the countries, the limits on the amount that can be contributed to a political party are related to an often annual non-election-specific timeline; in others, they are based on election periods. In general, the implementation of regulations on donation limits is weak.

Few Asian countries have limits on donations to candidates. Exceptions to this rule are found in Afghanistan, Bhutan, the Maldives and the four North-east Asian countries. Limits range from 50,000 afghanis (AFN) (I\$2,100) in Afghanistan and 100,000 ngultrum (BTN) (I\$4,800) in Bhutan up to 1.5 million Japanese yen (JPY) (I\$14,000) and 20 million South Korean won (KRW) (I\$24,000) in Japan and South Korea, respectively.[36]

Nearly two-thirds (65 per cent) of the Asian states examined do not limit donations to parties, with the exception of Afghanistan, Bangladesh, Bhutan, Indonesia and the North-east Asian countries (except for South Korea). The size of the limits on donations varies from BTN 100,000 (I\$4,800) in Bhutan to 7.5 billion rupiah (IDR) (I\$1.22 million) for firms in Indonesia.

The distinction between having contribution limits for parties and/or candidates is important, because the possibility of unlimited contributions to one but not the other creates a loophole that can be seriously abused. Bangladesh, Indonesia, the Maldives and South Korea fall under this category. By limiting contributions for one but not the other, the unrestricted actor (either the party or candidate) can circumvent the limits.

An unusual way to limit contributions is to restrict contributions relative to the donor's income (i.e., a relative restriction). Taiwan is an example of a state that employs this variation of contribution limits, and there the ceiling for donations to political parties during a non-electoral period is set quite high: 20 per cent of an individual's annual income or 200,000 Taiwanese dollars (TWD) (I\$11,000); and 10 per cent of an enterprise's annual income or TWD 3 million (I\$164,000).

Private sources of income

Membership dues

In Asia, party membership is often not clearly defined or is conceptualized as a privilege that is given by parties rather than chosen by citizens. This is rooted in the clientelistic and personalistic structure of political parties. In some countries, such as the Philippines, parties are perceived as personalistic networks without a real organizational base; thus party membership over a long period is an alien concept. In other countries, such as Malaysia, the majority of the adult population owns party membership cards, but dues are very small and membership is often only a way to access patronage networks. Consequently, membership dues are not a significant source of income for Asian parties (see Box 4.1.).

Box 4.1. Political party income in India

In India, the total income of parties for the period 2007/08–2010/11 evinces the minor role of membership dues.[37] The Indian National Congress has had the highest officially reported income of the Indian political parties (according to documents submitted to the income tax department), with 14.9 billion Indian rupees (INR) (I$886.27 million). This amount corresponds closely to the income reported for the sale of coupons[38] (INR 11.7 billion, I$695.78 million), donations and interest, demonstrating that membership dues are an insignificant source of income. The Nationalist Congress Party has a similar income composition with insignificant membership dues.

The Bharatiya Janata Party (BJP), a Hindu-nationalist party with stronger ideological linkages between representatives and followers or members, had a reported income of INR 7.7 billion (I$457.17 million), but was also overwhelmingly financed by 'voluntary contributions'. Membership dues form quite a small proportion of overall income, and have dwindled since the party lost power a few years ago.

Donations

Private donations are the most important source of income for Asian political parties and candidates, especially in countries without public funding. Some donors take over candidacies or leading positions within the parties; others use proxies to exercise control.

Companies are also known to have the pragmatic approach of donating money to several candidates or parties to ensure they receive some kind of 'back payment' from the winner after the elections.

In Indonesia, new regulations in 2008 and Law No. 8/2012 substantially increased allowable donations to IDR 1 billion (I$163,000) from individuals and IDR 7.5 billion (I$1.23 million) from groups or companies.[39] Yet these levels apparently are not generous enough, as entrepreneurs still circumnavigate the rules to make additional donations via sub-companies.[40] An alternative way of pumping money into the system is to gather a few hundred businesspeople and their representatives in a five-star hotel and ask for donations in cash.

Generally, the bulk of contributions comes from a small number of individuals and companies. In the Philippines, the Philippine Center for Investigative Journalism brought to light that in the May 2010 national elections only 308 people (out of a total 50.7 million registered voters) donated to the campaigns of the top candidates for president and vice-president.[41]

According to Transparency International India, corporations in India are expected to illegally donate more than the allowed 5 per cent of their profits. The donors 'control the politicians, and the politicians [become] more accountable to their sponsors than to their constituents'.[42] Reports suggest that around 2 billion US dollars (USD) in 'black money' would be spent to influence the Uttar Pradesh state elections of 2012.[43]

In Taiwan, even though campaign finance regulations were strengthened with the Political Donations Act in 2004 and its subsequent revisions, loopholes persist. Although there are limits to donations from individuals and corporations to candidates, money can avoid official scrutiny in various ways or can be delivered in cash if tax credits are dispensed with.[44]

Corporate donations are hard to pinpoint in most countries, especially if donors have the opportunity to remain anonymous (for example by splitting the contribution). Whereas the amount of donations is assumed to be rising in most countries, there are some counter-trends, as shown in Box 4.2.

Box 4.2. Japan–decreasing donations

In Japan, donations to the LDP by Keidanren—the powerful Japanese Business Federation that comprises 1,285 companies, 127 nationwide industrial associations and 47 regional economic organizations—dropped from JPY 9.38 billion (I$85.95 million) in 1992 to JPY 4.15 billion (I$38.02 million) in 1994 and JPY 2.25 billion (I$20.62 million) in 2009.

This is a result of the financial crisis in the 1990s, the party and political finance reforms in 1994, the declining power of the LDP, and the growing complexity of policy making that hampers a simple exchange of money for specific regulations or laws.[45]

Funding from the party leadership

In some countries, businessmen have taken over the leadership of political parties. They use the parties as vehicles with which to influence legislation. Sometimes their financial influence is so great that the entire existence of the party relies solely on their money.

In Indonesia, businessmen such as Yusuf Kalla and Aburizal Bakrie (Golkar Party), Sutrisno Bachir (National Mandate Party) and Surya Paloh (Nasdem Party) became (or have become) party chairmen. Some ex-generals, such as Prabowo Subianto and Wiranto, also used their fortunes to build their own parties (the Greater Indonesia Movement Party and People's Conscience Party) ahead of the 2009 elections. From a rational choice perspective, it is obviously most profitable to steer a political party directly. Besides, most Indonesian parties are predominantly represented by entrepreneurs or businessmen in the national parliament.[46]

In Thai politics, a new type of party emerged after the constitutional amendments of 1997. The TRT was founded, funded by and completely focused on the media mogul and billionaire Thaksin Shinawatra.[47] As a 'business firm party'[48] it transferred the logic of business administration directly into the world of party politics. The TRT won almost half the seats in the 2001 polls and gained a comfortable majority a few years later. The party strategy that concentrated on marketable issues was invented by media, marketing and advertising specialists.

In South Korea in 1993, the president of the Hyundai Corporation, Chung Ju Yung, set up the United National Party and ran as candidate in the presidential elections. He used money from his own corporation, but was defeated.[49]

Funding from electoral candidates and income from elected officials

In Pakistan, as is the case in most Asian countries, especially when public funding does not exist, campaigns are typically financed by the candidates themselves.[50] In Indonesia, they sometimes even have to buy their candidacies from the party leadership.[51] Party executives only rarely fund advertisements, posters, banners and rallies for their candidates. Candidates who spend their own money end up indebted, and have to repay their financial backers once they are in office.[52] Many actors in the process perceive this cycle of receiving and later repaying money for a candidacy as an investment in a business venture.

In the Philippines, local elites and candidates who are elected in single-seat electoral districts are often stronger than political parties, which might not even have a national headquarters or organizational structures in place. As in other Asian countries, popular candidates in the Philippines bargain with different parties and choose the party they wish to run for, as opposed to the party choosing and nominating its candidate.[53]

In countries where parties are no more than 'hollow shells', or where election laws effectively discourage new parties from being formed, independents make up the majority of the candidates. In Afghanistan, the major presidential candidates for the 2009 elections, as well as more than 80 per cent of provincial council candidates, 'stood for election as independents, as did all but 1.2 per cent of the 2,500-plus candidates for parliamentary elections'.[54]

Where political parties are stronger, they are in a position to make demands on their elected officials. In many countries, representatives have to pay levies deducted from their salaries (a glaring exception was the TRT in Thailand, which paid its MPs additional salaries). One of the consequences of the problematic financial situation of Indonesian parties, for example, is a more or less informal requirement for MPs to donate up to 50 per cent of their salaries to their party.[55]

Foreign funding

Donations by foreigners to political parties are usually banned in the region, with the exception of Malaysia and Sri Lanka. The rationale for this prohibition is fear of foreign influence on policy making. Bans do not apply to the same extent to donations to candidates, and eight of the 20 countries allow them.

Foreign funding is, however, not easy to control. In Afghanistan, for example, contributions from Iran, in particular, were thought to influence the 2010 election.[56] In Timor-Leste, foreign funding has been used by the ruling National Congress for Timorese Reconstruction (Conselho Nacional de Reconstrução de Timor, CNRT) in spite of a legal ban. The CNRT under Prime Minister Xanana Gusmão reportedly raised more than USD 2.5 million, partly from international companies or individuals, allegedly in relation to large government construction contracts.[57]

Contributions from overseas citizens and diaspora communities are sometimes hard to differentiate from foreign donations. This source of income is quite important for some parties, such as the Tamil parties in Sri Lanka and the Muttahida Qaumi Movement in Pakistan.[58]

Income from commercial activities

Money from commercial activities is a vital source of income for political parties, especially in authoritarian or transitional states such as Myanmar, Malaysia, Singapore and Cambodia, where ruling parties have direct access to state facilities, state credits and public licences.

In Malaysia, parties and politicians began acquiring their own firms in the 1970s, and by the 1990s a large proportion of politicians was involved in managing companies under their control. A large problem in relation to transparency in Malaysia is that government-linked companies do not have to report company accounts to public shareholders.[59] The United Malays National Organization (UMNO) and the Kuomintang (KMT), to give two examples, have opaque business conglomerates that serve as cash cows for the two parties. The KMT owns diverse real estate and financial holdings, but details about this conglomerate are not made public. According to the Taiwan Brain Trust, their dividend earnings in 2010 accounted for about USD 100 million.[60] After public pressure, the KMT began to divest its assets.

In other countries, laws that prevent parties from running their own businesses and limit parties' legal incomes are perceived as spurring corruption. In 2012, the speaker of the national parliament in Indonesia, Marzuki Alie, criticized the law's provision that the main source of funding for political parties is supposed to be members' contributions as unrealistic and demanded that parties be allowed to set up their own companies.[61]

In Japan, political parties are allowed to engage in commercial activities. Between 1998 and 2007 the Clean Government Party (CGP) or Kōmeitō raised around 17 per cent of its revenues through the sale of the *Kōmei Shinbun* and other publications. Likewise, the Social Democratic Party (SDP) sells a newspaper (*Shakai Shinpō*) and other party-related publications to finance its activities.[62] In Malaysia, the assets of the Malaysian Chinese Association (MCA), which is part of the ruling coalition, were estimated in 2011 at 2 billion Malaysian ringgit (MYR) (I$659.7 million); dividends from an investment in the country's biggest English-language newspaper, *The Star*, were MYR 50 million (I$16.5 million) a year.[63]

Public funding

Direct public funding

Public funding can have beneficial effects on the institutionalization of parties and party systems and the creation of a level playing field. It can, however, be problematic if it is concentrated on only a few main parties. In Europe, high levels of public funding have been said to contribute to the emergence of cartel parties.[64] Although this kind of development is less likely in most parts of Asia, public funding could strengthen clientelistic elites, especially if the funds are not made contingent on abiding by regulations that require intra-party reforms or transparent reporting. In any case, public funding is highly unpopular when parties are not adequately rooted in society.

There is a general trend toward expanding public funding in the region; the most generous funding regimes are found in North-east Asia. In total, eight countries in Asia regularly provide state subsidies (Indonesia, Japan, the Maldives, Mongolia, South Korea, Taiwan, Thailand and Timor-Leste), and two more supply these only in relation to campaigning (Sri Lanka and Bhutan).

In 2012, the National Election Commission in South Korea provided KRW 34.39 billion (I$41.15 million) in election subsidies to seven parties and KRW 1.13 billion (I$1.35 million) in female candidate nomination subsidies to two parties (see Table 4.1. and see further below in the subsection on political funding and women's representation).

Table 4.1. Subsidies provided to political parties in South Korea in 2012

Party	Election subsidies	Female candidate nomination subsidies
Total	**KRW 34.39 billion (I$41.16 million)**	**KRW 1.13 billion (I$1,357,000)**
Saenuri	KRW 15.78 billion (I$18.88 million)	KRW 744.60 million (I$891,000)
Democratic United	KRW 12.35 billion (I$14.78 million)	KRW 389.28 million (I$466,000)
Liberty Forward	KRW 2.48 billion (I$2.97 million)	–
United Progressive	KRW 2.20 billion (I$2.63 million)	–
Creative Korea	KRW 877.52 million (I$1.05 million)	–
Korea Vision	KRW 23.27 million (I$28,000)	–
New Progressive	KRW 687.89 million (I$823,000)	–

Source: Republic of Korea National Election Commission[65]

Public subsidies form the mainstay of party finances and account for at least half of the total revenues for the largest parties in Japan.[66] The LDP today has a slightly higher than average share of subsidies. Since 1994, when public funding was introduced, contributions have made up around 60 per cent of LDP income.[67]

Yet the subsidies in Japan have not had the desired effects, such as more party-centred campaigning. Instead, entrepreneurial politicians have managed to channel the party funds for their own benefit.[68] In addition, the effects of public funding are not uniform across and within specific party organizations. Within the CGP and the DPJ, private contributions to candidates remain much more important than subsidies.

Bhutan is a special case in which campaigns are fully funded by public money. The Public Election Funds Bill stipulates that every candidate is allocated BTN 100,000 (I$4,800), and for banners another BTN 20,000 (I$960). The electoral commission also sponsors posters and postcards for the candidates.[69] Candidates are not permitted other sources of finance, so both political parties complain that they lack resources.

There are also counter-trends to the general increase in public funding. In Indonesia, the Government Regulation on Financial Assistance to Political Parties funded a large part of the campaign expenses from 2001 to 2005. For example, from 2001 to 2004, the ruling PDI-P (Indonesian Democratic Party-Struggle) received an estimated USD 47 million in public money. However, the introduction of Government Regulation No. 29 in 2005 reduced funding by around 90 per cent, which forced many parliamentarians to dispense up to 50 per cent of their salaries to their parties' central executives. This led to an attempt to raise allowances for MPs by up to 300 per cent in order to compensate for the loss of income. This initiative, however, led to intense public criticism and was finally cancelled.[70] In the Philippines, the intense debate on the introduction of state subsidies continues.[71]

In some cases, public subsidies are earmarked for specific purposes. In Indonesia, 60 per cent of the funds have to be spent on voter education programmes.[72] In South Korea, non-electoral subsidies are designated for the operation of political parties, and may only be used for personnel costs, administrative furnishings and consumables, setting up and maintaining offices, public utility charges, policy development expenses, training of party members, organizational activity expenses, and advertising and election-related costs. At least 30 per cent of the subsidies must also be used for a party's policy development institute and not less than 10 per cent for promoting women's political participation.[73]

Sometimes public funding is intended to strengthen the party organization. In Thailand, according to the 1998 Political Party Act, public money is disbursed to defray the costs of establishing additional party branches in the regions. Unfortunately, this has led more often than not to the creation of mere shells.[74]

Indirect public funding

Indirect public funding includes free or subsidized access to media and tax reliefs for parties and/or donors. Media access is a very important subsidy, especially in countries where extremely expensive TV advertisements have to be financed by the political parties and candidates (such as the Philippines and Indonesia). In Indonesia, media magnates are often very closely linked with the political parties. The Bakrie Group (Bakrie is the chairman of one of the biggest parties, Golkar) owns Anteve and TVOne, while Surya Paloh (NasDem Party) owns Metro TV, and Hary Tanoesoedibjo (People's Conscience Party, Hanura) controls the Media Nusantara Citra Group that includes 20 TV stations.[75]

Free media access is guaranteed by law in Bangladesh, India, Japan, Mongolia, Nepal, South Korea, Sri Lanka, Taiwan and Thailand. In principle, this also applies to Cambodia, but the provision is not clear. In some countries, such as Bhutan, media access is highly regulated and controlled; the media have to follow Election Commission guidelines during campaigning in order to guarantee equal access for all political parties and candidates. Broadcasting time and space in the print media are allocated by the Bhutanese Commission, and a media arbitrator (the secretary of the Ministry of Labour and Human Resources) has oversight responsibilities.[76]

In addition to broadcasting opportunities as a form of indirect public funding, seven Asian countries provide tax relief: Bhutan, India, Japan, South Korea, Taiwan, Thailand and Timor-Leste. In Bhutan, the Election Commission also sponsors public debates, pamphlets and brochures, posters, advertisements and postage. In Timor-Leste, political parties are also exempt from legal charges and court costs. In India, parties are entitled to copies of the electoral register and other materials and items. Japan has provisions for producing posters and arranging public meeting places for candidates. In South Korea, citizens' halls, gymnasiums or cultural centres (owned or managed by the state or local governments) are placed at the disposal of candidates and parties. In Thailand, the Political Parties Act of 2008 gives taxpayers the chance to deduct 100 Thai baht (THB) (I$10) from their tax payments for supporting a political party. Although these donations are free, few taxpayers seize the opportunity.[77]

Figure 4.1. Asian countries where tax relief is provided to parties as a type of indirect public funding

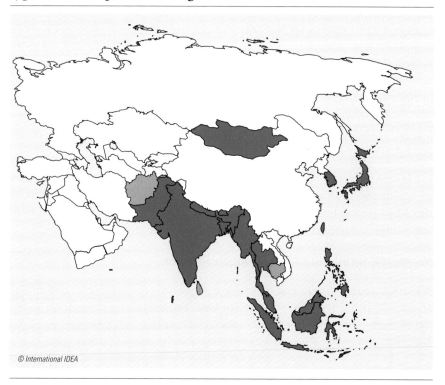

© International IDEA

■ Yes
■ No

Source: International IDEA. This map is based on data collected up to February 2014. Data are continuously updated on the International IDEA Political Finance Database. See http://www.idea.int/political-finance/question.cfm?field=279&region=42

In Indonesia, lawmakers recently proposed to allocate funds to independent monitors to supervise polling stations and ensure transparent vote counts. Currently, most parties pay for their own monitors. Under the new regulation, the Elections Supervisory Body (Bawaslu) would organize the monitoring.[78]

Abuse of state resources

In many countries, ruling parties use state resources to finance campaigns or to sustain their clientelistic networks. Similarly, incumbent parties take advantage of state media for campaigning or engage civil servants in party activities. All in all, clear boundaries between routine use and abuse of state resources are difficult to define, as the following examples illustrate.

In Malaysia, ahead of the 2013 elections, the government under Prime Minister Najib Razak from the ruling UMNO spent a total of MYR 58 billion (I\$30 billion) for populist policies such as salary increases and MYR 500 (I\$260) cash vouchers.[79] In Timor-Leste during the most recent elections, the CNRT was alleged to have massively misused the government machinery, although civil servants who tried to influence voters' choice risked facing a USD 1,000 to USD 2,000 fine and two to three years in prison.[80] In Cambodia, the ruling Cambodian People's Party (CPP) 'has displayed party logos on public buildings like government buildings and schools and used public premises for party meetings'.[81] Many civil servants who are members of the CPP, including police and military personnel, actively participated in the campaigning, including 'attending CPP party meetings and party gift-giving ceremonies and giving open pledges of loyalty to CPP during public events'.[82]

In Taiwan, a report published by *Next Magazine* uncovered an operation in which the head of the National Security Council ordered members of the Ministry of Justice Investigation Bureau to gather information about opposition campaign activities and meetings for the presidential office.[83]

Political funding and female representation

Although many Asian countries have legislated quotas,[84] the percentage of women in parliament is generally low. Yet female representation varies significantly, ranging from 5.8 per cent in Sri Lanka to 33.2 per cent in Nepal and 38.5 per cent in Timor-Leste.

Female candidates usually find it hard to attract financial support.[85] This seems to be particularly challenging in some parts of Asia for cultural reasons.[86] Gaunder, for example, shows that the non-partisan organization Women in the New World, International Network

> The regulatory frameworks in Asia usually do not specifically consider the disadvantages of women participating in politics or competing in elections.

(WIN WIN) in Japan (modelled after the US Political Action Committee 'EMILY's List') failed to raise funds to support female candidates, inter alia due to deeply rooted cultural patterns.[87]

The regulatory frameworks in Asia usually do not specifically consider the disadvantages of women participating in politics or competing in elections. The only exception in the 20 countries analysed here is South Korea, which gives additional subsidies to political parties that nominate women for district representative for the national parliament (see Table 4.1.).[88] In 2011, the National Election Commission provided KRW 1.13 billion (I$1.35 million) in female candidate nomination subsidies to two parties. An example of non-monetary support is the Sam Rainsy Party in Cambodia, which provided women candidates with clothing and a bicycle while campaigning.[89]

Spending by political parties and candidates

Spending limits

It is rare to set limits on party expenditure in the region. They are only applied in South Korea, Mongolia, the Philippines, Thailand, Bangladesh, Bhutan and Nepal. In Bangladesh, the spending limit is quite high (up to 45 million taka [BDT] [I$1,530,000]) during elections, depending on the number of candidates participating. In Bhutan, expenditures must not exceed the amount of money provided by the Election Commission, which is the only allowed source of income. In Mongolia, in the 2008 parliamentary elections, the General Elections Committee limited expenditures to between USD 226,000 and USD 870,000 per district, depending on the size of the district. In the Philippines, the limit for parties is calculated per voter (5 pesos [PHP] [I$0.2]) in each electoral district in which a political party has fielded a candidate. The candidates also have their own spending limits; however, the ceiling for presidential candidates is so low that in reality no candidate can abide by the regulation, which even the EMB has acknowledged.

Most countries (except Cambodia, Indonesia, Afghanistan, Sri Lanka and Timor-Leste) have spending limits for candidates. The ceiling amount ranges from a maximum per candidate of BDT 1.5 million (I$51,000) in Bangladesh and 1,500,000 Pakistani rupees (PKR) (I$46,000) for National Assembly elections in Pakistan, to 1,500 rufiyaa (MVR) (I$150) per eligible elector in each electoral district in the Maldives and 600,000 Singapore dollars (SGD) (I$551,000), or SGD 0.30 [I$0.28] per voter, in Singaporean presidential elections.

In Malaysia, candidates are allowed to spend MYR 200,000 (I$103,000) in the national parliamentary elections and MYR 100,000 (I$52,000) in elections to the state assemblies. However, it is probable that many candidates, especially those from the ruling National Front parties, spend much more.[90] This is a recurrent problem all over Asia. To give another example, Thailand's Electoral Commission limits campaign finance to THB 1.5 million (I\$90,000), but this limit 'was widely believed to be disregarded by virtually all candidates and their supporters'.[91]

Spending limits that are too low and regulations that are too strict may stifle campaigning, as has happened during assembly elections in Uttar Pradesh, Punjab and three other states in India. These polls were negatively affected by the strict enforcement of low expenditure caps for candidates by the Election Commission of India. Thus the Commission was forced to alter the rules so that publicity material (such as cardboard, paper caps, badges, etc.) could be used without bearing the name of the publisher.[92]

As noted above, unrealistically low limits constitute an incentive to circumvent the rules. Yet limits that are too high are also counterproductive. In the Maldives, the ceiling is so high that a level playing field can hardly be created. A candidate may spend the equivalent of MVR 1,500 (I\$150) per eligible elector in the electoral district on his/her campaign; in parliamentary elections this would amount to approximately MVR 7,500,000 (I\$747,000) and in presidential elections to MVR 312 million (I\$31.09 million).[93]

Actual spending

Parties and candidates spend their money primarily in two core areas. The first is campaigning, which includes costs for posters, banners, advertisements, gifts, payments for middlemen or vote canvassers, advisors, poll monitors, survey institutes, rallies, travel expenses, in-kind gifts, remuneration for attending meetings, buying votes and so forth. The second area of expenditure relates to routine party work such as conducting party congresses, workshops and training; producing brochures; and building and maintaining offices.

In countries with weakly institutionalized political parties, most money is spent ahead of and during elections because political parties are often dormant between campaigns. In addition, as noted before, candidates must fund their own campaigns under such circumstances.

> The so-called professionalization of campaigning has in recent years raised the expenses for advertisements in the mass media and payments for pollsters and 'spin doctors'.

All in all, there is a widespread perception that there has been a steep rise in campaign costs. The so-called professionalization of campaigning has in recent years raised the expenses for advertisements in the mass media and payments for pollsters and 'spin doctors'.[94]

Moreover, many campaign events in the region provide entertainment with local and national celebrities, lotteries and the distribution of food, cigarettes and small amounts of money (as 'compensation' for travel costs) and so on. In Indonesia, advertising expenditures alone increased more than tenfold from 1999 to 2009 to USD 117 million,[95] which is one of the reasons why a candidate running for governor spends up to USD 4 million. Another large chunk of this amount is spent on nominations by the party (or a coalition of parties) and surveys.[96] Candidates also have to spend large amounts of money on positive media coverage. During local elections in Bali, for example, the Bali Post Media Group charged candidates for these services.[97]

One of the main problems in tracing the spending patterns of parties and candidates is the lack of accessible and credible data.[98] This is especially true in South-east and South Asia. According to a 2009 election observation report by the International Republican Institute, to give just one example, campaign finance reporting in Bangladesh is notoriously unreliable, and even self-evident overspending is unchecked. The Bangladesh Election Commission frequently receives false documentation, but negates these transgressions.[99]

Vote buying

The definition of vote buying is controversial. Is it a direct exchange of a vote for a clearly defined service or payment, or does it include exchanges between a group of voters and a vote canvasser or a party/candidate? In Singapore, for example, publicly owned Housing and Development Board buildings are only upgraded if the majority of residents votes for the People's Action Party (PAP).[100]

Usually, vote buying is defined by a direct relationship between the buyer and seller. It is more or less banned all over Asia. Nevertheless, it is still a widespread practice; even Taiwan, which has a high per capita income, has a long history of trading votes.[101] The practice is also well known in many other countries, and the exchange of political support for money or gifts is especially expected among poor voters in rural areas. In Thailand, vote buying persists despite strict regulation of campaign expenditures and serious punishments for those who breach the law. The diverse methods of vote buying include 'in-kind gifts, cash handouts, electronic transfer of funds, payment to attend party rallies, politicians funding birthday parties, free telephone cards and supermarket coupons, transfer of money through fake wins at gambling, and free "sightseeing" trips to different parts of Thailand'.[102] Often the payments or gifts are only given after the elections, depending on the outcome. Vote canvassers pretend to be able to trace voting behaviour when they have a photocopy of the voter's *tabienbahn* (house registration), allowing them to check whether the voter has kept to her/his part of the vote-buying bargain.

According to a poll by India's Centre of Media Studies, 'in the 2009 election in Tamil Nadu, 33.4 per cent of voters received money from candidates' supporters for their vote … and in 2011, voters were lured to the polls with blenders, grinders and other household appliances'.[103]

A special form of vote buying is vote betting. In Taiwan, 'the candidate buying votes launders his or her money through an illegal gambling operation, which then offers voters odds that the candidate will lose. That is, the voter bets that the candidate will win and if the candidate does win the voter collects his bet at the generous odds offered by the "losing" candidate through the betting house'.[104] Traditional vote buying is also still rampant in the country, although hard data are difficult to find. In 2008, five members of the Legislative Yuan were convicted of vote buying and were forced to step down.[105]

Enforcement of political finance regulations

Disclosure requirements

As is the case for many other regulations, disclosure requirements also have to be connected to a country's electoral system. In majoritarian systems, campaigning is usually centred on individual candidates, while political parties are much more influential in proportional representation systems.[106] Reporting demands should be in line with this.

In the region, the financial reports submitted to EMBs or other bodies are frequently fragmentary. Although reporting is often unreliable, it has the potential to provide observers and auditors with important information. In all Asian countries except the Philippines and Malaysia, parties have to report their finances regularly. In most countries this is done on an annual basis, but Afghan parties only have to disclose income infrequently. In Indonesia, disclosure is limited to the use of public funds; however, these are not very significant in relation to private donations. These lax procedures stand in contrast to disclosure practices in Taiwan, where receipts of all contributions have to be sent to the tax authorities.

Parties must report on their election-related finances in only eight countries; in Bangladesh and Nepal this only applies to expenses. Candidates have to report on their campaign finances in 17 countries. Campaign finance reports are made public in 14 of the 20 countries assessed. In Bangladesh, reports submitted during the election period are made public and published on the website of the Electoral Commission. In other cases, reports are made available only upon request.

Reports from political parties and/or candidates must reveal the identity of donors in seven countries. In another nine countries, this has to be done only under certain circumstances (e.g., above a certain monetary limit). In India, for example, the Representation of the People Act requires parties to declare details of donors who contribute more than INR 20,000 (I$1,200) during a financial year. However, parties often circumvent this regulation by accepting multiple donations of INR 20,000 (I$1,200) from the same anonymous donor. The Bahujan Samaj Party (BSP) had an official income of INR 1.72 billion (I$102.15 million) between 2009 and 2011, but no single contribution of more than INR 20,000 (I\$1,200). For other parties, contributions of more than INR 20,000 (I\$1,200) have amounted to 1.39 per cent of a party's official income (in the case of the Communist Party of India-Marxist), 11.89 per cent (for the Congress Party) and 22.76 per cent (for the BJP).[107] Moreover, although political parties in India are exempted from paying tax if they maintain audited accounts, regional parties in particular fail to regularly report their annual income.[108]

Indonesia is one of many examples in the region where control has intensified over the years. The 2009 legislative election took place under stricter campaign finance reporting regulations than ever before; political parties were required to provide financial information both before and after the election.[109] Yet regulations are difficult to enforce because much campaign income and spending is done via informal campaign teams, who 'are not required to provide campaign income and expenditure reports as part of the financial reporting process'.[110] Indonesia Corruption Watch asserted that all major political parties in the country under-reported campaign funds and estimated that fraud totalled USD 62.7 million.[111]

Disclosure is not a widely accepted practice in Nepal, and political parties avoid making their finances transparent. According to Transparency International (TI), the same holds true in Bangladesh, where parties' internal bookkeeping is not properly carried out. The major political parties … tend to run their own accounts of income and expenditure through register books, but none of them has any registry of assets. Income from donations in cash and in kind is not usually officially registered'.[112]

In general, disclosure requirements are often loosely defined and infringements are endemic. This is especially true in countries with lax sanctioning and overburdened (or government-controlled) oversight bodies.

Scrutiny and enforcement

In many Asian countries, oversight bodies are unable to effectively scrutinize violations of regulations or enforce legislation. In Malaysia, Pakistan and Singapore, no specific institution has responsibility for examining financial reports and/or investigating violations; usually the EMB or an auditing agency or ministry has this job. This indicates very weak oversight and sanction mechanisms.

This problem is due in part to the fact that oversight agencies are not always independent. In Malaysia, the Election Commission, as a government-controlled body, is not willing to monitor party financing and campaigning closely. Candidates have to publish an account of their election expenses from nomination until polling day, but the Commission does not analyse these accounts.[113] The other extreme example is the Election Commission in Thailand, which has extraordinary powers. It can 'summon any relevant document or evidence from any person, or summon any person to give statements as well as to request the courts, public prosecutors, inquiry officials, state agencies, state enterprises or local government organizations to take action for the purpose of performing duties, investigating, conducting inquiries and passing decisions'.[114]

The role of the Indonesian Election Commission in auditing is limited because it only has the power to appoint public auditors, collect audit reports prepared by these firms and then publish the results.[115]

A country's regulatory framework is sometimes inconsistent or not well known by parties and candidates. In Timor-Leste, during the most recent elections, the legislation and regulations were unclear regarding party and campaign financing, particularly with regard to public funding.[116]

The lack of scrutiny and enforcement is a common problem in countries with authoritarian traits. The difference between regulatory frameworks and real politics is most glaring in these systems. In 2010, the Independent Election Commission of Afghanistan posted financial reports on its website after election day that listed specific contributions and expenditures, but 'without clear enforcement mechanisms the effect of the regulations at reducing illegal contributions and expenditures is unclear'.[117] In Pakistan, campaign financing restrictions were routinely ignored during the 2008 elections, and the Election Commission did not investigate the financial reports by candidates.[118] Sometimes political parties request oversight, such as the Uri Party in 2006 in South Korea, which asked the country's Election Commission to control the party's internal election campaigns because it was disclosed that 'in order to appear to be attracting more support, members of the major political parties paid party membership fees for others or for fake members'.[119]

Efforts are being made to improve expenditure monitoring. India's Election Commission introduced reforms including the mobilization of '"Flying Squads" of observers and videographers and Static Surveillance Teams to monitor, record, and report, as well as seize "black money" on the spot'.[120] In the Philippines, the Commission on Elections set up an Ad Hoc Campaign Finance Unit[121] in 2012 in order to better enforce the country's campaign finance regulations during elections.[122]

Established democracies in the region, such as South Korea, are generally more successful in oversight and enforcement. According to a 2009 Global Integrity Report, which measured the effectiveness of laws regulating individual and corporate donations to political parties (and the auditing of those donations and campaign expenditures), South Korea scored 84 in political finance (out of 100).[123] The Korean National Election Commission has independent power to investigate election offences. Political candidates disclose data relating to financial support and expenditures within a reasonable time period, and the

Commission audits their campaign finances. The Commission is somewhat limited in its ability to enforce the results of these investigations and impose penalties, because it needs to transfer the case to the public prosecutor, who decides on penalties.

Yet some established democracies have weaker enforcement and oversight. Japan, for example, received an overall score of 81 for integrity in the Global Integrity Report, but only 65 ('weak') for political finance.[124] Its regulations governing political financing were considered particularly ineffective, and received a low score of 42. The report stressed that Japan undertakes little independent monitoring of political financing and that the Ministry of General Affairs or the Election Control Commission receives financial reports from political parties and political organizations, but does not effectively monitor them. Moreover, there is no third-party entity to monitor the political financing process.

Sanctions

All countries have legal sanctions for political finance infractions, including fines, prison, loss of political rights, forfeiture, loss of nomination or elected office and deregistration of parties. In Japan, the principle of complicity (*renzasei*) means that in certain cases a candidate can be prosecuted for illegal fundraising by members of his or her staff. In Thailand, the Election Commission has extraordinary powers and can disqualify candidates, dissolve political parties and order new elections in any or all polling stations. According to ANFREL, the Thai Commission's powers led to unease when the certification of then-prime ministerial candidate Yingluck Shinawatra was delayed. There was even a widespread fear that the Commission would dissolve parties or disqualify a huge number of candidates and thus decide the outcome of the election.[125]

Liberal democracies in Asia, especially those with active multiparty systems, seem to have stricter regulations on donations, allow free media access, provide generous public funding and give EMBs strong oversight responsibilities. More authoritarian systems, on the other hand, have government-controlled EMBs that regulate political finance in such a way as to guarantee the predominance of the regime's party (e.g., Singapore, Cambodia, Malaysia, etc.).

Sometimes other institutions—such as the Corruption Eradication Commission in Indonesia—take over the enforcement and sanctioning tasks of the Election Commission. Ahead of the 2009 and 2014 elections, the former arrested dozens of lawmakers, government members and district heads for embezzlement and bribery in connection with campaign financing.

Lack of effectiveness also depends on other factors like the strength of the state. In Afghanistan, declaring assets and submitting reports are not enough because campaign finance regulation is inadequate in the Electoral Law[126] and enforcement and sanctions are weak: 'Non-submission or incomplete financial reporting is declared an "electoral offence" but there is no punishment beyond a ban on standing for future elections until such time as records are supplied. The [Afghan Election Commission's] ability to oversee such measures is also uncertain'.[127]

In some cases, effective legal prosecution is simply impractical because it would wipe out a large part of the political elite and could thus destabilize the whole political system. This situation probably impedes sanctioning, because defeated candidates and parties could use every legal opportunity to unseat newly elected incumbents.[128]

Civil society and the media

In many Asian countries, the media and civil society organizations are pressing for electoral reforms—especially to regulate the finances of parties and candidates—because there is a growing public awareness of fraud and corruption. Globalization means not only marketization and commercialization, but also the transfer of ideas. It has accelerated a trend toward tightening and deepening regulation (especially since the 1990s).[129]

Sometimes the quest for new legal norms is at the core of social movements that are demanding democratization. In Malaysia, in November 2007, July 2011 and April 2012 tens of thousands of people demonstrated in Kuala Lumpur calling inter alia for a clean-up of the electoral register, reform of the postal ballot system, the use of indelible ink, longer campaign periods, free and fair access to the mass media for all parties, strengthening public institutions, and a fight against corruption.[130] It is noteworthy that the demand for electoral reforms galvanized the whole opposition. The Coalition for Clean and Fair Elections (Gabungan Pilihanraya Bersih dan Adil)—an alliance of major opposition parties, NGOs and the Malaysian Trade Union Congress—organized the protests. Similar demands are expressed all over Asia, and are often spearheaded by opposition parties and/or NGOs that provide detailed information on electoral fraud, the non-enforcement of regulations, the lack of adequate sanctions and so on to the wider public.[131] The best-known alliance is probably the Bangkok-based ANFREL, which conducts election monitoring, education and training on election and democracy-related studies, research on election and democracy-related issues, campaigns and advocacy work, and strives to create an environment conducive to democratic development in the spirit of regional solidarity. Other examples are election watchdogs such as the Free and Fair Elections Foundation in Afghanistan, the Committee for Free and Fair Elections in Cambodia, the Indian Association

> In some cases, effective legal prosecution is simply impractical because it would wipe out a large part of the political elite and could thus destabilize the whole political system.

for Democratic Reforms, and the Pera at Pulitika 2010 Consortium in the Philippines,[132] which consists of the Consortium on Electoral Reforms, itself a national coalition of 47 organizations, the Philippine Center for Investigative Journalism, the Lawyers' League for Liberty (Libertas) and the Association of Schools of Public Administration in the Philippines. These movements and organizations directly cooperate with mainstream media in countries with a more liberalized environment. Within more authoritarian regimes such as Malaysia or Singapore, the Internet increasingly provides new opportunities to disseminate critical information.

Conclusions

This chapter has overviewed the regulatory frameworks in 20 Asian countries. It has also shown how parties and candidates raise and spend money, and what obstructs the effective implementation of these rules. The analysis has elucidated the enormous differences between these countries and the lack of clearly definable regional or sub-regional patterns.

It is difficult to arrive at holistic conclusions on political finance in this region, due to the great differences in levels of economic and political development and the cultures of the sub-regions and individual countries. Asia is one of the most diverse among the regions included in this global study.

Yet, arguably, there are some significant developments in most (or all) of the 20 countries. Most notable is the expansion of economic globalization and market mechanisms. From this follows a commercialization of politics linked to new forms of extremely expensive campaigning. Political finance is thus complicated by candidates who have weak affiliations to parties and the demands of cost-intensive political marketing in an environment of globalized economies with strong entrepreneurs seeking to influence policy making. Of course, the strength of these factors varies in different countries. In some cases, new parties are built on strong ideologies such as Islamism or Hindu-nationalism, while in other countries commercialization is still in its infancy, as in Bhutan.

It may be possible to differentiate between different types of party funding. On the one hand, there is a range of hegemonic parties that have, to a certain extent, captured the state apparatus. Past examples are the LDP in Japan, the KMT in Taiwan (though they have both since lost power), the PAP in Singapore, the CPP in Cambodia, the Bhutan United Party and the military-backed Union Solidarity and Development Party in Myanmar. In Malaysia, the ruling Barisan Nasional coalition, led by UMNO, has direct access to huge state funds. These parties are financially powerful and have set up vast patronage networks. Some of them own corporate enterprises and have access to local, state and national budgets. They also receive support from companies seeking benign relations with the government.

On the other hand, some parties are dominated by private business interests. Mongolian and Indonesian parties have been known to sell their candidacies, and each candidate has to finance his/her campaign privately. This practice significantly raises the number of businesspeople among MPs. In Bangladesh, the candidate selection process within the Awami League and the Bangladesh Nationalist Party favours rich individuals who unofficially buy party nominations. Entrepreneurs seek to gain party positions themselves or to influence decision making via huge donations. In India, despite two decades of economic liberalization, businesses remain highly vulnerable to discretionary government actions at both the central and the state levels. Unreported donations are given in return for governmental favours or to buy party goodwill.[133]

In some countries, these congeries of reinforcing mechanisms create or amplify processes in which 'guns, gold and goons' (Philippines) or 'money and muscle' (India) erode formal democratic procedures. In authoritarian states, elections are manipulated by the state or the regime party/coalition and regulations are skewed or not heeded by those in power. Many such examples have been presented above. Only in more advanced democracies is the possibility high that regulations will be adhered to. It follows that regulatory patterns alone do not tell us much about political finance 'on the ground'.

A recurrent problem for candidates and parties is a lack of money for party organization and campaigning, largely due to low membership dues and insignificant (or non-existent) public funding. One solution could be the full control of party/candidate finances by the state, as in Bhutan. Yet this is hardly implementable in most Asian countries, and could be perceived as a transgression of state power.

Private donations form the bulk of party and candidate income in most Asian countries and, as in the rest of the world, income from membership dues is in most cases insignificant. For political parties in South and South-east Asia, candidates often finance their campaigns independently from political parties.

Whereas some countries almost completely dispense with legal norms on political finance, others have established intricate sets of regulations. If there is a similarity among all the cases discussed, it is the gap between norms and reality. Even well-meaning reforms all too often encounter implementation problems. The predominance of clientelistic networks over programmatic linkages between politicians and voters, the uncontrolled flow of 'black money', non-compliance with and non-enforcement of legal norms, weak oversight and feeble sanctions are endemic features of political finance in Asia. However, this does not mean that rules are meaningless. Although the effects of reforms are hard to measure, new regulations often change the behaviour of donors and spenders.

But there is no fit-for-all solution. No single regulatory framework is suitable to different cultural, political and economic settings.[134] The legal prescriptions have to be adapted to the electoral and political system, the form of party and candidate competition, and the economic environment. In countries with a more candidate-centred electoral system, for example, it is understandably important to control candidates' expenses and incomes. In economies where double-entry bookkeeping is not routinely used, taxpayers form a small minority and money flows mostly as cash; therefore it will be more difficult to trace donations. And, of course, enforcement depends on the overall quality of democracy and the ethics of the players that act within it. The behaviour of party members and leaders is a main determinant for the possibility of establishing a clean system.

The independence of the enforcement agency, and the involvement of civil society in reporting abuse and educating the public about political finance, are additional key factors. Moreover, there are counterproductive measures and trade-offs between regulations. If income and expenses are tightly regulated, this may overburden parties and candidates and tempt them to circumvent the rules. Yet if ceilings are too low this may create a new 'black economy'. Too much control may also stifle political competition. Public funding can strengthen law-abiding behaviour, but it can also beef up party cartels and demobilize grass-roots members.

The solution to the poor state of political finance in most of the countries in this region should include a range of interconnected measures. Public funding should be expanded, but only if at the same time parties are becoming better organized and more transparent in their internal dealings. This may be a virtuous circle. Better-organized parties need more money, but the cash flow needs to be tightly controlled, which necessitates independent, strong oversight. In the Philippines, the not-yet-ratified Political Party Development Act of 2012 envisages exactly that: a strengthening of financial regulations through the public purse, stricter oversight and reporting, regulations on party organization, and an end to 'turncoatism', i.e., party switching immediately after being elected. But even these far-reaching reforms are open to all kinds of manipulation. The sequencing of interconnected reforms is, thus, important.

Recommendations

Policy makers[135]

1. Make sure the rules are not overly ambitious. Try to formulate consistent regulatory frameworks with clearly defined implementation rules. The legal framework must be consistent in order to avoid confusion among local election officials, political parties, candidates and observers.

2. Define clearly how parties/candidates have to report, and which agency is responsible for oversight and sanctioning. Give enforcement agencies effective power to scrutinize and penalize offenders. If possible, try to implement reporting rules for donors.

3. Sanctioning should not create an atmosphere of fear and paranoia or stifle political competition. The responsible agencies have to work independently of any influence from ruling parties.

4. If a country lacks a system of public funding, consider introducing one. Ensure that the disbursement of public money is strictly connected to compliance with other regulations, such as reporting requirements. If possible, try to make public funding contingent on political party reforms. This includes transparent and democratic intra-party processes and improved party institutionalization.

5. Provide free or subsidized media access to alleviate financial pressures for political parties/candidates. Promote the diversification of party/candidate income. Public funding is usually complemented by donations, membership dues and limited commercial activities such as the sale of publications.

6. Consider earmarking a portion of public finance for female candidates or for enhancing gender activities within political parties.

Monitoring and enforcement agencies

1. Finance regulatory bodies must be independent. Ensure that the government does not interfere, and cooperate with all relevant stakeholders, including opposition parties and civil society forces.

2. Try to communicate openly and provide transparency of your organization's internal affairs. Make all relevant information available to the wider public and actively involve civil society groups in spreading information about political finance problems.

3. Ensure that enforcement and sanctioning are fair and comprehensible to the wider public. Provide a comprehensive enforcement infrastructure in order to implement regulations effectively.

4. Bear in mind that monitoring has to include a gender perspective. This pertains to the composition of finance regulatory bodies and producing gender-aggregated data (i.e., men's and women's access to and use of money).

5. Try to engage the wider public. Everybody should be able to read detailed (but understandable) reports by parties/candidates. Reports should be independently audited and published on the Internet without undue delays.

Ruling parties

1. Fair and transparent political finance is based on a system of checks and balances that starts within political parties. Arrange for fully

democratic procedures within your party in terms of internal elections, selection of candidates, policy formulation and, in particular, finances. Avoid the sale of nominations and commercialized campaigns for party elections.

2. Provide for independent external auditing and disseminate detailed information on party and candidate financing.
3. Support female candidates financially or with specific training, including candidates seeking re-election.

Opposition parties

1. If you work within an authoritarian regime, cooperate with reformers within society. Expose infringements by governing parties and incumbents systematically and openly. Explain to the public why the playing field is not level.
2. Realize that political party reform has to be part of enhancing the control of illegal funding. This includes intra-party democracy and the transparency of internal procedures, particularly those related to financing. Try to establish well-institutionalized parties that can serve as role models in terms of financing practices and intra-party democracy. Seek to be independent from large donations and diversify your sources of income.
3. Make political finance regulations major elements of your platform and propose realistic and credible reforms. Think about setting expenditure limits for the election/nomination of candidates.
4. Consider establishing an internal party fund for female candidates for campaigning and/or training.

Civil society

1. Try to build alliances among civil society activists and groups to raise awareness and monitor problematic forms of party funding. Bear in mind that the situation in the countryside may differ from that in the capital. Connect to local, regional and national groups.
2. Cooperate internationally to learn how other civil society groups have tackled the issue of political finance in their countries. International cooperation can also be useful to help increase pressure on national elites.
3. Gather information on the organization of political parties and their financing. Document it systematically and present your findings to the wider public.
4. Campaign against obvious and widespread infringements of current regulations. Cooperate with the mass media and reformers within the business and political sectors.
5. Cooperate with political parties, but define clearly the boundaries between civil society and political society. Try to have an impact on

policy making and help improve the existing regulatory framework. Help state agencies scrutinize political finance.

6. Consider specific access to loans and training for female candidates. Establish fundraising networks such as EMILY's List.

7. Use different kinds of social media. Especially in authoritarian countries, this is often the only effective way to disseminate information and identify infringements of political finance regulations systematically.

Media actors

1. Try to establish a culture of investigative journalism, include citizen journalists and strive to make the media independent from political life.

2. Systematically expose infringements. Report in full on glaring forms of corruption, the undue influence of business on politics, the abuse of state resources, vote buying, and so on. Raise awareness among the wider public about political finance and corruption without presenting your findings in a sensationalized manner.

3. Avoid being part of the campaigning business. Develop a code of conduct that clearly punishes journalists who launch reports in return for secret payments.

4. Pay attention to gender issues in reporting on campaigns and party politics.

International actors

1. Try to perceive improvements in political finance as part of a comprehensive reform project that encompasses the organization of parties and the manifold linkages between entrepreneurs and politicians.

2. Consider country-specific political, economic and cultural circumstances. Regulations that work very well in one country may be disastrous in other countries.

3. Disseminate information on best practices and cooperate closely with reform-minded politicians and businessmen as well as local political scientists and activists. Strengthen civil society actors as well as reform factions within political parties and the government.

4. In many cases, election observation does not sufficiently take into account the major role of political financing. Try to gather much more information and include the analysis of party/candidate financing, regulatory frameworks and their implementation as important parts of observation missions.

References

ABS/CBN News (2010) 'Poll Spending Cap Outdated: Comelec Spokesman'.

Antara News (2012) 'Political Parties Should Be Allowed to Have Businesses', 16 July.

Arlegue, Celito and Coronel, John Joseph S. (2003) 'Philippines', in Peter M. Manikas and Laura L. Thornton (eds), *Political Parties in Asia: Promoting Reform and Combating Corruption in Eight Countries*, pp. 217–62. Washington, D.C.: National Democratic Institute for International Affairs.

Asian Network for Free Elections (ANFREL) (2008) *Mission Report 2008: Nepal Constituent Assembly Election.*

Asian Network for Free Elections (ANFREL) (2011) *Report of the International Election Observation Mission: Thailand.*

Asian Network for Free Elections (ANFREL) (2012a) 'Vision of a Blueprint for ASEAN Democracy, Free and Fair Elections', available at http://newmyanmarfoundation.blogspot.de/2012/02/vision-of-blueprint-for-asean-democracy.html

Asian Network for Free Elections (ANFREL) (2012b) 'ANFREL joined NDI and UNEAD for the official public launch of the Declaration of Global Principles for Nonpartisan Election Observation and Monitoring by Citizen Organizations (GNDEM)', available at http://anfrel.org/anfrel-joined-ndi-and-unead-for-the-official-public-launch-of-the-declaration-of-global-principles-for-nonpartisan-election-observation-and-monitoring-by-citizen-organizations-gndem/

Association for Democratic Reforms (ADR) (no date) *Analysis of Income of Political Parties in India*, available at http://adrindia.org/sites/default/files/Income%20of%20Political%20Parties_v4.pdf

Austin, Reginald and Tjernström, Maja (eds) (2003) *Funding of Political Parties and Election Campaigns*. Stockholm: International IDEA.

Balgos, Cecile C.A., Mangahas, Malou and Casiple, Ramon (eds) (2010) *Campaign Finance Reader: Money Politics and the May 2010 Elections*. Quezon City: Philippine Center for Investigative Journalism and the Pera at Pulitika 2010 Consortium.

Betz, Joachim (2005) 'Die Organisation und Finanzierung Indischer Parteien' [The Organization and Financing of Indian Parties], in Günter Schucher and Christian Wagner (eds), *Indien: Politik, Wirtschaft, Gesellschaft* [India: Politics, Economy, Society], pp. 31–51. Hamburg: Institut für Asienkunde.

Bhaskar, Utpal and Surseh, Appu Esthose (2012) 'Spending Limits Take the Buzz out of Poll Campaigns', *Livemint*, 29 January, available at http://www.livemint.com/Politics/T4ES5VOvoRUjsoHyFRvkAM/Spending-limits-take-the-buzz-out-of-poll-campaigns.html

Bjarnegård, Elin (2013a) 'Who's the Perfect Politician? Clientelism as a Determining Feature of Thai Politics', in Dirk Tomsa and Andreas Ufen (eds), *Party Politics in Southeast Asia: Clientelism and Electoral Competition in Indonesia, Thailand and the Philippines*. London and New York: Routledge.

Bjarnegård, Elin (2013b) *Gender, Informal Institutions and Political Recruitment: Explaining Male Dominance in Parliamentary Representation*. Hampshire: Palgrave Macmillan.

Bertelsmann Stiftung (BTI) (2012a) *Afghanistan Country Report*. Gütersloh: BTI.

Bertelsmann Stiftung (BTI) (2012b) *South Korea Country Report*. Gütersloh: BTI.

Butrsripoom, Atthayut (2011) 'Democrats Receive Most Donations from Taxpayers', The Nation, 28 March.

Carlson, Matthew (2012) 'Financing Democracy in Japan: The Allocation and Consequences of Government Subsidies to Political Parties', *Party Politics*, 18(3), pp. 391–408.

Carter Center (2009) *Final Report of the Carter Center Limited Observation Mission to the April 9, 2009 Legislative Elections in Indonesia*.

Chhibber, Pradeep (2013) 'Dynastic Parties: Organization, Finance and Impact', *Party Politics*, 19(2), pp. 277–95.

Committee for Free and Fair Elections in Cambodia (COMFREL) (2012) *Report on Misuse of State Resource for Political Party Purposes*, available at http://anfrel. org/wp-content/uploads/2012/06/Final_Misuse-of-State-Human-Resource_ Eng-correct.pdf

Da Cunha, Derek (2012) *Breakthrough. Roadmap for Singapore's Political Future*. Singapore: Straits Times Press.

Democracy International (2011) *Afghanistan Election Observation Mission 2010: Final Report*, available at http://www.democracyinternational.com/publications/ election-observation-mission-afghanistan-2010-parliamentary-elections-report

Dick, Howard (2011) 'Corruption in East Asia', in Mark Beeson and Richard Stubbs (eds), *Routledge Handbook of Asian Regionalism*, pp. 186–99. Oxon: Routledge.

EU Election Expert Mission (EU EEM) (2008) *Republic of the Maldives – Presidential Election, 8 and 28 October 2008. Final Report*.

EU Election Observation Mission (EU EOM) (2008a) *Bhutan 2008 : Final Report on the National Assembly Elections – 24 March 2008*, available at http://www. eeas.europa.eu/eueom/pdf/missions/eu__eom_bhutan_2008_final_report.pdf

EU Election Observation Mission (EU EOM) (2008b) *Pakistan 2008 Final Report National and Provincial Assembly Elections – 18 February 2008*, available at http://eeas.europa.eu/eueom/missions/2008/pakistan/index_en.htm

EU Election Observation Mission (EU EOM) (2012) *Timor-Leste 2012 : Final Report on the Parliamentary Election*, available at http://www.eueom.eu/files/pressreleases/english/east-timor-2012-final-report_en.pdf

Fackler, Martin (2009) 'Japan's Political Dynasties Come under Fire but Prove Resilient', *New York Times*, 14 March.

Ferdinand, Peter (2003) 'Party Funding and Political Corruption in East Asia: The Cases of Japan, South Korea and Taiwan', in Reginald Austin and Maja Tjernström (eds), *Funding of Political Parties and Election Campaigns*, pp. 55–69. Stockholm: International IDEA.

Gaunder, Alisa (2011) 'WIN WIN's Struggles with the Institutional Transfer of the EMILY's List Model to Japan: The Role of Accountability and Policy', *Japanese Journal of Political Science*, 12(1), pp. 75–94.

Global Integrity Report (2009) *Scorecard: Japan 2008*, available at http://report.globalintegrity.org/Japan/2008/scorecard

Gomez, Edmund T. (2012) 'Monetizing Politics: Financing Parties and Elections in Malaysia', *Modern Asian Studies*, 46(5), pp. 1370–97.

Gowda, M. V. Rajeev and Sridharan, E. (2012) 'Reforming India's Party Financing and Election Expenditure Laws', *Election Law Journal*, 11(2), pp. 226–40.

Halder, Nomita (2004) 'Female Representation in Parliament: A Case Study from Bangladesh', *New Zealand Journal of Asian Studies*, 6(1), pp. 27–63.

Hellmann, Olli (2011): *Political Parties and Electoral Strategy: The Development of Party Organization in East Asia*. Basingstoke: Palgrave Macmillan.

Heywood, Paul (1997) 'From Dictatorship to Democracy: Changing Forms of Corruption in Spain', in Donatella della Porta and Yves Mény (eds), *Democracy and Corruption in Europe*, London: Pinter, pp. 65–84.

Hicken, A. (2011) 'Clientelism', *Annual Review of Political Science*, 14, pp. 289–310.

Hilgers, T. (2011) 'Clientelism and Conceptual Stretching: Differentiating among Concepts and among Analytical Levels', *Theory & Society*, 40(5), pp. 567–88.

Indonesia Corruption Watch (ICW) (2009) *Tindak Lanjut Dugaan Manipulasi Dana Kampanye Pemilu Legislatif dan Pilpres 2009* [Follow-up on Alleged Manipulation of Campaign Funds in the 2009 Legislative and Presidential Elections], available at http://www.antikorupsi.org/docs/audit-dana-kampanye-legislatif-rev3.pdf

International Center for Research on Women (ICRW) and UN Women (2012) *Country Reviews, Women's Political Participation in South Asia (Bangladesh, Bhutan, Nepal, Pakistan and Sri Lanka)*.

International Committee for Fair Elections in Taiwan (ICFET) (2011) *Election Observation Mission 2012: Taiwan Elections Handbook*.

International Crisis Group (ICG) (2009) *Afghanistan's Election Challenges*, Crisis Group Asia Report No. 171.

International Election Observation Mission (IEOM) (2012) *Report on the National Election in Taiwan*.

International IDEA, Political Finance Database, available at http://www.idea.int/ political-finance.

International Republican Institute (IRI) (2009) *Election Observation Mission, Final Report: Bangladesh Parliamentary Elections, December 29, 2008*, available at http://www.iri.org/sites/default/files/Bangladesh's%202008%20 Parliamentary%20Elections.pdf

Irwanto, Ferry (2009) 'A Typically Well-Oiled Campaign Approach From a Well-Suited Team', *Jakarta Globe*, 9 June.

Kapur, Devesh (2012) 'The Puzzle of Poll Financing: Changing how Political Parties Fund their Election Battles is Essential to the Fight against Corruption', *Business Standard*, 8 October.

Katz, Richard and Mair, Peter (1995) 'Changing Models of Party Organization and Party Democracy: The Emergence of the Cartel Party', *Party Politics*, 1, pp. 5–28.

Klein, Axel and Winkler, Chris (2012) Japan. Schwalbach/Ts.: Wochenschau Verlag.

Kochanek, Stanley A. (2010) 'Corruption and the Criminalization of Politics in South Asia', in Paul R. Brass (ed.), *South Asia Routledge Handbook of South Asian Politics: India, Pakistan, Bangladesh, Sri Lanka, and Nepal*, pp. 364–81. Oxon: Routledge.

Koellner, Patrick (2009) 'Japanese Lower House Campaigns in Transition: Manifest Changes or Fleeting Fads?', *Journal of East Asian Studies*, 9(1), pp. 121–49.

Kompas (2010) *Wajah DPR dan DPD 2009-2014* [The Face of Parliament and Senate 2009–2014]. Jakarta: Penerbit Buku Kompas.

Kupferschmidt, David (2009) *Illicit Political Finance and State Capture*. Stockholm: International IDEA.

Lee, Eugene (2011) 'Of Money and Politics: The Political Donations Act (2011)', *Singapore Law Review*.

Lumanauw, Novi, Sihite, Ezra and Sihaloho, Markus Junianto (2013) 'Indonesia's Direct Local Elections on Chopping Block', *Jakarta Globe*, 2 April.

MacRae, Graeme and Putra, Nyoman Darma (2009) 'Not Just an Elite Game', *Inside Indonesia*, 97, available at http://www.insideindonesia.org/edition-97/not-just-an-elite-game

Mangahas, Malou (2013) 'Pera, Pulitika, at Eleksyon: Comelec Lays Down Rules', available at http://pcij.org/blog/2013/01/16/pera-pulitika-at-eleksyon-comelec-lays-down-rules

Mayberry, Kate (2013) 'Malaysia Opposition Battles Financial Odds', *Al Jazeera*, 29 April.

McCargo, Duncan and Pathmanand, Ukrist (2005) *The Thaksinization of Thailand*. Copenhagen: Nordic Institute of Asian Studies.

Mietzner, Marcus (2007) 'Party Financing in Post-Soeharto Indonesia: Between State Subsidies and Political Corruption', *Contemporary Southeast Asia*, 29(2), pp. 238–63.

Mietzner, Marcus (2008) 'Soldiers, Parties and Bureaucrats: Illicit Fund-Raising in Contemporary Indonesia', *South East Asia Research*, 16(2), pp. 225–54.

Mietzner, Marcus (2011) 'Funding Pilkada: Illegal Campaign Financing in Indonesia's Local Elections', in Edward Aspinall and Gerry van Klinken (eds), *The State and Illegality in Indonesia*, pp. 123–38. Leiden: KITLV Press.

National Election Commission (NEC) (Korea) (2012) 'Election Subsidies and Female Candidate Nomination Subsidies for Parties', 26 March, available at http://www.nec.go.kr/engvote/news/news.jsp?num=191

New Indian Express (2014) 'Can We Have a Cleaner Parliament in 2014?' Published 2 March 2014, available at http://www.newindianexpress.com/opinion/Can-We-Have-a-Cleaner-Parliament-in-2014/2014/03/02/article2085083.ece#.U0zwr_mH4vy

Ohman, Magnus (2012) *Campaign Finance Oversight in the 2009 Presidential Elections in Afghanistan*, IFES Political Finance White Paper Series No. 7. Kabul: IFES, 2009.

Paath, Carlos (2013) 'Legislative Candidates Need at Least Rp 1 Billion to Run in the Election: Priyo', *Jakarta Globe*, 23 April.

Paath, Carlos and Amelia, Rizky (2013) 'Activists Laud New Election Funding Rule Aimed at Better Transparency', *Jakarta Globe*, 6 May.

Philippine Center for Investigative Journalism (2010) 'Venture capitalists or true believers? Only 308 donors funded campaign for presidency', available at http://pcij.org/stories/only-308-donors-funded-campaign-for-presidency/

Philippine Center for Investigative Journalism (2013) 'Poll laws in limbo: Firms can't donate but owners bankroll bets', available at http://pcij.org/stories/poll-laws-in-limbo-firms-cant-donate-but-owners-bankroll-bets/

Phongpaichit, Pasuk and Baker, Chris (2009) *Thaksin*. Chiang Mai: Silkworm Books.

Pinto-Duschinsky, Michael (2002) 'Financing Politics: A Global View', *Journal of Democracy*, 13(4), pp. 69–86.

Qodari, Muhammad (2010) 'The Professionalisation of Politics: The Growing Role of Polling Organisations and Political Consultants', in Edward Aspinall and Marcus Mietzner (eds), *Problems of Democratisation in Indonesia: Elections, Institutions and Society*, pp. 122–40. Singapore: Institute of Southeast Asian Studies.

Quota Project (2014) Global Database of Quotas for Women, Country Overview, available at http://www.quotaproject.org/country.cfm

Radio Australia (2012) 'Timor PM's Party under Scrutiny over Political Donations', 20 May, available at http://www.radioaustralia.net.au/ international/radio/program/connect-asia/timor-pms-party-under-scrutiny-over-political-donations/946440

Reilly, Ben (2006) *Democracy and Diversity: Political Engineering in the Asia-Pacific*. Oxford: Oxford University Press.

Republic of Indonesia (2012) Law No. 8/2012 of the Republic of Indonesia on General Election of the Members of the House of Representatives, People's Representative Council and Regional House of Representatives, available at http://www.anfrel.org/wp-content/uploads/2012/08/IFES-Indonesia-Unofficial-Translation-of-Law-82012-on-Legislative-Elections-v1_2012-06-14.pdf

Sabarini, Prodita and Partogi, Sebastian (2013) 'Want to Run? Show Me the Money First', *Jakarta Post*, 9 April.

Santucci, Jack and Ohman, Magnus (2009) 'Practical Solutions for the Disclosure of Campaign and Political Party Finance', in Magnus Ohman and Hani Zainulbhai (eds), *Political Finance Regulation: The Global Experience*, pp. 25–41. Washington, D.C.: International Foundation for Electoral System.

Saragih, Bagus (2012) 'Govt Requires Parties to "Educate" Voters', *Jakarta Post*, 23 November.

Shrivastava, Rahul (2012) 'Who Funds India's Political Parties? Report Says Most Donors Anonymous', NDTV, 10 September, available at http://www.ndtv. com/article/india/who-funds-india-s-political-parties-report-says-most-donors-anonymous-265499

Shvedova, Nadezhda (2005) 'Obstacles to Women's Participation in Parliament', in Julie Ballington and Azza Karam (eds), *Women in Parliament: Beyond Numbers*, pp. 93–110. Stockholm: International IDEA.

Sihaloho, Markus Junianto (2013) 'House Makes Argument for Independent Poll Monitors', *Jakarta Globe*, 4 June.

Singaporeans For Democracy (SFD) (2010) *Report on Electoral Reform to UN Universal Periodic Review*, available at http://de.scribd.com/doc/40479745/Singaporeans-For-Democracy-report-on-Electoral-Reform-to-UN-Universal-Periodic-Review

Sirivunnabood, Punchada (2013) 'Building Local Party Organizations in Thailand: Strengthening Party Rootedness or Serving Elite Interests?', in Dirk Tomsa and Andreas Ufen (eds), *Political Parties in Southeast Asia: Clientelism and Electoral Competition in Indonesia, Thailand and the Philippines*, pp. 163–85. London and New York: Routledge.

Stubbs, Richard (2012) 'The Developmental State and Asian Regionalism', in Mark Beeson and Richard Stubbs (eds), *Routledge Handbook of Asian Regionalism*, pp. 90–9. Abingdon, Oxon: Routledge.

Suri, K.C. (2007) *Political Parties in South Asia: The Challenge of Change*. Stockholm: International IDEA.

Sustainable Governance Indicators (SGI) (2011) *Japan Report*, available at http://www.sgi-network.org/index.php?page=countries_status&country=JPN&pointer=1#point_1

Teehankee, Julio (2013) 'Clientelism and Party Politics in the Philippines', in Dirk Tomsa and Andreas Ufen (eds), *Political Parties in Southeast Asia: Clientelism and Electoral Competition in Indonesia, Thailand and the Philippines*, pp. 186–214. London and New York: Routledge.

Thompson, Nick (2012) 'International Campaign Finance: How Do Countries Compare?', 5 March, available at CNN.com

Times of India, (2012) 'The Indian National Congress is the richest political party', published August 12, 2012, available at http://timesofindia.indiatimes.com/city/bangalore/Indian-National-Congress-is-the-richest-political-party/articleshow/15455081.cms?intenttarget=no

Tomsa, Dirk (2013) 'What Type of Party? Southeast Asian Parties between Clientelism and Electoralism', in Dirk Tomsa and Andreas Ufen (eds), *Political Parties in Southeast Asia: Clientelism and Electoral Competition in Indonesia, Thailand and the Philippines*, pp. 20–39. London and New York: Routledge.

Tomsa, Dirk and Ufen, Andreas (2013) 'Introduction: Clientelism and Electoral Competition in Southeast Asia', in Dirk Tomsa and Andreas Ufen (eds), *Political Parties in Southeast Asia: Clientelism and Electoral Competition in Indonesia, Thailand and the Philippines*, pp. 1–19. London and New York: Routledge.

Transparency International (TI) (2006) *National Integrity Systems Country Study Report Republic of Korea 2006*, available at http://csis.org/images/stories/hills/06Korea_NationalIntegritySystems.pdf

Transparency International (TI) (2010) *Promoting Transparency in Political Finance: Bangladesh, Indonesia and Nepal*, available at http://archive.transparency. org/regional_pages/asia_pacific/current_projects/transparency_in_political_ financing_in_the_asia_pacific

Transparency International Malaysia (TI Malaysia) (2011) *Reforming Political Financing in Malaysia*. Kuala Lumpur: TI Malaysia.

Ufen, Andreas (2008) 'From Aliran to Dealignment: Political Parties in Post-Suharto Indonesia', *South East Asia Research* 16(1), pp. 5–41.

Ufen, Andreas (2010) 'Electoral Campaigning in Indonesia: The Professionalization and Commercialization after 1998', *Journal of Current Southeast Asian Affairs*, 4, pp. 11–37.

United Nations Development Programme and National Democratic Institute for International Affairs (UNDP/NDI) (2011): *Empowering Women for Stronger Political Parties: A Guidebook to Promote Women's Political Participation*, available at http://www.undp.org/content/dam/undp/library/gender/gender%20 and%20governance/Empowering-women-for-stronger-political-parties-eng.pdf

United Nations Office on Drugs and Crime (UNODC) (2013) *Afghanistan Opium Survey 2013, Summary Findings*, available at http://www.unodc.org/documents/ crop-monitoring/Afghanistan/Afghan_report_Summary_Findings_2013.pdf

Vaishnav, Milan (2011) *The Market for Criminality: Money, Muscle and Elections in India*. Working Paper, Columbia University, available at http://casi.ssc.upenn. edu/system/files/Market%2Bfor%2BCriminality%2B-%2BAug%2B2011.pdf

Wang, Chin-Shou and Kurzman, Charles (2007) 'The Logistics: How to Buy Votes', in Frederic Charles Schaffer (ed.), *Elections For Sale: The Causes and Consequences of Vote Buying*, pp. 61–78. Manila: Ateneo University Press.

Weintraub, Ellen L. and Brown, Samuel (2012) 'Following the Money: Campaign Finance Disclosure in India and the United States', *Election Law Journal: Rules, Politics, and Policy*, 11(2), pp. 241–66.

Welsh, Bridget (2013) 'Buying support – Najib's 'commercialisation' of GE13', blog article, available at http://bridgetwelsh.com/2013/04/buying-support-najibs-commercialisation-of-ge13

Widhiarto, Hasyim (2011) 'Politicians Plundering Public Funds to Keep their Parties Going', *Jakarta Post*, 15 August.

Zakaria, Hazlan (2013) 'PKR Accuses Zahid of Buying Votes, Huge Overspending', *Malaysiakini*, 12 June, available at http://www.malaysiakini. com/news/232722

Notes

1   Increased democracy can, in turn, help make political finance more transparent.

2   Afghanistan, Bangladesh, Bhutan, Cambodia, India, Indonesia, Japan, Malaysia, the Maldives, Mongolia, Myanmar, Nepal, Pakistan, the Philippines, Singapore, South Korea, Sri Lanka, Taiwan, Thailand and Timor-Leste.

3   See http://www.freedomhouse.org/regions/asia-pacific

4   For example, party politics in India have been commercialized and require increasing funds to pay for the political machinery. This is partly related to the growth in population and the resulting increase in the number of potential voters. However, it also has to do with the rising competitiveness of Indian elections, which is connected to the increase in the effective number of parties; the weakening of genuine cadre-based parties; and the growing number of local elections. Other factors that have spurred this development are the predominance of parties with minimal membership dues and the rise of identity politics as the main cleavage of politics (Betz 2005; Vaishnav 2011; Kapur 2012).

5   Clientelistic relations are often mediated by middlemen. Key elements of clientelistic exchange are iteration (not just single interactions between patron and client), status inequality, reciprocity, and voluntarism, though the latter characteristic is contested. Different studies have stressed these elements (see, for example, Hicken 2011; Hilgers 2011; Tomsa and Ufen 2013).

6   Dick 2011; Kochanek 2010.

7   Halder 2004; Bjarnegård 2013b.

8   Arlegue and Coronel 2003; Teehankee 2013.

9   See Chhibber 2013.

10 See, for example, Fackler 2009.

11 For more information on state capture and political finance, see Kupferschmidt 2009.

12 Heywood 1997, p. 77.

13 Bjarnegård 2013a, pp. 144ff.

14 Phongpaichit and Baker 2009.

15 Even in a 'developmental' state such as Japan, networking through personalized local support groups (koenkai) always became 'dangerously close to engaging in illicit financial and other transactions' (SGI 2011).

16 Stubbs 2012.

17 Gomez 2012.

18 BTI 2012b.

19 Gowda and Sridharan 2012, p. 237.

20 UNODC 2013.

21 New Indian Express 2014. See also Lumanauw, Sihite and Sihaloho 2013.

22 In Indonesia, parliamentarians are even paid by government departments that struggle to have their budgets approved, and by candidates for executive and judicial positions who need approval from parliament. Even the Banking Act was passed only after the Central Bank of Indonesia bribed a group of MPs (Mietzner 2008, p. 241).

23 ICRW and UN Women 2012, pp. 5, 14.

24 Bjarnegård 2013b.

25 Asian Network for Free Elections (ANFREL) 2012a. The Blueprint refers to Article 21 of the Universal Declaration of Human Rights, Article 25 of the International Covenant on Civil and Political Rights, and documents of the Inter-Parliamentary Union, which

have developed some standards and guidelines pertaining to democracy, elections and the working methods of parliaments.

26 See http://anfrel.org/wp-content/uploads/2013/04/The-Bangkok-Declaration-on-Free-and-Fair-Elections-Its-Endorsers-.pdf

27 Members are Afghanistan, Bangladesh, Bhutan, India, the Maldives, Nepal, Pakistan and Sri Lanka.

28 ASEAN members are Brunei, Cambodia, Indonesia, Laos, Malaysia, Myanmar, the Philippines, Singapore, Thailand and Vietnam.

29 Asian Network for Free Elections (ANFREL) 2012b. The Declaration is the result of a consensus achieved by regional networks of non-partisan election monitoring organizations from around the world.

30 See also Suri 2007, p. 102.

31 In the Philippines, corporate donations are banned, but executive officers of these corporations are allowed to bankroll candidates and parties (see Philippine Center for Investigative Journalism 2013).

32 Gaunder 2011, p. 87.

33 Lee 2011.

34 Law No. 2 on Political Parties, 2011.

35 Organic Act on Political Parties, B.E 2550, 2007.

36 Throughout this handbook, international dollars (I\$) are presented alongside amounts in national currencies. The international dollar is a hypothetical currency that takes into account purchasing power parity and is therefore suitable for comparisons between countries. For countries in which the purchasing power parity varies significantly from the United States (which is used as the baseline for the comparison), the I\$ exchange rate may be considerably different from the nominal exchange rate. No conversions are given for US dollars (as this is by default the same amount as the I\$) or for those instances where the original currency is unknown and a secondary currency such as the euro has been cited instead. For further information, see Annex V.

37 Times of India 2012.

38 Coupons as a confirmation of a smaller donation are used, for example, by shop owners to demonstrate their allegiance to a political party. The sale is more often than not based on a more or less gentle pressure.

39 Republic of Indonesia 2012.

40 Irwanto 2009.

41 Philippine Center for Investigative Journalism 2010.

42 See Thompson 2012.

43 Ibid.

44 ICFET 2011, p. 26.

45 Klein and Winkler 2012, pp. 117ff.

46 Kompas 2010.

47 McCargo and Pathmanand 2005, pp. 70ff.

48 Ibid.

49 Ferdinand 2003, p. 65.

50 EU EOM 2008b, p. 33.

51 Ufen 2008; Sabarini and Partogi 2013.

52 Ufen 2008.

53 Hellmann 2011, p. 115.

54 BTI 2012a, p. 10.

55 Mietzner 2008, 2011; Widhiarto 2011.

56 Democracy International 2011, p. 26.

57 Radio Australia 2012.

58 Suri 2007, p. 102.

59 Gomez 2012.

60 IEOM 2012.

61 Antara News 2012.

62 Carlson 2012, p. 397.

63 TI Malaysia 2011; Mayberry 2013.

64 Katz and Mair 1995. Cartel parties are closely connected to the state apparatus, estranged from society, try to fend off new competitors and share the spoils of office. Dependence on the public purse may weaken efforts to mobilize members, be unfair to opposition parties and ossify the party system.

65 NEC 2012.

66 The LDP, DPJ, CGP or Kōmeitō, SDP, the New Frontier Party, New Party Nippon and the People's New Party.

67 Carlson 2012, p. 398. Member dues also play a role for party income in Japan, especially in well-institutionalized parties such as the Communist Party of Japan (Klein and Winkler 2012, pp. 81ff). Public funds have been even more important for the DPJ, but much less so for the CGP (Carlson 2012, p. 398).

68 Carlson 2012.

69 EU EOM 2008a, pp. 8, 19.

70 Mietzner 2007, 2008; Ufen 2008.

71 See the proposal for the Political Party Development Act (Senate Bill 3214), which includes a plan to create a State Subsidy Fund amounting to PHP 350 million (I$13.96 million). It will provide money for campaigning and routine expenditures (for civic education, research and policy development, recruitment and training). At the same time, the bill limits contributions from natural persons and juridical persons (such as corporations) and boosts reporting standards. Moreover, state subsidies are given only if an equivalent amount of funds has been raised from membership dues and voluntary contributions (see 'Public Funding for Political Parties', *Manila Times*, 25 November 2012).

72 Saragih 2012.

73 Political Fund Act, No. 10395, 23 July 2010.

74 Sirivunnabood 2013.

75 'Stricter Rules Sought as Media Moguls Enter Presidential Race', *Jakarta Post*, 6 July 2013.

76 EU EOM 2008a, p. 22.

77 Butrsripoom 2011.

78 Sihaloho 2013.

79 Welsh 2013

80 EU EOM 2012, p. 4.

81 COMFREL 2012, p. 4.

82 Ibid., p. 4.

83 International Committee for Fair Elections in Taiwan 2011, p. 24.

84 Quota Project 2014.

85   Shvedova 2005; UNDP and NDI 2011.

86   For Bangladesh, see Halder 2004.

87   Gaunder 2011

88   NEC 2012.

89   UNDP and NDI 2011, p. 28.

90   See, for example, Zakaria 2013. The PKR accuses Ahmad Zahid Hamidi, the minister of home affairs, of spending more than MYR 2 million (I$1.03 million) on his campaign.

91   ANFREL 2011, p. 50.

92   Bhaskar and Surseh 2012.

93   EU EEM 2008, p. 22.

94   In Japan, as a North-east Asian example, political parties increasingly use voter-chasing strategies that target independent voters and include a media-spin approach (Koellner 2009).

95   Qodari 2010, p. 123.

96   Ufen 2010. According to Paath (2013), a candidate for the national parliament easily needs more than USD 100,000 [I$100,000].

97   MacRae and Putra 2009.

98   South Korea is an exception to this rule; its Election Commission posts party expenditures on its website.

99   IRI 2009, p. 56.

100 Da Cunha 2012, p. 30.

101 Wang and Kurzman 2007.

102 ANFREL 2011, p. 54.

103 Thompson 2012.

104 IEOM 2012.

105 ICFET 2011, p. 27.

106 Santucci and Ohman 2009, p. 28.

107 Shrivastava 2012.

108 ADR [no date].

109 Carter Center 2009, p. 27.

110 Ibid., p. 30.

111 ICW 2009.

112 TI 2010, p. 18.

113 TI Malaysia 2011.

114 ANFREL 2011, p. 10.

115 Carter Center 2009, p. 30. Yet recently the Commission started to formulate new regulations that would require candidates and parties to disclose all their finances. One party, the Indonesian Democratic Party-Struggle, requires its candidates to create separate bank accounts for their campaigns (Paath and Amelia 2013).

116 EU EOM 2012.

117 Democracy International 2011, p. 26.

118 EU EOM 2008b, p. 25.

119 Transparency International 2006, p. 46.

120 Weintraub and Brown 2012, p. 265.

121 The Ad Hoc Campaign Finance Unit's work is defined by the January 2013 Resolution No. 9616 of the Commission on Elections ('General Instructions for the Implementation of Campaign Finance Laws') as well as some parts of the Omnibus Election Code and The tair Elections Act.

122 Mangahas 2013.

123 Global Integrity Report 2009.

124 Ibid.

125 ANFREL 2011, p. 36.

126 Ohman 2012.

127 ICG 2009, p. 21.

128 Cf. Mietzner 2011, p. 131.

129 It is well known that, at the same time, there has been a tendency to alter electoral systems in many Asian countries in recent years in order to improve the institutionalization and nationalization of parties and the representativeness of parliaments, and to weaken traditional elites and clientelism. Reilly (2006) noted a marked trend to choose mixed-member electoral systems that combine elements of proportional representation and plurality systems. In South Korea, Taiwan and Japan, mixed systems replaced the single non-transferable vote; in the Philippines and Thailand they replaced plurality or plurality-like systems (see also Tomsa 2013).

130 There have recently been other cases of anti-corruption movements. See, for example, the victory of the newly established Aam Aadmi Party (Common Man Party) in the December 2013 Delhi elections or the protests in Thailand, Cambodia and against pork-barrel politics in the Philippines.

131 See also SFD 2010.

132 Cf. Balgos, Mangahas and Casiple 2010.

133 Gowda and Sridharan 2012, p. 237.

134 Pinto-Duschinsky 2002.

135 Policy makers are defined as those involved in the drafting, amending and adopting of political finance policies, either from the executive or m the legislative arm of government. The focus is therefore on the role policy makers play rather than on a particular institution.

CHAPTER 5

Latin America

Juan Fernando Londoño and Daniel Zovatto*

Introduction

Money plays an increasingly important role in politics in Latin America[1] as a result of the region's recent economic growth, the increase in foreign direct investment and the rise of the middle class. Between 2003 and 2008, for example, the region experienced an average annual growth rate of gross domestic product (GDP) of almost 5 per cent.[2] It witnessed a 31 per cent increase in foreign investment between 2010 and 2011[3] and greater social mobility: the middle class represented 20 per cent of the region's population in 1995 and 30 per cent in 2009.[4]

Although the rising importance of money in politics has coincided with the consolidation of democratic values and institutions throughout the region, the issue continues to be associated with corruption scandals and the influence of criminal or illegitimate interests (and the authorities' inability to deal with it) rather than with the potential to invest money to strengthen democratic institutions and level the political playing field.

Several important studies have examined the role of money in Latin American politics in recent decades.[5] These studies confirm that there is a gap between the dense legal *regulations* that exist in nearly all countries in the region and the role of money in the political and electoral life of Latin American democracies. Although complete, current and easily comparable data are available on regulations for financing, practical, quantitative information about the *amounts* of financing (especially their real origin and their impact on democratic life) is not available.

---

* The authors would like to thank Luis Alfredo Rodríguez for his research assistance and choice of useful material; Juanita Betancourt, for the systematization of the information; Omar Darío Peña Niño, consultant and researcher specializing in political economy; and International IDEA's Latin America and the Caribbean team, which provided comments and contributions.

Attention to the amount of money spent on campaigns is increasing in the region, and the issue ranks high on several civil society organizations' agendas.[6] The past couple of years have seen regular citizens' mass protests occur in several countries across the continent, closely connecting the issue of money and politics with the overall quality of democracy and the distribution of welfare. In Brazil, citizens have taken their discontent with corrupt politicians to the streets. These protests clearly indicate that political representatives who cannot effectively address issues such as vote buying, corruption or limits to corporate donations may be faced with severe political or legal consequences.

This chapter provides an initial overview of political financing regulation and implementation in the region.

Problems of political finance in Latin America

The problems of political finance in the region appear to stem not from a lack of regulation but from an inability to enforce those regulations. This is not exclusively a problem of finance, but is characteristic of the evolution of the rule of law in Latin America. Nor is this a one-dimensional situation; rather it results from a convergence of variables—including cultural factors, excessive and inadequate regulatory designs, institutional incapacity and a lack of mechanisms for public, political and legal oversight—which together would ensure an adequate degree of compliance with norms and true accountability.

The solution to this problem requires political will, and monitoring and enforcing agencies must have adequate institutional flexibility to cooperate with other state actors involved in combating illicit finance. The main challenges to understanding and effectively tackling the issue of undesired money in politics are linked.

The region's overall return to democracy in the 1990s after decades of military juntas in many of the region's countries—and subsequent efforts to consolidate democracy—have since produced the greatest progress in regulation thus far. Today regional bodies such as the Organization of American States (OAS) are increasingly focusing on the issue of money in politics and finance regulation.

Lack of transparency and reliable information

In Latin America, most countries require political parties to disclose their income either annually (84 per cent) and/or in relation to election campaigns (75 per cent). Around half of the countries have the same requirement for candidates. The consistency of this requirement, however, contrasts with scant knowledge of the origin of the funds and a lack of discussion about money in campaigns. In practice, there is also a lack of compliance regarding disclosure, due to poor access to public information.[7] The absence of national sources of information about campaign income and expenditures makes in-depth comparative analysis difficult. The failure to disclose funds makes it more likely that political parties and candidates will exceed their limits and makes political corruption more likely. A lack of transparency increases the likelihood of impunity or the infiltration of illicit funds, and erodes political parties' public credibility. Yet the issue of money in campaigns is generally not part of the electoral debate, except in certain situations (e.g., infiltration of international or illicit funds); politicians tend to claim that party funds should be considered internal affairs.

Poorly conceptualized regulations

The region lacks regional standards (adopted by international accord) for political finance. The Inter-American Convention against Corruption, ratified in 1997, does not include specific norms for political finance. Article 5 of the Inter-American Democratic Charter, signed in 2001, states that political parties are crucial for democracy and that special attention should be paid to 'the problems associated with the high cost of election campaigns and the establishment of a balanced and transparent system for their financing', but it offers no prescription for doing so.

In many cases, the legal frameworks in Latin America include loopholes or are rigid to the point that they cannot be incrementally reformed. More often than not, due to poor conceptualization or understanding of their implications, the regulations do not achieve the desired results or address the root causes of the problem. For example, even if regulations include limits on donations or expenditures, they are insufficient to address the electoral inequalities that come with very different access to resources. And if regulations are too strict and unrealistic, they risk encouraging evasion.

Infiltration of illicit financing

Illicit financing, mainly from drug trafficking, is a particular problem in this region: it contributes to the destabilization of the political systems and their institutions. Illicit organizations have a strong foothold, especially in the drug-trafficking corridor that stretches from the Andean region to Mexico. The extreme case is Colombia, where during the past two decades the lack of an appropriate regulatory framework has created a vacuum that criminal organizations have used to their advantage. Later, the capture of the state by paramilitary groups in some areas of the country made it difficult to prevent these groups from financing political campaigns, or to keep politicians from indirectly funding activities of such groups because of their local influence. To the extent that drug trafficking exists in other countries in the region, the infiltration of money associated with that illicit trade into political life and electoral processes has become a generalized risk.[8]

Absence of strong monitoring and enforcement agencies

Across the region, it is clear that there is a gap between the existence of regulations and the degree to which they are effectively implemented.[9] The lack of enforcement has its roots in a dearth of strong monitoring and enforcement institutions. If monitoring institutions fail to create standards and guidelines for reporting and then do not even properly review the reports they get, it undermines their ability to enforce rules on parties and candidates. To a degree, this is caused by a lack of resources and staff, which makes it difficult for them to adequately detect violations.

The main issue related to lack of enforcement in the region can most likely be attributed to an overall lack of political will to address the issue of political finance, especially with regard to the (often very considerable) illicit financing available to politicians. Thus, in addition to their lack of resources, the enforcement agencies lack the independence and legal mandate to do their job: they are tasked with controlling the same actors who grant them their powers, which both undermines and delegitimizes them. Therefore few sanctions are imposed in the region for breaches of finance regulation. When violators are not punished, a sense of impunity prevails and that, in turn, becomes an incentive for others to also evade regulations. The impunity ultimately jeopardizes the credibility of political finance regulation.

Sources of income for political parties and candidates

Contribution bans

Latin American countries have an extensive repertoire of bans on contributions, especially donations to candidates. One of the most widely used bans relates to foreign donations to both parties and candidates (88 per cent of countries ban foreign donations to parties and 77 per cent to candidates). Latin America has a long history of foreign interventions, and these bans seek to avoid undue interference by foreign interests in the countries' democratic lives. Foreign companies and governments have been found donating to political parties and candidates across the region, from Argentina in the south to Mexico in the north. For example, there has been a steady flow of funds from abroad into Nicaragua to finance politics.[10] Former presidents Enrique Bolaños (2002–07) and Arnoldo Alemán (1997–2002) were both accused of receiving donations from Taiwanese banks for their election campaigns.[11] In Ecuador, former President Lucio Gutiérrez and the leaders of his political party admitted to accepting 15,000 US dollars (USD) from Taiwan for the 2002 elections.[12]

In Venezuela, the current government (which has been accused of financing campaigns and political parties in other countries in the region) accused the opposition of receiving foreign funding, especially from organizations that promote democracy. As a result, the government approved the Law of Defence of Political Sovereignty and National Self-Determination,[13] which prohibits organizations with political goals (i.e., political parties) and organizations that defend political rights from receiving foreign donations.

Yet foreign 'democracy assistance' is generally allowed. The most significant examples of authorized international financing are funds for technical assistance that various organizations and countries disburse as a form of cooperation—via organizations such as the German party foundations, the International Republican Institute, the National Democratic Institute for International Affairs and International IDEA—which are devoted to supporting political parties or political party systems.

Countries in the region also widely prohibit contributions from government contractors. Donations from companies that have government contracts or partial government ownership are banned in 67 per cent of countries to parties and in 72 per cent of countries to candidates. Such bans are meant to prevent conflicts of interest, guarantee impartiality in public functions, avoid corruption and maintain the state's neutrality. Nevertheless, relationships between government contractors and political finance persist; these types of corporations may have a financial stake in the election results.[14] The challenge with designating organizations or individuals as 'undesired donors' is to determine whether the bans will merely drive these relationships further into the shadows. In practice, many instances of violations of this regulation are detected. In one case from Brazil in 2011, the media reported a 4.6 million Brazilian real (BRL) (I$2.5 million)[15] donation from the Andrade Gutiérrez construction company (the third-largest government contractor, which had contracts totalling BRL 393.2 million [I$209.9 million]) to the Partido dos Trabalhadores.[16]

A high percentage of countries in the region also bans anonymous donations: 72 per cent of countries for parties and 70 per cent for candidates. These donations are banned due to the principle that voters have the right to know what interests a party or candidate represents by revealing the origins of their funding, including its legality. Without bans or limits on anonymous donations, it is easier for illicit money to enter the system or for money laundering to occur. Chile has a unique mechanism known as 'reserved contributions', which requires anonymous contributions from companies to a party to be channelled through the Chilean Electoral Service, which then delivers the contributions to the party without revealing the source of their funds.[17] Through this mechanism, in which the Electoral Service becomes a de facto middleman between the recipient and donor, contributions can be monitored and potentially corrupt exchanges can be stifled—while respecting anonymity.

Figure 5.1. The percentage of states in Latin America that ban anonymous donations to political parties and candidates

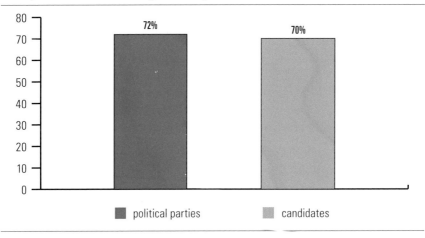

Source: International IDEA. This chart is based on data collected up to February 2014. Data are continuously updated on the International IDEA Political Finance Database. See http://www.idea.int/political-finance/question.cfm?field=292&region=19

Private sources of income

Contributions from party members

Latin American countries generally have a fragmented party landscape, and many parties in the region only emerged during or after the region's general transition to democracy in the 1990s.

Therefore it is very difficult to find parties that have organized themselves along the lines of more established and traditional European mass-membership parties, which (to a large extent) were dependent on their members' loyalty or dues. Membership dues are a declining source of income for parties around the world; large private or corporate donations and public funding are becoming more important. This global trend can be observed in the Latin American context, where political parties are in many regards more similar to those in the United States of America (USA) than to their counterparts in Europe.

Highly centralized parties are also on the decline in Latin America and are being replaced by parties that are more loosely structured and operate informally. This trend affects parties' ability to collect membership fees, which are normally based on official membership.[18]

The Frente Amplio in Uruguay requires payment of membership dues before members can participate in internal elections for the party's national leadership.[19] Yet Brazil prohibits mandatory fees; a legal ruling held that charging dues would threaten the wages of party members, especially those working in the public sector.[20]

The lack of funding from party members could also be attributed to the reduction in party identification that has occurred in much of the region. This trend is connected to a lack of public trust in parties, as reflected in various opinion polls and studies.[21] Another reason could be the failure of parties to motivate their members.[22]

Arguably, the value of member contributions lies less in the amount donated, which in most cases is not very high, than in the sense of empowerment it gives party members. If members contribute from their own pockets, they will be better able to demand accountability from the party leadership in administration, finance and political management. Parties should therefore implement strategies to enhance transparency and incentives for members through positive compensation,[23] and should have an appropriate infrastructure for handling donations.[24]

Small donations, sales and in-kind contributions

Seeking many small donations is arguably the most accepted formula for political finance contributions, because it keeps large donors from gaining excessive influence over a party or candidate. Avoiding such influence justifies the setting of ceilings on donations; 83 per cent of countries in the region limit the amount a single donor can give to a party over a certain period of time (not election specific). Yet only 50 per cent of countries limit the amount a donor can give to a candidate.

Another type of income is the small amounts of money that parties receive for the sale of items and materials, for example campaign-related materials. Other innovative ways of allowing people of limited economic means to contribute financially to political parties and election campaigns include in-kind contributions from farmers and donations of works of art. Bolivian President Evo Morales received donations of coca and *chuño* (freeze-dried potatoes) from farmers and grass-roots organizations for his 2009 campaign.[25] The main candidates in the 2002 Colombian presidential campaign—Álvaro Uribe, Horacio Serpa and Noemí Sanín—sold products with campaign slogans to raise small amounts of money. One person who ran a shop for the Uribe campaign raised 300 million Colombian pesos (COP) (I$218,000) in just two months.[26]

It is difficult to measure the exact importance of small donations to the electoral process in general or to a particular campaign. Since all parties use these innovative fundraising methods, especially during election seasons, their effects should not be underestimated.

Large donations

Although some countries seek to limit the size of donations in order to avoid undue influence by the few in politics, ceilings on election-related donations to parties are found in only five countries (Brazil, Chile, Colombia, Ecuador and Paraguay). It should be noted that for politicians, large donations represent an economy of scale, because they require less effort to collect. The flip side, as noted above, is the power that donors acquire when a candidate's political survival depends on them.

Large private donors often contribute to several political groups. In Chile, family enterprises of the Luksics, Mattes and Saiehs contribute to nearly all the parties except the Partido Comunista, which could be seen as either a strategy for financial diversification (to maintain influence regardless of who wins) or as a form of democratic philanthropy.[27] In many cases, businesses prefer not to reveal their political 'preferences'. In a survey of 151 businesspeople, 54 per cent said they had made in-kind contributions instead of cash donations because they are more difficult to trace and identify.[28] Just 56 per cent of businesses record such donations in their financial accounting, which makes it impossible to compare information from donors and recipients.

Civil society groups in Latin America are, however, paying increasing attention to these issues. A non-governmental organization representative in Panama, when discussing contributions from convicted donor David Murcia,[29] stated that: 'Freedom and democracy have a cost; either we, the citizens, pay, or Murcia pays. If we pay, we will be the masters of our freedom and democracy. If Murcia pays, he will be the master of our freedom and our democracy.'[30]

> It is often claimed that the problem with large donations is not their size but the lack of transparency that often surrounds them. Future efforts to control them should therefore focus on making them transparent and the information accessible to the public.

Unlike small donations, which are often perceived as politically correct but require a major logistical effort, large donations are seen as lacking the same legitimacy and based on political pragmatism. It is often claimed that the problem with large donations is not their size but the lack of transparency that often surrounds them. Future efforts to control them should therefore focus on making them transparent and the information accessible to the public.

Funds from party leaders

There is a markedly personalist tradition in Latin American politics, and the strong, populist and adversarial caudillo leader has been a key figure during populist periods of history. Although a number of millionaires participate in regional and national politics, few parties depend on the finances of their major leaders. Two examples of this dependence are found in Mexico and Colombia. In Mexico, former Vice-president Vicente Fox was called a 'financial asset'[31] of the political party Acción Nacional. In Colombia, most of the COP 1.76 billion (I$1.28 million) collected by Colombia Democrática in 2006 was a loan that the candidates and party leaders, Mario Uribe and

José Gonzalo Gutiérrez, had to guarantee with their own personal assets.[32] However, party leaders' influence generally stems more from their charisma and political talent than from the money they contribute to the party.

Candidates' own funds

> To the extent that individuals finance their own campaigns, the party's weight in decisions is diluted, even once the candidate reaches office.

A candidate's personal financial contribution is distinct from her or his fundraising ability, which is mainly tied to his or her prospects of winning. This section discusses the use of candidates' personal funds in election campaigns. While party leaders generally play a small role in party financing, many candidates at all electoral levels (but especially the local level) finance their own campaigns.[33] This practice underscores the personal nature of politics and the institutional weakness of parties. To the extent that individuals finance their own campaigns, the party's weight in decisions is diluted, even once the candidate reaches office.

How much money candidates should be allowed to contribute to politics is an issue that does not appear to have been settled across the region. A significant example of the use of candidates' own funds is found in Argentina, where various parties depend on their candidates' fortunes. During the local elections in 2009, Unión-Propuesta Republicana (PRO) candidate Francisco Narváez said 'The campaign costs a lot of money, and it is all, but all, mine'.[34] Countries such as Colombia exempt candidates—except in presidential campaigns—from abiding by limits on donations, although they are required to respect total ceilings on expenditures established for the various campaigns.

In Colombia, two-thirds of the COP 362 billion (I$262.6 million) financing for regional campaigns in 2011 came from the candidates and their relatives.[35] In Costa Rica, the Partido Movimiento Libertario's top candidate and leader, Otto Guevara, placed his personal fortune at the service of the party, even mortgaging his house to raise money for the campaign.[36] This example suggests the potential financial benefits of being in politics, to the extent that a politician is willing to risk personal bankruptcy. In this, as in other cases, there is no clear line between contributions from the party leader and the candidates, since Guevara was both. A case from Chile demonstrates the importance of the candidates' own contributions. Between the 2005–06 and 2009–10 campaigns, the candidates' own contributions rose from 3.4 per cent to 9 per cent of total campaign funds, while private contributions rose from 50 per cent to 59 per cent and public funding increased from 13.6 per cent to 16 per cent.[37]

Besides the parties' scant ability to contribute to candidates' campaigns, there is the impossibility of demanding appropriate accountability. The candidate builds his or her own political capital through closeness to voters, which is difficult for the party to influence. This means that election prospects are largely tied to the candidate's own financial capacity, which acts as a barrier to access and, in the worst case, makes politics more elitist and oligarchic. This is a problem not only for electoral equality but also for the participation of certain groups in politics, particularly women, whose access to large amounts of money is often more limited.

Funds from elected officials

An alternative form of income for parties is dues, either via compulsory payments or via deductions from the salaries of those who represent the party in elected office or government positions. While this practice is generally prohibited across the region, several countries still use it. In Argentina, the Radical Civic Union party in the capital region keeps information about party income, which is published on its official website. Figures from 2008 to 2012 indicate that dues or payroll deductions from party members working as civil servants represented about 40 per cent of the party's income, while dues from members represented some 20 per cent. Gustavo Torrico, a Movement Toward Socialism parliamentarian in Bolivia, said that contributions to the party depend on monthly income, and that, in the past two elections, parliamentarians contributed 40 per cent of the last two salaries they received before the election.[38]

Some countries have also prohibited parties from requesting dues or payroll deductions from party members working as civil servants. In Brazil, for example, Superior Electoral Tribunal Resolution No. 22 025 ruled mandatory payroll deductions illegal and unconstitutional.[39]

Illicit money

The infiltration of illicit money into the financial and political system poses severe challenges for the Latin American democracies. Through parties' and candidates' acceptance of black money, the financiers may develop a 'creditor' relationship with the recipient, in which the party or candidate becomes 'owned' by the donor in a sense. Financiers, for example, may pressure a party to install a candidate who will comply with their demands.

The level of infiltration of black money into the national economies is reaching substantial proportions of overall GDP, especially in Mexico and Colombia. In Mexico, 77 per cent of GDP from the formal economic sectors has reportedly been infiltrated by organized crime; in Guatemala, the problem is even greater, at 82 per cent.[40] In Mexico, money laundering now totals between USD 10 billion and USD 12 billion a year, yet it is only illegal in three states in the country.[41] Traffickers of narcotics and actors involved in organized crime in Mexico have been known to infiltrate local governments by financing mayoral campaigns or bribes.

In Colombia, the cocaine trafficking business in 2008 moved approximately COP 13.6 billion (I$9.87 million), equivalent to 2.3 per cent of the country's GDP.[42] Colombia has experienced severe scandals of politicians interacting with paramilitary groups and receiving money from the drug trade.[43] Infamous drug trafficker Pablo Escobar created his own political party in order to enter the political arena.[44] While some experts consider Colombia a success story in combating illicit financing from drug trafficking in politics because of its effective sentences and specific reforms to address the problem, it has received increasing criticism for its lack of action.[45]

The problem in Latin America is exacerbated by the fact that scandals involving illicit money are seldom investigated, and politicians who accept money from drug trafficking often go unsanctioned. In Argentina there have been numerous scandals involving political candidates, some of whom have been investigated, but none has resulted in sanctions. In the case of the Medicine Cartel, the National Electoral Chamber demanded that the electoral judges hand down rulings in those cases of illicit financing.[46] Far from being an exception, however, such delays seem to be the rule, with an average 14-year delay in sentencing for crimes committed by politicians.[47]

Electoral authorities in the region play a secondary role in investigating these types of crimes, which are generally handled by offices of attorneys general or prosecutors. Therefore, greater coordination between electoral management bodies (EMBs) and special prosecutors has been suggested as a way to curb the influence of illicit money.[48] Experts have also recommended implementing the four pillars of the Palermo Convention and the recommendations of the Financial Action Task Force[49] on Money Laundering.[50]

Since the influence of illicit drug money in political finance in Latin America has deep roots in organized crime, the problem cannot be separated from addressing the broader issues related to criminal networks and their activities.

Limits on contributions

A handful of the countries—Argentina, Bolivia, Ecuador, Guatemala, Peru and Uruguay—limit contributions to political parties during non-campaign periods. Meanwhile, 61 per cent of the countries place limits on donations to political parties (and 50 per cent limit donations to candidates) during the electoral campaign period. These limits seek to avoid undue influence by certain donors and to ensure more egalitarian participation in political life. They are extremely difficult to enforce, however, especially because of in-kind donations that tend not to be recorded.

Funding limits are continuously exceeded across the region; some argue that they encourage 'pathologically creative' accounting practices and mechanisms to circumvent the regulations.[51] In Mexico, a civic organization collected funds that exceeded the donation ceiling, which were then used to pay for advertising in support of Vicente Fox;[52] sanctions were ultimately imposed in this case.[53]

Public financing

Direct public financing

One way to counteract potential corruption resulting from private contributions is to provide direct public financing. Overall, the introduction of public financing in 88 per cent of the region appears to have helped create more equitable political competition. Public money also strengthens institutional solidity and is, at least in theory, important to enable female politicians to participate in the political process, as it gives candidates a minimum amount of funding, regardless of gender, to help level the playing field. Yet these changes do not seem to have led to a reduction in perceived corruption in the region.[54]

The fact that 88 per cent of countries in the region legally prescribe direct public financing reflects its importance for party financing although, as will be discussed below, the weight it carries in the parties' actual finances remains to be determined. Public financing was introduced early in this region starting with Uruguay (1928). Thereafter followed Costa Rica (1949), Argentina (1957 indirect and 1961 direct) and Peru (1966 indirect and 2003 direct). Nicaragua followed in 1974 and Mexico in 1977. The subsequent spread of democracy enabled other countries to introduce such regulations: Ecuador in 1978, Honduras in 1981, El Salvador in 1983, Colombia and Guatemala in 1985, Paraguay in 1990, Brazil in 1995, and Panama and the Dominican Republic in 1997. The cases of Venezuela and Bolivia are atypical, because after introducing public financing in 1973 and 1997, respectively, both countries later eliminated it, Venezuela in 1999 and Bolivia in 2008.[55]

While public funding is often necessary for the survival of parties, it may sometimes make parties too dependent on the state, whereas fundraising within society enables them to maintain channels of communication with citizens. Although there is little comparative information regarding private funding, there is evidence of the growing importance of public funds as a percentage of parties' and candidates' total income.

Table 5.1. Party dependency on public funding in Latin America, by country

Country	Year/election	Relative dependency on public funding (%)
Argentina	2003 (presidential)	44
	2007 (presidential)	36
	2009 (legislative)	23
	2010 (presidential)	60
Chile	n/a	16–20
Colombia	2006 (presidential)	89
Costa Rica	2010 (presidential)	33

Dominican Republic	2000	58
Guatemala	2011 (presidential)	12[56]
Honduras	1997	10
Mexico	2012 (presidential)	95
Nicaragua	2006 (presidential)	51
Panama	1999	30
Uruguay	2009 (presidential)	80

Source: Bértoa, Molenaar, Piccio and Rashkova 2014

Table 5.1. shows that the relative dependency on public funding varies significantly between countries, from being marginal in Honduras and Guatemala to dominating party campaign income in Colombia and Mexico.

Although public financing is important for equality and institutional solidity, there is a dilemma between giving to everyone and rewarding those who win voter support. Larger parties generally believe that the fairest formula is to reward electoral performance, while small parties believe that equal distribution is the ideal approach.

One good example of equal disbursement of public funds is from Colombia, where the introduction of advance disbursement in 2006 gave all candidates who met the legal criteria the same amount of public money for their campaigns, meaning that election performance would depend more on the candidates' abilities and less on the funds obtained.[57] This change, combined with ceilings for both total expenditures and individual contributions, significantly levelled the playing field.

Parties in Costa Rica, on the other hand, have experienced the uncertainty of financing through public debt bonds. This has led some parties to resort to obtaining bank guarantees calculated on the basis of polls, which meant that parties that had a lower showing in voter surveys received fewer funds. However, some parties made risky deals, assuming that they would receive a larger number of votes than they actually did and that this would enable them to obtain large amounts of public funds, which they could later use to repay the debt.[58]

The timing of the disbursement of funds is a challenge, because it makes all the difference when it comes to real opportunities for competing. In Colombia, the vote-based system disburses public funds months after the election based on the number of votes won, potentially leaving parties with few resources for the campaign. In Costa Rica, parties have complained that a lack of guidance from election authorities led them to submit incorrect financial reports, which interrupted their EMB payments.[59]

There are also examples of the misuse of public funds, lack of sufficient state budgets, or subsidies not being paid due to a lack of public or executive will.

In Peru, even though there is a provision for public funding, political parties do not receive any public funds in practice due to the discretionary nature of the provision, as disbursement of funds is subject to budgetary considerations and decisions by the executive branch. This body normally considers it politically costly to authorize disbursements to political parties, which suffer from low public credibility. Some party leaders also resist accepting such resources out of fear of internal party pressures. Lack of compliance with the norm has led the OAS to recommend the 'regularisation of public financing, ensuring delivery on the grounds that the debt to parties helps guarantee that political parties have the resources and conditions necessary for participating in elections'.[60]

Some countries have special forms of public funding. All Chilean parties receive public contributions, and some receive additional indemnities from the state for crimes committed during the dictatorship. Indemnities to the Partido Comunista for goods and money in 2008 and 2010 amounted to a total of about USD 10 million.[61]

Public funding and gender equality

Political gender equality remains a distant goal in most Latin American countries. To alter this, approximately one-third of the countries in the region have introduced earmarking of public resources to promote gender equality among candidates or within parties, which is a higher percentage than elsewhere in the world.

These financial resources are designed to level the playing field and enable women to participate successfully in elections. A Brazilian study comparing the income of male and female candidates found that in the 2006 elections for state deputies, women had lower fundraising rates than men in all areas except 'individual donations'. Also in that year, in the election for federal deputies, women did not have higher rates from any sources; they only received an equal amount of funds 'from committees'. In 2010, the differences in the rates increased in all funding categories, and women did not have higher rates than men in funding from any source.[62] The imbalance between male and female candidates' access to financial resources and the media is discussed further below.

In Costa Rica, parties must provide a certificate of egalitarian use of training resources for both genders; otherwise the expenditures may not be covered by public funds. In Honduras, parties are required to develop a policy of non-discrimination on the basis of gender and submit it to election authorities; if they do not do so, they can be fined 5 per cent of the public funds they receive. In Brazil, 5 per cent of public funds must be used to promote women's participation. In Colombia, 15 per cent of public funds received by parties must go to activities that include promoting women's participation. In Mexico, each party must dedicate 2 per cent of its funds annually to promoting women's leadership. Finally, Panama establishes that 10 per cent of resources earmarked for civic education and training must be spent on education for women.[63] In 2009, Brazil introduced a novel mechanism—earmarking a percentage of the free media advertising slots for female candidates.[64]

Some political parties have designed measures to address the funding deficit for female candidates. In Costa Rica, the by-laws of the Partido Liberación Nacional and the Partido Acción Ciudadana include provisions for earmarking funds for gender training, some of which are more ambitious than those required by law. In El Salvador, in 2007, female candidates from the Frente Farabundo Martí de Liberación Nacional organized a fundraising strategy to promote women's candidacies. In Panama, the Association of Parliamentarians and Former Parliamentarians holds training activities to strengthen female candidates' capacity to raise and access funds.

There is little analysis of the effectiveness of these measures, because many are recent. Nevertheless, a study on Mexico concluded that '2 per cent of public funds allocated for women is turning out, like compliance with quotas, to be a practice of simulation and a matter of mere rhetoric'.[65] Since there are no clear rules regarding the use of those resources, they are often being put to other uses, and when they are used for activities related to women, oversight has not been exhaustive.[66] In any event, the combination of gender quotas and public financing indicates that some countries have the political will to promote higher levels of inclusion and equality for women in politics, although much remains to be done.

Indirect public financing – the importance of access to media

Overall, 78 per cent of the countries in the region have provisions for some sort of indirect public funding, while 22 per cent either have none or have eliminated it (Bolivia, Guatemala, Panama and Paraguay comprising the latter group). Of the countries that do provide indirect public finance, all except Costa Rica, Honduras and Venezuela have provisions related to subsidized media access. With increasing campaign costs, media access is arguably one of the more important subsidies for parties and candidates.

There are two forms of subsidized media access. The first gives free slots to parties; neither the state nor the parties must pay for the slots because they are a legal obligation. The second involves public slots paid for with government funds, as in Mexico. In some countries, such as the Dominican Republic, El Salvador, Guatemala, Nicaragua and Panama, free access only applies to state-run media. The other countries use a system of free slots in both public and private media. In Argentina, Ecuador and Mexico, the purchase of additional advertising time is prohibited.

A controversial issue related to media access is the mechanism for allocating airtime and free slots. In Brazil there was a debate over the allocation of free advertising in the media based on the number of seats in Congress. The candidate for governor of Paraná, Avanílson Araújo (Partido Socialista dos Trabalhadores Unificado, PSTU), objected that he had 50 seconds during three days of the week, while other candidates, such as Beto Richa (Partido da Social Democracia Brasileira, PSDB) and Omar Dias (Partido Democrático Trabalhista, PDT), had six minutes.[67]

> ... the combination of gender quotas and public financing indicates that some countries have the political will to promote higher levels of inclusion and equality for women in politics, although much remains to be done.

Another issue related to access to media slots is the space or airtime that media donate to political parties and candidates. In many cases, the media are tied to strong business groups with major economic interests. This relationship between the media and politicians tends to be controversial, because of biases toward certain candidates in an effort to curry favour. In Uruguay the three private television channels are owned by a family consortium that offers discounts of up to 95 per cent off the usual rate for parties and candidates. Another approach is that parties and candidates do not have to pay anything and the cost is regarded as a campaign contribution.[68]

In Guatemala, 'over-the-air television has been monopolized for more than a decade by a private operator, the businessman Remigio Ángel González'.[69] This monopoly has given him considerable political influence. During the 1999 presidential campaign, González put all the power of his monopoly at the service of the campaign of the eventual winner, Alfonso Portillo, and received public positions for relatives in return.[70]

These cases inevitably lead to reflection about the relationship between parties and the media, and underscore the complicated mutual dependence between the media and politicians. Another problem is the misuse of official advertising for political propaganda, which will be discussed further in the section on abuse of government resources.

Media access and gender

It is particularly useful to examine media access from a gender perspective, as this could shed light on alternative, gender-sensitive models for providing media access via public financing. Specialized gender studies of the 2006 and 2010 elections in Peru indicate a gender disparity between media coverage and expenditures for media access. With a 30 per cent gender quota in Peru, one could assume that the media coverage of female candidates would at a minimum match this ratio. This was not the case, and the coverage varied significantly depending on media type. In the 2006 elections, coverage of female candidates (in the Lima electoral district) was 19 per cent in the print media, 22 per cent on television and 26 per cent on the radio.[71] On average among the candidates studied in the Lima district, male candidates spent 4.6 times as much on advertising as female candidates. Women's purchase of advertising was 19 per cent in print media, 12 per cent on radio and just 4 per cent on television.[72] For the 2010 elections there was a considerable advance in terms of televised media advertisements for women, as they purchased 32 per cent of TV advertisements. In advertising spending in all media, however, women accounted for just 20 per cent.[73]

A recent study[74] of media monitoring during the presidential and/or legislative campaigns in eight countries in the region[75] noted that, despite progress in the way gender-related news is covered, there is still inequality in the coverage of women and gender-related issues. Public media, in particular, have not met the goal of being pluralistic and gender inclusive.

Coverage of female candidates for the lower houses of parliament was less than the percentage of women on electoral lists in all countries except in Chile (which had 18 per cent coverage and 16 per cent female candidates). In coverage of candidates for the upper house, the percentage of coverage exceeded the percentage of female candidates in only two of four countries. In the Dominican Republic, 12 per cent of the candidates were women, and they received 36 per cent of the coverage, while in Colombia women represented 19 per cent of candidates and received 23 per cent of coverage.[76]

In Argentina, Bolivia, Chile, Costa Rica, Guatemala and Peru, coverage of gender issues in the state-run media was lower than in the private media. Coverage of female candidates for the lower house in the state-run media in Argentina, Chile, Costa Rica, Guatemala and Peru was either far less than in the private media or non-existent.[77] Nevertheless, as noted above, there was qualitative progress in the tone of news coverage of issues related to gender equality. In all countries except Peru, such issues were addressed in a positive or neutral tone (in Peru, the tone was negative 54 per cent of the time).[78]

Abuse of government resources

The misuse of government resources is a complex issue, and the situation in Latin America is further complicated by the expansion of countries that allow immediate presidential re-election, which permits the incumbent to hold on to the advantages of power for another term. So far, only Colombia has established a legal framework to constrain the president from abusing public resources during all electoral periods.[79]

The abuse of power can take various forms. For example, the media can be used for partisan purposes. During the 2012 election campaign in Venezuela, President Hugo Chávez had 60 hours of airtime, 47 television networks and an average of 47 minutes of coverage a day, while opposition candidate Henrique Capriles had only three and a half hours, or a total of three minutes a day.[80] There were also complaints about the use of government programmes for political purposes.[81] Likewise, during the 2010 elections in Bolivia, public authorities of all political affiliations engaged in propaganda activities.[82]

State resources can also be abused by extracting donations via deductions from the salaries of public servants. There are reports from Bolivia and Nicaragua that the ruling parties have instituted mandatory wage deductions from civil servant salaries to support the government parties. In Bolivia, a former vice-minister of mining complained about a 10 per cent deduction from their wages to finance the Movimiento Al Socialismo Bolivia (MAS) campaigns.[83] In the Nicaraguan case, the wage deduction was equivalent to one-quarter of the public servants' salaries.[84]

Spending by political parties and candidates

Spending limits

In Latin America, only about one-third of countries establish spending limits for political parties, while approximately one-quarter do so for candidates. Spending limits have to be set at a reasonable level in order to be respected and effective. In Colombia there is a widespread perception that these limits are not respected, partly because they are artificially low,[85] and partly because this type of regulation requires the capacity to determine actual campaign expenditures. The difficulties in doing so make it challenging to detect violations of the regulations.

Therefore Colombia's Party Law of 2011 created an Electoral Crimes Unit in the Attorney General's Office to investigate complaints about overspending and other election-related crimes.

In Brazil the spending ceilings appear to be fairly realistic in terms of the investments by politicians. For example, the expenditures declared by candidates in the elections in Goiania (all declared that they spent only 50 per cent of the maximum allowable amount) were realistic for an election in a smaller city in the interior of the country.[86]

While spending limits should not be set too low, as this will hinder parties and candidates from effective campaigning and encourage clandestine spending, no limit (or a too-high limit) may create an uneven playing field that would allow the richer candidates and parties to use their wealth more aggressively. The right limits thus vary according to the conditions in different countries.

Actual expenditures

A number of countries in Latin America are witnessing a general increase in election expenditures. Several organizations and experts see this as a disturbing trend and raise warnings about the 'steady increase in costs associated with greater operational complexity (organization and administration of the campaign command, consultants, marketing, publicity, surveys and communication technologies)'.[87] Total spending on election campaigns varies by country, ranging from a maximum of USD 2.5 billion for general elections in Brazil in 2006 to USD 301 million in Mexico in 2006, followed by Uruguay in 1999–2000, with USD 38.8 million, and Costa Rica in 2010 with USD 27 million.[88]

These sometimes exorbitant amounts indicate the need to better understand what explains these differences and why, for example, per-vote spending is five times higher in Brazil than Mexico (USD 19.90 compared to USD 4.20) and twice the per capita level of campaign spending in Costa Rica (USD 19.90 compared to USD 9.60).[89]

A high percentage of campaign funds is generally spent on advertising, especially on television. In Argentina in 2007, electoral spending on advertising amounted to 80 per cent, of which spending on television represented 54 per cent[90] (although a subsequent 2009 political finance law banned the purchase of advertising time). In the 2009 elections in El Salvador, TV advertising expenditures reportedly amounted to 90 per cent of the total.[91] In Guatemala in 2011, spending on advertising reportedly amounted to 71 per cent and TV expenditures represented 57 per cent of overall campaign spending.[92]

But does the party or candidate that spends the most win the election? The anecdotal evidence is mixed. In Argentina, the campaign with the highest expenditures (Cristina Fernández de Kirchner's) won the presidential election in 2007, but the second-place finisher was not Jorge Sobisch (who had the second-highest expenditures), but Elisa Carrió.[93] In Peru, there was no correlation between the parties' TV expenditures and seats won.[94]

Vote buying

The majority of countries in the region prohibit and punish vote buying. The offer of money or goods in exchange for a vote on election day differs slightly (but cannot completely be separated from) the more structural relationship of patronage, in which a political leader provides a series of favours in return for political loyalty. The percentage of people that reported having received an offer of benefits in exchange for their votes in 2010 was highest in the Dominican Republic (22 per cent) and lowest in Chile (6 per cent).[95]

This type of electoral crime is common, but those involved are rarely prosecuted. Although the purpose of vote buying remains the same, the goods or favours provided vary from country to country. In Brazil, Deputy-elect Asdrúbal Bentes bought votes from women in exchange for tubal ligations and abortions.[96] In Mexico, the National Action Party (PAN) engaged in indirect vote buying by arranging discounts for members with businesses and other institutions including travel agencies, mechanics, hospitals, universities and cinemas.[97] While vote buying is not illegal in Venezuela, in 2010 the opposition denounced the practice by the Chávez government in indigenous communities.[98]

Compliance with political finance regulations

Transparency

The problem in Latin America is not so much the formal requirements for political parties (and to some extent candidates) to submit financial reports, but rather compliance with the given regulations. All the countries studied—except Belize, El Salvador and Venezuela—require periodic reporting of party financing, yet there are few cases on the continent in which the information submitted has been used to further investigate violations and ultimately impose sanctions.[99]

Figure 5.2. Countries in Latin America that require periodic reporting of party financing

© International IDEA

■ Yes
■ No

Source: International IDEA. This map is based on data collected up to February 2014. Data are continuously updated on the International IDEA Political Finance Database. See http://www.idea.int/political-finance/question.cfm?field=288&region=19

The Crinis Project led by Transparency International evaluated compliance with the three stages of financial reporting (accounting, submission of reports to EMBs and public access to the reports). It found that in Argentina, as in the other countries studied, the reliability of the official data was limited. In reports submitted by parties before the general election, there were gaps between the information provided and actual income and expenditures. The study also

> ... the most significant transparency initiatives on the continent come from civil society efforts. Organizations in various countries have created and improved methodologies that make it possible to obtain better information about election spending.

found that the requirement that parties submit financial reports in standard electronic format, in effect since the 2005 elections, did not improve the presentation of data.[100] Colombia had the most effective regulations and the most consistent data; registered auditors regularly review the parties' legally required internal accounting. Costa Rica received a 'fair' rating because of its lack of standard formats for reporting, but it received a satisfactory score on compliance with requirements for submitting information.[101] Other countries, such as Guatemala and Nicaragua, make public funding conditional on the submission of financial reports but do not stipulate their format or time frames for submission. The Crinis investigation also noted that information from political parties and candidates in Panama,[102] Paraguay and Peru,[103] especially in relation to private contributions, is not very reliable.

The majority of Latin American countries legally require that financial information from parties and candidates is made public.[104] In practice, however, there are often other obstacles to accessing this information, or the information provided in response to requests is incomplete or incorrect. For example, in Chile it is difficult to access information and its quality is often poor. The information is available after elections in a format that is difficult to access, and after a certain time it is removed from the Internet. Information must be requested in writing, and when a breakdown of information is requested, the person making the request must pay for photocopies.[105] Although this may not constitute a very high barrier, it suggests that authorities are not prioritizing transparency.

Although several EMBs in the region have announced that they will post information on the Internet, very few have done so. At the time of writing, only Costa Rica and Mexico have electronic portals with easy access to this type of information, and only Costa Rica presented the information in standardized formats that allow it to be managed easily in data software.

It should be noted that the most significant transparency initiatives on the continent come from civil society efforts. Organizations in various countries have created and improved methodologies that make it possible to obtain better information about election spending. For example, the methodologies used by Acción Ciudadana (Guatemala), Poder Ciudadano (Argentina), Transparencia Perú and FUNDE (El Salvador) to estimate election expenditures have made it possible to determine that spending on political campaigns is much higher than indicated in reports to EMBs.[106] In Venezuela, the opposition plays a monitoring role and often investigates to present or request clarification of the finances of *chavista* candidates or to denounce the misuse of election funds. Although these demands are usually rejected, some fines have been imposed on state-run enterprises and government agencies.[107] In addition, political parties may also lack internal transparency. For example, information about Guatemalan parties' income during elections is often not shared even among the party leaders or members.[108]

Oversight and compliance

Transparency is a necessary—but not sufficient—precondition for effective oversight. Although the organizational set-up of the monitoring agencies varies from country to country, these bodies lack the ability to impose sanctions, with the partial exception of Mexico.[109]

There are several reasons for this. One is related to the origin of some of the EMBs and the fact that they grew out of the political parties. In other cases, the EMBs simply lack technical capacity or the ability to impose sanctions.

As these bodies are often criticized for being ineffective, there is a continuous debate about how they can be empowered. EMBs have demanded special powers in Mexico[110] and they have established partnerships and agreements with other government oversight bodies in Peru[111] and delegated special functions to police agencies in Brazil to address vote buying.[112] Colombia's Electoral Crimes Unit was created because of the ineffectiveness of measures taken by the National Electoral Council (Consejo Nacional Electoral, CNE). In the 2006 elections, legislation was limited to requiring the CNE to ensure that paperwork was submitted correctly and that campaign expenditure ceilings were not exceeded. Any other aspect had to be addressed by the judiciary.[113]

Most countries in the region require political parties to have specialized internal bodies or treasurers to manage party funds.[114] By law, these treasurers must be registered when the candidate registers. That requirement usually is a mere formality, however, and in some cases it is ignored altogether. For example, for the National Assembly elections in Ecuador, in the province of Guayas only 12 of 36 groups with candidates had registered their campaign treasurers, even though the deadline for registration had been extended.[115]

The institutional functions and capacities of the bodies responsible for electoral administration need to be better defined in a vast majority of Latin American countries. Their inability to act has been offset by the judiciary in some cases, but in the future they must find more effective strategies such as coordinating with other oversight agencies in the country. If candidates and/ or parties violate the law without repercussions, public confidence in them suffers.

Sanctions

All countries in this sample, except the Dominican Republic, have a plethora of legal sanctions available; they vary from fines to criminal sanctions for severe breaches of the law to administrative sanctions (e.g., deregistration of parties or candidates).

Yet there are problems related to implementation, for example abuse or lack of enforcement. No monetary, criminal or administrative sanctions have ever been imposed in El Salvador or Chile because there is no institutional practice of electoral auditing of any political party.[116]

In some cases, sanctions are too lenient. For instance, in Guatemala sanctions were limited to fines for pre-campaign propaganda and reprimands for exceeding the spending limit. These fines were minimal, barely 1 per cent of overall expenditures (or less than one day of television advertisements).[117] In Panama, the fines of USD 25,000 for those who receive dirty money or funds from foreign sources to finance their campaign have been called 'ridiculous'.[118]

Sanctions have also been used as a political tool. In Argentina they have reportedly been motivated by political bias, and the electoral judges issuing them are accused of being political players.[119] Naturally this makes political contestants worry about the abuse of such measures.[120] In Bolivia, the highest-profile case involving political sanctions occurred in 2009, when the National Electoral Court disqualified two parties (the Nationalist Democratic Action (ADN) and the Revolutionary Left Front (FRI)) from the presidential race because they had not submitted their financial reports.[121] The existence of regulation is not enough unless it is seriously and fairly implemented. Toothless regulation can also be an issue. If the sanctions for wrongdoing hurt less than committing the unlawful act, the incentive to remain on the right side of the law decreases.

Conclusions

Latin American countries have a complex web of regulations, many of which appear to be easily violated. Accusations of misconduct seldom lead to formal requests for action by the responsible authorities, and the few investigations that are launched rarely result in punishments. On the rare occasions when a sanction is imposed, its proportionality to the violation leaves much to be desired. A system with a low possibility of sanctions and minimal punishment does little to deter misconduct, since there is little political or financial cost.

Parties in some countries in the region are becoming increasingly reliant on public money for their operations, which is provided based on electoral performance (e.g., votes received in the previous election or seats in parliament). In contrast to, for example, Germany, it is not common practice in Latin America to reward parties that are more efficient at fundraising by matching their fundraising efforts with state grants. Parties therefore have no incentive to increase the amount they collect, which jeopardizes their link with society, public confidence and legitimacy.

The relationship between politics and the business sector is often perceived as donations made in exchange for favours or favourable policies.[122] Many Colombian donors consider donations advance payment for perks, therefore 94 per cent of companies surveyed in a recent study believe that donations to political campaigns are a corrupt practice.[123] Two elements related to large private donations should be considered in future analyses: (1) donor preference generally focuses on local elections rather than national elections and (2) donations often target multiple candidates, including rivals, so the donors can hedge their bets.

Illicit financing is a dangerous factor in the region. The most visible aspect of such financing lies in the relationship with drug trafficking, but other criminal organizations are also interested in building relationships with the political world.

The main risk for many countries is the weakness of the state and its authorities in certain parts of the country, which allows criminal organizations to establish clandestine (but effective) control that provides them with refuge and a base for operating and expanding illicit business.[124]

Given its murky origin, illicit finance is difficult to document and prevent. However, under-reporting of campaign expenditures can be an important clue, since it may obscure the sources and amount of income.[125] Yet under-reporting is not necessarily intended to hide illicit income: the often-low spending caps (and the threat of being sanctioned if the caps are exceeded) can lead contestants to misrepresent their spending from legitimate sources. However, if political parties and candidates receive income they do not want to make public, they have to under-report their expenses to ensure that their official income and spending match. Because this money does not flow via traceable routes, the opportunity cost for criminal groups to fund politics is much lower. Criminal groups often have plenty of money (in cash) that cannot enter legal circuits, so its use in political campaigns is doubly beneficial: they buy political support and launder the money at the same time. Ernesto Samper's 1994 presidential campaign in Colombia, which sought donations from the Cali cartel, is a well-known example.[126] Efforts to tackle organized crime must therefore take into consideration the money flowing through the political arena.

Most countries in the region show a clear upward trend in campaign spending,[127] partially due to the enormous costs related to electoral advertising. To counteract this upward spiral—and to make political races more equitable—it is important to better regulate the use of media, as has been done recently in Mexico, Ecuador, Colombia and Venezuela.

Even with new regulations, the parties in power continue to have major financial advantages. The tendency to use official resources to gain a political advantage appears to have been aggravated by the introduction in several countries of the possibility of immediate re-election. Once the incumbent decides to enter the race, the temptation to tip the balance by misusing media coverage of government activities seems irresistible. Several countries have regulations governing the incumbent's electoral behaviour: Colombia, for example, introduced a legal framework of constraints on the president.

One related issue is the abuse of power by agents of the state. This is a very complex issue, because it involves the legal powers of public administration, which gives governing parties a natural advantage. However, there is a grey area between the legitimate actions of a government that must respond to citizens' demands and the use of those actions for electoral advantage. The distinction between these actions is even more complex because of the ingrained tradition of political patronage in many countries in the region.

The general norms designed to avoid misuse of public resources are undermined by the lack of effective investigation and sanctions. This situation is aggravated when the state commits the abuses, for example with government advertising, use of the government payroll or the management of social programmes around election time.

There is a great deal of information about the formal legal regulation of political finance in the region, and adequate systematization of the existing information. However, this information generally does not address the impact of financing on specific areas, such as promoting equality in elections, strengthening party institutions or preventing the influx of illicit money. In addition, it is difficult to trace parties' income. In many countries, parties must submit reports to the electoral body, but these are not necessarily comprehensive or made available to the public, nor do they account for the illicit money that in many cases sustains the parties and candidates. There is also a lack of comparative information, and national analysis is scant. Yet there is an emerging consensus about the need to move into a new phase of studies and analysis of political finance that focuses more specifically on the quantitative and practical aspects of money in politics.[128]

Recommendations

Three criteria are important regarding political finance recommendations. First, it is very difficult to make general recommendations, given the different challenges in each country and the varying degrees of institutional development. Second, reforms should be addressed prudently, bearing in mind that 'the more difficult it is for parties and candidates to raise funds by legal means, the more likely it is that they will do it using murky and questionable procedures'.[129] Third, recommendations should emerge from practical assessments of the role of money in politics, which are lacking in the region. With these caveats in mind, some suggestions can be made about areas of action for the future of political finance in the region.

Policy makers[130]

During the consolidation of democracy that has characterized Latin America's development in recent decades, important reforms have resulted in better regulation of political finance. These reforms have mainly been marked by the need to adjust political or party systems that have emerged or that have required configuration. In future developments of the party system, reforms should focus on the following aspects.

Fostering equality

1. Given the growing trend of immediate re-election of the incumbent president, it is important to give priority to norms that allow rivals to compete in elections on equal terms. These should include the provision of public resources as a basis for more equal competition in elections, and prohibitions aimed at avoiding the abuse of power by the incumbent and members of the government.

2. Mechanisms should be developed that enable women and other social groups, especially minorities, to overcome obstacles to their participation. In addition to gender quotas and opportunities for minorities, attention should be given to the lack of financial resources for these groups' participation, which becomes a vicious circle of lacking access to either of the two reinforcing components: financial support and political power. Creating special public funds to finance female candidates as part of gender-equality policies would be a great help in breaking this vicious circle.

3. Mechanisms for prior financing of campaigns also have a significant effect on equality. Post-election public funding compensation based on the number of votes won forces candidates to make the same effort to raise money as the systems in which no public financing is provided.

4. Policy makers should also consider introducing or strengthening laws that oblige the media to provide pluralistic information. This is a difficult issue, given the tradition of partisan media in the region and the economic interests associated with the media, which often make them political contradictors rather than sources of information. This requires combining legal regulations on media slots with voluntary media commitments to give equal opportunity to candidates.

Protect politics from organized crime

1. Political systems must be shielded from the destabilizing power of organized crime and the money that comes with it. No country is free of the effects of the illicit economy; the extreme case of Colombia should serve as a cautionary tale. Political systems need adequate incentives and sanctions to keep criminal activity from further penetrating political life in the region. Isolated candidates are clearly easy prey for a criminal organization, but a party with strong institutions is much more difficult to co-opt.

2. An appropriate institutional model in this area should close the opportunity gaps that allow the relationship between crime and politics to flourish, for example, by providing public funding and reducing the time frame for campaigns in order to reduce expenditures. The model also requires close coordination with electoral institutions and other institutions in areas such as economics and finance—including, for example, ministries or secretariats of finance, offices of superintendents of financial affairs, or agencies dedicated to controlling money laundering.

3. The transparency of financing and political spending should also be improved by requiring reports to be submitted during campaign periods, because although it is nearly impossible to trace illicit funds in a campaign (because they are submitted in cash and at private meetings or through secret intermediaries), it is at least easier to trace expenditures.

4. Unless the candidate uses illicit money for his or her personal enrichment, the normal route is for the money to be invested in the campaign, where it can be observed and monitored more easily. The media's role in monitoring and revealing possible relationships between campaigns or candidates and organized crime should be highlighted and strengthened. Most of the examples mentioned in this chapter came to light because of media reports of cases that were later investigated by the appropriate authorities. Even when there is no subsequent official investigation, the political cost of relationships reported in the media often serves as more of a disincentive than a legal investigation.

Monitoring and enforcement agencies

1. It is necessary to evaluate the difficulties facing institutions set up to oversee political finance in the region and determine whether these difficulties are due to problems of institutional design, a weak mandate or lack of technical capacity. A thorough assessment will make it possible to determine the best solutions.

2. Even though no EMB in Latin America faces exactly the same challenges as another, the main challenge for EMBs in the region is to reinforce their role as guardians of order. This implies that they play an active role in preventing and sanctioning all violations related to electoral finance. EMBs require more resources and staff, but especially with regard to combating illicit finance, the challenges are so great that only with a high degree of political will and freedom to cooperate with other bodies (such as special prosecutors) will they be able to fully carry out the task that the political system has entrusted to them.

3. Political finance information should become more accessible, which requires the involvement of the private sector and banks as well as mechanisms for tabulating and recording information in databases that

promote transparency. Making the information publicly accessible—and improving mechanisms for consulting the information—would contribute greatly to transparency and control and public and media oversight. It is important to establish quality guidelines for the information, including conditions related to categories, methods of gathering information, and parameters for breaking down the information to provide data about gender or other issues of interest for public policy. This should be supplemented by mechanisms for real-time disclosure of parties' and candidates' financial information, especially during campaigns.

4. EMBs must assume that overseeing all activities of all parties and all candidates is impossible; they must therefore seek mechanisms to set priorities without creating biases that undermine the credibility of their efforts. These mechanisms could include risk mapping (to determine where in the country to focus attention) and random monitoring, which randomly chooses candidates and parties for closer scrutiny. It is important that the selection rules do not allow monitoring to become a tool for political persecution.

5. Finally, it is important to increase and enhance efforts to create a political culture that helps highlight the civic values that are part of the democratic ethos. This could involve broader training, but mainly requires better methodologies for targeting work, especially with young people, who develop their social relationships within the parameters of the digital age. Social media can play an important role in reaching younger voters.

Civil society

In recent years, civil society organizations have usually led efforts to improve transparency and accountability in campaign fundraising and spending in Latin America. It is very important to continue advancing these efforts and to better share methodologies in order to develop standard protocols for long-term comparison and monitoring. Innovations made in one country can often be perfected thanks to their implementation in others, in a process of constant feedback. Organizations such as the Lima Accord[131] play a key role, not only in sharing these oversight experiences, but in being at the forefront of an issue on which those in power will always be reluctant to act.

Media actors

The media must continue to speak up for the public interest and improve their ability to cover elections; avoiding a focus on anecdotal evidence is crucial for the quality of public debate about electoral choices. Citizens have a right to know where party resources originate, and should keep in mind that a lack of transparency of legal money is the best smokescreen for the entry of illicit money. The media can improve the quality of their coverage of election campaigns; expand their commitment to pluralism, giving opportunities to candidates from across the spectrum; and create mechanisms for joint coordination to encourage civic practices.

International actors

Research and knowledge

1. National and comparative analyses of election expenditures in the region would be useful further work in the field—beginning, for example, with a review of public spending on elections. Because such expenditures are included in each country's budget, the information should be relatively accessible through budget offices of their ministries of economy. This would increase understanding of how much the state supports parties and election processes, and would make it possible to better determine the percentages of public and private financing.

2. A second step would be to compile the information provided by candidates and parties—for example information on expenditures in presidential campaigns, since almost all the countries in the region require such reporting. A study of this nature would add value to earlier studies of regulations and gradually compile a repository of information about real election expenditures. Helping to improve the EMB reports on their websites—for example by developing standards for presenting and systematizing the information—would also be extremely useful. Only a few electoral management bodies currently present this information, and it is usually done in a way that is confusing and difficult to use.

3. A study in each of these countries would make it possible to establish a baseline for more precise monitoring of election information; this would also become a powerful incentive for greater transparency and encourage countries to provide more information. It would also be a powerful tool for civil society organizations and the media, which have taken on the task of monitoring these issues in each country, and which could use the information to exercise greater oversight of politics, significantly contributing to the fight against corruption.

4. International bodies could create an interactive, collaborative portal (a 'Wikipedia of political finance') that would provide real-time information about political finance from a variety of scattered sources and connect networks, organizations and experts in a common effort to supplement existing sources, such as Agora, the ACE Electoral Knowledge Network, iKNOW-Politics and the International IDEA Political Finance Database. Because much of the problem is the amount of scattered information that exists, especially in the media, it would be very important to undertake a networked initiative with social

organizations, researchers and even public officials (from government, EMBs, parliament).

Policy initiatives

1. Regional organizations in Latin America should increase their monitoring of political finance and perfect their electoral observation reporting. This is a recent and growing trend. Governments—especially governing officials involved in campaigns—may be reluctant to participate. But given the evidence of inequities in campaigns and the need to promote appropriate reforms, it is important to adopt protocols that make it possible, for example, to reach an international agreement on campaign expenditures, perhaps using the Inter-American Democratic Charter as a basis. Once that is achieved, it will be important to develop methodologies and skilled work teams to carry out the tasks of monitoring and reporting.

2. Regional bodies could also continue to raise the issue of political finance in forums for discussing issues related to combating corruption, for example by requesting reports that could be assessed by the Mechanism for Follow-Up on the Implementation of the Inter-American Convention against Corruption.

3. Cooperation should more decisively support efforts by national electoral observation organizations and initiate specific actions for addressing issues related to monitoring of finance—for example, support for initiatives to define and coordinate a common, comparative methodology for monitoring financing.

4. International donors should keep in mind that the enormous amount of resources currently dedicated to combating corruption should be divided more strategically between punitive and preventive actions. If the goal is to avoid corruption and encourage politicians to exercise greater (and better) political control, transparent political finance is absolutely necessary. Combating organized crime in its various forms (drug trafficking, contraband, human trafficking, money laundering, new forms of illicit economy) requires complementary efforts to help expose the political networks that these criminal organizations construct and those who benefit from illicit money.

References

Acción Ciudadana (2012) *¿Cuánto costó la campaña electoral?* [How Much Did the Election Campaign Cost?]. Guatemala: Acción Ciudadana, available at http://www.accionciudadana.org.gt/?wpfb_dl=116

A Hora do Vale (2012), 'Polícia flagra compra de votos em jantar' [Police catch votes being sold during dinner], *A Hora do Vale*, 10 August, available at http://www.jornalahora.inf.br/?oxi=lerNoticia&noticiaId=1476&jid=347

Agostini, C. (2012) 'Financiamiento de la política en Chile: Campañas electorales 2009–2010' [Political Finance in Chile: Election Campaigns 2009–2010], in *Propuesta de Reforma a los Partidos Políticos de Chile* [Proposal to Reform the Political Parties of Chile]. Santiago de Chile: CIEPLAN, available at http://www.cieplan.org/biblioteca/detalle.tpl?id=297

Álvarez, L. (2010) 'Roberto Courtney: Bono sólo abona a la ilegalidad de Ortega' [Roberto Courtney: Bonuses Only Pay the Illegality of Ortega], *El Nuevo Diario*, 4 May, available at http://www.elnuevodiario.com.ni/nacionales/73687

Artiga-González, A. (2011) 'La financiación de los partidos políticos en El Salvador' [The Financing of Political Parties in El Salvador], in *Financiamiento de los Partidos Políticos en América Latina* [Funding of Political Parties in Latin America]. Mexico: IFE, International IDEA, OAS.

Bértoa, Fernando C. B., Molenaar F., Piccio, D. and Rashkova, E. (2014). 'The World Upside Down: De-Legitimising Political Finance Regulation', *International Political Science Review*, Vol. 35, no. 3, 355-375.

Bossi, J. (2009) '¿Sabe cómo se financia la campaña?' [How to Know How the Campaign is Financed?], *Crítica de la Argentina* [Critique of Argentina], 31 May, available at http://criticadigital.com/impresa/index.php?secc=nota&nid=25212

Brown Araúz, H. (2010) 'La política de la Reforma Electoral en Panamá' [The Politics of Electoral Reform in Panama], in *Las reformas electorales en Panamá: claves de desarrollo humano para la toma de decisiones* [Electoral Reform in Panama: Keys to Human Development in Decision Making]. Panama: UNDP.

Canales, A. (2012) 'Multan a partidos pero ninguno supera topes de campaña: IFE [Federal Electoral Institute]', in *La Silla Rota* [The Empty Chair], available at http://www.e-consulta.com/2012/index.php/nacionales/item/multan-a-partidos-pero-ninguno-rebaso-topes-de-campana-ife

Cárdenas Morales, N. (2011) *El financiamiento público de los partidos políticos nacionales para el desarrollo del liderazgo político de las mujeres* [Public Financing of National Political Parties for the Development of Women in Political Leadership]. Mexico: Tribunal Electoral del Poder Judicial.

Cardoso, V. (2012) 'La ley antilavado, una vacilada, dice Buscaglia' [The Law against Money Laundering a Farce, Says Buscaglia], *La Jornada*, 17 October, available at http://www.jornada.unam.mx/2012/10/18/politica/003n1pol

Carquez, C. (2012) 'CNE: Medios no pueden hacer campaña por cuenta propias' [CNE: The Media Cannot Conduct Their Own Campaigns], *El Nacional*, 11 July, available at http://impresodigital.el-nacional.com/ediciones/guardar/guardar2.asp?archivo=n1_2n120120711&C=&P=&N=&fechaEd=7/11/2012

Carter Center (2012) 'Regulacion de campañas electorales. El caso de Colombia. Ponencia presentada en el seminario Campañas electorales: una mirada comparativa en el hemisferio' [Regulation of Election Campaigns: The Case of Colombia. Argument Presented at a Seminar on Electoral Campaigns: A Comparative View of the Hemisphere]. Caracas, November.

Casas, K. and Zovatto, D. (2004) 'Financiamiento político en Centroamérica, Panamá, República Dominicana y México' [Political Finance in Central America, Panama, Dominican Republic and Mexico], in *De las normas a las buenas prácticas* [From Norms to Good Practice]. San José: International IDEA, OAS.

Casas, K. and Zovatto, D. (2011) 'Para llegar a tiempo: Apuntes sobre la regulación del financiamiento político en América Latina' [To Arrive on Time: Notes on Political Finance Regulation in Latin America], in *Financiamiento de los Partidos Políticos en América Latina* [Funding of Political Parties in Latin America]. Mexico: IFE, International IDEA, OAS.

Chasquetti, D. (2011) 'Financiamiento Político en Uruguay' [Political Finance in Uruguay], in *Financiamiento de los Partidos Políticos en América Latina* [Funding of Political Parties in Latin America]. Mexico: IFE, International IDEA, OAS.

Corcuera, S. (2011) 'El financiamiento político en Argentina' [Political Finance in Argentina], in *Financiamiento de los Partidos Políticos en América Latina* [Funding of Political Parties in Latin America]. Mexico: IFE, International IDEA, OAS.

Cordero, L. A. (2003) *Análisis comparativo sobre financiamiento de campañas y partidos políticos Costa Rica* [Comparative Analysis of Campaign Financing and Political Parties in Costa Rica]. Unidad para la Promoción de la Democracia OAS, International IDEA.

Corporación *Arco Iris* (2011) 'Parapolíticos, influencia en la Costa' [Beyond Politicians, Influence from the Coast], Arco Iris, 21 November, available at http://www.arcoiris.com.co/2011/11/parapoliticos-influencia-en-la-costa/

Corporación Colectivo de Abogados (2009) 'José Alvear Restrepo', in *Obstáculos a la aplicación de Justicia* [Obstacles to the Implementation of Justice]. Colombia: Colectivo de Abogados José Alvear Restrepo.

Dador, J. and Llanos, B. (eds) (2007) *La igualdad esquiva: Una mirada de género a las elecciones generales 2006* [Evaded Equality: A Gender Perspective on the General Elections 2006]. Peru: International IDEA, Asociación Civil Transparencia.

Diario Hoy (2009) 'Hay que esperar 14 años para que un corrupto sea condenado' [A Fourteen-year Wait until Corruption is Punished], *Diario Hoy*, available at http://pdf.diariohoy.net/2009/11/02/pdf/cuerpo.pdf

Donoso, P., Ramos., P. and Riquelme, P. (1999) *Mecanismos Alternativos para el Financiamiento de los Partidos Políticos* [Alternative Mechanisms for the Funding of Political Parties]. Chile: Centro de Estudios Públicos, available at http://www.cepchile.cl/dms/archivo_3519_1749/refor1_08_donoso.pdf

Dragonetti, M. (2011) 'Campañas en offside' [Offside Campaigns], *Plaza de Mayo*, 4 July, available at http://www.plazademayo.com/2011/07/campanas-en-offside/

Economic Commission for Latin America (ECLAC) (2012) *Foreign Direct Investment in Latin America and the Caribbean 2011*. Santiago de Chile: United Nations.

El Día de Santa Cruz de Bolivia (2010) 'Polémica por descuentos para la campaña del MAS' [Controversy over discounts for MAS campaign], *El Día de Santa Cruz*, available at http://www.eldia.com.bo/mobile.php?cat=280&pla=7&id_articulo=8335

El Diario (2011) 'Ex Viceministro denuncia "diezmo" obligatorio para candidatos masistas' [Ex Vice-minister Denounces the 'Ten Per Cent' Obligation for Independent Candidates], *El Diario*, 23 September, available at http://www.eldiario.net/noticias/2011/2011_09/nt110923/2_02plt.php

El Nacional (2012) 'Instruyeron a los partidos para rendir cuentas de la campaña' [Parties Were Instructed to Account for the Campaign], *El Nacional*, 21 May, available at http://www.contextotmt.net/base/krafts/index2.php?option=com_content&do_pdf=1&id=37688

El Tiempo (2007) 'Así financian sus campañas los seis candidatos a la Alcaldía de Bogotá que puntean en las encuestas' [This Is How the Campaigns of the Six Main Candidates to the Mayor of Bogota Were Funded, According to the Polls], 7 October, available at http://www.eltiempo.com/archivo/documento/CMS-3757033

El Universo (2005) 'Partidario de SP niega que donación de Taiwán haya sido usado en campaña' [Supporter of SP Denies that Donation from Taiwan Was Used in the Campaign], *El Universo*, 15 February, available at http://www.eluniverso.com/2005/02/15/0001/8/D8E1593146B9471F93BEB10E6F9C9F8F.html

El Universo (2007) 'En el TEG se registraron solo 12 tesoreros' [In TEG only 12 people were registered as treasurers], *El Universo de Ecuador*, 21 August, available at http://www.eluniverso.com/2007/08/21/0001/8/7A2D43D6F8DF4A7B95A4B120ADF1AE4D.html

Evertsson, N. (2010) *Report of Survey on Electoral Campaign in Colombia*. Stockholm: Stockholm University.

Faughman, B. and Zechmeister, E. (2011) 'Vote Buying in the Americas', in *AmericasBaromoter Insights*, 57, pp. 1–8.

Freidenberg, F. and Levitsky, S. (2007) 'Organización informal de los Partidos en América Latina' [Informal Organization of Political Parties in Latin America], *Desarrollo Económico* [Economic Development], 46(184), pp. 539–68.

Freitas, C. (2012) 'Candidatos a prefeito de Goiânia devem gastar R$ 51,25 milhões em campanha' [Candidates to the Region of Goiânia Need to Spend R$51.25 Million in the Campaign], *Diário Mahná*, 29 July, available at http://www.maisgoias.com.br/noticias/politica/2012/6/29/25579.html?Candidatos+a+prefeito+de+Goiania+devem+gastar+R$+51,+25+milhoes+em+campanha+

Fuentes, C. (2011) 'Financiación de Partidos Políticos en Chile' [Political Party Funding in Chile], in *Financiamiento de los Partidos Políticos en América Latina* [Funding of Political Parties in Latin America]. Mexico: IFE, International IDEA, OAS.

Garay Salamanca, L. J. and Salcedo Albarán, E. (2012) *Narcotráfico, corrupción y Estados: Cómo las redes ilícitas han reconfigurado las instituciones en Colombia, Guatemala y México* [Narcotraffic, Corruption and States: How Illicit Networks Have Reshaped Institutions in Colombia, Guatemala and Mexico]. Bogotá: Random House Mondadori.

Geuna, L. (2010) 'Intiman a los jueces electorales a resolver sobre gastos de campaña' [Appointment of Electoral Judges to Resolve Questions of Campaign Expenses], *El Clarín*, 6 October, available at http://www.clarin.com/politica/Intiman-electorales-resolver-gastos-campana_0_348565159.html

Global Integrity (2007) *Global Integrity Report: Country Scorecard 2007. Washington, D.C.: Global Integrity.*

Global Integrity (2008) *Global Integrity Report: Country Scorecard 2008. Washington, D.C.: Global Integrity.*

Global Integrity (2009) *Global Integrity Report: Country Scorecard 2009. Washington, D.C.: Global Integrity.*

Global Integrity (2010) *Global Integrity Report: Country Scorecard 2010. Washington, D.C.: Global Integrity.*

Global Integrity (2011) *Global Integrity Report: Country Scorecard 2011. Washington, D.C.: Global Integrity.*

Grupo Cívico Ética y Transparencia (2011) 'Valoración técnica final del Proceso Electoral para Presidente y Diputados Nicaragua 2011' [Final Technical Evaluation of the Electoral Process for President and Members of Parliament in Nicaragua 2011'], available at http://www.conexiones.com.ni/files/86.pdf

Gutiérrez, P. and Zovatto, D. (2011) 'Balance Regional: Financiamiento político en América Latina 2004–2010' [Regional Balance: Political Finance in Latin America 2004–2010], in *Financiamiento de los Partidos Políticos en América Latina* [Funding of Political Parties in Latin America]. Mexico: IFE, International IDEA, OAS.

Hurtado, S. (2010) 'Correa: Ley que limita financiamiento de ONG pretende desaparecerlas' [Correa: The Law that Limits the Funding of NGOs Aims to Make Them Disappear], *El Nacional*, 22 December.

International IDEA, Political Finance Database, available at http://www.idea.int/political-finance

Kupferschmidt, D. (2009) *Illicit Political Finance and State Capture*. Stockholm: International IDEA.

La Razón (2009) 'Evo se refuerza con invitados para su lista legislativa' [Evo is Reinforced by His Legislative List], *La Razón*, 8 September, available at http://educamposv.lacoctelera.net/post/2009/09/08/evo-se-refuerza-con-invitados-su-lista-legislativa

La Segunda (2012) '¿Quiénes son los mecenas de la política chilena?' [Who are the Financial Backers of Chilean Politics?], *La Segunda,* 14 April, available at http://www.lasegunda.com/Noticias/Impreso/2012/04/737898/los-mecenas-de-la-politica

Llanos, B. (2012) *Ojos que (aún) no ven: Nuevo reporte de ocho países: género, campañas electorales y medios en América Latina* [Eyes That Do Not (Yet) See: A New Report from Eight Countries. Gender, Electoral Campaigns and Media in Latin America]. Lima: International IDEA.

Llanos, B. and Tello, P. (eds) (2012) *Igualdad: ¿para cuándo? Género y elecciones peruanas 2011–2012* [Equality: When? Gender and Peruvian Elections 2011–2012]. Lima: International IDEA.

Londoño, Juan Fernando (forthcoming) 'Colombia: garantías y equidad en una competencia desigual' [Colombia: Warrants and Equity in an Unequal Competition], in *Campañas electorales, ventajismo y reelección presidencial en América Latina* [Electoral Campaigns, Opportunism and Presidential Re-election in Latin America]. Venezuela: The Carter Center.

Los Angeles Times (1997) 'Yes, Drug Lords, There's a Santa', *Los Angeles Times*, 19 December.

Lugo-Galicia, H. and Hinds, A. (2012) 'Evaden debate de soberanía, pero dan fondos a promotores del PSUV' [They Evade Debate on Sovereignty, but Donate Funds to Supporters of PSUV], *El Nacional*, 6 June, available at http://www.contextotmt.net/base/krafts/index2.php?option=com_content&do_pdf=1&id=38132l

Martínez, R. (2012) 'Desplaza prensa al estado en indagar infiltración del narco en política: Buscaglia' [The Media Replace the State in Investigating the Infiltration of Drugs in Politics: Buscaglia], Proceso, 2 March, available at http://www.proceso.com.mx/?p=299864

Mejía, D. and Rico, D. M. (2011) 'La microeconomía de la produccíon y el tráfico de cocaína en Colombia' [The Microeconomy of Production and Traffic of Cocaine in Colombia], in A. G. Uribe and D. Mejá (eds), The Political Fight against Drugs in Colombia: Successes, Failures and Diversions. Bogota: Universidad de los Andes.

Mendevil, L. (2011) 'Colombia: Cómo lo hicieron?' [Colombia: How Did They Do It?], Crónica, 2 September, available at http://www.cronica.com.mx/notaOpinion.php?id_nota=602659

Menéndez, M. (2002) 'Mercados Persas en las campañas Políticas' [Persian Markets in the Political Campaigns], El Tiempo, 30 April, available at http://www.eltiempo.com/archivo/documento/MAM-1357355

Meyer Dos Santos (2005) 'Partidos políticos: repensar financiamentos e finaças' [Political parties: rethink financing and finances], 1 August, available at http://jusvi.com/artigos/16590 and http://www.boletimjuridico.com.br/doutrina/texto.asp?id=769

Noticias UOL (2011) '77. STF condena deputado Asdrúbal Bentes (PMDB-PA) por esterilização de eleitoras' ['77. STF Prosecutes Deputy Asdrúbal Bentes (PMDB-PA) for 'Sterilization' of the Electorate], 8 September, available at http://noticias.uol.com.br/politica/escandalos-no-congresso/stf-condena-deputado-asdrubal-bentes-pmdb-pa-por-esterilizacao-de-eleitoras.htm

Ohman, M. (2011) 'Global Trends in the Regulation of Political Finance', IPSA-ECPR Joint Conference, Sao Paulo, 16–19 February.

Organisation for Economic Co-operation and Development (OECD) (2012) Latin American Economic Outlook 2012, available at http://www.oecd.org/dev/americas/48965859.pdf

Organization of American States (OAS) (2011) Politics, Money and Power: A Dilemma for Democracy. Mexico: FCE, OAS.

Peschard, J. (2006) 'Control over Party and Campaign Finance in Mexico', Mexican Studies, 22(1), pp 83–106.

Poder Ciudadano (2008) Informe de Monitoreo del financiamiento de la Campaña Electoral Presidencial 2007 [Report on the Monitoring of the Funding of the Presidential Electoral Campaign 2007]. Argentina, Poder Ciudadano, available at http://poderciudadano.org/informe-sobre-el-financiamiento-de-la-campana-presidencial/

Quirós Gallegos, J. (2012) 'Achacan culpas al TSE por irregularidades en campaña' [Blame TSE for Irregularities in the Campaign], *Diario Extra*, 27 March, available at http://www.diarioextra.com/2012/marzo/27/nacionales05.php

Ramos, C. (2007) 'La manipulación de la capacidad de inversión económica de los partidos derivada de la financiación privada indirecta' [The Manipulation of Parties' Capacity for Economic Investment Derives from Indirect Private Funding], Thesis for licentiate in legal and social sciences, San Carlos University of Guatemala.

Regalado Florido, E. (2005) 'Taiwán: fuente de financiamiento de corrupción centroamericana' [Taiwan: Source of Financial Corruption in Central America], *El Catoblepas Revista Crítica del Presente*, 35, available at http://www.nodulo.org/ec/2005/n035p16.htm

Rivera, A. (2012) 'México, el número dos en flujo de dinero ilícito' [Mexico, Number Two in the Flow of Illicit Money], *Milenio*, 30 September, available at http://edomex.milenio.com/cdb/doc/noticias2011/ace9c075d1834834a98f806b01a0e71e

Rodríguez, M. (2009) *La propaganda electoral en El Salvador (2008–2009): monitoreo y propuesta para transparencia* [The Electoral Campaign in El Salvador (2008–2009): Monitoring and Proposals for Transparency]. San Salvador: National Democratic Institute and Fundación para el Desarrollo.

Rodríguez-Raga, J. C. and Seligson, M. (2012) *Cultura Política de la democracia en Colombia y las Américas* [Political Culture of Democracy in Colombia and the Americas]. Bogotá: USAID, Universidad de los Andes, Vanderbilt University.

Romero Ballivián, S. (2011) 'La corta y sobresaltada historia del financiamiento público a los partidos políticos en Bolivia' [The Short and Shaky History of Public Funding of Political Parties in Bolivia], in *Financiamiento de los Partidos Políticos en América Latina* [Funding of Political Parties in Latin America]. Mexico: IFE, International IDEA, OAS.

Rosales Valladares, R. (2010) 'Financiamiento de los partidos políticos y las campañas electorales en Panamá' [Political Party Funding and Electoral Campaigns in Panama], in *Las reformas electorales en Panamá: claves de desarrollo humano para la toma de decisiones* [Electoral Reform in Panama: Keys to Human Development in Decision Making]. Panama: UNDP.

Sacchet, T. (2011) *Political Parties and the (Under) Representation of Women in Legislative Spheres: A Study on Electoral Recruitment and Campaign Finance.* Paper presented at the IPSA-ECPR Joint Conference, Universidade de Sao Paulo, Brazil, 16–19 February.

Sánchez, J. A. (2011) 'Discreto proselitismo del priísmo Queretaro [Gentle Proselytism of the PRI in Queretaro], *Enlace México*, 14 March, available at http://www.enlacemexico.info/index.php?option=com_content&view=article&id=1536:discreto-

Saúl, L. (2012) 'Revelan top dc partidos más multados por el IFE' [The Parties Most Fined by IFE Are Revealed], *Red Política*, 13 March, available at http://www.redpolitica.mx/ruta-electoral/revelan-top-de-partidos-mas-multados-por-ife

Semana (2006) 'Pasando el sombrero' [Passing the Hat], *Semana*, 10 March, available at http://www.semana.com/wf_ImprimirArticulo.aspx?IdArt=93081

Servicio Electoral Chileno (SERVEL) (2010) *Informe de ingresos de campaña electoral 2009. Base de datos* [Report on Election Campaign Income 2009]. Chile: SERVEL.

Siu, M. and Quirós, J. (2012) 'TSE investiga gastos de campaña del PAC' [TSE Investigates the Campaign Costs of PAC], *Diario Extra*, 13 April.

Terra (2012) 'Jornal: PT recebeu R$ 50 milhões de doações em 2011' [Jornal: PT Receives R$50 Million in Donations in 2011], Terra, 26 May, available at http://noticias.terra.com.br/eleicoes/2012/noticias/0,,OI5796275-EI19136,00-Jornal+PT+recebeu+R+milhoes+de+doacoes+em.html

Transparencia Colombia (2012) *Candidatos a elecciones territoriales reportaron más de 348 millones de pesos de gastos en campaña, revela informe de transparencia* [Candidates to Regional Elections Reported More Than 348 Million Pesos in Campaign Expenses, Transparency Report Reveals]. Colombia: Transparencia por Colombia, available at http://www.transparenciacolombia.org.co

Transparency International and Carter Center (2007) *The Crinis Project: Money in Politics: Everyone's Concern.*

Tuesta Soldevilla, F. (2011) 'El financiamiento de los partidos políticos en Perú' [The Funding of Political Parties in Peru], in *Financiamiento de los Partidos Políticos en América Latina* [Funding of Political Parties in Latin America]. Mexico: IFE, International IDEA, OAS.

United Nations Development Programme (UNDP) and Organization of American States (OAS) (2010) *Nuestra Democracia* [Our Democracy]. Mexico City: UNDP and OAS.

Urcullo Cossío, L. G., Moya Díaz, E. J. and Engel Goetz, E. (2009) *Control delfinancimento y gasto electoral en Chile* [The Monitoring of Electoral Funding and Expenses in Chile]. Chile: Chile Transparente and Inter-American Development Bank.

Vizcaíno, I. (2010) 'Dineros privados ganan peso en la última fase de la campaña' [Private Funds More Important in the Final Phase of the Campaign], *Nación*, 25 January, available at http://wvw.nacion.com/ln_ee/2010/enero/25/pais2236148.html

World Bank (2013) *Economic Mobility and the Rise of the Latin American Middle Class*. Washington, D.C.: World Bank.

Zermiani, B. and Goetten, C. (2010) 'Distribuicao do tempo no horario eleitoral divide opinioes' [Time Allocation in the Electoral Schedule Divides Opinion], *Journal Comunicacao*, 27 September, available at http://www. jornalcomunicacao.ufpr.br/materia-8853.html

Notes

[1] In this chapter, Latin America will be considered as including Argentina, Belize, Bolivia, Brazil, Chile, Colombia, Costa Rica, Ecuador, El Salvador, Guatemala, Guyana, Honduras, Mexico, Nicaragua, Panama, Paraguay, Peru, Suriname, Uruguay and Venezuela.

[2] OECD 2012.

[3] The region's economic growth is faster than the global average (ECLAC 2012).

[4] World Bank 2013.

[5] See, for example, Gutiérrez and Zovatto 2011.

[6] Organizations working in this area on the regional and national levels are: Transparency International (through the Crinis Project), the Organization of American States, Poder Ciudadano in Argentina, Auditoría Ciudadana in Costa Rica and Acción Ciudadana in Guatemala.

[7] Transparency International and Carter Center 2007.

[8] Garay Salamanca and Salcedo Albarán 2012.

[9] This confirmation is based on information from Global Integrity, an organization that compares regulations and the degree to which they are implemented, examining their effectiveness and the accessibility of information about political finance. Both variables are calculated on a scale of 0 to 100. According to the 2011 report, in Colombia, the existence of regulations is 100 (very strong), while implementation is 77 (moderate); in Mexico, the degree of regulation is 90, while implementation is only 44 (very weak); and in Venezuela, regulation scores 36.5, while implementation scores just 4.5. For 2010, Argentina has a score of 100 for regulations and 77 for implementation; in Guatemala the scores are 80 and 0; and in Peru, 74 and 59. For 2009 in Brazil, the scores are 53 and 54; in Chile, 77 and 43; and in Ecuador in 2008, 70 and 27. Finally, in Costa Rica in 2007, the scores are 100 and 52. Global Integrity 2007, 2008, 2009, 2010, 2011.

[10] Grupo Cívico Ética y Transparencia 2011.

[11] Regalado Florido 2005.

[12] *El Universo* 2005.

[13] Hurtado 2010.

[14] Evertsson 2010.

[15] Throughout this handbook, international dollars (I$) are presented alongside amounts in national currencies. The international dollar is a hypothetical currency that takes into account purchasing power parity and is therefore suitable for comparisons between countries. For countries in which the power purchasing power parity varies significantly from the United States (which is used as the baseline for the comparison), the I$ exchange rate may be considerably different from the nominal exchange rate. No conversions are given for US dollars (as this is by default the same amount as the I$) or for those instances where the original currency is unknown and a secondary currency such as the euro has been citied instead. For further information, see Annex V.

[16] *Terra* 2012.

[17] SERVEL 2010.

18 Freidenberg and Levitsky 2007.

19 Chasquetti 2011, p. 517.

20 Meyer Dos Santos 2005.

21 Rodriguez-Raga and Seligson 2012, p. 157.

22 Donoso, Ramos and Riquelme 1999, p. 336.

23 Positive compensation could include invitations to internal debates on all issues, invitations to sessions held by deputies, participation in internal elections, etc.

24 Donoso, Ramos and Riquelme 1999, p. 340.

25 *La Razón* 2009.

26 Menéndez 2002.

27 *La Segunda* 2012.

28 Transparencia Colombia 2012.

29 A Colombian businessman convicted of money laundering in the USA, who made contributions to several presidential candidates in Panama.

30 Brown Araúz 2010, p. 41.

31 He was called this by Germán Martínez Cázares (president of the National Executive Committee of the Partido Accíon Nacional, PAN, in 2008).

32 *Semana* 2006.

33 The fact that most Latin American countries used electoral systems based on proportional representation, which is normally seen as placing less emphasis on individual candidates, does not seem to affect the nature of fundraising.

34 Bossi 2009.

35 Transparencia Colombia 2012.

36 Quirós Gallegos 2012.

37 Agostini 2012, p. 3.

38 *El Día de Santa Cruz de Bolivia* 2010.

39 Meyer Dos Santos 2005.

40 Martínez 2012.

41 Rivera 2012.

42 Mejía and Rico 2011, p. 16.

43 In Colombia, since 2006, 133 members and former members of Congress have been implicated with paramilitaries; of these, 71 have been called for questioning, 50 were detained, 42 resigned from Congress, 18 are on trial, 13 pleaded guilty to the charges against them and were sentenced, and seven were convicted (Corporación Colectivo de Abogados 2009, p. 14). Since 2009, other politicians have been accused and convicted of parapolitics (Corporación Arco Iris 2011).

44 Kupferschmidt 2009, pp. 16–17.

45 Part of Colombia's 'success' can be attributed to the fact that the four pillars of the Palermo Convention against Organized Crime are applied (Mendevil 2011): (1) prosecution, (2) prevention in society, (3) prevention of high-level political corruption and (4) confiscation of property in the private sector through civil (not criminal) cases. Others are more sceptical about calling Colombia a success because, although there are more sentences handed down in that country than in many others, relationships between politics and criminals still exist (Garay Salamanca and Salcedo Albarán 2012). In Mexico, meanwhile, during the Calderón administration, policy focused mainly on the pillar of prosecution (Mendevil 2011).

46 Geuna 2010.

47 *Diario Hoy* 2009.

48 Martínez 2012.

49 The United Nations Convention against Transnational Organized Crime, adopted by General Assembly Resolution 55/25 of 15 November 2000, is an international instrument in the fight against transnational organized crime and was signed in Palermo, Italy in December 2000. The Financial Action Task Force (FATF) is an intergovernmental body established in 1989. Its objectives are to set standards and promote effective implementation of legal, regulatory and operational measures for combating money laundering, terrorist financing and other related threats to the integrity of the international financial system.

50 Cardoso 2012.

51 Rodríguez 2009, p. 14.

52 Peschard 2006.

53 Casas and Zovatto 2011, pp. 45–6.

54 Bértoa et al. 2013.

55 Ohman 2011, p. 7.

56 Acción Ciudadana's report on these elections argued that public funding represented only 2.4 per cent of the total campaign income (Acción Ciudadana 2012, p. 78).

57 In the 2002 election, when the system was still one of post-election reimbursement based on votes received, the winning candidate (Alvaro Uribe) received 55 per cent of public funds, the runner-up 33 per cent, and two other candidates 6 per cent each. In 2006, with the introduction of advance disbursement, the situation was very different, because each candidate received 33 per cent of the public funds. For the first round of balloting in the 2010 election, the winner received 24 per cent of public financing, and others 20 per cent, 15 per cent, 14 per cent, 14 per cent and 13 per cent, respectively.

58 OAS 2011, p. 145; Vizcaíno 2010.

59 Siu and Quirós 2012.

60 OAS 2011, p. 145.

61 *La Segunda* 2012.

62 Sacchet 2011, pp. 24–6.

63 Further information is available in the International IDEA Political Finance Database.

64 OAS 2011, p. 58.

65 Cárdenas Morales 2011.

66 Ibid.

67 Zermiani and Goetten 2010.

68 OAS 2011, p. 99.

69 Ibid., pp. 99–100.

70 Ibid.

71 Dador and Llanos 2007, p. 101.

72 Ibid., p. 122.

73 Llanos and Tello 2012, p. 95.

74 Llanos 2012.

75 Bolivia 2009, Chile 2009, Costa Rica 2010, Colombia 2010, Dominican Republic 2010, Peru 2011, Guatemala 2011 and Argentina 2011.

76 Llanos 2012.

77 Ibid.

78 Ibid.

79   Londoño (forthcoming).
80   Garay Salamanca and Salcedo Albarán 2012.
81   Lugo-Galicia and Hinds 2012.
82   OAS 2011, p. 148.
83   *El Diario* 2011.
84   Álvarez 2010.
85   For example, according to Enrique Peñalosa, former candidate for mayor of Bogotá, 'For a campaign in a city of 7 million inhabitants, the ceiling on expenditures is very low' (*El Tiempo* 2007).
86   Freitas 2012.
87   UNDP and OAS 2010, p. 118.
88   OAS 2011, p. 123.
89   The OAS study compares different types of elections, so only data from general elections are noted here. Some data are probably also under-reported.
90   Poder Ciudadano 2008.
91   Artiga-González 2011, p. 289.
92   Acción Ciudadana 2012.
93   Corcuera 2011, p. 87.
94   Tuesta Soldevilla 2011, p. 466.
95   Faughman and Zechmeister 2011.
96   *Noticias* UOL 2011.
97   Sánchez 2011.
98   *El Nacional* 2012.
99   There is no information in International IDEA's Political Finance Database for the Dominican Republic.
100 Transparency International and Carter Center 2007, p. 48.
101 Ibid., p. 56.
102 In Panama, submission of financial reports is not mandatory, but is done upon legal request (ibid., p. 68).
103 In Peru, only five of 32 parties submitted reports in 2006 (ibid., p. 76).
104 The exceptions to this 'rule' are Belize, Bolivia, the Dominican Republic, El Salvador, Panama, Paraguay and Venezuela.
105 Fuentes 2011, p. 170.
106 Cordero 2003, p. 13.
107 Carquez 2012.
108 Ramos 2007.
109 In recent elections in Mexico, most parties were fined for irregularities in financial reports, except for the Partido Verde Ecologista. These fines ranged from a maximum of 5 million Mexican pesos (MXN) (I$579,000) for the Partido Revolucinario Democratico (PRD) to a minimum of MXN 6,000 (I$690) for the Partido Revolucinario Institucional (PRI) (Canales 2012). Based on data from the Federal Electoral Institute (Instituto Federal Electoral, IFE), Lilia Saúl published figures for fines imposed on political parties and media by the IFE. Since the reform in 2007, the IFE has fined parties MXN 863 million (I$99.9 million), while fines for electronic media have amounted to only MXN 3 million (I$347,000) (Saúl 2012).

[110] After the scandals of Pemexgate and 'Fox's friends', the IFE improved the oversight system, giving it the powers and resources for appropriate enforcement. Nevertheless, in 2006, the IFE had agreements with just 21 of 32 state electoral institutes (Peschard 2006, p. 97).

[111] In Peru, collaboration agreements were signed with the Ministry of Justice's Financial Intelligence Unit (Tuesta Soldevilla 2011, p. 475).

[112] In Brazil, the electoral authority has granted military brigades the autonomy to handle cases of vote buying (*A Hora do Vale* 2012).

[113] *Semana* 2006.

[114] Casas and Zovatto 2004.

[115] *El Universo* 2007.

[116] Artiga-González 2011, p. 294; Urcullo Cossío, Moya Díaz and Engel Goetz 2009, p. 78.

[117] Acción Ciudadana 2012, p. 91.

[118] Rosales Valladares 2010, p. 267.

[119] Dragonetti 2011.

[120] Transparency International and Carter Center 2007, p. 51.

[121] Romero Ballivián 2011, p. 102.

[122] Evertsson 2010

[123] Evertsson 2010

[124] Garay Salamanca and Salcedo Albarán 2012.

[125] Acción Ciudadana 2012.

[126] *Los Angeles Times* 1997.

[127] Poder Ciudadano 2008; Agostini 2012; Artiga-González 2011; Acción Ciudadana 2012.

[128] Gutiérrez and Zovatto 2011, p. 14.

[129] Casas and Zovatto 2011, p. 53.

[130] Policy makers are defined as those involved in the drafting, amending and adopting political finance policies, either from the executive or from the legislative arm of government. The focus is therefore on the role policy makers play rather than a particular institution.

[131] The Lima Accord is a network of civic movements in Latin America and the Caribbean, which was established in 2000 with the goal of strengthening democracy. It facilitates and promotes the sharing of experiences, provides a system for mutual support in political and technical aspects of election monitoring, and carries out joint activities and projects (see http://www.acuerdodelima.com).

CHAPTER 6

CHAPTER 6

Eastern, Central and South-eastern Europe and Central Asia*

Introduction

This chapter analyses political finance regulations and practices in Eastern, Central and South-eastern Europe and Central Asia.[1] Countries in these regions have very diverse sizes, political regimes, constitutional models and political cultures. They range from consolidated democracies in the central and eastern parts of Europe, including European Union (EU) member states, to more autocratic regimes in Central Asia.

Although there may be no single specific feature that all these countries share, they undoubtedly have 'family resemblances', partly due to their communist legacy.[2] Many have long histories of authoritarian and even totalitarian rule, and generally weak traditions of democracy and constitutionalism. After the fall of communism in 1989–91, many of them experienced rapid democratization. Since then, the countries covered in this chapter have been involved in a considerable effort to regulate money in politics, and Western European countries have in many cases served as a model. However, the regulatory systems introduced have taken on their own logic. Generally speaking, the regions feature elaborate systems of rules, restrictions on contributions and expenditure, and disclosure mechanisms. However, the efficacy and enforceability of these regulations are uneven, and there is a general sense of dissatisfaction with the current levels of transparency.

The meaning of regulatory measures differs depending on a country's political and constitutional setting. In countries that lean toward authoritarianism, extensive and elaborate political finance regulation can be used to weaken the opposition and prevent the emergence of new and powerful political actors. Therefore it is clearly difficult to discuss party finance regulations without

---

* This chapter is based on a paper entitled 'Political Finance in East, Central and South East Europe & Central Asia' by Daniel Smilov. The original paper was edited by Fredrik Sjöberg.

specifying the broader constitutional and political contexts in which they operate. After all, one of the central tasks of party and campaign finance regulation is to ensure healthy and pluralistic democratic competition; in several of the reviewed countries, this is not the case.

Regional problems with money in politics

While the countries in this region differ from each other in several respects, many share certain traits that create particular problems for ensuring transparency and control over the role of money in politics. Examples of problems from the more authoritarian countries discussed here are hard to come by, as they rarely become public, not least due to the suppression of investigative journalism.

Abuse of state resources

Using state funds for political purposes is not unique to the regions analysed here. However, a strong argument can be made that these regions have more problems than any other with the abuse of state resources. It even has its own terminology: *administrativnyi resurs* in Russian is the commonly used term to indicate abuse of office for electoral advantage.

During one-party communist rule, from which most of the countries in these regions emerged, state funds and party funds were impossible to differentiate. This problem was recognized as early as 1990, when the states participating in the Conference on Security and Co-operation in Europe agreed on the Copenhagen Document.[3] This and other similar statements signalled a departure from this legacy and stipulated that there must be 'a clear separation between the State and political parties; in particular, political parties will not be merged with the State'.[4] Unfortunately, such abuse is still widely prevalent and may even be on the rise in some countries. This issue is discussed at greater length below.

State control over the political arena

Closely related to the issue of the abuse of state resources is *government* control over the political process in some countries in these regions. The major political cleavage has not been between left-wing labour parties and right-wing market-oriented parties, but between government and *opposition* parties. In a number of countries, political finance rules have been designed to favour the ruling parties.[5]

The regions discussed feature a wide range of countries that represent different shades of the democratic spectrum, from authoritarian Central Asian states to more established democracies in Central Europe and the Baltic states, and others somewhere in between.[6]

Russia is an example of a country that has exerted greater state control over politics in recent years. While in the 1990s Russia had a relatively competitive, albeit chaotic, political scene, in the 2000s it experienced a democratic backsliding.[7] Over time, power was successfully centralized in the presidential administration, and the parties in power dominated the Duma. Gradually, political parties became so regulated that only a handful could register with the relevant authorities. This process was driven by the ruling party, United Russia, in an attempt to make it more difficult for new parties and challengers to emerge.[8] The 'managed democracy' that was installed features elections in which the outcome is known well in advance, an appointed 'convenient opposition', and tight control over the means of communication.

In such an environment, standard political finance regulations such as bans on foreign funding, limits on independent expenditure, and regulation of the links between parties and non-governmental organizations (NGOs) acquire a different meaning from their meaning in other contexts, since they may be used to suppress political activity.

Private-sector kickbacks and buying government favours

Private-sector kickbacks in return for government favours have been behind serious party funding scandals in even some of the more established democracies, such as the Czech Republic, Poland and Hungary[9]. The political orientation of certain parties (or factions in the legislature), coupled with their close links to specific *corporate* interests, reveal that one principal raison d'être of these political actors is to lobby for their corporate sponsors. Analysts have described some of the legislatures, such as the Ukrainian Parliament, as de facto corporate representatives—that is, businesspeople are elected to parliament in order to safeguard business interests.[10] Instances of corporate representation are also present in more party-centred systems, albeit probably to a lesser degree.

Many of the party financing scandals in the regions are more related to personal enrichment than to enrichment of a particular political party. This was the case in the 2007 'buying the law' scandal in Estonia, where one of the country's most prominent business figures donated considerable funds to several political parties while he was involved in building a power plant for renewable energy sources. The subsequent passage of a bill that granted government subsidies to such projects led to accusations of corruption.[11]

The Lazarenko scandal in Ukraine (see Box 6.1.) is a good illustration of personal enrichment through privatization kickbacks and other corrupt behaviour. Such scandals have also occurred elsewhere in the regions under consideration. All of the above-mentioned political finance problems are related to the larger phenomenon of the high costs of politics in the area studied. Business interests can easily influence legislatures and regulatory agencies in some of the less institutionalized polities.[12]

Illegal and illicit funding

Illegal and illicit funding finds its way into politics in many of the countries under review, including funding from organized crime and the direct involvement of criminal actors in political party affairs and elections. Countries that are strategically located along drug trade routes—in Central Asia and the Balkans, as well as EU border countries—are especially vulnerable to this type of influence.

Dodging rules and avoiding transparency

The countries in these regions have generally struggled to implement effective political finance regulation. At the beginning of the transition from communism, many countries were characterized by rather crude forms of violations of the rules and ineffective regulation. Unrecorded cash transactions have been relatively common in political financing: where money has changed hands in suitcases or bags rather than through bank transactions, this has made the enforcement of disclosure, expenditure and contribution limits almost meaningless. With the modernization of the banking systems across the regions and the expansion of a middle class that uses bank accounts and credit cards, the importance of these crude forms of rule evasion has diminished.[13] However, illicit networks have adapted to new realities by using increasingly sophisticated techniques to evade rules and scrutiny.[14]

> ## Box 6.1. The Lazarenko scandal[15]
>
> Pavlo Lazarenko, a Ukrainian politician and former prime minister, amassed a fortune while in office, allegedly charging 50 per cent of the profits from businesses for his patronage. The case is well documented, since Lazarenko was tried and convicted in a US District Court on charges of fraud, conspiracy to launder money, money laundering and transport of stolen property.

Overview of political finance regulations

There have been remarkable developments in party and campaign finance regulation in Eastern Europe, the Caucasus and Central Asia over the last 20 years. Starting practically from zero, most of the countries have introduced relatively comprehensive regulatory models. There seems to be a strong preference for limiting expenditures and contributions, which suggests that the belief in the regulatory power of the state is still strong. The aggregate score for all the bans and limitations of the countries covered in this chapter—from International IDEA's Database on Political Finance (Political Finance Database)—show that they are the most regulated of the world's regions. This clearly illustrates the popularity of comprehensive political finance regulation in these regions. Yet there is a serious discrepancy between normative

> **Although much has been achieved in terms of transparency in many of these countries, the enforcement of rules is still problematic in most cases.**

commitments and compliance. Although much has been achieved in terms of transparency in many of these countries, the enforcement of rules is still problematic in most cases. The introduction of models of public financing has also been widespread in these regions, although disbursement is limited in practice due to obstacles that restrict the allocation of such funding.

Political finance regulations in the regions discussed here are influenced by standards from the Council of Europe (CoE), the EU, and other organizations such as the Organization for Security and Co-operation in Europe (OSCE). This influence varies, and is weakest in Belarus and Central Asia. For Central and Eastern Europe and Turkey, the CoE and EU are of primary normative importance. Some of these countries are subject to intense monitoring by EU and CoE bodies regarding their compliance with common standards.[16] Political finance regulation has not been completely harmonized, although various instruments contain important sets of rules. One of the weaknesses of international efforts has been their apolitical, technical approach to party funding and campaign finance, and the excessive focus on corruption as a primary concern for regulation. As a result, political finance has become a patchwork of increasingly complex rules, the rationales of which are often inexplicable.

The CoE has been the most involved in introducing international standards in the area of political finance in Europe. It has adopted a series of documents concerning the regulation of party financing, with the main text being the 2003 *Recommendation of the Committee of Ministers on Common Rules against Corruption in the Funding of Political Parties and Electoral Campaigns*.[17] This recommendation firmly establishes the principle that caps on expenditure are legitimate in Europe. Other distinct features of the document are discussions about the admissibility of corporate financing and making private donations tax deductible.

The attempt to produce a pan-European normative framework for political finance is commendable and serves a useful purpose. However, many of the countries covered in this chapter generally meet the CoE and OSCE recommendations already; it is unclear whether the recommendations would require the introduction of new regulations. The effectiveness of the regulations depends on the quality of the work performed by the monitoring teams and enforcement agencies responsible for their implementation. As is often the case with common international standards, the desire to reconcile different legal traditions leads to abstract and general norms, with varying degrees of effectiveness in implementation and supervision.

The OSCE/Office for Democratic Institutions and Human Rights (ODIHR) and CoE Venice Commission's Guidelines on Political Party Regulation provide some specific guidance on reporting requirements and the all-important issue of the abuse of state resources.[18] On reporting requirements, the Guidelines state that 'it is good practice for [such] financial reports to be made available on the Internet in a timely manner'.[19] They also specify that parties should submit annual disclosure reports in non-campaign periods that itemize contributions and expenditures. On the abuse of state resources, the issues of intimidation and workplace mobilization are highlighted. The Guidelines note that 'it is not unheard of for a government to require its workers to attend a pro-government rally'. The OSCE/ODIHR Guidelines explicitly state that the law should expressly and universally ban such practices.

It can be problematic and not always appropriate to transplant models or specific institutions from more established democracies. This process often takes place without a good understanding of all the background factors that make these models or institutions efficient in their original context. Thus many of the transplants acquire completely different meanings or result in completely different outcomes when they are adapted to the local context.

Sources of income for political parties and candidates

The regions under review heavily regulate the funding of campaigns and parties. Yet the impact of such regulations on how political parties and election candidates actually raise money is another matter.

Contribution bans

Two types of regulation of contributions are almost universal in the regions covered in this chapter: bans on foreign funding and anonymous donations (anonymous donations are banned to increase transparency and to facilitate monitoring of compliance with other regulations). Bans on foreign funding are introduced, at least in theory, to insulate domestic political processes from foreign influence. Yet the extent of these bans differs from country to country. Especially in Central Europe, these bans aim to prevent direct foreign donations to parties and candidates, especially in the electoral process. Foreign party-related or independent NGO donations are normally allowed, and could be used for party-related activities such as seminars, training of party leaders, the organization of events and so on. In fact, there is quite active cooperation between political parties in Central and Eastern Europe and the Balkans with German political foundations (e.g., the Konrad Adenauer Stiftung and Friedrich Ebert Stiftung) and US organizations (e.g., the National Endowment for Democracy, National Democratic Institute for International Affairs, International Republican Institute). With the accession of the Central European countries to the EU, similar forms of cooperation have continued and even intensified.

In contrast, in the former Soviet republics, bans on foreign funding are more far-reaching and generally aim to insulate all political activities from foreign sponsorship, including the work of pro-democracy NGOs. This is particularly evident in countries with authoritarian or semi-authoritarian governments. In Kazakhstan, for example, the ban on foreign funding of political parties extends to receiving funds from local organizations that have in turn received foreign funding, or have foreign membership or participation. In Russia, a 2012 law compels organizations that receive foreign funding to register as 'foreign agents' and generally aims to restrict their political activities.[20] Even in countries without such legislation, the same effect could be achieved through very tight control of NGOs, refusal to register them, or banning and dissolving them for failure to disclose funding.[21]

Contribution limits

A majority of countries in the regions studied feature limits on contributions.[22] These limits vary in terms of the size of the contribution, the timing of donations and the recipient. In general, countries that do not provide considerable public funding rely on sizeable corporate donations, and countries that have introduced extensive public funding schemes have more stringent restrictions on contributions. Ukraine has had no public funding since 2007–08, and limits on contributions are set very high. An individual in Ukraine can contribute up to 400 times the minimum monthly wage (I$58,400) to a party and up to 20 times the minimum wage (I$2,920) to a single candidate for election to the parliament in a single-mandate election district.[23] In the United States, the equivalent numbers are 5,000 and 2,600 US dollars (USD) per annum,[24] which is the equivalent of four times and twice the minimum wage, respectively.[25] It should be noted, however, that a comparison with the United States is complicated by the prevalence of political action committees that allow for multiple smaller donations in the USA, which in total can significantly exceed the aforementioned limit. Comparisons with Western Europe are difficult since few countries in that region limit individual donations to parties in relation to an election. One that does is France, where individual donations for the funding of election campaigns are limited to 4,600 euros (EUR) (I$5,400), which is equivalent to about three times the minimum wage (and about one-tenth that of Ukraine).[26]

Figure 6.1. Limits on the amount donors can contribute to candidates in Eastern, Central and South-eastern Europe and Central Asia

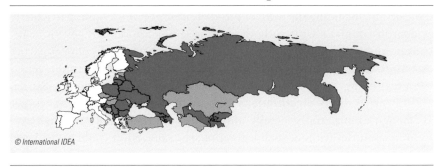

© International IDEA

■ Yes
■ No

Source: International IDEA. This map is based on data collected up to February 2014. Data are continuously updated on the International IDEA Political Finance Database. See http://www.idea.int/political-finance/question.cfm?id=268

Significant public funding coupled with unlimited corporate funding for political parties is not common, although some countries in Central Europe have adopted this approach. Most notably, the Czech Republic provides public subsidies and has no limits on expenditures or contributions. Slovakia and Hungary follow suit with public funding and unlimited contributions, but both of these countries have expenditure limits.

The regions covered here tend to rely on limiting contributions and expenditures. To compensate for such restrictions, 83 per cent of the countries have public funding schemes. The overall model comes close to the French approach, which provides public funding and limits contributions and expenditures.

Sources of private income

Political parties in the regions covered here rely predominantly on two types of sources of income: public funding and large private (and in some cases corporate) donations. In some countries, the distinction between illicit funding and corporate funding is not always clear, either in the regulations or in practice.

Membership dues and small donations

Party income from membership fees and small donations from individuals is generally low. Moreover, political parties in these countries are often fragile and short-lived organizations: even in Central Europe, many of the 'established' parties of the transition period have already disappeared and been replaced by newcomers. Thus loyalty to political parties is generally low, and there are no good examples of parties being able to create a sizeable fund by collecting membership fees. All in all, membership dues and fees constitute a marginal part of the income of most political actors in the reviewed regions. But in some of the countries in Eastern Europe—such as Ukraine and Hungary, where there is no upper limit to membership fees—using membership fees to bypass donation limits or disclosure requirements could potentially be a very important source of income for parties.[27]

Large (and corporate) donations

As membership contributions and small donations are a largely insignificant form of political fundraising, political parties must rely on public funding and large donations. Large donations normally mean corporate donations, even if funds come from an individual businessman rather than directly from a business.

There is no limit on corporate donations to either political parties or candidates in a majority of the countries covered here. The exceptions are Bulgaria, Poland and Russia. Some countries have partial bans on corporate donations to either candidates or parties; such bans are problematic because they provide a loophole for channelling funds via one actor to another. In Azerbaijan and Russia, corporations cannot donate to parties but can donate to candidates. In Armenia, Ukraine and Uzbekistan the situation is the reverse.

Large or corporate donations are a problem in these regions since they are often connected to kickback bribes. There have been scandals in this area, for instance in the Czech Republic where the government of Vaclav Klaus fell due to allegations of kickback bribes.[28] In Latvia, widespread perceptions of corruption and undue influence of oligarchs led the country's then president, Valdis Zatlers, to call a referendum on dissolving parliament in 2011.[29] Estonia, which is perceived as one of the least corrupt in this sample, has also experienced party funding scandals. In 2012 a former member of parliament (MP), Silver Meikar, admitted to channelling EUR 7,600 ($10,200) in questionable donations to the ruling Reform Party in 2009 and 2010.[30] Meikar claimed that the money had come from a fellow MP and party member, and that other members of the Reform Party also donated funds in a similar fashion.[31] No criminal case was pursued, since accepting covert funding is not criminally punishable under Estonia's Political Parties Act. The ultimate source of the money has never been revealed.

In Russia, it was widely alleged that the support given to President Boris Yeltsin by so-called oligarchs in the 1996 election was in exchange for presidential favours connected with the preservation and expansion of business empires established through murky privatization deals.[32] In the 2000s, presidents Putin and Dmitrii Medvedev established firm control over the oligarchs, and at present only those who do not seriously threaten the governing parties seem to be able to operate, which calls the concept of 'private' ownership of the big magnates into question.

The size of a country and the existence of oligarchs have an important influence on political finance. Wealthy entrepreneurs can affect domestic politics regardless of the type of political finance regulation, which suggests the ineffectiveness of such regulation. The phenomenon of 'oligarchic parties', or parties set up by wealthy individuals, is quite widespread in many of the countries discussed here, as is illustrated by the case of the Georgian election of 2012, which will be further discussed below. Even EU member countries are by no means immune to such developments; take, for instance, the case of Latvia.[33]

Two caveats need to be addressed here. First, many believe that the existence of 'oligarchic parties' per se is not a problem for democracy. According to this view, wealthy individuals should be allowed to start up political projects of their own. The obstruction of such activities through regulatory, administrative or penal means, as was allegedly done in the case of Mikhail Khodorkovsky,[34] could constitute deliberate efforts to restrict democratic freedoms. But entrepreneurial political projects become problematic when they are the result of, or aim to achieve, illegitimate links between power and money or when they result in governmental favouritism vis-à-vis specific economic interests. Arguably, many of the countries in the regions covered here, especially those in the post-Soviet space, have such problems. The very word 'oligarch' suggests the illegitimate fusion of power and wealth, which complicates the issue of entrepreneurial political projects. Yet it must be kept in mind that such problems with oligarchs can be a sign that a country has a degree of political competition: in non-competitive authoritarian regimes (such as Belarus and parts of Central Asia) this problem does not exist because opposition-minded oligarchs are more aggressively targeted by the justice system.[35]

> Wealthy entrepreneurs can affect domestic politics regardless of the type of political finance regulation, which suggests the ineffectiveness of such regulation.

Second, political finance rules cannot effectively deal with the influence of oligarchic structures on their own; much more substantive constitutional and legal reforms are needed. If oligarchs have considerable influence in a polity, their money will find its way into the coffers of parties and candidates regardless of what type of legal framework regulates contributions and expenditures. The question is how visible this process is. Curiously, in Eastern Europe—especially in Russia and Ukraine (which has no public funding and no limits on expenditure)—the funding process is quite visible, and people directly associate political players with specific corporate interests.

Illicit funding

Illicit funding of political parties and election campaigns has been a problem in the regions since the fall of communism. All conclusions regarding this issue are to a certain extent speculative since this is an informal sector, although some tentative generalizations are possible. For politicians in some countries, many of their most enthusiastic party donors have a criminal record and a suspect agenda. Little of the crime–politics nexus is properly documented, but recent arrests might result in more tangible evidence.[36] In addition, there are cases of high-profile political assassinations that could be interpreted as circumstantial evidence of the involvement of organized crime in politics. Those assassinated include Zoran Djinjic,[37] serving prime minister of Serbia; Andrey Lukanov, a former prime minister of Bulgaria; and Iliya Pavlov,[38] one of the richest persons in Eastern Europe and a sponsor of politicians and political parties in Bulgaria.[39]

In Kyrgyzstan, illicit funding has played an important role in election campaigns and in the political liberalization of the country more generally.[40] It lies on a major drug-trafficking route between Afghanistan and Europe. Organized criminal groups and their leaders reportedly played an important role in destabilizing the rule of President Askar Akaev during the so-called Tulip Revolution.[41] After the president was toppled, criminal bosses continued to defy the new rulers openly. Similar dynamics have been witnessed elsewhere in the regions where groups involved in trafficking and the drugs trade become involved in electoral politics.[42]

Public funding

Public funding is the only viable alternative to corporate funding in most of the countries under review. Only a few countries lack direct public funding schemes for political parties or candidates: Belarus, Moldova, Ukraine, Kyrgyzstan and Turkmenistan. Belarus and Turkmenistan have no competitive democratic processes or freedom of association, so the lack of public funding is simply another way to discourage independent political activity. Moldova has passed a law on public funding, and such support was about to be introduced at the time of writing.[43]

In certain cases, such as that of Ukraine, the decision not to provide significant public funding is probably driven by a desire on the part of the governing parties or politicians to preserve their competitive advantage. In Serbia, this logic was adopted most explicitly by former President Slobodan Milosevic, who attempted to starve the opposition of political funding by providing minimal public support, banning foreign donations and controlling the business sector by delaying privatization.[44]

It is difficult to classify the states according to the generosity of their public funding schemes. Generally, the Central European states—the Czech Republic, Slovakia, Hungary, Poland, Bulgaria and Romania—have rather generous direct subsidies.[45] In some Central European states (with the exception of Poland) corporate financing is allowed, which puts the political parties in a more comfortable position. The situation is similar in Turkey, where parties rely on both the public budget and corporate donors.

In the post-Soviet space, public funding for political parties is less widespread and generous, yet it has been increasing in Latvia, Lithuania and Russia. In Russia, dominance of President Putin and the executive branch over the legislature has meant that public funding chiefly benefits the pro-presidential political forces. Political parties that receive at least 3 per cent of the votes in State Duma elections receive public funding and some access to public media. According to a report on Russia by the Group of States against Corruption (GRECO):

> ...the most recent increase has substantially improved the parties' overall financial situation. The percentage of state funding in the parties' annual budgets had grown: for the Communist Party—from approximately 40% to over 50%, for 'Fair Russia'—from 7% to 25%, for the Liberal Democratic party—from below 40% to over 83%, and for 'United Russia'—from 23% to 36%.[46]

Note that none of the parties listed above belongs to the opposition in Russia. Needless to say, the parties that benefitted from the increases in public funding are those that are formally registered as parties, and the liberal democratic opposition in Russia has faced serious obstacles to registration throughout the post-Soviet period.[47] Here it should be noted that a 3 per cent threshold for receiving public funding is not among the higher thresholds. For instance, in Turkey parties need 7 per cent of the votes in the preceding elections to be eligible for public funding. Yet they do not face the same kinds of challenges in registering as opposition parties do in Russia.

In some more autocratic states—for instance Kazakhstan, Uzbekistan and Azerbaijan—public funding schemes for opposition parties serve as an instrument for suppressing, monitoring and controlling the political competition. In practice, public funding in this political context normally goes to docile or regime-friendly opposition parties, or is provided in such a way as to benefit the ruling party disproportionately.

As in the rest of the world's regions, the predominant model of disbursing public funding is direct subsidies distributed on the basis of the number of seats in parliament or votes won in the last election. None of the countries examined in this chapter employs complex allocation formulae that match public subsidies with small donations or membership fees. In addition to direct subsidies, the vast majority of the countries discussed have elaborate schemes of indirect, in-kind support to parties and candidates. The most important type of in-kind support is subsidized access to the media—which has become common practice in all the countries covered here except Estonia—providing free or subsidized access to the media for parties, candidates or both.[48]

The abuse of state resources

Abuse of state resources in the regions

The abuse of state resources is a major challenge, especially in countries that have an excessive concentration of power in the executive branch or limited media or judiciary independence. This structural bias in favour of the executive branch puts the governing parties in a privileged position not only in the more autocratic countries such as Belarus, Azerbaijan and the states of Central Asia, but also in others such as Armenia and Georgia.[49]

Even in more competitive democracies, such as those in Central Europe, governments have attempted to use state resources in their favour. However, the phenomenon is more accentuated in less democratic cases. For instance, in the most recent Armenian elections the OSCE/ODIHR documented several cases of local administration offices being used for the incumbent president's re-election campaign.[50] The OSCE Armenia report further notes that lax enforcement of existing regulations allowed for the abuse of administrative resources, and therefore 'did not provide for a level playing field among candidates'.[51]

One form of abusing state resources is the practice of government parties 'extorting' money from state-owned enterprises. The fact that one-third of the countries discussed here allow public enterprise donations to candidates is a strong indication of the abuse of state resources. Even in countries that ban donations from public enterprises to candidates,[52] such prohibitions have proved ineffective, and have become a further motivation to evade transparency and disclosure requirements.[53]

Donations by public enterprises are facilitated by widespread political patronage in the appointment of the managing directors and board members of publicly owned enterprises in the regions.[54] While there are few specific examples of public enterprises funding party activities, the parties sometimes disclose information that reveals illegitimate connections between public enterprises and parties. For example, in Serbia, the Democratic Party's list of donors in its publicly available financial reports includes individuals that the party appointed to leading positions in public enterprises.[55] This is an example of so-called party taxation: party members who were appointed to public enterprises have to pay a share of their salary back to the party. There have also been cases where donors listed by the parties on their own websites include some in leading managerial positions in state-owned enterprises.[56]

It should be noted that dubious connections between state-owned enterprises and parties have been reported in countries that give some degree of freedom to investigative journalists. Yet this practice also probably takes place in countries where investigative journalism is suppressed and there is not the level of media freedoms or transparency laws to allow such facts to emerge.

> In many countries in the regions discussed here, incumbent parties have shown great inventiveness in using public resources to support the party's electoral chances.

Private companies that have privileged access to the markets can also be a problem. Politicians or their close relatives sometimes own private companies that benefit from such access. Given the deficiencies in procurement processes, companies often get valuable contracts on questionable grounds. In Serbia, for instance, a security company owned by the husband of one of the highest officials in the Democratic Party reportedly has several contracts with different state institutions, including the National Employment Service and the Tax Administration; the company also donated around EUR 40,000 to the party in 2011–12.[57]

Finally, it has to be said that the issue of the abuse of state resources can hardly be discussed as a narrow political finance matter; it relates to the overall constitutional structure of the political regime. All the countries under review here have provisions banning the use of state resources (other than those legally provided as subsidies and in-kind support) by political parties and candidates. Yet the impact of these provisions is different in different settings. Incumbent candidates invariably have a competitive edge: they are more visible in the media and have the opportunity to use resources such as transport, security, interpretation and so on for their own ends. Competitive democracies have other instruments to check the abuse of state resources: for instance, parliamentary commissions examining government use of facilities, means of transport and so on. Especially after a change of government, this is usually done whenever there are suspicions of illegitimate use of state resources.

In many countries in the regions discussed here, incumbent parties have shown great inventiveness in using public resources to support the party's electoral chances. In 2013, the newspaper *Dan* in Montenegro published the transcripts of secret recordings of meetings between senior government party officials. In one of the recordings, a party official expressed satisfaction with 'the number of internships that the Ministry of Education, the Ministry of Health and the Agency for Environmental Protections gave us, and I believe it gave us additional strength and better results in these elections'.[58]

Abuse of state resources and the media

A particular problem throughout several of these regions is control over the media. Control over the media is related to the issue of political finance through the access of political parties to public media. A lack of media access for political parties can manifest itself in many ways, from outright censorship to more subtle forms of public media restrictions and incentives for media conglomerates.

Recent reports of unequal access to public media and unbalanced coverage in favour of the incumbent regime have been made in Azerbaijan, Belarus, Montenegro and Kazakhstan. Complaints about biased media coverage were also made in Bosnia and Herzegovina.[59] In Azerbaijan, the OSCE found that candidates for the 2013 presidential election were provided with insufficient access to the media and that the disproportionate coverage received by the president contributed to a non-level playing field.[60] And in the 2012 parliamentary election in Belarus, despite rules providing for the allocation of free and equal media coverage in the state media (both print and broadcast), the OSCE found that reporting from state-owned media outlets focused heavily on the ruling party and president. Indeed, opposition parties and candidates only received 2 per cent of the coverage in the state-owned print media.[61]

In Georgia, the opposition successfully challenged the incumbent in 2012 partly by aggressively investing in the media sector and thereby balancing an otherwise biased media environment. President Mikheil Saakashvili had the benefit of a state-owned channel (Channel 1) with coverage across the territory. There were also two privately held pro-government channels, Rustavi-2 and Imedi, which together dominated TV viewing in Georgia.[62] In the 2012 elections the billionaire Bidzina Ivanishvili led the opposition coalition Georgian Dream. His wife and brother invested heavily in opposition-minded TV companies, TV9 and Global TV, respectively. In the months leading up to the election, many TV companies faced difficulties: one company was fined after a tax audit, satellite antennas were seized in another over vote-buying allegations, and technical equipment belonging to a third company was allegedly damaged while waiting for customs clearance.[63] There was suspicion of political motivations behind such actions, which the authorities vehemently denied. In the end, the opposition's financial clout produced a more balanced media space in Georgia.

Spending by political parties and candidates

Spending limits

The general preference in the regions is for overall spending limits. Some countries have no spending limits, including the Czech Republic, Turkey, Ukraine, Kazakhstan, Turkmenistan and Uzbekistan. In other countries, the spending limits are so high that they have no impact on political competition.

In Hungary, a party can spend a maximum of 386 million Hungarian forints (HUF) (I$2,670,000), or HUF 1 million (I$6,900) per candidate, while in Moldova the equivalent amounts are (in 2009) around 12 million Moldovan lei (MDL) (I$2 million) and MDL 500,000 (I$87,000), respectively. By contrast, in Russia the limits are 250 million roubles (RUB) (I$12.9 million) for parties.

In some cases, especially where the government party uses state resources to unofficially fund its activities, spending limits have been used to obstruct the opposition, for example Ivanishvili's challenge to Saakashvili in Georgia in 2012. Much of the state machinery under Saakashvili was mobilized against the challenger, including the parliament. Under new legislation passed at the end of 2011, evidently to prevent Ivanishvili from spending his own money on his campaign, a cap of 60,000 Georgian lari (GEL) (I$77,000) was placed on the amount individuals could donate to political parties.[64]

In Kyrgyzstan, political parties may not spend more than 1 million monthly salaries (the exact amount is not specified). Using the country's minimum wage of 600 Kyrgyz som (KGS) (I$40) per month,[65] the spending limit is very high relative to the regions considered here: 1 million minimum-wage monthly salaries equals I$36 million. Similarly, spending limits for candidates are 500,000 times the minimum, or I$18 million.

Actual spending

Level of spending

In the 60 per cent of states under review that have limits on expenditures, according to their official reports parties normally comply with these limits. Yet virtually everywhere experts and analysts insist that official reports reflect only a fraction of actual expenditures. One factor that complicates the calculation of electoral costs is the murky situation in the media sector. Most of the analysis of costs uses standard advertising rates for political advertisements. Yet political actors may use preferential rates or discounts, which could seriously change the estimates. Whether such discounts are legal, and whether they are granted to all participants in elections on a fair basis, are also matters of concern.

The Ukrainian case also helps to illustrate the level of spending on elections. According to official reports, during the 2012 parliamentary elections political parties jointly spent more than 600 million Ukrainian hryvnia (UAH) (I$207.14 million).[66] The Party of Regions spent about UAH 218 million (I$75.26 million), the Fatherland UAH 107 million (I$36.94 million), the Ukrainian Democratic Alliance for Reform more than UAH 33.7 million (I$11.63 million), the Communist Party of Ukraine UAH 72 million (I$24.86 million), Our Ukraine UAH 63 million (I$21.75 million) and Ukraine–Forward! UAH 60.6 million (I$20.92 million).[67]

The Ukrainian situation reveals modest spending if we limit our analysis to official reports. Yet analysts estimate much higher figures for the real cost of elections in Ukraine in 2012: from USD 850 million to the rather astronomical figure of USD 2.5 billion.[68] The political scientist Artem Bidenko reports that the Party of Regions spent around USD 850 million, Ukraine–Forward! some USD 150 million and the rest of the political parties USD 350 million, while candidates in single-member districts had spent approximately USD 900 million on the campaign.[69] Only about half of the single-member district candidates submitted reports on their campaign spending.[70]

If these speculative estimates are close to the real level of political spending in Ukraine, the situation would not be too dissimilar to that of that of established democracies. Admittedly, the calculation of electoral expenditure is not an exact science, and is sometimes connected to political spin and propaganda. Even so, there is reason to believe that campaign spending, and especially overspending, in Ukraine and many other countries in the regions is significant. This is also the case in Hungary, where overspending has occurred in recent times. Transparency International reports that the five parliamentary parties in the 2006 election spent, according to conservative estimates, a combined total of HUF 7.3 billion (I$50.07 million). In this election, the two biggest parties alone allegedly spent ten times the legal limit of HUF 386 million (I$2.65 million).[71]

Another factor that complicates reporting on actual spending is the difficulty of capturing vote buying. There are numerous anecdotal cases of vote buying, but it is notoriously difficult to document; new information technologies like mobile phone cameras can help. In the Balkans, vote buying is still fairly widespread, for instance in areas populated by minorities such as the Roma.[72] In some cases the candidates themselves even admit to having paid voters a bribe. For instance, in the 2012 parliamentary elections in Georgia, a ruling party candidate in a single-member district admitted to having assisted a local resident with GEL 500 (I$300).[73] List experiment surveys that guarantee respondents anonymity have recently been used to estimate the extent of vote buying.[74] The International Foundation for Electoral Systems (IFES) collaborated with a local survey organization to conduct a list experiment survey on the 2012 parliamentary elections in Ukraine. One in ten voters admitted in the survey that vote buying affected their vote choice in the single-member district elections.[75] The study also included a detailed analysis of crowd-sourced reports on vote buying.

Official reports from across the regions covered by this chapter suggest that a significant portion of campaign expenditures is spent on TV and media advertising.[76] In Moldova, almost 80 per cent of publicly disclosed expenditures went to advertising, and a majority of that went to TV advertising.[77] The standards for reporting are often not strictly adhered to. While some parties report spending on billboards and other unspecified 'election materials', others are more explicit and report spending on calendars and other specific types of promotional material.

Third-party spending

Because of the enormous weight of large corporate donations in the incomes of political actors, direct transactions are probably not the preferred means of obtaining funds. Accordingly, money might instead be channelled through party-related foundations, which are usually not subject to the same restrictions as political parties with regard to the size and origin of donations. They are therefore convenient instruments for 'legalizing' money obtained from publicly owned enterprises, foreign donors or large corporate sponsors. Sometimes the legislation is rather lax, making it easy to use foundation money for straightforward political purposes. More commonly, however, funds are disbursed under the pretext of seminars, training for party officials or honoraria for services never performed, for example.

For instance, party-affiliated NGOs in Latvia were set up to circumvent spending limits when enforcement was tightened. US Embassy-funded research in Latvia summarizes the effect of third-party spending as: 'non-governmental organisations, established by the organisers of their election campaigns, for their advertising, has ruined the political party financing system developed in 2004'.[78]

Another challenge is monitoring and enforcing restrictions on private in-kind donations. In some cases, cars and mobile phones are provided for electoral campaigns or for the routine use of political parties.[79] In Kosovo, political parties were obliged to disclose in-kind contributions exceeding EUR 1,500 in the early 2000s. A detailed audit by the OSCE suggests that the parties that reported their contributions largely stayed within the limits for in-kind contributions.[80]

Enforcement of political finance regulations

Many analyses of political finance have concluded that enforcement is generally the weakest link in the system. In the regions under discussion there are no exemplary models in terms of enforcement, and there are a number of widespread challenges—including often-ambiguous mandates, insufficient resources, and unclear reporting procedures for parties and candidates. Moreover, all of the approaches to enforcement used by countries in this chapter suffer from a considerable disparity between regulation and actual practices. Either state audit offices or electoral management bodies are generally tasked with enforcing the laws. In both cases, some degree of transparency is achieved, especially regarding public funds. Civil society monitoring projects have also been carried out in many states, especially in Central Europe, but their efficiency is not well documented. In any case, civil society monitoring cannot replace the role of formal institutions in performing their oversight role. In addition, civil society pressure for political finance reform is not very strong in the regions analysed, perhaps because the public has little understanding of the vagaries of political finance beyond what has been revealed by a few media scandals.

One dilemma, when analysing enforcement, is whether to treat political parties as civil society organizations or state constitutional bodies. If political parties are seen as civil society organizations, they may claim a right to privacy regarding their funding matters. From this point of view, parties have the right to regulate their internal affairs, including funding matters, without limitations and restrictions imposed by the state. Generally speaking, parties in these regions enjoyed considerable privacy during the first ten years after the fall of communism, due in part to the poor quality of regulatory efforts to ensure a degree of transparency and enforceability[81]. However, given the prevalence of corruption there is a general trend toward requiring transparency in party and candidate funding. By contrast, if political parties are treated as quasi-state bodies, then their finances should be just as transparent as those of budgetary organizations. In such cases, access-to-information legislation that is applicable to state bodies should regulate access to party income and expenditure data, which should be available to citizens upon request.

There are four main types of institutional enforcement arrangements. First, state audit offices can be used for enforcement, but they may lack sufficient resources and prerogatives to properly audit the internal affairs of political parties.[82] In theory, they might be efficient at controlling the state aid received by parties, but might not be able to control private funding. A second option is a parliamentary commission, as in the Czech Republic. Yet such a commission's lack of independence—and conflicts of interest between parties—can render it ineffective.

The judiciary as the enforcement force is a third option, but generally has not been widely utilized in the regions discussed here. One reason is that party financing is seen as a 'partisan' matter, one with which the judiciary (which is supposed to be unbiased) should not interfere.[83] However, a deeper reason is that many countries in the regions, such as Bulgaria and Romania, have a very low level of public trust in the judiciary, which is perceived as one of the most corrupt branches of power. The fourth institutional option, independent commissions such as electoral commissions, is used in countries such as Albania and Bosnia and Herzegovina. Unfortunately, this option has suffered from most of the weaknesses of the other options discussed above, and has in some cases led to very low levels of activity from the enforcing institution (such as in Georgia and Serbia before the mandate was moved to the State Audit Office and the Anti-Corruption Agency respectively).

Some countries have created hybrid institutional arrangements. For example, the Former Yugoslav Republic of Macedonia (FYROM) has two oversight agencies: the State Commission for Prevention of Corruption and the State Auditor's Office.[84] One practical concern with such a set-up is independence from political parties. Technically, members of the State Commission cannot be removed for political reasons, but a commission member was dismissed in 2012 for alleged abuse of office, without parliamentary approval.

A Transparency International report notes that the dismissal was 'in clear contravention of the regulations'.[85] Furthermore, the mandate of the Auditor's Office in the FYROM is quite broad, but its audits are reported to be rather superficial.[86]

Figure 6.2. Institutions responsible for examining financial reports and/or investigating violations in Eastern, Central and South-eastern Europe and Central Asia

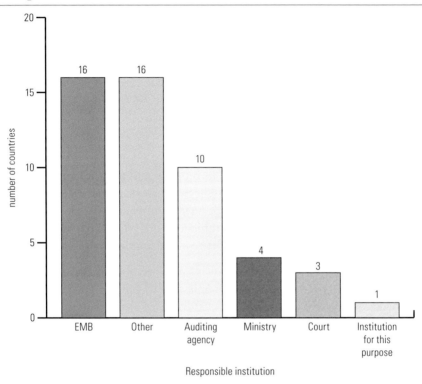

Note: As some countries have more than one institution, the total number is higher than the number of countries.
Source: International IDEA Political Finance Database.

In Eastern Europe and Central Asia, there are a lot of rules and regulations, but selective enforcement is a problem[87]—and is compounded by the incumbent advantage in countries with poor rule of law. The Georgian case is worth considering further. After new legislation was introduced, opposition leader Ivanishvili and his affiliates were fined more than GEL 80 million (I$102 million) for allegedly violating campaign funding rules,[88] which produced several accusations of biased enforcement against his party.[89]

The role of civil society organizations and the media

The role of civil society organizations

Many international donor organizations have placed their hopes on NGOs in the fight against corruption and for transparent political finance. However, it is far from certain that civil society organizations can induce the reforms necessary to eliminate pro-government bias in political finance in the regions or enforce the rules more generally.[90] The political will for such reforms is lacking, especially in the more autocratic countries. However, in addition to their advocacy work, NGOs also play an important role in monitoring compliance with existing rules and standards. NGOs can use innovative measurement and outreach strategies to make it more difficult for political actors to use loopholes or otherwise exploit existing political finance regulations.

Recent examples include projects that monitor the use of administrative resources in Georgia. The local branch of Transparency International examined the use of administrative resources in the 2010 local elections[91] and found increased spending on social services by local governments during the election year, and reported that public officials who had formally taken leave for the duration of the campaign continued to use office resources. Elsewhere, methods have been developed to track actual party spending on print, radio and TV media.[92] Realistic assessments of expenditures, which account for possible discounts, make it more difficult for parties to spend beyond the formal limits. Such reports will hopefully demonstrate the extent of the abuse of public office for partisan purposes during elections. In contrast to other monitoring projects, which have focused on the lack of transparency, these new approaches promise to tackle a real problem behind the veil of public ignorance, which will undoubtedly be a step forward.

The role of the media

It is commonly stated that engaged media are necessary for political finance transparency.[93] Yet some of the countries covered here (particularly the post-Soviet states) do not have independent media or unimpeded media access, which hampers the unveiling of political finance scandals. In autocratic states such as Belarus and most of Central Asia, access to the media—be it public or private—is strictly controlled by the administration.[94] Thus, while over 90 per cent of the countries analysed have subsidized media access that is supposed to be allocated equitably, it is often reserved for pro-presidential parties and the convenient 'opposition'.[95] Poland and Romania are notable in that they take into account the number of proposed candidates when calculating subsidized media access.

In the more competitive post-Soviet states, pockets of media independence exist, but they are generally marginalized by pro-government forces. Central

Europe has greater media independence, but the Hungarian example has recently demonstrated that majoritarian governments still see the public media as an instrument of propaganda.[96] In the Balkans and Turkey, government influence in the media sector is very visible: for instance, news about the protests against Prime Minister Recep Tayyip Erdogan in Turkey only made it to the public channels with great difficulty.[97] It should be noted that the lack of coverage by established media was offset by the use of social media in this case. Bulgaria and Romania are also typically cited as offenders against media independence, although both of these countries have pluralistic and vibrant media sectors.[98]

Party funding scandals emerge more easily in competitive political systems and where the opposition exercises some degree of control over the government, especially with the help of an independent judiciary. One study reports: 'it is no coincidence that the more consolidated democracies—such as the Czech Republic and Poland —produce scandals, while the other types of system produce mainly extensive allegations of scandalous doings'.[99] It is no surprise then that Russia was more capable of producing political finance scandals in the 1990s than in the 2000s, as the political regime has become less competitive.

Thus, it is difficult to generalize on the link between political finance and media freedom over such a vast part of the world. Central Europe and parts of the Balkans have a more competitive and pluralistic media environment; freedom of speech and information is suppressed in Belarus, Central Asia and Azerbaijan; and Russia and Ukraine have regressed and become more autocratic.

Conclusions

The regions of Eastern, Central and South-eastern Europe and Central Asia are diverse and contain countries with fundamentally different regimes. Some countries are consolidated democracies, while others are outright autocracies. There is also considerable variation in political finance regulation throughout the region, but there are some interesting similarities. The two major categories of political finance violations are (1) evasion of expenditure and/or contribution restrictions and (2) major parties' exploitation of their access to the government to secure financial benefits for party members and the party treasury, including access to state media.

Generally, the electoral and party finance agencies lack adequate enforcement mechanisms, especially in cases of systematic violations of expenditure and contribution restrictions. Another problem is vague and gap-ridden (or even conflicting) laws. Rules are often not conducive to increased political pluralism and transparency. In some cases, expenditure and contribution limits are set very low in order to make their observance difficult—which invites the selective use of the sanctions regime to keep political opponents out. Selective implementation of strict regulations is a hallmark of the more autocratic regimes in the area. The opposite also happens: setting the restrictions so high that even the richest political party could not violate them.

The provision of public funding in some of the countries analysed here is modest and does not sufficiently cover the parties' costs, especially for those without access to the government machinery. Admittedly, one of the reasons for the low level of public funding is the economic plight of many of the countries in these regions.

The experience in these regions shows that strict regulations are not sufficient to create control over (or transparency of) political finance. Rules that are better adapted to each country's situation—and implemented by well-resourced and dedicated public entities—are needed. Even then, effective oversight is unlikely without the engagement of civil society groups and independent media.

Recommendations

Policy makers[100]

1. Further specify requirements for reporting on finances for both parties and candidates. *More* regulation is not necessarily needed, but rather *more specific guidelines* on how to comply with existing regulations.
2. Require parties to comply with all regulations to be eligible for public funding.
3. Expenditure and spending limits should be reasonable and indexed for inflation.
4. Focus the regulatory apparatus on a few items that can realistically be implemented without stifling political competition.
5. Provide indirect public funding to all eligible parties—including the opposition.
6. Seek parity between government and opposition parties in the broadcast media, especially if the public media control large sections of the online market.
7. Consider matching small donations and membership dues to political parties with the same amounts of public funding.
8. Further specify the authorization of oversight bodies. They should be able to apply fines for breaches of regulations.
9. Oversight and regulatory bodies need sufficient human and financial resources to perform their duties properly.

Monitoring and enforcement agencies

1. Address transgressions throughout the campaign period and inform the voters in a timely fashion, prior to voting if applicable.
2. Develop standard reporting templates that provide enough detail for meaningful public scrutiny.
3. Provide candidates and parties with clear instructions on how to complete reporting templates. If needed, provide training for candidates and parties.
4. Publish standardized, detailed reporting online, allowing for public scrutiny. Provide financial reports in a spreadsheet format that facilitates comparisons.
5. Create incentives for donors to disclose their identity and the nature of their donation.
6. Do not overburden parties and candidates with reporting requirements during the critical stages of the campaign.
7. Consider ways in which investigative journalism can be supported.

Political parties and politicians

1. Government parties should strive to avoid abusing public resources in order to maintain their public legitimacy and avoid large-scale public protest that may destabilize the entire country; political finance protests in Ukraine, Romania and the Czech Republic are a case in point. Such abuse not only entails a significant waste of public funds, it also entrenches a political culture that makes it less likely that a party can regain power in the future if an election is lost.
2. Opposition parties should realize that exposing the abuse of state resources by the ruling party is one of the most effective ways of appealing to large groups of citizens. Cooperate with civil society and the media for proper investigations that provide you with solid proof. Given that the quality of political finance legislation is often reasonable, opposition parties should invest in understanding and using the available law as much as possible to scrutinize ruling party behaviour.

Civil society and media actors

1. Focus especially on monitoring abuses of administrative resources for partisan purposes.
2. Further develop methods to measure actual spending levels, accounting for preferential advertising rates and discounts.

International actors

1. Do not support a political finance regulatory regime that stifles political competition.
2. When supporting the fight against corruption, include measures that address the lack of political will for political finance reforms.

3. Support the use of innovative measurement strategies and outreach by NGOs working on political finance transparency.

References

Bajovic, V. and Manojlovic, S. (2013) *Corruption and Financing of Political Parties: Case of Serbia*. Observatório de Economia e Gestão de Fraude.

Balkan Insight (2009) 'Serbian Political Party Financing Not Transparent', 21 April, available at http://www.balkaninsight.com/en/article/serbian-political-party-financing-not-transparent

Baykurt, B. (2013) 'The Gezi Protests Have Shown the Rampant Institutional Bias in Turkey's Media Which Now Leaves Little Room for Facts', available at http://blogs.lse.ac.uk/europpblog/

Chicago Tribune (1997) 'To Keep Power, Milosevic Switches Jobs', 24 July, available at http://articles.chicagotribune.com/1997-07-24/news/9707240217_1_slobodan-vuksanovic-slobodan-milosevic-serbian

Čigāne, L. (2007) *9th Saeima Election Finances: Political Party and Third Party Election Campaign Expenditure*, Riga, 27 February.

CNN (2011) 'Russia Refuses to Register Liberal Party; U.S. "Disappointed"', 22 June, available at http://www.cnn.com/2011/WORLD/europe/06/22/russia.party.elections/index.html

Conference on Security and Co-operation in Europe (CSCE) (1990) *Document of the Copenhagen Meeting of the Conference on the Human Dimension of the CSCE*.

Council of Europe (2003) *Recommendation Rec(2003)4*, adopted by the Committee of Ministers on 8 April at the 835th meeting of the ministers' deputies.

De Waal, T. (2012) 'A Crucial Election in Georgia'. Washington, D.C.: Carnegie Endowment for International Peace, available at http://carnegieendowment.org/2012/09/11/crucial-election-in-georgia/drlp

Estonian Public Broadcasting (2012) 'Reform Party Caught Up in "Dirty Money" Scandal', 22 May, available at http://news.err.ee/politics/660921d5-6410-43a1-b01e-ec47e2d3550f

Federal Election Commission (2013) The FEC and the Federal Campaign Law - Contribution Limits, available at http://www.fec.gov/pages/brochures/fecfeca.shtml#Contribution_Limits

Freedom House (2004) *Freedom in the World Report 2004*, 'Russia', available at http://www.freedomhouse.org/report/freedom-world/2004/russia

Freedom House (2013) *Nations in Transit 2013: Authoritarian Aggression and the Pressures of Austerity*.

Gonzalez-Ocantos, Ezequiel et al. (2012) 'Vote Buying and Social Desirability Bias: Experimental Evidence from Nicaragua', *American Journal of Political Science*, 56(1), pp. 202–17.

Grigas, A. (2012) *Legacies, Coercion and Soft Power: Russian Influence in the Baltic States*, Briefing Paper. London: Chatham House.

Group of States against Corruption (GRECO) (2011) *Third Evaluation Round, Evaluation Report on the Czech Republic on Transparency of Party Funding*, adopted by GRECO at its 50th plenary meeting, Strasbourg, 28 March– 1 April 2011.

Group of States against Corruption (GRECO) (2012) *Third Evaluation Round, Evaluation Report on the Russian Federation Incriminations* (ETS 173 & 191, GPC2), adopted by GRECO at its 54th plenary meeting, Strasbourg, 20–23 March 2012.

Grzymala-Busse, Anna (2003) 'Political Competition and the Politicization of the State in East Central Europe', *Comparative Political Studies*, 36(10), pp. 1123–47.

Human Rights Watch (2012) Memorandum to the European Union on Media Freedom in Hungary, available at http://www.hrw.org/news/2012/02/16/ memorandum-european-union-media-freedom-hungary

Human Rights Watch (2013) *Laws of Attrition Crackdown on Russia's Civil Society after Putin's Return to the Presidency*, available at http://www.hrw.org/sites/ default/files/reports/russia0413_ForUpload.pdf

International Foundation for Electoral Systems (IFES) (2010) *Campaign Finance in Moldova: Big Money, Few Donors, Undeclared Expenses – Reform Needed!* Washington, D.C.: International Foundation for Electoral Systems.

International IDEA, Political Finance Database, available at http://www.idea.int/ political-finance

International IDEA (2013) *Illicit Networks and Politics in the Baltic States*. Stockholm: International IDEA, available at http://www.idea.int/publications/ illicit-networks-and-politics/

Karadaku, L. (2013) 'Accused Crime Boss Arrest Is a "Kick" to Regional Drug Trade', *Southeast European Times*, 9 May.

Koppel, K. (2012) 'Tarand: Meikari väidetes ei ole midagi üllatavat' [Tarand: Meikar's Allegations Are Not Surprising], *ERR*, 22 May, available at http:// uudised.err.ee/index.php?06253397

Kupatadze, A. (2008) 'Organized Crime before and after the Tulip Revolution: The Changing Dynamics of Upperworld-Underworld Networks', *Central Asian Survey*, 27(3-4).

Kyiv Post (2012a) 'Candidates Spent $2.5 Billion on Election Campaign, Says Expert', 2 November, available at http://www.kyivpost.com/content/politics/candidates-spent-25-billion-on-election-campaign-says-expert-315462.html

Kyiv Post (2012b) 'Media: Parties Report to CEC on Election Costs', 15 November.

Kyiv Post (2012c) 'Parties Spend over Hr 600 Million on Elections, According to Report', 16 November, available at http://www.kyivpost.com/content/politics/parties-spend-over-hr-600-million-on-elections-according-to-report-316205.html

Kyiv Post (2012d) 'Campaigns File Dodgy Spending Declarations', 8 December.

Kyiv Post (2013) 'Hiring Law Firm to Chase Lazarenko Assests is a New Waste of Money', 7 November.

Kynev, A. (2011) *State Duma Elections 2011 and the Marginal Role of Russian Parties.*

Leviev-Sawyer, C. (2011) 'Andrei Lukanov, Red Baron of Bulgaria', *Sofia Echo*, 11 February, available at http://sofiaecho.com/2011/02/11/1041549_andrei-lukanov-red-baron-of-bulgaria

Matuszak, S. (2012) 'The Oligarchic Democracy the Influence of Business Groups on Ukrainian Politics', *OSW Studies*, 42, September.

Mladenovic, N. (2012) 'Transnational Organized Crime: The Failed Divorce of Serbia's Government and Organized Crime', *Journal of International Affairs*, 66(1), Fall/Winter.

Nassmacher, K.-H. (2003) 'Party Funding in Continental Western Europe', in M. Tjernström and R. Austin (eds), *Funding of Political Parties and Election Campaigns*. Stockholm: International IDEA.

Network for Affirmation of NGO Sector (MANS) (2013) *Building Trust in the Election Process in Montenegro*, December, available at http://www.mans.co.me/en/about-mans/publications/building-trust-in-the-election-process-in-montenegro

Ohman, Magnus (ed.) (2013) *Political Finance Oversight Handbook*. Washington, D.C.: International Foundation for Electoral Systems (IFES), Training in Detection and Enforcement.

Orenstein, M. A. (2001) *Out of the Red: Building Capitalism and Democracy in Postcommunist Europe*. Ann Arbor, MI: University of Michigan Press.

Organisation for Economic Co-operation and Development (OECD) (2013) *Fighting Corruption in Eastern Europe and Central Asia Anti-corruption Reforms in Eastern Europe and Central Asia: Progress and Challenges, 2009-2013*, OECD Publishing.

Organization for Security and Co-operation in Europe (OSCE Kosovo) (2004) *Report on Political Party Annual Financial Reports for Years 2002 and 2003*, Department of Elections, Political Party Registration Office.

Organization for Security and Co-operation in Europe (OSCE Kosovo) (2007) *Report on Political Entity Campaign Financial Disclosures for 2007 Kosovo Elections*, Political Party Registration Office.

Organization for Security and Co-operation in Europe, Office for Democratic Institutions and Human Rights (OSCE/ODIHR) (2009) *Republic of Uzbekistan Parliamentary Elections Election Assessment Mission: Final Report*.

Organization for Security and Co-operation in Europe, Office for Democratic Institutions and Human Rights (OSCE/ODIHR) (2011) *Guidelines on Political Party Regulation*.

Organization for Security and Cooperation in Europe, Office for Democratic Institutions and Human Rights (OSCE/ODIHR) (2012) *Republic of Belarus, Parliamentary Elections: OSCE/ODIHR Election Observation Mission Final Report*.

Organization for Security and Co-operation in Europe, Office for Democratic Institutions and Human Rights (OSCE/ODIHR) (2013a) *Review of Electoral Legislation and Practice in OSCE Participating States*.

Organization for Security and Co-operation in Europe, Office for Democratic Institutions and Human Rights (OSCE/ODIHR) (2013b) *Republic of Azerbaijan, Presidential Election, 9 October 2013*, OSCE/ODIHR Election Observation Mission Final Report, Warsaw, 24 December 2013.

Organization for Security and Co-operation in Europe, Office for Democratic Institutions and Human Rights (OSCE/ODIHR) (2013c) *Needs Assessment Mission Report: Republic of Azerbaijan Presidential Election*.

Organization for Security and Co-operation in Europe, Office for Democratic Institutions and Human Rights (OSCE/ODIHR) (2013d) *Statement of Preliminary Findings and Conclusions, Republic of Albania Parliamentary Elections*.

Organization for Security and Co-operation in Europe, Office for Democratic Institutions and Human Rights (OSCE/ODIHR) (2013e) *Republic of Armenia Presidential Election 18 February 2013: Election Observation Mission Final Report*.

Radio Free Europe, Radio Liberty (RFE/RL) (2013) 'Controversial Tajik Tycoon Falls from Grace', 25 December, available at http://www.rferl.org/content/tajikistan-zayd-saidov-convicted/25212375.html

Schroder, H.-H. (1999) 'El'tsin and the Oligarchs: The Role of Financial Groups in Russian Politics Between 1993 and July 1998', *Europe-Asia Studies*, 51(6).

Service-Public.fr (2014) 'Salaire minimum de croissance (Smic)' [Minimum wage], available at http://vosdroits.service-public.fr/particuliers/F2300.xhtml

Shelley, L. (1998) 'Organized Crime and Corruption in Ukraine: Impediments to the Development of a Free Market Economy', *Demokratizatsiya*.

Sindelar, D. (2013) 'How Far Will Nazarbaev Go To Take Down Mukhtar Ablyazov?', *RFE/RL Features*, 7 June.

Sjoberg, F. M. (2011) *Competitive Elections in Authoritarian States: Weak States, Strong Elites, and Fractional Societies in Central Asia and Beyond*, PhD Dissertation. Uppsala: Uppsala University.

Sjoberg, F. M. and Herron, E. (2013) 'Electoral Systems and Fraud: Evidence from Ukraine's 2012 Parliamentary Election', working paper.

Smilov, D. (2002) 'Governmental Favouritism in Bulgaria and Russia', in Stephen Kotkin and Andras Sajo (eds), *Political Corruption of Transition: A Sceptic's Handbook*. Budapest: Central European University Press.

Smilov, D. and Toplak, J. (2007) *Political Finance and Corruption in Eastern Europe: The Transition Period*. Aldershot: Ashgate Publishing Ltd.

Teleradio Moldova (2013) 'Moldovan Political Parties to Get State-budget Funding', 19 June, available at http://www.trm.md/en/politic/partidele-politice-ar-putea-sa-fie-finantate-din-bugetul-de-stat/

Transparency International (2009) *Political Finance Regulations: Bridging the Enforcement Gap*, available at http://www.transparency.org/whatwedo/pub/policy_position_no._02_2009_political_finance_regulations_bridging_the_enfo

Transparency International (2013) *Buying Influence: Money and Elections in the Balkans*, available at http://www.transparency.org/whatwedo/pub/buying_influence_money_and_elections_in_the_balkans

Transparency International Georgia (2010) *The Use of Administrative Resources for Election Campaign 2010 Local Self-Government Elections*, available at http://gateway.transparency.org/tools/detail/105

Transparency International Georgia (2012a) *Pre-Election Period Monitoring Results, August 1 to September 27*, available at http://transparency.ge/sites/default/files/post_attachments/Pre-Election%20Period%20Monitoring%20Results.pdf

Transparency International Georgia (2012b) *Georgia's Television Landscape August 2012*, available at http://transparency.ge/sites/default/files/post_attachments/Georgian%20Television%20Landscape%20Report%20English_0.pdf

Transparency International Hungary (2008) 'Transparent Campaign Financing!', 26 September, available at http://www.transparency.hu/Transparent_Campaing_Financing_?

Tynan, D. (2008) 'Freedom House Media Report Paints Bleak Picture for Central Asia', Caucasus, 28 April, available at http://www.eurasianet.org/departments/insight/articles/eav042908b.shtml

Ukrainian News Agency (2008) 'Experts Estimate Costs of Party's or Bloc's Campaign in Snap Rada Elections at USD 25–100 Million', 22 October.

United States Department of Labor (2009) Wages: Minimum Wage, available at http://www.dol.gov/dol/topic/wages/minimumwage.htm

US Department of State (2013) 'Country Reports on Human Rights Practices for 2012: Secretary's Preface', available at http://www.state.gov/j/drl/rls/hrrpt/humanrightsreport/index.htm#wrapper

Wilson, A. (2011) 'Latvia's Unnoticed Revolution: Analysing the Elections', 22 September, available at http://www.opendemocracy.net/od-russia/andrew-wilson/latvias-unnoticed-revolution-analysing-elections

Notes

1 For the purposes of this chapter, Eastern, Central and South-eastern Europe and Central Asia refers to (in alphabetical order) Albania, Armenia, Azerbaijan, Belarus, Bosnia and Herzegovina, Bulgaria, Croatia, Czech Republic, Estonia, the Former Yugoslav Republic of Macedonia (FYROM), Georgia, Hungary, Kazakhstan, Kyrgyzstan, Latvia, Lithuania, Moldova, Montenegro, Poland, Romania, Russia, Serbia, Slovakia, Slovenia, Tajikistan, Turkey, Turkmenistan, Ukraine and Uzbekistan.

2 This does not hold for Turkey, a country with no communist legacy.

3 CSCE 1990.

4 Ibid., p. 4.

5 Smilov 2002.

6 See http://www.freedomhouse.org/regions/central-and-eastern-europeeurasia

7 As evidenced by, for instance, the Freedom House scores for the time period. See Freedom House 2004.

8 Kynev 2011.

9 Smilov and Toplak 2007.

10 Matuszak 2012.

11 Koppel 2012.

12 Grigas 2012; OECD 2013, p. 145.

13 Smilov and Toplak 2007.

14 International IDEA 2013.

15 Kyiv Post 2013.

16 See, for instance, reports from the Group of States against Corruption (GRECO), established in 1999 by the CoE to monitor states' compliance with the organization's anti-corruption standards.

17 Council of Europe 2003.

18 OSCE/ODIHR 2011. The ODIHR is the main institution responsible for the 'human dimension' of security in the OSCE.

[19] OSCE/ODIHR 2011.

[20] Human Rights Watch 2013.

[21] The recent case of the main domestic election observation organization in Azerbaijan, the Election Monitoring and Democracy Studies Center (EMDS) illustrates this point. The EMDS has observed elections since the 2000s, but still has not been officially registered. See OSCE/ODIHR 2013c.

[22] According to the International IDEA Political Finance Database, 55 and 59 per cent of the countries covered in this chapter have a limit on the amount a donor can contribute to a political party over a non-election-specific time period and an election period, respectively, while 62 per cent have a limit on the amount a donor can contribute to a candidate.

[23] Throughout this publication, international dollars (I$) are presented alongside amounts in national currencies. The international dollar is a hypothetical currency that takes into account purchasing power parity and is therefore suitable for comparisons between countries. For countries in which the power purchasing power parity varies significantly from the United States (which is used as the baseline for the comparison), the I$ exchange rate may be considerably different from the nominal exchange rate. No conversions are given for US dollars (as this is by default the same amount as the I$) or for those instances where the original currency is unknown and a secondary currency such as the euro has been cited instead. For further information, see Annex V. In 2012 the minimum wage in Ukraine, as determined by the Social Policy Ministry, was USD 146 per month.

[24] Federal Election Commission 2013.

[25] United States Department of Labor 2009. Calculation based on the US hourly minimum wage of USD 7.25 (I$7.25) per hour.

[26] Service-Public.fr 2014.

[27] So-called membership fees in Russia are of particular interest in this regard. The 2012 GRECO report explains how membership fees are distinct from donations and that they can be given without any upper limit, as opposed to specific caps established for monetary donations. The report's authors were 'made aware of important sums of money being voluntarily given as membership fees to political parties by influential business persons and elected members of parliament'. The existing legal framework in Russia creates ample opportunities for circumventing disclosure rules: see GRECO 2012.

[28] The case is best illustrated by a quotation: 'In particular, the party [Klaus' party, the Civic Democratic Party, CDP] received several large gifts from two fictitious donors (including a dead Hungarian) that actually proved to come from a businessman, Milan Srejber, who had won a successful bid to gain ownership of one of the major Moravian steelworks under the CDP government'. Orenstein 2001.

[29] International IDEA 2013.

[30] Estonian Public Broadcasting 2013.

[31] The Reform Party leadership has disputed the details in Meikar's story.

[32] Schroder 1999.

[33] Wilson 2011.

[34] As head of the petroleum company Yukos, Khodorkovsky was one of the richest men in Russia in the early 2000s. Around the time of Putin's ascendancy he started to finance human rights groups and parties that were critical of the Kremlin. He was charged with fraud in 2003, convicted two years later and imprisoned until the end of 2013. Some have argued that the legal case against Khodorkovsky was politically motivated.

[35] An illustrative case is that of Zayd Saidov, a prominent Tajikistani businessman who was imprisoned on multiple charges in December 2013 after he announced earlier that year the creation of a new political party (see RFE/RL 2013). Another example is the case of the oppositional Kazakh businessman Mukhtar Ablyazov, whose wife and six-year-old

daughter were deported from Italy in a move that suggested political pressure from the authorities in Kazakhstan. See Sindelar 2013.

36   For instance, the alleged narcotics boss Naser Kelmendi, who was arrested, is speculated to have connections to the ruling party in Montenegro. See Karadaku 2013.

37   Mladenovic 2012.

38   Leviev-Sawyer 2011.

39   Smilov and Toplak 2007

40   Sjoberg 2011.

41   Kupatadze 2008.

42   Shelley 1998.

43   Teleradio Moldova 2013.

44   *Chicago Tribune* 1997.

45   For example, in the Czech Republic political parties received a total subsidy of 866,445,067 koruny (CZK) (I\$59.67 million) in 2010. See GRECO 2011.

46   GRECO 2012, p. 26.

47   CNN 2011.

48   Ibid.

49   OSCE/ODIHR 2013a, p. 21.

50   OSCE/ODIHR 2013e.

51   Ibid.

52   For donations to parties, 87 per cent of countries outlaw them.

53   Smilov and Toplak 2007.

54   Grzymala-Busse 2003.

55   *Balkan Insight* 2009.

56   Ibid.

57   Bajovic and Manojlovic 2013.

58   Network for Affirmation of NGO Sector 2013, p. 6. A parliamentary committee was set up as a result of these tape recordings, but it concluded its work without reaching any conclusions, and the prosecutor's office concluded that there had been no corruption among senior party officials.

59   OSCE/ODIHR 2013a, p. 26.

60   OSCE/ODIHR 2013b, p. 16.

61   OSCE/ODIHR 2012, p. 15.

62   De Waal 2012.

63   Transparency International Georgia 2012b.

64   De Waal 2012.

65   US Department of State 2013.

66   *Kyiv Post* 2012c.

67   Ibid.

68   *Kyiv Post* 2012a, 2012d; Ukrainian News Agency 2008. In October 2008, Ukrainian experts estimated that a small political party that wanted to win seats in parliament would spend up to \$30 million (I\$30 million) on the campaign and that large political parties would spend up to USD 100 million (I\$100 million). Political analyst Pavlo Bulhak stated that a party's election budget would be spent on advertising on television, bribing voters, organizing rallies and party propaganda.

69 *Kyiv Post* 2012a.

70 *Kyiv Post* 2012d.

71 Transparency International Hungary 2008.

72 For a reference to vote buying in the Roma community, see OSCE/ODIHR 2013e.

73 The transaction took place during a public holiday event organized by the government-affiliated local governor. See Transparency International Georgia 2012a.

74 Gonzalez-Ocantos et al. 2012.

75 Sjoberg and Herron 2013.

76 See for instance OSCE Kosovo 2007.

77 IFES 2010.

78 Čigāne 2007.

79 Smilov and Toplak 2007.

80 The OSCE report appendix lists all the in-kind contributions. See OSCE Kosovo 2004.

81 Smilov and Toplak 2007.

82 Nassmacher 2003.

83 Smilov and Topak 2007.

84 Transparency International 2013.

85 Ibid.

86 Ibid.

87 See, for example, the cases described in Ohman 2013, pp. 175–80.

88 De Waal 2012.

89 It should be noted that the Georgian Dream falls into the category of 'oligarchic parties', which is widespread in the post-Soviet space. One wonders what the overall assessment of the regime should be if it takes a billionaire to offset the self-entrenchment efforts of political parties.

90 Smilov and Topak 2007.

91 Transparency International Georgia 2010. The organization has also monitored the same issue in subsequent elections.

92 Čigāne 2007.

93 Transparency International 2009.

94 Tynan 2008.

95 For instance in Uzbekistan, where no genuine oppositional parties are allowed to participate in elections, each of the officially sanctioned parties is entitled to 40 minutes per week on state-funded TV and radio, and half a page twice per week in the three daily state newspapers. Media monitoring by the OSCE/ODIHR notes that media companies generally complied with this obligation. See OSCE/ODIHR 2009.

96 Human Rights Watch 2012. This document outlined several concerns about media freedom in Hungary, including the independence of the Media Council, self-censorship by independent media and political interference in public television editorial content.

97 Baykurt 2013.

98 Freedom House 2013.

99 Smilov and Toplak 2008.

100 Policy makers are defined as those involved in the drafting, amending and adopting political finance policies, either from the executive or from the legislative arm of government. The focus is therefore on the role policy makers play rather than on a particular institution.

CHAPTER 7

CHAPTER 7

Northern, Western and Southern Europe

D. R. Piccio[*]

Introduction

Financial resources play a crucial role in determining which actors participate in the political process in modern democracies. The importance of the ways in which political parties access and use financial resources has stimulated the regulation of political finance around the world, including in Northern, Western and Southern Europe.[1] This chapter identifies the most important challenges of political finance legislation in these countries and compares European regulatory patterns (implementation and effectiveness in particular) to those in other regions.

Northern, Western and Southern Europe are among the richest regions in the world; their democratic institutions have progressively stabilized since the end of World War II. Parties in these regions were traditionally founded on a mass-membership basis with ties to civil society such as trade unions and church organizations. Although this historical model is changing, and party membership is declining, it has influenced the process of finance regulation, which was introduced to solve common social, financial and political needs of political parties. On the one hand, regulation was introduced alongside public funding for political parties and candidates to allow all elements of society to access the political arena, and to help counteract the decline in party membership and defray the increased costs of politics. On the other hand, states aimed to use such regulation to control the inflow of money into politics in order to prevent corruption and limit the influence of powerful donors.

The established liberal democracies in Northern, Western and Southern Europe have been less inclined to regulate political finance than the

* The author would like to thank Ingrid van Biezen and her colleagues in the research team of the 'Re-conceptualizing Party Democracy project (http://www.partylaw.leidenuniv.nl) for the many fruitful discussions on topics related to this paper. The usual disclaimer applies.

neighbouring post-communist democracies in Central and Eastern Europe. Countries that have more recently made the transition to democracy after a non-democratic experience have been found to be more inclined to regulate political parties than earlier democratizers.[2]

Despite having common needs and concerns, the diverse traditions, political philosophies and social attitudes toward the role that political parties should play in representative democracies have so far prevented the establishment of a homogeneous regulation in Northern, Western and Southern Europe. However, there is a trend toward greater harmonization of regulation, especially with regard to transparency requirements.

Challenges and problems of political finance in Northern, Western and Southern Europe

European governmental and non-governmental organizations agree that regulating the financial management of political parties is essential for promoting the principles of democracy and the rule of law.[3] Yet political finance regulation still faces significant challenges. First, such regulation has not provided a solution to some of the underlying problems, such as political corruption and illicit financial practices in politics. In recent years, scandals related to the issue of money in politics have been revealed in Northern, Western and Southern Europe that are as great as anywhere else on the globe: Spain, Greece, the United Kingdom (UK)[4] and France, for example, have battled multimillion-euro political finance scandals involving the abuse of government funds, illegal donations flowing into the parties or slush funds set up to buy favours from elected politicians.

Second, there is weak oversight and enforcement of regulations, with political actors able to exploit loopholes in the legislation. A third problem relates to parties' growing dependency on the state after the introduction of a widespread (and generous) public funding system for political parties and candidates. The final challenge is the persisting gender gap in the region.

Political corruption

Political corruption remains a major problem in Europe. Reform to curb corrupt behaviour is often initiated in the aftermath of political finance scandals and public outcry. The level of corruption in Europe is thought to have risen in recent years,[5] which suggests that the political finance regulations have not achieved their aims. Indeed, countries that have adopted more political finance rules—such as Greece, Portugal and Spain—are perceived as having the most corrupt parties, while countries with less rigorous regulation—such as Denmark, Switzerland and Sweden—have the lowest levels of perceived corruption.[6]

> If not adequately drafted, political finance rules may have the opposite effect: instead of preventing corrupt practices, they may motivate political actors to circumvent the rules or become more sophisticated in concealing illicit donations, thereby undermining the democratic values and principles behind political finance regulation.

Yet the relationship between political finance regulation and political corruption is complex, and very much depends on the quality of regulation itself; it is difficult to establish causal relationships between the two. High levels of political finance regulation may be adopted to combat high levels of corruption.[7] If not adequately drafted, political finance rules may have the opposite effect: instead of preventing corrupt practices, they may motivate political actors to circumvent the rules or become more sophisticated in concealing illicit donations, thereby undermining the democratic values and principles behind political finance regulation.

Weak enforcement

The mere presence of political finance regulation does not guarantee its implementation. The Group of States against Corruption (GRECO) emphasizes two main problems in its recommendations to Northern, Western and Southern European countries. The first is that few oversight organs are granted effective monitoring and enforcement powers. Financial audits often lack investigative power and focus on procedural aspects, and are therefore unable to trace the actual sources of income and expenditures. Moreover, insufficient cooperation between the investigative and auditing authorities allows political actors to engage in illegal financial practices with little risk of being sanctioned. The second problem relates to the loopholes that are still present in much of the political finance legislation.

Parties' state dependency

The acknowledgement that (1) money in politics matters, (2) the political process should be accessible by all political actors and (3) the organizational continuity of political parties, which matters for party system stability, has motivated the introduction of public funding of political parties and candidates in the region. While public funding has helped political parties survive and face the growing costs of politics, it has also made them financially dependent on state resources. Given the declining linkages between political parties and citizens in Europe, high financial dependence on the state may appear paradoxical: states help maintain political organizations that have loosening linkages with society, at the risk of (generously) sustaining political actors that are present only at the institutional level.

Gender inequality

The under-representation of women in political life is a persistent problem in Northern, Western and Southern Europe. The Council of Europe has urged member states to support gender balance in political life and public decision making, and to adopt special measures to achieve balanced participation and to representation in all sectors of society, including legally binding quotas.[8] Yet Northern, Western and Southern Europe still lack binding requirements for promoting women's representation, and few countries in the region have political finance mechanisms that aim to promote women's representation. Linking public funding to gender equality requirements would help encourage parties to address women's political empowerment and level the playing field among (male and female) candidates. This issue is discussed further below.

Overview of political finance regulations

This section discusses the regional standards in political finance regulation. First, it provides an overview of regulation since the end of World War II. Second, it examines the main traditions of political finance legislation in the area and identifies the main patterns of legislative intervention. Finally, it highlights recent trends in political finance reforms, including harmonization of the different legal frameworks.

The growing regulation of political finance

The degree to which states should intervene in financing political parties and candidates touches on an underlying debate about how political parties are (and ought to be) conceived. Liberal tradition envisages political parties as private associations that should be free of state interference, including in their financial management. Another body of thought perceives parties as private entities that function as 'public utilities'; state intervention is seen as a necessary means of guaranteeing the fair functioning of democratic processes.[9] The laissez-faire treatment of political parties has typically characterized countries with a longer democratic experience.[10] For example, Sweden has a long history of democratic institutions; its constitution contains no codification of political parties, it has no laws regulating party activity or organizational functioning, and legislation regulating parties' income was introduced for the first time in 2014. Spain is an example of the opposite—after the Franco dictatorship, it developed a strong tradition of party regulation, reflected in various laws concerning party activity.

The growing regulation of political parties in various sources of party law seems to indicate the decline of the liberal tradition.[11] This is particularly true for political finance regulation, as the introduction of public funding for political parties and candidates has justified increasing state intervention in their internal (financial) management. There is growing consensus around the principle of *do ut des*: the idea that there must be a balance between privileges that political parties obtain and the constraints to which they are subject. Hence, as states grant public financing to political parties and candidates, the latter must adhere to more specific rules.[12] The introduction of direct public subsidies for political parties and the adoption of rules on party income and expenditure prompted a growing number of countries to introduce comprehensive legislation concerning different aspects of political finance (see Figure 7.1.).

Figure 7.1. Year of introduction of political finance laws for parties and candidates in Northern, Western and Southern Europe

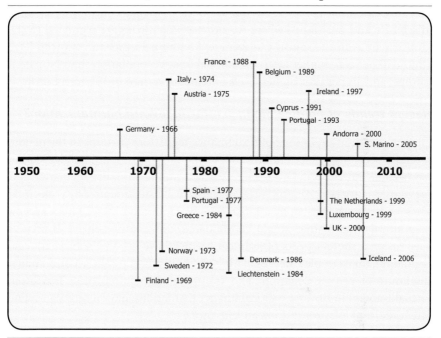

Source: Piccio 2012.

Since the first regulation was adopted in Germany in 1966,[13] there has been a considerable increase in the number of party finance laws in the region. At the end of the 1970s, only eight countries had introduced a law on political finance; two decades later 17 countries had done so. Today only three countries in the region do not have a specific political finance act, two of which are European micro-states.[14] Andorra and San Marino adopted their first political finance laws in 2000 and 2005, respectively, whereas Malta, Monaco and Switzerland have not established any.

Traditions of political finance regulation

Older liberal democracies in the region have historically been more reluctant to infringe on the freedom of association of political parties and have introduced less stringent regulation over political parties' (financial) activities than the neighbouring Eastern European democracies. Yet there is considerable variation in the regulatory patterns within Northern, Western and Southern Europe. Examining the main clusters of political finance rules—including the regulation of income and spending, and enforcement and oversight mechanisms—reveals that countries in Southern Europe generally have higher levels of political finance regulation than those in the north and west. The only exception is the regulation of political finance control mechanisms (disclosure and oversight), where the northern countries are regulated to the same extent as in the south. On average, Southern European countries have almost 10 per cent higher levels of political finance regulation than Northern Europe, and 16 per cent higher levels of regulation than in Western Europe.[15]

Recent trends of political finance reform: toward harmonization?

Despite the variation in the political finance regulatory patterns in the region, several aspects suggest a trend toward greater harmonization. First, legislation has become more specific over time. Whereas political finance regulation was previously dispersed among several legislative instruments (e.g., electoral acts, media laws), legislators are increasingly combining the different aspects of political finance into single consolidated and comprehensive legislative acts. Second, more aspects of political finance have become subject to legal regulation, for example rules regulating mechanisms of public accountability, disclosure of private donations and transparency requirements. The latter, virtually absent in the first political finance regulations, have received growing attention from Western European legislators.

The European Union (EU) and various governmental and non-governmental organizations (such as the Council of Europe, the Organization for Security and Co-operation in Europe/Office for Democratic Institutions and Human Rights [OSCE/ODIHR], the Venice Commission, GRECO and Transparency International) have played an important role in promoting the harmonization of legislative frameworks on political finance. In the last decade especially, EU actors have issued an increasing number of reports and recommendations aimed at establishing 'good practices' and 'common principles' related to the transparency of (and public access to) the financial management of political parties and candidates.[16]

Sources of income of political parties and candidates

In order to give all political parties and candidates the opportunity to participate in the electoral competition on an equal basis, and translate into practice the democratic principle of the level playing field, states have introduced various means to control the inflow of money in political life. Private sources of income, traditionally the most important avenues for political funding, range from membership fees to small and larger private donations to income from elected officials. Public sources of income include direct funding for political parties, candidates or election campaigns from the state, as well as indirect state financing through the provision of media access, tax deductions, or the provision of other financial or logistic advantages to political actors. Despite the regulations in force, however, illicit practices of political funding still remain a common and persistent problem throughout the region.

Private funding of political parties

Private funding (membership fees, donations, salary deductions from elected officials, candidates' personal funds) has traditionally accounted for most of political party income, but this is shifting toward public funding. Membership fees and small contributions to political parties and candidates are generally considered beneficial, and serve as a civil society endorsement of political party legitimacy. Together with voter turnout, party membership and party identification figures, 'grass-roots financing' is an expression of citizens' political engagement. Large donations, especially from legal persons (i.e. non-human entities such as corporations, trade unions or other organized interest associations that are treated as persons for limited legal purposes), are perceived as having a pernicious influence. Indeed, private funding is one of the most evident ways in which individual or special interests may 'buy' political representatives in exchange for financial concessions, benefits and favours.

Membership fees and small donations

Membership fees currently account for only a small portion of political parties' income, which represents a shift in some countries. In Norway, for example, membership fees accounted for over half of total party income in the 1950s and 1960s, but now comprise approximately 5 per cent.[17] This drop might be explained by the extreme decrease in party membership that Norwegian parties have experienced since the 1990s.[18] In other countries, membership fees have always constituted a practically irrelevant source of income; membership levels have always been low in Portugal, and only 1 to 2 per cent of political parties' total income in the early 1990s derived from membership fees.[19]

As Table 7.1. shows, for the period between 1950 and 1990, the importance of membership fees has declined over time in the majority of the larger Northern, Western and Southern European countries, in some cases even shrinking to one-third of the original share in party income. More recent figures show how this trend has continued until today.

Table 7.1. Membership fees as a percentage of total party income in Northern, Western and Southern Europe, 1950–90

Country	1950s	1960s	1970s	1980s
Austria	88	87	45	26
Denmark	61	59	48	44
Finland	2	2	3	3
Ireland	45	31	45	39
Italy	43	30	14	17
The Netherlands	84	78	73	73
Norway	55	54	28	32
Sweden	25	15	7	8
UK	13	15	21	37

Source: Krouwel 1999, p. 68 (adapted by the author).

In the UK, where longitudinal data point to an increasing significance of membership fees as a percentage of total party income from the 1950s to the 1980s, current figures show a share of 11 per cent. Recent estimates from different sources reveal that membership fees constitute 5 per cent of total party income in Belgium, 13 per cent in France, and 5 per cent in Greece.[20] In Sweden, long known for grass-roots involvement in party politics, voluntary income disclosure by the parliamentary political parties indicates that only 3 per cent of their income came from membership dues in 2011.[21] Political parties still very much rely on membership fees in Ireland, Germany and the Netherlands. In Ireland and Germany, over one-third of total party income derives from membership fees. In the Netherlands they accounted for over 45 per cent of total party income in 2000.[22]

Party income from membership fees may vary significantly not only across countries or over time, but also across political parties. In France, for example, income from total party membership fees in 2004 ranged from 719,133 euros (EUR) (I$849,000) for the Ligue Communiste Révolutionnaire to EUR 8,172,652 (I$9,650,000)[23] for the Parti Socialiste, constituting 30 and 18 per cent respectively of the parties' total incomes.[24] The most recent available data for Norway (2009) show total membership fees ranging from 21,150 Norwegian krones (NOK) (I$2,300) for the Christian Coalition Party to NOK 2,895,481 (I$316,000) for the Christian Democratic Party, constituting 3 and 8 per cent, respectively, of the two parties' total income.[25]

In addition to membership fees, political parties receive income from voluntary contributions by party members and donations from non-members. Obtaining comprehensive and consistent data on these smaller donations and contributions to political parties has always been challenging due to the lack of available information.[26] Moreover, official figures (as well as subsequent analyses) frequently merge membership fees and small donations[27] since it is impossible to distinguish between the two. More recently, the increased importance of transparency in Northern, Western and Southern Europe has improved access to information on all donations to both political parties and candidates. In some cases this stems directly from regulations prescribing compulsory formats in which smaller donations must also be reported and made publicly accessible. Since a 2007 amendment to its political finance law, for example, political parties in Luxembourg have been obliged to disclose information on individual donations exceeding EUR 250 (I\$290). This provides the opportunity to assess private donation levels in greater detail, and to compare the ratio between small and large donations to political parties. Is it the case, as is commonly acknowledged, that private funding to political parties mainly consists of large donations, and that smaller donations no longer constitute a relevant source of income to political parties?

Table 7.2. Reported donations to political parties in Luxembourg, 2009–11

	2009*	2010	2011
<EUR 1,000 (I\$1,200)	EUR 26,009 (I\$30,000) (29%)	EUR 18,748 (I\$22,000) (71%)	EUR 103,802 (I\$120,000) (63%)
>EUR 1,000 (I\$1,200)	EUR 63,885 (I\$74,000) (71%)	EUR 7,513 (I\$8,700) (29%)	EUR 61,894 (I\$72,000) (37%)
Total amount of donations reported	EUR 89,894 (I\$104,000) (100%)	EUR 26,261 (I\$30,000) (100%)	EUR 165,696 (I\$191,000) (100%)
Total number of reported donations	<EUR 1,000 (I\$1,200): 63 >EUR 1,000 (I\$1,200): 24 Total: 85	<EUR 1,000 (I\$1,200): 61 >EUR 1,000 (I\$1,200): 6 Total: 67	<EUR 1,000 (I\$1,200): 169 >EUR 1,000 (I\$1,200): 43 Total: 212

Source: Chambre des Députés du Grand-duché de Luxembourg.

*Election year: national parliamentary elections and elections to the European Parliament

The breakdown of donations reported in Table 7.2. shows how small donations[28] represent a larger proportion of Luxembourgish political parties' income than large donations. For both 2010 and 2011, they accounted for over 60 per cent of total donations received. The figures were reversed in 2009, when both national elections and elections to the European Parliament (EP) took place: larger donations—including two donations exceeding EUR 10,000 (I\$12,000)—accounted for almost three-quarters of total donations.

The increased attention being given to transparency principles has also encouraged (or sometimes required) more political parties to publish their annual financial statements on their website, often including detailed information on donations received. For example, since 2003 the Dutch Social Democratic Party (Partij van de Arbeid, PvdA) has posted its annual financial accounts on its website, including donations above EUR 500 (I\$610).

Table 7.3. Reported donations to the Dutch Social Democratic Party, 2010–12

	2010*	2011	2012*
<EUR 1,000 (I$1,200)	EUR 21,241 (I$26,000) (37%)	EUR 7,500 (I$9,100) (39%)	EUR 15,910 (I$19,000) (31%)
>EUR 1,000 (I$1,200)	EUR 35,443 (I$43,000) (63%)	EUR 11,850 (I$14,000) (61%)	EUR 35,313 (I$43,000) (69%)
Total amount of donations reported	EUR 56,684 (I$69,000) (100%)	EUR 19,350 (I$23,000) (100%)	EUR 51,223 (I$62,000) (100%)
Total number of reported donations	<EUR 1,000 (I$1,200): 37 >EUR 1,000 (I$1,200): 20 Total: 57	<EUR 1,000 (I$1,200): 14 >EUR 1,000 (I$1,200): 6 Total: 20	<EUR 1,000 (I$1,200): 29 >EUR 1,000 (I$1,200): 22 Total: 51

Source: http://www.pvda.nl/

*Election year: national parliamentary elections

Although large donations appear to make up the bulk of total party income from private contributions to the PvdA, smaller donations accounted for almost one-third of private contributions to the party in 2010, 2011 and 2012. Yet in both Luxembourg and the Netherlands, private contributions represent only a small portion of total party income. In Luxembourg, the most important source of party income is state funding (see Figure 7.5.). In the case of the PvdA, state funding accounts for almost 40 per cent of total income.

Small donations are not an important source of income in Austria, France, Norway, Greece or Belgium. This might be explained by the general trend of disenchantment with political parties in Northern, Western and Southern Europe,[29] which has resulted in a decline in citizen contributions. Belgium has seen a steady decline in both the amounts of donations to political parties (they accounted for only 0.3 per cent of total party income in 2007) and the number of donations to candidates.[30]

Large donations and corporate contributions

Overall, the 'beneficial' sources of private income have been declining, as membership fees and small donations no longer constitute a reliable source of income for parties in Northern, Western and Southern Europe. But do the 'pernicious' sources of private income play a relevant role in parties' financial inflows? Information on large donations to political parties is now more easily accessible. Transparency requirements have been introduced to give citizens information about the larger financial flows to political parties, in particular from companies and business enterprises.

Previous research has reported a pattern of corporations withdrawing from politics, indicating a decline in corporate contributions as a source of political funding.[31] Evidence of a long-term decline has been observed in Germany and Sweden, but also in the UK, where corporate donations formerly constituted the most relevant source of party revenue, especially for the Conservative Party. According to recent analyses, the proportion of donations to the Conservatives from the financial services sector has now dropped to 51.4 per cent of total income, from 60–90 per cent in the 1950s to the late 1980s.[32] The decline of corporate donations to the UK Conservative Party since the 1990s has been explained by the Labour Party's ideological changes—in particular its departure from socialism (which meant that there was less cause for companies to make significant donations to the Conservatives)—and by a growing negative perception of corporate donations on the part of the public: businesses perceived such donations as a controversial practice to be avoided.[33] Ireland has also experienced a decline in corporate contributions. Comparing the 2011 political parties' donations statements with those from 2002,[34] it is remarkable to observe that not only the total amount of reported donations decreased considerably (from EUR 265,800 [I$301,000] in 2002 to EUR 30,997 [I$35,000] in 2011), but also the number of corporate donations has dropped. Noticeably, the most relevant source of income among the private contributions disclosed by Irish political parties is contributions from members of the Dáil Éireann (House of Representatives) and members of the EP (MEPs). Recent data published by the Treasury of the Italian Chamber of Deputies show similar figures. Of the reported private contributions by the two major Italian political parties (Partito Democratico and Popolo della Libertà) for 2012, no large or corporate contributions appear, despite the lowering of the reporting threshold from EUR 50,000 (I$62,000) to EUR 5,000 (I$6,200) in 2012. While there may be some undisclosed corporate donations that are not revealed by the official data, there does appear to be a trend of reduced corporate donations, which could be attributed to an overall drop in support for politics and political parties. Alternatively, large donors may simply have been scared off by the heightened transparency requirements. This decrease in corporate contributions appears to be offset by individual contributions from individual members of parliament (MPs) and MEPs.[35] Large donations also constitute only a small part of the total income of political parties in Greece, the Netherlands, Sweden and Norway.

Further sources of private income for political parties and candidates may derive from the activity of 'third parties', that is, issue advocacy groups or individuals that campaign for individual candidates, political parties or issues. Continental Western Europe has so far had very little third-party regulation; Ireland and the UK are the only countries in the region that have established donation ceilings and expenditure limits for third parties. Spain has a specific ban on third-party donations.

Bank loans are another source of income. Greek political parties have been borrowing from banks since the end of the 1990s, providing (future) state financing as a guarantee. Over time, this type of income has become increasingly more significant. In 2001, bank loans accounted for 33 and 11 per cent of the total income of the two main political parties in Greece

(PASOK and Nea Democratia); in 2007 bank loans accounted for 63 and 42 per cent, respectively.[36]

Large donations and contributions from companies are considered potentially dangerous for democratic political processes. Thus states have introduced different types of rules to prevent or limit the possibility that private companies or wealthy individuals can influence the political arena, and to enable political parties to maintain sufficient independence from the private interests of a wealthy few. This has been done by imposing qualitative and/or quantitative restrictions on the private income of political parties and candidates.

Qualitative restrictions: contribution bans

The sources of private funding that have been most frequently subject to restrictions are foreign entities, corporations, (semi-)public institutions and trade unions. A large number of states also prohibit political parties and candidates from accepting anonymous contributions and set limits on cash donations. According to the Committee of Ministers of the Council of Europe, states should introduce qualitative restrictions on the sources of private funding to political parties in order to avoid prejudicing the activities of political parties, and to ensure their independence.[37]

Three findings can be derived from an analysis of five common contribution bans (donations from trade unions, anonymous sources, semi-public organizations, foreign entities and corporations) in Northern, Western and Southern Europe.

First, most Northern, Western and Southern European countries prohibit donations from foreign entities, companies with mixed public and private capital, and anonymous donations. Second, bans on contributions to political parties or candidates are significantly more common in Southern European countries (over 45 per cent), whereas less than 30 per cent of Western European and Nordic countries restrict private donations. This may be explained in part by the Southern European countries' overall higher levels of regulation. Third, there is no significant distinction between regulating parties and regulating candidates, which is common in other parts of the world.

In practice, however, the mere presence of contribution bans in the political finance legal framework does not ensure that rules are indeed implemented, or that financial flows do not take place outside the regulated area—particularly when mechanisms of rule enforcement and sanctions are poorly developed. Portugal (along with France and Greece) has introduced the greatest number of restrictions on private donations to political parties and candidates. Through various amendments introduced in the political finance legislation since the mid-1990s, all the main sources of donations discussed above have been banned in Portugal (including corporate donations, since 2000). Yet illegal donations to parties and candidates still take place, and circumvention of the rules is commonplace.[38] Figure 7.2. shows the number of infractions related to private donations, as identified by external financial audits.

Figure 7.2. Infractions related to annual private donations in Portugal, 1994–2007

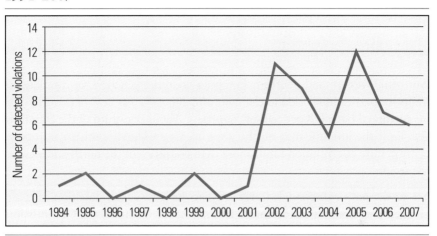

Source: De Sousa 2012, p. 15 (adapted by the author).

Figure 7.2. shows that the number of detected violations on private donations to political parties and candidates has increased considerably in Portugal during the last ten years. This trend can be explained in part by the strengthening of the political finance supervision that was established in Portugal in the mid-1990s. After being unmonitored for almost 20 years, party financial activity came under the supervision of a newly established independent body and became more accurately controlled.[39] Yet this figure also shows how rules restricting private donations have all but encouraged political actors to rely on illegal practices. For example, an inquiry was opened in 2005 after party officials of the Christian Democratic Party allegedly made a list of non-existent names to justify the origin of 105 cash donations deposited in their electoral accounts.[40] In March 2010, the Christian Democratic Party and two other parties were fined for irregularities in campaign financing, including illicit funding.[41]

Quantitative restrictions: contribution limits

The Committee of Ministers of the Council of Europe recommended that states should set contribution limits.[42] European countries have established comparatively high levels that eligible donors are allowed to contribute to political parties or candidates (see Table 7.4.).

Table 7.4. Annual limits on contributions to political parties in Northern, Western and Southern Europe*

	Belgium	Cyprus	Finland	France	Greece	Iceland	Ireland**	Portugal	Spain
Euros	4,000 (I$4,700)	8,000 (I$11,000)	30,000 (I$32,000)	7,500 (I$8,900)	15,000 (I$20,000)	2,800 (I$20)	2,500 (I$2,800)	10,650 (I$15,000)	100,000 (I$135,000)

Source: International IDEA Political Finance Database.

*Donations from natural persons only
**As of the 2012 political finance reform

Northern, Western and Southern European countries generally set contribution limits for parties in relation to election campaigns (42 per cent of countries) or on an annual basis (38 per cent of countries). About one-third of the countries also limit the amount that can be given to a candidate. Southern European countries use contribution limits more than countries in the north and west of the region.

Yet, as the political scandals in recent years have revealed, donation caps are violated and legally circumvented. In France, for instance, the Commission Nationale des Comptes de Campagne et des Financements Politiques (CNCCFP) reported on the circumvention of donation caps by establishing 'satellite parties'.[43] Under French legislation, while a donor may contribute a maximum of EUR 7,500 (I$8,900) to a political party per year, no regulation prevents donations up to this amount to several political groups, and no regulation prevents the beneficiary parties from transferring donations to another political movement. Thus, the Commission warned that these 'satellite' groups (which increased in number from 28 in 1999 to 255 in 2004) act as financial conduits for individual donations and allow larger parties to circumvent the maximum ceiling on individual donations.[44] Despite this loophole in legislation, the CNCCFP more recently reported that there is no evidence of substantial financial flows from satellite parties to larger parties; on the contrary, a large number of satellite parties benefit from funding from larger parties.[45]

Public funding of political parties

Indirect public funding

State funding is provided to political parties and candidates in two main forms: direct funding of party organizations and campaign activities, or indirect funding, e.g. media access in public broadcasting, tax benefits, use of public town halls for meetings, etc.[46] Depending on which type of indirect public funding is available, it can be a sensible cost-efficient complement (or alternative) to direct public funding, which involves direct monetary transfers that in many cases can be used freely by the recipient. Thus indirect public funding has another major benefit: it can more easily be targeted to help level the playing field in a specific area.

Northern, Western and Southern European countries do not provide free or subsidized media access more than countries in other regions in the world. While two-thirds of these European states offer this provision to parties, only one-third do so for candidates. Thirty per cent of the states that do offer media provisions offer it equally to all eligible parties. It would be unrealistic to provide it to all candidates.

All Northern, Western and Southern European states except Liechtenstein offer some type of indirect public funding provisions—tax benefits are the most common—and these provisions are much higher than elsewhere in the world. Such funding provisions can, however, differ significantly in scope and generosity. Examples range from the modest Swedish provision, whereby party secretaries enjoy free access to technical equipment and premises in the Riksdag (the parliament), to Cyprus, where public funding and private donations to parties are exempt from taxation. Other countries, such as Iceland, offer tax relief for donors in order to incentivize grass-roots donations. Space for placing campaign materials is another popular type of indirect public funding; it is offered in seven states, most commonly in the form of free designated spaces to display campaign posters.

Direct public funding

Figure 7.3. Northern, Western and Southern European countries that offer direct public funding for political parties

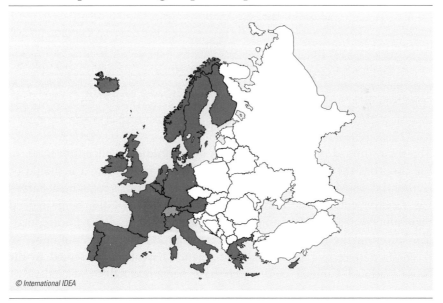

© International IDEA

■ Yes
■ No

Source: International IDEA. This map is based on data collected up to February 2014. Data are continuously updated on the International IDEA Political Finance Database. See http://www.idea.int/political-finance/question.cfm?id=270

Of the 24 European countries considered in this chapter, only three offer no direct public funding to cover organizational expenses, campaign expenses, or both: Andorra, Malta and Switzerland. Figure 7.4. shows the year in which direct public funding was introduced in 17 of these countries.

Figure 7.4. The introduction of direct public funding of political parties in Northern, Western and Southern Europe

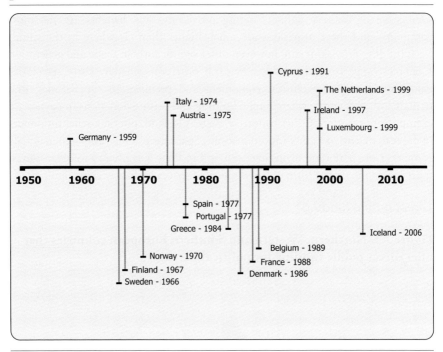

Source: http://www.partylaw.leidenuniv.nl

The trend toward introducing direct public subsidies is uncontroversial; in the countries that do not have it, there is debate over whether it should be introduced. In Malta, the introduction of public subsidies to political parties has recently entered the political agenda.[47] In Switzerland, while federal regulation is absent, two cantons (Geneva and Fribourg) have introduced legislation on the reimbursement of campaign expenses, and a number of recent initiatives to regulate political finance have been presented to the Swiss National Council (and so far have been rejected).[48] Switzerland is restrictive about introducing public funding due to its liberal tradition of non-interference by the state in the private sphere of political party activities. In the UK, which has very limited direct public funding of political parties, the possibility of introducing a more solid system of public funding has been intensively discussed, especially in the last 20 years.[49] However, this debate has not led to any major changes, partially due to the fear that parties would lose touch with their members once they are no longer financially dependent on them.

If levelling the playing field of electoral competitions is among the fundamental justifications for introducing direct public funding, thresholds for accessing this funding and deciding how the funds are distributed are crucial for its implementation.

As in most countries around the world,[50] most political finance regulations in Northern, Western and Southern Europe have defined eligibility for public funding based on a combination of two criteria: the share of votes obtained in parliamentary elections, and representation in the elected body. Only five countries in these regions (Spain, Belgium, the Netherlands,[51] Finland and the UK) provide direct public funding to just parliamentary parties. This approach has been criticized, as it undermines the principle of levelling the playing field: it makes it harder for new parties to enter the political arena and compete under fair conditions with the better-established parties. Indeed, under the OSCE/Venice Commission guidelines on party regulation, the pay-off threshold for public funding should be lower than the electoral threshold.[52]

The degree to which this criterion is harmful (or not) for the pluralism of political parties depends on the electoral threshold used. In Finland and the Netherlands, where the electoral threshold is particularly low,[53] the eligibility criterion of representation in an elected body clearly does not constitute a problem in terms of political pluralism. It may raise concerns in Spain and Belgium, where the electoral threshold is 3 and 5 per cent of the votes, respectively.

Northern, Western and Southern European countries' distribution criteria for public funding are also in line with those elsewhere in the world. The most common allocation procedure entails an equal sum distributed equally to all parties that meet the eligibility threshold ('absolute equality') and an additional variable sum, which is distributed in proportion to the votes or seats obtained in the most recent parliamentary elections ('equitability').

The German and Dutch allocation mechanisms include incentives to encourage citizens' political participation and stimulate political parties to maintain a social anchorage.[54] In Germany, funds are distributed based on both a party's success in the most recent elections and the amount of private donations received (the 'matching funds' rule). Under the German regulation, only a given percentage of the parties' income can be provided by the public purse, and public subsidies cannot be higher than the private funds raised by the party. This regulatory requirement plays a crucial role in keeping the state dependency of political parties in Germany the second-lowest in Western Europe. In the Netherlands, funds are distributed based on three criteria: a fixed amount is distributed to all parties represented in parliament; additional funds are distributed depending on the number of seats obtained; and a further amount is distributed in proportion to the number of contributing party members.

There is greater variation across countries with respect to provisions for how public funds should be used. Nearly half of the countries in Northern, Western and Southern Europe do not earmark public funds. Those that do prescribe their use in very general terms (i.e., 'campaign spending' or 'ongoing party activities'). Exceptions include Germany and the Netherlands, which earmark funds for membership education, research initiatives or women's wings.

Public funding and parties' dependency on the state

Of the sources of income for political parties, public funding probably attracts the most vivid discussion among policy makers, academics and society at large since it is now (quantitatively) the most important source of revenue for parties in the region; it accounts for an average of 67 per cent of the total income of political parties in Europe (see Figure 7.5.). These data are striking, especially when compared to other areas of the world. In South America, for instance, the percentage of state dependency is only 35 per cent.[55]

Figure 7.5. The dependency of political parties in Northern, Western and Southern Europe on state funding

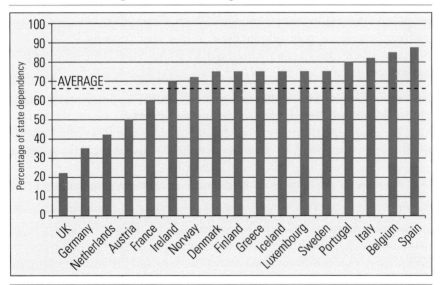

Source: GRECO evaluation reports. Transparency and Party Funding (adapted by the author).
Note: Figures refer to 2007–11 except for the UK (2012). Averages are computed when range estimates are reported by GRECO. Data were unavailable for Cyprus, Liechtenstein, Monaco and San Marino.

Unsurprisingly, state funding accounts for the lowest proportion of total party income in the UK.[56] Between 2000 and 2010, public funding varied from

2 per cent for the Labour Party (since it was in government) to 51 per cent for the Democratic Unionist Party. For the Conservative Party, which was in opposition during that period, state funding accounted for 15 per cent of total party income.[57] In Germany and the Netherlands, the percentage of state funding is also comparatively low, which suggests the success of allocation procedures that include incentives to promote political involvement from the citizenry (the 'matching funds' system). While private contributions have remained the most important source of income for Dutch political parties— even after the introduction of direct public funding in 1999—there is a trend toward increasing party dependence on state resources in the Netherlands. Public funding accounted for only 26 per cent of total parties' income in 2000, but accounted for 42 per cent in 2005–06.[58] In Spain, Belgium, Italy and Portugal, public funding accounts for over 80 per cent of total party income.

The growing amount of public funds available to political parties is the source of frequent criticism. Politics may have become more costly because of its increasing commercialization and reliance on the media,[59] challenging the maintenance of the 'heavy' and bureaucratized party structures that traditionally characterized Northern, Western and Southern European countries. Yet the weight of public funding as a proportion of total annual party income, which in some parties exceeds 90 per cent of total revenues, is hardly justifiable. Indeed, while encouraging the provision of public funding to political parties as a means of levelling the playing field of electoral competition, the Council of Europe equally stressed that public financing should not be the only source of income for a political party, because such a scenario would weaken the link between voters and parties.[60]

Party finance regulation is unique in that the parties are the principal agents of their own legal rules. Academics have often stressed the inherent conflict of interest, as legislators are also partisans.[61] In one of the most influential propositions developed in the political science literature in recent decades, Katz and Mair's 'cartel party' thesis asserts that public subventions enable parties to guarantee their own financial interests and organizational survival while further withdrawing from society.[62] Others have questioned whether the revenue maximization logic ought to be the sole possible explanation for political finance regulation.[63] Self-serve logic would not explain, for example, the convergence toward greater transparency of political finance rules in Europe or the reduction of party subsidies.

In fact, it is worth mentioning that a number of Northern, Western and Southern European countries (noticeably those that have been hard hit by the financial crisis) have reduced the amount of public funding to parties. In line with broader government austerity measures, party subsidies have been reduced in Italy (in 2007 and 2012), Portugal (in 2010) and Spain (in 2012).[64] This seems to substantiate the role of environmental and societal factors in political finance reforms, and suggests that political parties may be more responsive to citizens than is often assumed.

Political funding and women's representation

The percentage of women represented in the lower (or single) houses of parliament in the 24 countries under observation in this study is 29 per cent, on average.[65] Contrary to conventional wisdom, differences between Northern, Western and Southern Europe and other regions in the world are not very significant in this respect: the percentage of women represented in lower or single houses of parliament ranges from 24 per cent in the Americas and 21 per cent in sub-Saharan Africa to 18 per cent in Asia and 16 per cent in the Arab states.

In order to promote the participation of women in politics, a large number of countries around the world have introduced legislated quotas or gender balance regulations. Europe, however, despite the persistence of a gender gap, has mainly voluntary party quotas. Only six countries have national-level regulations promoting gender balance:[66] Belgium, France, Greece, Ireland, Portugal and Spain. Of the 21 countries that provide state funding to parties, only France, Ireland, Portugal and Italy link direct public funding to parties with gender equality.

France has the most established tradition in this respect. After the constitutional revision adopted in 1999,[67] the French legislature amended the 1988 political finance law to require all French political parties to field an equal number (50 per cent) of male and female candidates in elections at all levels. Under the amended political finance law from 2000, if parties fail to field an equal percentage of male and female candidates and the difference exceeds 2 per cent of the total number of candidates on the list, they face financial sanctions.[68] These provisions seem to have played a role in increasing female representation in France: from 12 per cent in 2002, to 19 per cent in 2007, to 27 per cent in 2012.[69] It was estimated that in 2012 the Union for a Popular Movement (Union pour un Mouvement Populaire, UMP) lost over EUR 4 million (I$4.7 million) for fielding only 26 per cent female candidates.[70]

Allocation procedures in France require that the total amount of funding is divided into two equal portions: the first half is distributed according to the percentage of votes obtained by each party, and the second is distributed to political parties represented in the National Assembly and Senate proportionally to the number of MPs that support one of the political parties eligible for the first allotment. Financial sanctions, however, are only applied to the first category of public funding. This approach means that the regulation acts as an effective constraint for small parties, but the cost of non-compliance, especially for the largest parties, is substantially reduced. Indeed, a EUR 4 million (I$4.7 million) deduction of public funding is a minor percentage of the average public funding that larger political parties receive (in 2011, the UMP received EUR 33.3 million [I$39.4 million]).[71] According to a UMP party official, 'We still prefer to pay fines than lose elections!'.[72] If parties expect to be more electorally successful in fielding a male candidate, they would arguably not mind the reduction in public funding.

In Ireland, under the Electoral (Amendment) (Political Funding) Act of 2012, public subsidies to political parties are reduced by 50 per cent unless at least 30 per cent of the candidates of each political party are female. This figure will rise to 40 per cent in subsequent general elections.[73] In Portugal, parties that do not have at least 33 per cent of each gender represented among their candidates can lose 25 to 80 per cent of their public funding.[74] In Italy, while no legislated quotas have been introduced at the national level, political funding regulation prescribes a reduction in subsidies to parties that do not spend at least 5 per cent of their public funding to promote initiatives aimed to increase the active participation of women in politics.[75]

Despite the persistent gender gap in Northern, Western and Southern Europe—and parties' exceptional reliance on state resources—legislators in this region have largely overlooked the possibility of linking public funding of political parties to gender equality. Moreover, the few that have enacted such provisions do little to address some of the key barriers that women in politics have encountered, particularly in relation to fundraising in the earlier stages of election cycles. Indeed, women have less access to financial resources and moneyed social and professional networks, which (especially in candidate-centred systems) affects their capacity to generate resources and thus their likelihood of being elected.[76] Different women's organizations and networks have been established to support female candidates. Drawing on the North American experience of EMILY's List, women's 'sister organizations' offering financial grants to female candidates have also been flourishing in Europe. In some cases, individual parties have set up initiatives to channel funds to female candidates (such as the Spanish Gender Equality Office or the Labour Party in Ireland). Yet there are remarkably few legislative prescriptions in this direction.

Increasing attention has been paid in recent years to gender-balanced representation. The 2010 Guidelines on Party Regulation and the EP 2012 resolution on women in political decision making asserted that gender parity must be among the 'reasonable' minimum requirements for receiving public funding.[77] The EP resolution also tackles the important challenge of fundraising for female candidates by encouraging member states to increase measures to support women's organizations, including by providing them with adequate funding and creating platforms for cooperation and gender campaigning in elections.[78]

> Despite the persistent gender gap in Northern, Western and Southern Europe—and parties' exceptional reliance on state resources—legislators in this region have largely overlooked the possibility of linking public funding of political parties to gender equality.

A particular case linking women's representation and public funding to political parties is the Dutch orthodox protestant party, the Staatkundig-Gereformeerde Partij (SGP). Based on its interpretation of the Bible, the SGP did not allow female party members and did not grant women passive suffrage. A court decision in September 2005 established that excluding women from party membership was in violation of the Convention on the Elimination of All Forms of Discrimination against Women (CEDAW)[79] and suspended public funding to the SGP, which would have cost the party about EUR 800,000 (I$971,000) a year.[80] The case provoked an important legal debate in the Netherlands on the relationship between different constitutional rights: the right of association, political opinions and religious belief on the one hand, and the right to non-discrimination on the other.[81] In December 2007 the court of second instance abrogated the previous ruling and reintroduced (retroactively, for 2006 and 2007) public subsidies to the SGP. The SGP changed its internal statutes to allow women to become party members from 2006.[82]

Regulation of spending by political parties and candidates

The regulation of spending by parties and candidates is based on the same underlying principles as the regulation of private donations and the provision of public funding to parties: reducing the advantages of those with access to more financial resources and levelling the playing field—and, hence, protecting the democratic process. In other words, legislation should ensure that all political parties and candidates are able to run election campaigns, and that no expenditure on behalf of any candidate or party is disproportionate.[83] Northern, Western and Southern European countries have introduced several restrictions on party and candidate spending, with varying degrees of effectiveness. This section will also discuss the underlying tension between political spending limits and citizens' fundamental rights, such as the freedom of expression.

Spending regulations can restrict the total amount that a political party or a candidate may spend, as well as restrict particular forms of spending. Bans on vote buying are common in these regions, and in most cases are regulated not under political finance laws, but rather in electoral codes (Belgium, France, Italy) or penal codes (Denmark, Germany, Greece, Sweden). Moreover, prohibitions on vote buying were often introduced at the very earliest stages of the establishment of European democracies.

On the other hand, spending limits for parties or candidates are not very common in Northern, Western and Southern Europe. Fewer than half of the countries in the region have introduced any such limits. These figures match the world trends: 29 per cent of Northern, Western and Southern European countries regulate spending by parties (the same as the world average), and 42 per cent of countries in the region regulate spending by candidates (2 per cent less than countries in other regions).[84] Eastern European countries have introduced greater regulation of political finance.[85]

Most Northern, Western and Southern European countries that have spending restrictions apply them to both regular party spending and campaign spending. Only four countries in the region (France, Iceland, Ireland, Spain) restrict only one type of spending. This is a remarkable difference from other regions, where legislators have distinguished between types of spending, which may provide opportunities to circumvent regulations easily.

Problems related to rule implementation and effectiveness also apply to spending rules. Bans on vote buying have proved to be ineffective in Italy,[86] where diverse forms of exchanging economic, material or occupational benefits for votes have continued for over half a century, including the 'vote packages' organized by criminal organizations in exchange for financial benefits and policy favours.[87] In France in the late 1990s, violations of spending limits did not necessarily lead to sanctions, after an amendment was included that allowed judges to opt out if 'the good faith of the defendant could be established'.[88] In Spain, expenditure limits have been ignored; the Court of Auditors recently denounced the country's systematic under-reporting.[89]

Expenditure limits can also be circumvented. For example, if spending limitations are restricted to a brief time frame, parties may push campaign expenditures forward to avoid them. This has been the case in Ireland, where the Standards in Public Office Commission signalled the problem of 'front loading'. According to the Commission, the parties' behaviour both undermines the purpose of expenditure limits and risks discrediting the provisions of the Act.[90]

Finally, the purpose of restricting expenditure may be undermined when the limits are set excessively high. This has been argued to be the case in the UK. While national spending limits were introduced in the 2000 Political Parties, Elections and Referendums Act (PEERA) in order to reduce campaign spending and narrow the spending disparity between the larger and smaller parties,[91] excessively high ceilings have arguably obscured both goals.[92]

Yet the establishment of excessively low spending ceilings is also problematic, as they may artificially restrict voters' access to information. The establishment of overly strict spending limits has received much attention in anglophone countries, in particular after the *Bowman v. UK* case, the outcome of which resulted in a raising of spending ceilings for third-party contributions to election campaigns in the PEERA. The European Court of Human Rights found that a very strict restriction on spending related to an election by a private person (at the time of the ruling, 5 pounds sterling [GBP] [I$8]) was an unreasonable infringement of freedom of expression as protected by Article 10 of the European Convention on Human Rights.[93] In two similar cases, the Court had to decide—ultimately ruling in both cases for their compatibility with the Convention—whether the ban on paid broadcasting in Switzerland and the UK infringed the right to freedom of expression.[94] As with the case of the Dutch party refusing women's passive suffrage discussed earlier, these examples show how political finance regulations have direct implications on citizens' fundamental right of political expression, and how legislators need to carefully balance regulations accordingly.[95]

Levels and types of spending

According to conventional wisdom, political parties and candidates spend more money than they used to, and will spend as much as they are allowed to. Increases in party and candidate expenditure have often been related to campaign professionalization processes and technical changes. Comparative analyses on party spending from the 1970s to the 1990s confirm a trend of rising campaign expenditure in Northern, Western and Southern European countries.[96] Table 7.5. shows the costs of French presidential elections from 1981 to 2002.

Table 7.5. The costs of French presidential elections, 1981–2002

	1981	1988	1995	2002
Total cost (in million EUR)	47.6 (I$56.2)	114.4 (I$135)	133.5 (I$157.6)	200.5 (I$236.7)
Average cost per registered voter	EUR 1.31 (I$1.54)	EUR 3 (I$3.54)	EUR 3.34 [I$3.94]	EUR 4.86 (I$5.75)

Source: Conseil constitutionnel.[97]

Over the last 20 years in France, the number of candidates running in presidential elections has increased (from 10 in 1981 to 16 in 2002), while the average cost of a presidential campaign for each registered voter has quadrupled. Similar figures apply to the Netherlands. In 1989, political parties spent just over EUR 2 million (I$2.43 million) on their election campaigns, and the figure rose above EUR 8 million (I$9.71 million) in 2012—decreasing from the 2010 peak of almost EUR 10 million (I$12.14 million).[98] This drop is probably explained by the fact that two elections took place so close together and that by 2012 the parties had already depleted their war chests. The most recent figures from the UK provide an interesting example in the opposite direction. In the 2010 UK general elections the overall aggregate party expenditure on the national level was 26 per cent lower than in the previous elections in 2005. This also applied to party spending for the EP elections in 2009, which was also significantly lower than it was in the previous elections of 2004.[99]

In addition to the problem of finding reliable data sources, any comparative analysis of levels of party and candidate spending implies a number of further methodological problems. First, party and candidate spending differs substantially depending on whether it is measured in election years or non-election years. Second, for an overall assessment of how much democracies cost and spend, it is crucial to take the size of the countries into account. Finally, floating currencies and variable exchange rates are additional problems.[100]

Reporting, external oversight and enforcement of political finance regulations

Rules on private donations, earmarked funding, or spending limits for political parties and/or candidates are of little importance unless they are backed up by an effective enforcement system—which includes reporting mechanisms, a body responsible for monitoring political parties' financial accounting, and sanctions. This section will assess the regulations on reporting by political parties and candidates, the institutions responsible for oversight of the parties' accounts and the sanctions in force in Northern, Western and Southern Europe. Moreover, it will discuss the extent to which these regulations are effectively implemented.

Reporting requirements

Reporting rules are crucial for ensuring that political parties and candidates comply with the political finance legislation, and for guaranteeing that their financial conduct is subject to external scrutiny. The Council of Europe's Committee of Ministers recommends that parties should report to an independent authority at least annually.[101]

Compared to elsewhere in the world, Northern, Western and Southern Europe show a higher degree of regulation on reporting, both in relation to the requirement of regular reporting of political parties (often annually) and of party and candidate campaign finances. This could be explained by the particular logic of party politics in these countries, where party organizations have been particularly important as permanently active membership bodies vis-à-vis the more electoral-based logic in other regions in the world.[102] Countries in this region appear, however, seem to have regulated less than the world average on candidate disclosure, and on requirements for political parties and candidates to disclose donors' identities.

The only three countries in Northern, Western and Southern Europe that do not require political parties to present financial accounts—Andorra, Malta and Switzerland—are also the only countries in the region that do not provide direct public funding to political parties (although Andorra provides public funding in relation to electoral campaigns). In the only two Swiss cantons that provide public funding to political parties (Ticino and Geneva), parties are required to meet certain transparency obligations. This shows how political finance legislation in the region is characterized by the integration of two fundamental components of political funding: (1) the financing of political actors by the state, which facilitates their organizational survival, and (2) the restrictions to compel political actors to comply with a number of rules favouring greater transparency.

According to the Council of Europe, parties and candidates should be subject to similar prescriptions.[103] Yet there is a marked difference between the reporting requirements for parties and candidates. Of the 24 countries in the area, almost all require parties to present financial accounts, while only half require candidates to report. This distinction is particularly noteworthy, because—like the establishment of spending limits discussed above— excluding one of the two from the duty to report may present an easy way to circumvent political finance regulations: funds can be channelled through the stakeholder that does not have to report, thus obscuring an important element of political financing. This is the case for national-level candidates in Portugal;[104] for Norway, where the legislation concerning funding and reporting only applies to registered political parties; and for Germany, which also treats parties and candidates differently in this respect.[105]

Two final important aspects related to reporting relate to whether party financial reports must be disclosed to the public, and whether information on the source of donations to political parties and candidates should be reported. Public disclosure is considered a further means of enhancing the transparency of parties' and candidates' financial management.

Almost all countries in Northern, Western and Southern Europe require that party reports are made available to the public, with the exception of Malta, Monaco and Spain.[106]

Figure 7.6. Northern, Western and Southern European countries that require political party reports to be made available to the public

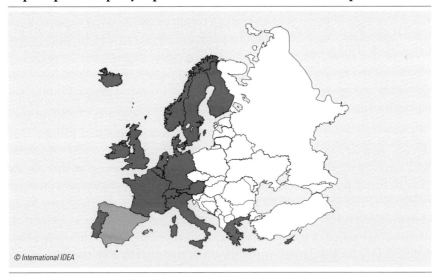

© International IDEA

■ Yes
■ No

Source: International IDEA. This map is based on data collected up to February 2014. Data are continuously updated on the International IDEA Political Finance Database. See http://www.idea.int/political-finance/question.cfm?field=291&region=50

The Council of Europe has often stressed that information should not just be available, but should also be timely and 'citizen-friendly'—clear and easily accessible to the general public. The United Kingdom offers one of the best examples of public disclosure of political parties' financial accounts through the website of the Electoral Commission. The central register of Statistics Norway, the French CNCCFP and the Irish Standards in Public Office Commission provide a similar service to citizens, publishing party annual accounts, political finance statistics and analytical reports on their websites.

In seven of the 24 countries analysed here—Malta, Andorra, Switzerland (which do not provide direct public funding), Cyprus, Monaco, Liechtenstein and France—political parties and candidates are not required to reveal donors' identities, which is a lower percentage than elsewhere in the world. Yet transparency requirements have been increasing, especially during the last decade. As a possible consequence of the various recommendations and party regulation guidelines, the debate in Northern, Western and Southern European countries centres not on whether donations should be disclosed, but rather on the threshold for disclosure; the regional average is currently around EUR 3,500.

Of course, the existence of a law requiring political parties and/or candidates to report income and expenditures says little about the reliability, detail and comprehensiveness of the reporting practices. Three main points stand out in this regard. First, most countries in this region lack a standardized and uniform reporting format.[107] Therefore political parties combine different sources of income and expenditure under different (non-comparable) labels. Second, European countries vary in the amount of detail that their financial reports include. In terms of transparency, it makes a substantial difference if, for instance, parties are required to itemize all income and expenses, or if they must simply report aggregated total amounts. Finally, the financial reports often do not include all entities that are related to the parties' spheres of activity. Political finance legislation has often paid little attention to local parties, political party foundations or other parties' organizational units. This has been the case in the Netherlands, for instance, where transparency requirements did not apply to the regional or local levels until recently.[108]

Monitoring authorities

Another fundamental aspect of the enforcement of political finance regulations relates to the different institutions responsible for monitoring and controlling existing regulations. Effective monitoring is among the most important features of political finance regulation; it is ultimately the crucial means by which the legislation can claim to be effectively implemented. Yet there is wide variation across Northern, Western and Southern European countries with respect to monitoring institutions; the legislative frameworks seem to have the most problems.

First, some countries lack an authority to control parties' finances: Malta, Switzerland, Liechtenstein and Denmark. In the Nordic countries, there has been a tradition of relying on transparency and the traditional culture of high public trust in political parties—a tradition that is fading, however, as Finland, Norway and Sweden have all introduced stricter regulations in recent years.

Second, there is variation in the monitoring authorities' independence from the political process. Independence and freedom from political influences are crucial for the credibility and effectiveness of monitoring mechanisms.[109] The bodies responsible for supervising political funding must be as independent as possible from the political parties.

In this region, few countries have enforcement institutions that are truly independent from political influence. The control of political finance appears to be mainly exercised by parliamentary commissions or by the executive branches, either directly or through institutions or special commissions that are accountable to them. When executive branches control supervisory bodies, they cannot claim independence or impartiality from the political process because ministers are often elected members of the party in power; they may use political finance rules to favour the party in power or sanction the opposition. However, in many of these countries the independence of the enforcement body is not an issue of public debate. In countries that have relatively high public perceptions of financial integrity and public trust in political institutions, many feel that the mere suspicion of, for example, a ministry abusing its power to harm an opponent would severely damage the ruling party's reputation.

Third, in most Northern, Western and Southern European countries, different institutions may be responsible for receiving and examining financial reports from parties and candidates. In Finland, for example, the Ministry of Justice oversees the applications concerning the parties' regular reporting, and the National Audit Office checks reports for election campaigns and for candidates. In Italy, until the 2012 reform, the Board of Comptrollers of Election Expenses at the State Audit Court was responsible for expenditures; the Board of Auditors in the parliament checked parties' annual financial reports; and the Regional Electoral Guarantee Board checked candidates' electoral expenditures. These institutions often cannot impose sanctions. A similar dispersion of monitoring institutions can be observed in Greece and Portugal. While the variety of oversight institutions within individual countries depends on the countries' specific constitutional and legal traditions (and the broader economic and organizational management of existing resources), their dispersal, and their limited mandate over specific areas of political finance, may hamper inter-institutional coordination and effectiveness.

The proper functioning of enforcement mechanisms is essential for the entire legal framework on political finance. If such mechanisms do not serve their purpose, it may severely jeopardize the credibility, the effectiveness and the very raison d'être of the political finance regulatory framework as a whole.

Sanctions for political finance violations

Few countries in the world have not established sanctions for political finance violations. The only country in the region without such sanctions is Switzerland.[110] Fines, loss of public funding and imprisonment are the most common sanctions in Europe. Party suspension or deregistration, probably the most extreme sanction available, and loss of active and passive political rights (including ineligibility, loss of nomination of candidate or loss of elected office) are less common.

Proportionality is among the most important characteristics that political finance sanctions should aim to achieve: sanctions should be sufficiently dissuasive and proportionate to the offence (and to the size and financial resources of the various political parties). This is not always the case. In Portugal, for example, although the legal framework prescribes penal sanctions (one year of imprisonment for the party treasurer or leader for accepting illegal donations), financial misdemeanours have often been converted into financial fines that are not proportional to the size of illegal donations received. For example, in June 2007, the Constitutional Court fined the centre-right Social Democrat Party EUR 35,000 (I$49,000) for accepting an illegal donation from the Somague company of EUR 233,415 (I$328,000).[111] In France, violations of private donation rules (and specifically, donations from a banned source, or exceeding the maximum legal limit of EUR 7,500 [I$8,900]) are sanctioned 'with a maximum fine of EUR 3,750 [I$4,400] and a one-year prison sentence, or only one of these two penalties'.[112] GRECO observed that a EUR 3,750 (I$4,400) fine may not deter acceptance of a sizeable illegal donation, especially since such donations to political parties cannot be confiscated.[113] Ineffective sanctions are also found in Belgium, where the penalty for exceeding the thresholds on campaign expenditure is a suspension of public funding for up to four months.

Sanctions may also be so severe that they are seldom applied in practice. For example, in Iceland violations of the political finance law are punished by six years' imprisonment—which will probably never be sought.[114] Criminal penalties are rarely applied in Belgium, Cyprus, Finland, France, Greece or the UK. Indeed, the fact that sanctions are not applied does not necessarily indicate their dissuasiveness; it may also reflect their ineffectiveness.[115]

The civic watchdogs: civil society and the media

A recent large-scale political finance scandal took place in Spain in February 2013, after the newspaper *El Pais* published the unofficial accounting records of the Partido Popular party. The published documents suggest that the party kept parallel accounting books for over 20 years, hiding secret contributions from businesses that were then redistributed to leading party members.[116] Several political finance scandals in Western Europe have emerged because of media coverage. In turn, the emergence of scandals plays a major role in stimulating political finance reforms. Political corruption scandals create more critical (or hostile) public opinion, which influences parties' behaviour and promotes political finance reforms that lead to greater transparency of parties' and candidates' financial management.[117] Thus the media constitute an important element of political finance supervision, which has successfully managed to keep up with its fundamental task of being the 'watchdog of democracy'. Yet only about 35 per cent of Western Europeans consider themselves to be informed about the level of political corruption in their country,[118] which suggests the need for greater media attention to these politically sensitive issues.

Conclusions

The process of political finance regulation in Northern, Western and Southern Europe began before World War II, when political parties in numerous countries were provided with indirect financial support in the form of free broadcasting time on radio, reduced postal rates or tax deductions on party donations. After the war, countries in the region started adopting broader and increasingly comprehensive legal frameworks on the financial management of political parties and candidates. These regulations were often introduced alongside the decision to provide political parties with direct public funding.

The provision of public funding and the regulation of political finance signify a changing conception of political parties and their role in society: from private and voluntary associations to public utilities.[119] Political parties are often seen as essential for democracy.[120] This positive conception has justified both the provision of growing levels of state funding to political parties and their management through public law.

However, in political finance law-making there is an inherent conflict of interest because legislators are also partisans.[121] Political parties should bear this in mind, and provide substantive evidence of impartiality when establishing political finance rules.

Northern, Western and Southern European countries have different legal frameworks and traditions with respect to state intervention in party activity. Yet there is a trend toward greater harmonization of political finance regulations among countries, especially with regard to rules regulating the mechanisms of public accountability and transparency. Lowering the threshold for the public disclosure of private donations and making political parties' annual statements more accessible are increasingly perceived as fundamental requisites of political finance laws. EU-level reports and recommendations to establish 'common principles' and 'good practices' in the different political finance legislative frameworks have been an important stimulus in this direction.

This chapter has discussed the main rationale behind the introduction of public funding to political parties and candidates and the establishment of rules on political finance: to prevent illicit funding practices, level the playing field for all political parties and help political parties cope with the rising financial costs of politics. Yet these provisions are not immune from criticism and concerns.

The most influential criticism of public funding regimes in the political science literature holds that state support is a means by which the established political parties grant themselves opportunities for organizational survival and electoral victory, while keeping power resources out of the reach of outsiders. This argument notably reverses the democratic justification of public funding: rather than promoting and sustaining effective democracy, public funding would constitute a tool for disadvantaging the challengers and self-perpetuating the political status quo.[122] Little evidence was found to support this argument in terms of the eligibility and allocation criteria for public funding in Northern, Western and Southern Europe. The legal frameworks for provision of public funding in the region appear to take into account both the need for party organizational stability and the importance of political pluralism through the funding of smaller and newer political parties.[123]

The introduction of public funding has undeniably made political parties very dependent on state resources. Compared to other areas of the world, figures for Northern, Western and Southern Europe are striking: overall, state funding accounts for almost three-quarters of total party income. Considering party membership decline, and the worrisome and increasing figures on disenchantment with political parties,[124] high state dependency may risk sustaining political actors that are out of touch with the social reality. A final (and equally important) criticism of public funding is that it has not solved the fundamental problem of political corruption—which was, in most cases, the fundamental justification for its introduction.

If political finance regulation has proved not to be the panacea it promised, part of its ineffectiveness can be blamed on the quality of the legislation itself. Political finance legislation has increased in this region and has become more comprehensive, regulating more candidate and party financial activities, but it is still full of loopholes that candidates and parties have proved willing to exploit. Greater regulatory complexity, when badly drafted, may undermine the very democratic values and good governance that political finance regulation in principle supports. This is not only a problem for rule implementation. When ineffective, political finance legislation is highly detrimental to the public image and credibility of the representative institutions. The following recommendations provide guidelines for political finance reforms for monitoring authorities, individual political parties and media actors.

Recommendations

Policy makers[125]

The design of political finance legislation has a significant impact on rule implementation, on the effectiveness of the overall system, and consequently on the legitimacy of political institutions. Political actors will often be tempted to find new ways to exploit loopholes in the legislation, so it must be carefully crafted. Two types of recommendations can be addressed to legislators: formal law-making guidelines in relation to political finance, whose realization has often proved insufficient; and guidelines specifically related to the content of political finance legislation.

A. The three main principles for political finance law-making are:

1. *Internal coherence.* While regulation of political finance in Northern, Western and Southern Europe has grown in scope and detail, it has not evolved in a coherent manner. Political finance legislation should address all the main aspects of political parties' and candidates' financial management, and should give equal attention to the different clusters of regulation. It makes little sense, for example, to strictly regulate the sources of private income when the monitoring authorities have no power to investigate, and controls are merely formal (Italy); or to establish strict rules on party income but not regulate income from candidates or elected officials (Portugal, Norway, Germany); or to establish financial sanctions for failure to comply with gender parity requirements that are so low that the regulation is broadly ignored (France).

2. *Explicitness.* Rules on political finance should leave no room for ambiguity and should avoid opaque, non-prescriptive and discretionary formulations. For example, Article 13 of San Marino's political finance law permits only 'modest amounts' of anonymous donations. Political actors may lawfully profit from such ambiguous wording, thus undermining the very essence of political finance regulations.

3. *Comprehensiveness.* A number of countries have a legislative framework of political finance that is fragmented and dispersed among several legislative instruments. The adoption of a single act—including a comprehensive regulation of the different areas of party funding—is an important way to improve clarity and transparency.

B. The five recommendations regarding the content of political finance legislation are:

1. *Balancing private and public funding.* The provision of state funding to political parties is an important tool for promoting political pluralism and levelling the field of electoral competition. Yet political parties must not lose touch with their constituents. Legislation should therefore aim to balance public and private sources of income for

parties and candidates, and provide financial incentives to establish close connections with citizens.

2. *Anchor public funding to gender requirements.* Regulatory frameworks linking public funding to parties and gender equality are rare in Northern, Western and Southern Europe. Given the parties' high dependency on state resources, public funding regulation has great potential to change their incentive structures and influence their internal practices. Legislation should include measures to ensure de facto equality between men and women, including levelling the playing field for candidate selection and fundraising.

3. *Reporting.* Political finance legislation should require parties and candidates to provide standardized financial reports that include specific sources of income and expenditure. Larger donations (>EUR 4,000) should be reported separately, including the details of the donor. Reporting requirements should not, however, be so strict that they impose an undue administrative burden that may in turn limit the effective freedom of political organizations.

4. *Monitoring authorities.* The authorities monitoring the parties' and candidates' financial management should be as removed as possible from political power. Monitoring is still either directly or indirectly linked to parliaments in many European countries. The establishment of single independent monitoring institutions (such as the CNCCFP in France or the Electoral Commission in the UK) should stimulate other countries to set up similar agencies. This would prevent problems of inter-institutional cooperation, improve the standardization of training and expertise on auditing political finances, and provide greater transparency to the public. These authorities should publish political finance information in a timely and citizen-friendly manner.

5. *Sanctions.* Sanctions constrain political actors only when effective costs for non-compliance are put in place. Political finance sanctions should be proportional to the specific nature of the violation (and to the size of the parties) as well as dissuasive.

Monitoring and enforcement agencies

1. *Avoid dispersion.* The majority of Northern, Western and Southern European countries have separate authorities that control the parties' and candidates' financial management. Inter-institutional coordination should be improved in order to make monitoring more cost-efficient, timely and effective.

2. *Promote specialization.* The quality of the control and the timeliness of the conclusions are highly dependent on the specialization of agency staff. Training of personnel should be prioritized in order to create and maintain expertise and proficiency at all levels.

3. *Join forces.* The diversified political finance legal frameworks in Europe

provide the opportunity to learn from other monitoring authorities' experiences. Establish international networks that promote focused training and workshops.

4. *Publish information online.* Within the limits of the law, candidates' and parties' financial statements should be easily accessible on monitoring agencies' websites. Yearly reports should be issued that summarize the main outcomes of agencies' findings using standardized formats to allow citizens, media actors, and researchers to compare information across parties and over time.

Political parties and politicians

1. *Promote pluralism.* Parties should make sure that political finance legislation does not prevent new political actors from emerging.
2. *Show 'good practices'.* The legislative process is time-consuming, and it often takes several years to approve political finance reforms. Even in the absence of formal legislation, political parties can show good practices. For example, the Italian Partito Democratico voluntarily established best practice accounting procedures, and other parties have adopted voluntary quotas.
3. *Do not become too reliant on public funding.* Party membership in the region is rapidly falling, which is reducing membership contributions and increasing parties' reliance on public funding. Although dealing with one big donor (the state) is easier in the short run than dealing with thousands of small donors, a diversified funding base in the long run makes parties less vulnerable to sudden shocks in public funding availability.
4. *Be accountable to your voters.* Citizens' growing distrust of parties has led to the creation of citizen protest movements and anti-establishment parties that are challenging the existence of traditional parties across Europe. To regain voter confidence (and thus ensure their own survival), political parties should strengthen their regulatory frameworks and improve internal integrity standards.

Media actors

1. *Keep up with expectations.* The media have played an important role in uncovering the illicit and illegal financial practices of political parties, candidates and elected officials. By informing citizens, they help maintain democratic accountability.
2. *Provide 'informed information'.* More countries in the region have established independent monitoring authorities with the task of publishing citizen-friendly reports. Since these institutions rely heavily on data from the media, they must provide high-quality, accurate information based on official documents, legislation and statistics—and avoid the temptation to create a financial scandal for the sake of publicity.

3. *Keep political finance at the top of your editorial agenda.* Media attention to political finance comes and goes; the timing is often determined by election campaigns or political finance scandals. The media should question an array of sources (including smaller-party actors) regularly and keep citizens informed.

4. *Stay independent of the donors that fund political parties.* Media outlets in several countries in this region have become intertwined with politics over the years, either directly (e.g., Italy, where media and political parties can be run by the same people) or indirectly, i.e., ownership is separate but the same donors fund media outlets and political parties (e.g., Sweden, where until 2009 LO, the Swedish trade union confederation, which has strong links with the Social Democratic Party, owned a majority stake in one of Sweden's largest daily newspapers). All media should therefore verify that there is no such conflict of interest.

References

Barkhuysen, T. (2004) 'Politieke participatie van discriminerende partijen: ondersteunen, gedogen of bestrijden?', [Political participation of discriminatory parties: support, tolerate or fight?] in M. M. Groothuis (ed.), *Grondrechten in de pluriforme samenleving* [Fundamental Rights in the plural society], pp. 42–54. Leiden: Stichting NJCM-Boekerij.

Casal Bértoa, F., Piccio, D. R., Molenaar, F. and Rashkova, E. (2014). 'The World Upside Down: De-Legitimising Political Finance Regulation', *International Political Science Review*, Vol. 35, no. 3, 355-375.

Clift, B. and Fisher, J. (2004) 'Comparative Party Finance Reform: The Cases of France and Britain', *Party Politics*, 10, pp. 677–99.

Clift, B. and Fisher, J. (2005) 'Party Finance Reform as Constitutional Engineering? The Effectiveness and Unintended Consequences of Party Finance Reform in France and Britain', *French Politics*, 3, pp. 234–57.

Colombo, E. (2013) 'Superflop per le donazioni private 2012' [Superflop for Private Donations 2012], *Il Messaggero*, 6 June.

Commission Nationale des Comptes de Campagne et des Financements Politiques (CNCCFP) (2010) *Treizième rapport d'activité* [Thirteenth Activity Report], available at http://www.cnccfp.fr/docs/commission/cnccfp_activite_2010.pdf

Commission Nationale des Comptes de Campagne et des Financements Politiques (CNCCFP) (2005–2006) *Neuvième rapport d'activité* [Ninth Activity Report], available at http://www.cnccfp.fr/docs/commission/cnccfp_activite_2005-2006.pdf

Commission Nationale des Comptes de Campagne et des Financements Politiques (CNCCFP) (2011), *Avis relatif à la publication générale des comptes des partis et groupements politiques au titre de l'exercice 2010* [Review of the overall report of political parties and groups for the year 2010], p. 6, available at http://www.cnccfp.fr/docs/partis/comptes/cnccfp_comptes_2010.pdf

Committee on Standards in Public Life (UK) Annual Reports, available at http://www.public-standards.gov.uk/our-work/annual-reports/

Committee on Standards in Public Life (UK) (1998) *Fifth Report of the Committee on Standards in Public Life* (the 'Neill Report').

Committee on Standards in Public Life (UK) (2011) *Thirteenth Report of the Committee on Standards in Public Life: Political Party Finance: Ending the Big Donor Culture.*

Council of Europe (2001a) *Guidelines and Report on the Financing of Political Parties*, available at http://www.osce.org/odihr/37843?download=true

Council of Europe (2001b) *Financing of Political Parties*, Parliamentary Assembly, Rec. 1516, available at http://assembly.coe.int/Main.asp?link=/Documents/AdoptedText/ta01/EREC1516.htm

Council of Europe (2003) *Recommendation Rec(2003)4 of the Committee of Ministers to Member States on Common Rules against Corruption in the Funding of Political Parties and Electoral Campaigns*, available at http://www.coe.int/t/dghl/cooperation/economiccrime/cybercrime/cy%20activity%20interface2006/rec%202003%20%284%29%20pol%20parties%20EN.pdf

Council of Europe (2009) 'Declaration: Making Gender Equality a Reality', Committee of Ministers, CM(2009)68, available at https://wcd.coe.int/ViewDoc.jsp?id=1441675&Site=CM

Council of Europe (2010) 'Increasing Women's Representation in Politics through the Electoral System', Parliamentary Assembly, Rec. 1899, available at http://assembly.coe.int/Main.asp?link=/Documents/AdoptedText/ta10/EREC1899.htm

Crouch, C. (2004) *Post-Democracy*. Cambridge: Polity Press.

Dalton, R. and Wattenberg, M. (eds) (2002) *Parties Without Partisans: Political Change in Advanced Industrial Democracies*. Oxford: Oxford University Press.

De Saambinder (2005) 'SGP en non-discriminatie' [SGP and non-discrimination], 22 September, pp. 4–5.

De Sousa, L. (2005) 'Challenges to Political Financing Regulation: Sound External Monitoring, Enforcement and Sensible Internal Party Accountability'. Paper prepared for the international conference *Corruption Control in Political Life and the Quality of Democracy: A Comparative Perspective Europe – Latin America*, ISCTE, Lisbon, 19–20 May.

De Sousa, L. (2012) 'New Challenges to Political Financing Supervision: The Case of the Portuguese Entity for Accounts and Political Financing (EAPF)'. Paper presented at the APCP Panel on Party Regulation in Southern Europe: Portugal in Comparative Perspective, Lisbon, 1–3 March.

Doublet, Y. M. (2011) 'Fighting Corruption: Political Funding'. Thematic Review of GRECO's Third Evaluation Round, Council of Europe.

Dragstra, L. (2008) *Enige opmerkingen over partijfinancering* [Some Remarks on Party Finance]. Doctoral dissertation, University of Amsterdam.

Dupont, Thierry (2010) 'Micro-partis, Maxi-Fric', *L'Express*, 1 July, available at http://www.lexpress.fr/actualite/politique/micro-partis-maxi-fric_903396.html

El Pais (2013) 'Dos decades de notas Ilenas de incógnitas' [Two Decades of Notes Full of Unknowns], 3 February, available at http://politica.elpais.com/politica/2013/02/02/actualidad/1359819189_845362.html

Electoral Commission (UK) (2008) *Party Finance and Expenditure in the United Kingdom. The Government's Proposals: The Electoral Commission's Response.*

Electoral Commission (UK) (2011) *General Election 2010: Campaign Spending Report.*

Epstein, L. D. (1986) *Political Parties in the American Mold*. Madison, WI: University of Wisconsin Press.

Eurobarometer (2012a) *Corruption on the Rise?* European Commission Press Release.

European Commission (2011) *Fighting Corruption in the EU*, available at http://ec.europa.eu/dgs/home-affairs/what-is-new/news/pdf/1_act_part1_v121_en.pdf

European Parliament (EP) (2012) Resolution of 13 March 2012 on Women in Political Decision-making – Quality and Equality (2011/2295(INI)).

Ewing, K. D. and Ghaleigh, N. S. (2006) 'The Cost of Giving and Receiving: Donations to Political Parties in the United Kingdom', available at http://www2.law.ed.ac.uk/file_download/publications/2_31_thecostofgivingandtaking.pdf

Farrell, D. M. and Webb, P. (2002) 'Political Parties as Campaign Organizations', in R. J. Dalton and M. P. Wattenberg (eds), *Parties without Partisans: Political Change in Advanced Industrial Democracies*, pp. 102–28. Oxford: Oxford University Press.

Fisher, J. (2001) 'Campaign Finance: Elections Under New Rules', in P. Norris (ed.), *Britain Votes 2001*, pp. 125–36. Oxford: Oxford University Press.

Griner, S. (2005) 'The Delicate Balance between Political Equity and Freedom of Expression', in *Political Party and Campaign Financing in Canada and the United States*, pp. 61–70. Stockholm: International IDEA.

Group of States against Corruption (GRECO) (2007) Evaluation Report on Transparency and Party Funding. Third Evaluation Round Reports, available at http://www.coe.int/t/dghl/monitoring/greco/evaluations/round3/ReportsRound3_en.asp

International IDEA, Political Finance Database, available at http://www.idea.int/political-finance.

Inter-Parliamentary Union (IPU) (2012) 'Women in Parliament in 2012: The Year in Perspective', available at http://www.ipu.org/pdf/publications/WIP2012e.pdf

Katz, R. S. and Mair, P. (1995) 'Changing Models of Party Organization and Party Democracy: The Emergence of the Cartel Party', *Party Politics*, 1(1), pp. 5–28.

Katz, R. S. and Mair, P. (2009) 'The Cartel Party Thesis: A Restatement', *Perspectives on Politics*, 7(4), pp. 753–66.

Koole, R. (2001) 'Political Finance in Western Europe: Britain and France', in K. H. Nassmacher (ed.), *Foundations for Democracy: Approaches to Comparative Political Finance*, pp. 73–91. Baden-Baden: Nomos.

Koß, M. (2008) 'Party Goals, Institutional Veto Points and the Discourse on Political Corruption: The Evolution of the German Party Funding Regime', *Journal of Elections, Public Opinion and Parties*, 18(3), pp. 283–301.

Krouwel, A. (1999) *The Catch-all Party in Western Europe 1945–1990. A Study in Arrested Development*. Doctoral dissertation, Vrije Universiteit Amsterdam.

Lei da Paridade, Lei Orgânica nº 3/2006, de 21 de Agosto [Parity Law, Organic Law No. 3/2006 of 21 August, Portugal.

Loi nº 88-227 du 11 mars 1988 relative à la transparence financière de la vie politique, art. 11-5 [Law No. 88-227 of 11 March 1988 on the Financial Transparency of Political Life, France].

Mair, P. (1998) 'Representation and Participation in the Changing World of Party Politics', *European Review*, 6(2), pp. 161–74.

Mair, P. (2003) 'Political Parties and Democracy: What Sort of Future?', *Central European Political Science Review*, 4(3), pp. 6–20.

Mathiason, Nick (2011) 'Hedge Funds, Financiers and Private Equity Make Up 27% of Tory Funding,' Bureau of Investigative Journalism, 30 September, available at http://www.thebureauinvestigates.com/2011/09/30/hedge-funds-financiers-and-private-equity-tycoons-make-up-27-of-tory-funding/

Murray, R. (2007) 'How Parties Evaluate Compulsory Quotas: A Study of the Implementation of the "Parity" Law in France', *Parliamentary Affairs*, 60(4), pp. 568–84.

Nassmacher K.-H. (1993) 'Comparing Party and Campaign Finance in Western Democracies', in A. B. Gunlicks (ed.), *Campaign and Party Finance in North America and Western Europe*, pp. 233–67. Boulder CO: Westview Press.

Nassmacher K.-H. (ed.) (2001) *Foundations for Democracy*. Baden-Baden: Nomos Verlagesellschaft.

Nassmacher, K.-H. (2003) 'Party Funding in Continental Western Europe', in R. Austin and M. Tjernström (eds), *Funding of Political Parties and Election Campaigns*, pp. 117–37. Stockholm: International IDEA.

Nassmacher, K.-H. (2009) *The Funding of Party Competition: Political Finance in 25 Democracies*. Baden-Baden: Nomos Verlagesellschaft.

'Notitie Herijking Wet subsidiëring politieke partijen', Kst. 27442 [Memo and Revision of the Law on the Public Funding of Political Parties: The Netherlands].

Ohman, M. (2012) *Political Finance Regulations Around the World: An Overview of the International IDEA Database*. Stockholm: International IDEA.

Oomen, B., Huijt, J. and Ploeg, M. (2010) 'CEDAW, the Bible and the State of the Netherlands: The Struggle over Orthodox Women's Political Participation and their Responses', *Utrecht Law Review*, 6(2), pp. 158–74.

Organization for Security and Co-operation in Europe (OSCE) Office for Democratic Institutions and Human Rights (ODIHR) (2010) *Guidelines on Political Party Regulation*.

Piccio, D. R. (2012) 'Party Regulation in Europe: Country Reports', Working Paper Series on the Legal Regulation of Political Parties, No. 18, available at http://www.partylaw.leidenuniv.nl/uploads/wp1812.pdf

Piccio, D. R. (2013) 'Restraint in Party Regulation? Confronting the Rhetoric and the Reality of Party Regulation in the Netherlands', Working Paper Series on the Legal Regulation of Political Parties.

Piccio, D. R. (2014) 'A Self Interested Legislator? Party Regulation in Italy', *South European Society and Politics*, Vol. 19, no. 1, pp. 135-52.

Piccio, D. R. and van Biezen, I. (2014, forthcoming) 'More, and More Inclusive, Regulation: The Legal Parameters of Public Funding', in R. Boatright (ed.), *The Deregulatory Moment? A Comparative Perspective on Changing Campaign Finance Laws*. Ann Arbor, MI: University of Michigan Press.

Pinto-Duschinsky, M. (2002) 'Financing Politics: A Global View', *Journal of Democracy*, 13(4), pp. 69–86.

Rechtbank's-Gravenhage [District Court of the Hague] (2005) *LJN:AU2088, HA ZA 03/3395*.

Saviano, R. (2013) 'Quel voto di scambio che uccide la democrazia' [The Vote-buying that Kills Democracy], *La Repubblica*, 11 February.

Scarrow, Susan E. (2004) 'Explaining Political Finance Reforms: Competition and Context', *Party Politics*, 10, pp. 653–75.

Scarrow, Susan E. (2007) 'Political Finance in Comparative Perspective', *Annual Review of Political Science*, 10, pp. 193–210.

Schattschneider, E. E. (1942) *Party Government*. New York: Farrar and Rinehart, Inc.

Seiradaki, Emmanouela (2012) 'In Midst of Crisis, State Funding for Greek Political Parties Increases', 13 January, *Greek Reporter*, available at http://greece.greekreporter.com/2012/01/13/in-midst-of-crisis-state-funding-for-greek-political-parties-increases/

Standards in Public Office Commission of Ireland (2007) *Submission to the Minister for the Environment, Heritage and Local Government concerning spending limits at local elections*, available at http://www.sipo.gov.ie/en/About-Us/Our-Policies/Review-of-Legislation/Submission-to-the-Minister/

Statistics Norway (2005–2011), available at http://www.ssb.no/forside

Sustainable Government Indicators (2011), available at http://www.sgi-network.org/index.php?page=indicator_quali&indicator=S1_4

Svåsand, L. (1992) 'Norway', in Richard S. Katz and Peter Mair (eds), *Party Organizations: A Data Handbook*, pp. 732–80. London: Sage.

Ten Napel, H. M. (2011) 'Finishing the Work Begun by the French Revolution: A Critical Analysis of the Dutch Supreme Court Judgment on the Political Reformed Party and Passive Female Suffrage', *European Public Law*, 17(1), pp. 61–70.

Testo Unico delle Leggi Elettorali D.P.R (1957) [Consolidated Text of the Electoral Law, Decree of the President of the Republic (D.P.R.)] 30 marzo 1957, n 361, art. 96 [Law No. 361, 30 March 1957, Article 96. Italy].

The 1979 Election of Members to the House of Representatives Law [Law No. 72/79, Cyprus] (1979).

Times of Malta (2009) 'Openness and Transparency in Party Funding', 18 December, available at http://www.timesofmalta.com/articles/view/20091218/opinion/openness-and-transparency-in-party-funding.286431

Van Biezen, I. (2004) 'Political Parties as Public Utilities', *Party Politics*, 10(6), pp. 701–22.

Van Biezen, I. (2011) 'Constitutionalizing Party Democracy: The Constitutive Codification of Political Parties in Post-war Europe', *British Journal of Political Science*, 42, pp. 187–202.

Van Biezen, I. and Nassmacher, K. H. (2001) 'Political Finance in Southern Europe: Italy, Portugal and Spain', in K. H. Nassmacher (ed.), *Foundations for Democracy: Approaches to Comparative Political Finance*, pp. 131–54. Baden-Baden: Nomos Verlagesellschaft.

Van Biezen, I. and Kopecký, P. (2007) 'The State and the Parties: Public Funding, Public Regulation and rent-seeking in Contemporary Democracies', *Party Politics*, 13(2), pp. 235–54.

Van Biezen, I., Mair, P. and Poguntke, T. (2012) 'Going, Going ... Gone? The Decline of Party Membership in Contemporary Europe', *European Journal of Political Research*, 51, pp. 24–56.

Van Biezen, I. and Molenaar, F. (2012) 'The Europeanisation of Party Politics? Competing Regulatory Paradigms at the Supranational Level', *West European Politics*, 35(1), pp. 632–56.

Van Biezen, I. and Piccio, D. R. (2013) 'Shaping Intra-Party Democracy: On the Legal Regulation of Internal Party Organizations', in R. S. Katz and W. Cross (eds), *The Challenges of Intra-Party Democracy*, pp. 27–48. Oxford: Oxford University Press.

Vernardakis, C. (2012) 'From Mass Parties to Cartel Parties: The Evolution of the Structure of Political Parties in Greece through Changes in their Statutes and Systems of Financing', Working Paper Series on the Legal Regulation of Political Parties, No. 18, available at http://www.partylaw.leidenuniv.nl/uploads/wp2712.pdf

Voerman, G. (2012) 'Over de toekomst van de politieke partij' [On the Future of the Political Party]. Oratie [lecture], Rijksuniversiteit Groningen, 18 September.

Weekers, K. and Maddens, B. (2009) *Het geld van de partijen* [The Parties' Money]. Leuven: Acco.

Widfeldt, A. and Pierre, J. (1992) 'Sweden', in Richard S. Katz and Peter Mair (eds), *Party Organizations: A Data Handbook*, pp. 781–836. London: Sage.

Women's Environment and Development Organization [WEDO] (2007), 'Women Candidates and Campaign Finance', available at http://www.wedo.org/wp-content/uploads/women-candidates-and-campaign-finance-report-final.pdf

Notes

[1] The 24 countries included in this chapter are divided into three sub-regions: (1) Northern Europe: Denmark, Iceland, United Kingdom, Ireland, Norway, Finland and Sweden; (2) Southern Europe: Italy, Andorra, Cyprus, Portugal, Greece, Malta, San Marino and Spain; and (3) Western Europe: Austria, Germany, Monaco, Belgium, Liechtenstein, the Netherlands, France, Luxembourg and Switzerland.

[2] Van Biezen 2011; Casal Bértoa et al. 2013.

[3] Council of Europe 2001a.

4   The UK and Ireland are included in this chapter as well as Chapter 8 on the established anglophone democracies. The rationale for including them here is that the two countries offer useful comparisons with other Western European EU countries. In addition, as some readers may choose only to read this chapter, it was deemed prudent to include the UK and Ireland in both chapters.

5   Eurobarometer 2012a; European Commission 2011, p. 3.

6   Casal Bértoa et al. 2014. See also Pinto-Duschinsky 2002; Scarrow 2007.

7   Van Biezen and Kopecký 2007; Ohman 2012.

8   Committee of Ministers of the Council of Europe, Recommendations (2003)3&4; (CM(2009)68); Recommendation 1899(2010).

9   Epstein 1986; van Biezen 2004.

10 Van Biezen 2011.

11 Van Biezen and Piccio 2013.

12 OSCE/ODHIR 2010, p. 11.

13 Although party funding was introduced in Germany in 1958, the first regulation was introduced in 1966. Similar cases in which a legal framework on political finance was established by law after the introduction of public funding for political parties are Norway and Sweden (Svåsand 1992; Widfeldt and Pierre 1992) and The 1979 Election of Members to the House of Representatives Law (Law 72/79).

14 The absence of a specific political finance law does not mean that no political finance regulation exists. The latter may be regulated in a variety of other legal acts (such as media laws or electoral laws).

15 Based on analysis of the International IDEA Political Finance Database. The percentage of countries that has such regulations is defined as those with positive answers to questions 1–13, 15, 17, 19, 22–3, 29–31, 33, 35–39, 41, 43.

16 Van Biezen and Molenaar 2012; Piccio 2012.

17 Data for the 1950s and 1960s: Krouwel 1999, p. 68. For current data, see Statistics Norway (2005–11).

18 Van Biezen, Mair and Poguntke 2012.

19 Van Biezen and Nassmacher 2001, p. 138.

20 For recent figures on Norway see Statistics Norway (2005–2011); for the UK: Committee on Standards in Public Life (annual reports 2000–10); for Belgium (2007): Weekers and Maddens 2009; for France: CNCCFP (2004–11); and for Greece, 1997–2007: Vernardakis 2012.

21 Calculated from the 'intäktsredovisning' (income reporting) voluntarily published by all parliamentary parties apart from the Sweden Democrats.

22 Dragstra 2008, p. 204.

23 Throughout this handbook, international dollars (I$) are presented alongside amounts in national currencies. The international dollar is a hypothetical currency that takes into account purchasing power parity and is therefore suitable for comparisons between countries. For countries in which the power purchasing power parity varies significantly from the United States (which is used as the baseline for the comparison), the I$ exchange rate may be considerably different from the nominal exchange rate. No conversions are given for US dollars (as this is by default the same amount as the I$) or for those instances where the original currency is unknown and a secondary currency such as the euro has been cited instead. For further information, see Annex V.

24 Data based on the 2004 statement of accounts (CNCCFP 2005–6).

25 Statistics Norway.

26 Nassmacher 2009, p. 215.

27 See for instance Koole 2001; van Biezen and Nassmacher 2001.

28 There is no specific accepted threshold defining small donations (Scarrow 2007, p. 197). The legal definition of 'small donations' in Germany—EUR 3,300, I$4,200—has rightly been considered excessively high (Nassmacher 2009, p. 216). In this Chapter I define small donations as under EUR 999.

29 Mair 1998, 2003.

30 Information on Austria, France, Norway and Belgium is based on Nassmacher 2001; Koole 2001; Statistics Norway; Weekers and Maddens 2009.

31 Nassmacher 2009, pp. 261–9.

32 Mathiason 2011; Nassmacher 2009, p. 262.

33 Ewing and Ghaleigh 2006.

34 Both 2002 and 2011 were election years, and the same legislation applies for both. The 2012 Irish political finance law lowered donation ceilings to EUR 2,500 (I$2,800), required that donations over EUR 1,500 (I$1,700) must be declared, and banned corporate donations over EUR 200 (I$230) unless the donors meet specific requirements. Data are published by the Standards in Public Office Commission (SIPO), an independent body established in 2001, which supervises the disclosure of donations, election expenditures and the expenditure of state funding received by the Irish political parties (see http://www.sipo.gov.ie/en/).

35 Colombo 2013.

36 Vernardakis 2012.

37 Council of Europe 2003b, p. 4.

38 GRECO 2007, p. 17.

39 The Entity for Accounts and Political Financing was created in 2003 by Law 19/2003 and established in 2005.

40 This case is known to the public as the 'Portucale affaire'.

41 Sustainable Government Indicators 2011.

42 Council of Europe 2003b, Article 3.

43 CNCCFP 2005–6.

44 Dupont 2010.

45 CNCCFP 2010, p. 101.

46 This section will not deal with the public funding that political parties or party-related organizations receive for supporting political parties or party systems in other countries. Such funding is, for example, provided in Denmark, Germany, the Netherlands, Sweden and the UK.

47 *Times of Malta* 2009.

48 Nassmacher 2003. See also http://www.parlament.ch/ab/frameset/f/n/4813/321237/f_n_4813_321237_321507.htm

49 Piccio 2012, pp. 88–9.

50 Ohman, 2012, p. 25.

51 The Netherlands is the only country in Western Europe that explicitly provides public funding to political parties based on party membership requirements. In order to receive public funding, political parties must have at least 1,000 members (Piccio 2013). However, in a number of other countries minimum requirements of societal support are implicit, as they are necessary conditions for political parties to register (Finland, Norway, Sweden and Portugal) (Piccio 2014).

52 According to the OSCE/Venice Commission Guidelines, '(a)t a minimum, some degree of public funding should be available to all parties represented in parliament. However, to

promote political pluralism, some funding should also be extended beyond those parties represented in parliament to include all parties putting forth candidates for an election and enjoying a minimum level of citizen support. This is particularly important in the case of new parties, which must be given a fair opportunity to compete with existing parties' (OSCE/ODIHR 2010, pp. 71–2).

53   No official thresholds exist in Finland or the Netherlands. The two countries' effective thresholds are 0.35 and 0.67 per cent, respectively.

54   Nassmacher 2003; Piccio 2013.

55   The countries included in this analysis are Argentina, Brazil, Chile, Colombia, Costa Rica, El Salvador, Guatemala, Honduras, Mexico, Nicaragua, Paraguay, Peru, Uruguay and Venezuela (see Casal Bértoa et al. 2014, forthcoming).

56   Direct forms of public funding are the 'Short' and 'Cranborne' money that is granted to opposition parties of the House of Commons and the House of Lords (introduced in 1975 and 1996, respectively), and the 'policy development grants' to finance policy research to parties that hold at least two seats in the House of Commons (introduced in 2000).

57   Committee on Standards in Public Life 2011, p. 36.

58   Average percentages are adapted from Dragstra (2008, p. 306) and 'Notitie Herijking Wet subsidiëring politieke partijen', Kst. 27442, nr. 6. See Piccio 2013.

59   Crouch 2004.

60   Council of Europe, Rec. 1516(2001), 2001.

61   Nassmacher 1993; Katz and Mair 1995; Scarrow 2004; Piccio 2014. As Katz and Mair (2009, p. 756) underlined, political parties are privileged organizations, 'and they are unique in that they have the ability to devise their own legal (and not only legal) environment and, effectively, to write their own salary checks'.

62   Katz and Mair 1995.

63   For a discussion, see Nassmacher 1993; Scarrow 2004; Koß 2008.

64   Seiradaki 2012.

65   Adapted from data of the Inter-Parliamentary Union, available at http://www.ipu.org/wmn-e/arc/classif010213.htm

66   Available at http://www.quotaproject.org/

67   Constitutional Act No. 99-569 of 8 July 1999.

68   Law no. 88-227 of 11 March 1988 on financial transparency in political life (Article 9-1).

69   IPU 2012, p. 3.

70   Ibid.

71   CNCCFP 2011, p. 6.

72   Murray 2007, p. 571.

73   Electoral (Amendment) (Political Funding) Act of 2012, section 27. See http://www.partylaw.leidenuniv.nl

74   Lei da Paridade, Lei Orgânica nº 3/2006, de 21 de Agosto [Parity Law, Organic Law no. 3/2006 of 21 August].

75   Law No. 96 of 6 June 2012, Article 9.6. See http://www.partylaw.leidenuniv.nl

76   WEDO 2007.

77   OSCE 2010, p. 75; EP 2012.

78   EP 2012, section 18.

79   Rechtbank's-Gravenhage, 2005, LJN: AU2088, HA ZA 03/3395. Under CEDAW, 'States Parties shall take all appropriate measures to eliminate discrimination against women in

the political and public life of the country and, in particular, shall ensure to women, on equal terms with men, the right: (a) to vote in all elections and public referenda and to be eligible for election of all publicly elected bodies' (Art. 7).

80 *De Saambinder*, 22 September 2005, pp. 4–5.

81 Barkhuysen 2004; Ten Napel 2011; Oomen, Huijt and Ploeg 2010.

82 More recently, and after new judicial rulings on women's discrimination by the SGP, the party also changed its internal statutes, allowing women passive suffrage. The decision was taken in March 2013.

83 OCSE/ODHIR 2010, pp. 75–6.

84 Ohman 2012, pp. 35–7.

85 See Chapter 6 in this Handbook and van Biezen 2004.

86 Testo Unico delle Leggi Elettorali D.P.R. 30 marzo 1957, no 361, Art. 96.

87 Saviano 2013.

88 Clift and Fisher 2004, p. 690.

89 GRECO 2007, p. 18.

90 Standards in Public Office Commission of Ireland, 2007. See http://www.sipo.gov.ie/en/About-Us/Our-Policies/Review-of-Legislation/Submission-to-the-Minister/

91 Committee on Standards in Public Life (UK) 1998.

92 See Fisher 2001; Clift and Fisher, 2005. In 2004, the Electoral Commission proposed to lower the spending limits from GBP 20 million (I\$32.7 million) to GBP 15 million (I\$24.5 million). For a review of the discussion on expenditure limits in the UK, see Electoral Commission 2008, pp. 40–6.

93 *Bowman v. United Kingdom*, App. No. 24839/94, 26 Eur. H.R. Rep. 1 (1998).

94 See http://www.loc.gov/law/help/campaign-finance/uk.php#issues

95 See Griner 2005 for an analysis of this subject in relation to Canada and the United States.

96 Farrell and Webb 2002. The countries included in their analysis are Austria, Belgium, Denmark, Finland, Ireland, Italy, the Netherlands, Norway, Sweden and the United Kingdom.

97 See http://www.conseil-constitutionnel.fr/conseil-constitutionnel/francais/documentation/dossiers-thematiques/2007-election-presidentielle/faq/financement-et-prise-en-charge-de-la-campagne-electorale/quel-est-le-cout-des-elections-presidentielles.98832.html

98 Voerman 2012.

99 Electoral Commission (UK) 2011, pp. 23–4. The main reduction in spending related to the Labour Party, which according to its financial report spent only GBP 8 million (I\$13 million) in 2010, compared to GBP 18 million (I\$29 million) in 2005.

100 Nassmacher 2009, Chapters 2–4.

101 Council of Europe (2003).

102 Nassmacher 2001, p. 11.

103 Doublet 2011, p. 7.

104 De Sousa 2005.

105 GRECO 2007, p. 23.

106 It should be mentioned, however, that although the complete balance of assets of political parties is not available to the public in Spain, the Court of Audit publishes annual reports that include findings and remarks in connection with the monitoring of political finance, and an annex with summary information on the annual accounts of political parties.

107 GRECO has urged the establishment of a single computerized format for the accounts of Spain, Luxembourg, Andorra, Ireland, Netherlands, Norway, Portugal and the UK (Doublet 2011, pp. 20–1).

108 This was recently amended in the new political finance law, 'Wet financiering politieke partijen', adopted in March 2013.

109 Council of Europe 2003b. Article 14 of the recommendation calls for an independent monitoring system for the funding of political parties and electoral campaigns.

110 The International IDEA Political Finance Database includes no data on this issue for Liechtenstein.

111 De Sousa 2012.

112 Loi n° 88-227 du 11 mars 1988 relative à la transparence financière de la vie politique, Art. 11-5 [Law No. 88-227 of 11 March 1988 on the financial transparency of political life, Art. 11-5].

113 GRECO 2007, p. 33.

114 Ibid., p. 18.

115 Doublet 2011, p. 53.

116 *El Pais* (2013).

117 See, for example, Koß 2008.

118 Eurobarometer 2012a.

119 Epstein 1986; van Biezen 2004.

120 Schattschneider 1942, p. 1.

121 Katz and Mair 2009, p. 756.

122 This is among the best-known arguments behind the 'cartel-party' hypothesis (Katz and Mair 1995).

123 See Piccio and van Biezen 2014, forthcoming.

124 See the World Values Survey data reported in Dalton and Wattemberg 2002, p. 265.

125 Policy makers are defined as those involved in drafting, amending and adopting political finance policies, either from the executive or from the legislative arm of government.

CHAPTER 8

CHAPTER 8

The Established Anglophone Democracies

Karl-Heinz Nassmacher

Introduction

This chapter focuses on the six established anglophone democracies of Western Europe, North America and Oceania: Australia, Canada, Ireland, New Zealand, the United Kingdom (UK) and the United States of America (USA).[1] Despite differences in size and geographical location, these countries have historical, cultural and legal similarities that should make it easy to compare their experiences in handling the common problems of modern democracy, especially with regard to financial matters. Although they are all old democracies, they have not solved all problems related to money in politics. Enduring problems include unlevel playing fields, dependency on corporate and trade union donations, and largely uncontrolled spending by actors other than political parties and candidates ('third parties'). Different loopholes in each country have allowed stakeholders to avoid various regulations and have harmed transparency in political finance.

All six countries are members of the Organisation for Economic Co-operation and Development (OECD) with high incomes. They are also English speaking[2] and share a joint legal tradition (the 'common law').[3] All have enjoyed a long, uninterrupted tradition of free elections, popular government and the rule of law. Political parties have alternated between the roles of government and opposition. All countries were at some point part of the British Empire—the USA until 1776–83 and Ireland until 1916–20—and the others are still members of the Commonwealth.

Yet they also have important differences, especially in relation to their political systems. Three countries (the USA, Canada and Australia) have federal (plus state/provincial) governments,[4] and the other three (the UK, New Zealand and Ireland) have unitary systems with a central government.[5]

Only the USA uses a *presidential system* that separates the three branches of government (legislative, executive and judiciary). This separation of powers does not require joint action by parliamentary parties, which affects party discipline and parties' overall positions in the political system. In the USA, individual candidates are at the centre of the electoral process; political parties play a limited role in the candidate selection process due to the primary electoral system used in most US states.

The other five countries are *parliamentary democracies*, adhering to the 'Westminster model', with its fusion of legislative and executive powers in a majority-based cabinet. Political parties in these countries have stronger positions in parliament and government; the systems in three of the five countries are also partially candidate-centred due to the majority-based electoral systems used there.[6] The 'Westminster model of political finance' is characterized by fewer regulations, frequent spending limits (for constituency candidates) and a general absence of public subsidies. This model applies the concept of transparency 'to campaign expenditures by candidates and not to party incomes and expenditures in general'.[7] One aim of this chapter is to examine the applicability of this model to the countries analysed.

The USA and UK instituted political finance regulations as early as the 19th century. In 1883, both countries enacted legislation for the purpose of protecting electoral politics; the USA created a statutory ban on the abuse of civil servants in elections, and the UK banned the distribution of alcoholic drinks in connection with election campaigns.[8] Canada, Australia and New Zealand initiated their own versions of some of the early British rules to regulate spending in constituency campaigns; Ireland followed suit later. Later amendments to existing legislation concerned spending by parties and other bodies, transparency of sources, creation of a monitoring agency, and contribution bans and limits.

Current challenges of political finance

Although the current regulation of political finance is different for all six countries, there are some general issues to discuss before addressing specific regulations and regulatory measures. Do spending and contribution limits unduly interfere with civil liberties or constitutional rights? Can the possible abuse of state resources for partisan advantage be prevented? Do specific parties need corporate or trade union contributions? Are parties and candidates the only actors in the electoral process that need to be regulated?

Unequal access to resources

Political differences between parties include their unequal appeal to voters and donors. Because parties are linked with different segments of society (e.g., business and trade unions), not all of them will have the same resources at

> The freedom to use unrestricted amounts of money and other resources in politics transfers the unequal distribution of income and wealth among members of a modern society to the political process. This endangers equality (one person, one vote), an essential aspect of all democratic politics.

their disposal. However, unequal access to political funding may bring about skewed competition, especially during elections. By contrast, reliable access to sufficient resources for all competitors means a more level playing field, which is an important precondition of fair elections. The freedom to use unrestricted amounts of money and other resources in politics transfers the unequal distribution of income and wealth among members of a modern society to the political process. This endangers equality (one person, one vote), an essential aspect of all democratic politics.[9]

The unequal appeal to different segments of society can be partially equalized by public funds, which provide income floors for all relevant competitors. In many countries public subsidies come with strings attached, such as requiring more transparent funding or banning/limiting specific financial activities.

'Free speech' vs 'fair elections'

Freedom of expression is one of the most highly respected civil liberties protected by democratic constitutions. Unfortunately, this freedom can sometimes conflict with the principle of fair elections. In the course of political finance legislation, supreme courts in three of the countries studied have had to decide which principle represents the overriding value for a specific democracy. In Australia and the USA, the highest courts of the land have held that 'free speech' may not be infringed upon to provide a level playing field between political competitors. People who intend to express their views may want to spend money to be heard by others, and they may speak up collectively to promote their political views without restriction. Therefore the US Supreme Court[10] ruled that money is an important dimension of 'speech' and that organizations enjoy the freedom of expression, too. Or, in short, money can be speech and organizations can also speak.

The case that the Australian High Court had to decide was different, but with some similarities. In 1991 the Australian Labor government passed the Political Broadcasts and Disclosure Act, which banned paid TV and radio advertising by political parties and required free campaign broadcasts of commercial radio and TV operators.[11] In 1992 the High Court ruled that these provisions were unconstitutional.[12] However, this has not meant a complete ban on party spending limitations; three Australian states have enacted spending limits for political parties and candidates.

The Supreme Court of Canada[13] holds the opposite view: the overriding aim of fair elections demands that all views shall be heard in an election campaign, and subsequently the use of financial resources should be limited to avoid unequal opportunities for the political competitors.[14] High courts in New Zealand and the UK have not yet had to take sides on the conflict between the two principles, and statutory limits for parties and candidates have not been challenged in court. The same is true for Ireland, which has introduced spending limits for candidates (though not for political parties) to improve the fairness of elections by levelling the playing field for all competitors.

Abuse of state resources

A further issue in fair elections is the behaviour of incumbents (governments and politicians) during their re-election bids. Every incumbent running in an election has to face a difficult conflict of interest between being both the office holder and the candidate. Incumbent abuse of state resources is a classic problem of political funding. Office holders are entitled to privileges, services and powers that are not available to all other candidates. What prevents an incumbent from using resources that her or his opponents lack access to? The voting public and competing candidates would probably be reluctant to rely solely on the incumbents' sense of fairness.

Yet incumbents have always been able to use public funds to support their re-election bids. Whereas the distribution of public subsidies opens up opportunities for opposing parties and candidates, the abuse of state resources for electoral gain is by no means limited to such extreme cases as paying for partisan publicity from secret government funds,[15] sending a tax inspector to harass opposition candidates or excessive coverage of government actions in the publicly-owned media.[16]

In Canada and the UK, state institutions (e.g., corporations in public ownership, called 'crown corporations' in Canada) are not considered 'permissible donors' to political contenders. For Australia and the USA, the International IDEA Database on Political Finance (Political Finance Database) shows a cross-section of regulations aimed to prevent common types of abuses. Both countries have a detailed list of campaign activities that may not be performed by public employees. A wealth of potential assistance to parties and candidates is expressly banned for civil servants, especially those on duty. In the UK, civil servants must not 'undertake any activity which could call into question their political impartiality, and 'ministers must not use Government resources for party political purposes'.[17]

Nevertheless, in Australia, as in other democracies, 'government advertising has become a significant incumbency benefit' and the majority of High Court judges have allowed 'the use of taxpayers' funds for partisan political purposes'.[18] However, some High Court judges have 'expressed grave concern at practices such as advertising government policy before parliamentary consideration of related legislation'.[19]

In New Zealand, 'about 1200 staff are employed by the Ministerial and Parliamentary Services, many of whom carry out party political research, marketing and organising. .... regional party organisers (previously paid for by the party organisation) have been replaced by electorate agents (paid for by the Parliamentary Service)'.[20]

Dependence on corporate and trade union contributions

Whereas Canada has banned corporate as well as trade union contributions to political parties and candidates, the USA (despite similar bans in 1907 and 1943, respectively) has developed ways to channel such funds into the political process, which will be discussed further below. However, in three anglophone countries, corporate and union contributions are the traditional mainstays of the two major parties' revenue. The Conservatives in the UK, the Nationals in New Zealand and the Liberals in Australia rely heavily on business contributions, including contributions from individual businessmen. The Labour parties in all three democracies were established as political arms of the trade union movement, and are traditionally funded by the unions, although this is no longer their only source of revenue.[21] In Ireland, Labour is a minor party, but its funding does not differ from that of its sister parties.[22]

In New Zealand and the UK (and possibly in Australia and Ireland), the 'class-conscious' tradition of political funding (trade union affiliation fees and business contributions as 'institutional sources') of the two major parties is an obvious obstacle to an outright ban of (or possibly even limit on) 'institutional' donations, as has been enacted in Canada and the USA.[23]

Third-party campaigning

In a free country, actors that are neither political parties nor candidates may want to spend funds in order to influence political discourse in general or the outcome of an election in particular. Such political spending by individuals, groups or organizations (most often called 'third parties' or occasionally 'parallel campaigners') poses serious problems in terms of the amount of corporate and interested money that can be channelled into the political process. Transparency may also suffer, since these indirect expenditures are more difficult for monitoring institutions to track during election periods. Some regulatory systems do not regulate third-party spending (in our sample, this applies only to Ireland), which gives interest groups a significant role in political spending,[24] although campaign spending by parties and candidates is subject to statutory limits.

Australia and the USA have not limited political spending by parties, candidates[25] or third parties. The US *Citizens United vs the Federal Election Commission* ruling increased opportunities for third-party involvement. One estimate from the 2012 presidential election indicates that, while Barack Obama's campaign received only 10 per cent of its donations from third parties, more than one-third of the funds spent in relation to the Mitt Romney campaign went through third parties.[26] Both the USA and Canada do, however, require third-party spending to be reported to the public.

Canada,[27] New Zealand[28] and the UK[29] have moved one step further. They stipulate statutory limits not only for parties and candidates but also for certain political spending by third parties during campaign periods. The implementation of effective controls for parties and candidates stimulates the need to apply additional measures to other areas. However, data from Canada show two relevant trends. First, over three electoral cycles both the number of (registered) third parties and their expenses have increased. Second, compared to total campaign spending by parties and candidates, the overall outlay for third-party activity remains negligible.[30] The latter was also true for political spending in the British 2010 campaign, as third parties represented less than 6 per cent of political parties' election expenditures.[31]

Overview of political finance regulation

All political finance regimes are composed of several regulative, distributive and incentive elements, including controls and enforcement strategies.[32] The six anglophone democracies use several methods to regulate money in politics, yet—in contrast to the notion of a common Westminster model of political finance regulation—there is no common pattern of regulation that applies to all of them. Nonetheless, the countries discussed in this chapter have rules that in many respects are more advanced than those in the other groups of countries included in this global study.[33]

Introduction of relevant regulation

Since the late 19th century, countries have created rules concerning the role of money in politics. With hindsight, such individual measures were elements of a general process of transforming political parties from private associations to 'public utilities'.[34] As long as 'parties were regarded as private associations largely immune from mandatory legal regulation', they were 'open to every abuse that unscrupulous men … incredible wealth and dictatorial power could devise'.[35] Such abuse was not limited to the USA, which enacted major rules concerning campaign funds in 1883, 1907, 1943 and 1971. Starting in Canada in 1974, the term 'political party' entered the statute law of the other anglophone countries (Australia in 1984, New Zealand in 1993, Ireland in 1997 and the UK in 1998). Much like the business world, the political sphere of civil society requires public regulation of competitive practices. As a consequence, political parties are today treated like 'public utilities' (i.e., private organizations under some sort of public supervision) in the established anglophone democracies—and many others.

Can reform waves be identified? Among the six countries, Canada and the USA started to update their rudimentary political finance rules in the early 1970s and went through a second round of tightening regulations after 2000. Australia followed in the 1980s and 1990s, and recent changes at the state level may indicate that additional reforms are to come at the national level. However, the fact that after more than five years, the 2008 green paper on regulatory reform still has not made it through the Senate serves to dampen optimism in this area. The UK did not make substantial changes between 1883 and 2000,[36] but has enacted a rash of reforms recently (2000, 2006, 2009). New Zealand (2010) and Ireland (2012) have produced the most recent amendments to their legislation.

Political finance continues to be an issue.[37] Since 2000 a general improvement in regulation has occurred in five of the six countries.[38] A common motivation for all these measures was that the government of the day wanted to overcome some sort of media outcry ('campaigners spend too much' or 'politics is too sleazy'). The regulatory activity in Canada, Ireland, New Zealand and the UK since 2000 demonstrates the general paradox of reform measures. Implementation of reform legislation breeds the need for more (and more complex) reform legislation. The e laborate restrictions designed to control the flow of funds into the political process have encouraged professional politicians to engage in a creative search for loopholes either in the application of the existing law or, when necessary, by drafting amendments. Only Australia and the USA, most probably because of their restrictive court rulings that certain types of regulations are unconstitutional, have so far not bowed to demands by the media and public opinion for reforms. It remains to be seen how long both countries can hold out against the pressure for reform.

> The elaborate restrictions designed to control the flow of funds into the political process have encouraged professional politicians to engage in a creative search for loopholes either in the application of the existing law or, when necessary, by drafting amendments.

Two possible patterns

In understanding the regulations in the countries discussed in this chapter, it is useful to employ a typology that contrasts an 'expense-centred pattern' with a 'revenue-centred pattern'.[39] A revenue-centred pattern would require disclosing sources or enacting contribution bans/limits or both—but would completely neglect political spending. Australia fits the revenue-centred pattern, as does the USA (if the voluntary limits on presidential campaign spending, which have become highly symbolic, are ignored). Both countries require the reporting of revenue, while the USA adds some contribution limits. Ireland, which requires a donors' list and limits spending by parliamentary candidates (but not by political parties) comes rather close to a pattern that is centred on revenue.

Two major factors suggest that Canada, New Zealand and the UK fall under the 'expense-centred' category. All three countries limit campaign spending by parties, candidates and third parties. All three countries also require reporting on financial transactions by all these participants in campaign activities. While Canada also restricts contributions, the other two countries are quite liberal in this respect. This indicates that these two patterns are closer to the core intentions of regulatory systems in the countries studied here: (1) to level the playing field by limiting campaign spending, thus preventing the 'buying' of an election and ending the potential 'arms race' between competitors;[40] or (2) to reduce the influence of 'fat cats' (wealthy donors) and the hazards of corruption by disclosure of donors and/or contribution limits.

Sources of income for political parties and candidates

Sources of political revenue are frequently subject to political finance regulation. These rules aim at specific sources and are deemed to counteract undue or illicit influence on political parties and politicians. Such influence can be corrupt in principle or unwanted by some competitors. Control measures either ban selected types of donors from making contributions in order to preclude all potential hazards or limit the amount that can be donated in order to make sure that political actors do not become dependent on specific donors.

Contribution bans

The International IDEA Political Finance Database offers information on five types of contribution bans: foreign interests, trade unions, corporations, anonymous donors and government contractors (or corporations in partial public ownership) may be legally banned from contributing to parties or candidates. Australia does not operate any of these bans, which—given the role of mining in the Australian economy—could become a serious problem, although the mining and petroleum sectors have been unlikely to make political donations in that country.[41] In New Zealand, foreign donations are allowed if they are below 1,500 New Zealand dollars (NZD) (I$1,000),[42] and government contractors (and possibly state-owned enterprises) are also allowed to donate. Ireland and the UK deviate slightly from this pattern because they ban foreign contributions.[43] Canada and the USA have the strictest regulation in this respect: they ban all foreign contributions to parties and candidates, as well as donations from trade unions and corporations.[44] However, in the USA many political action committees (PACs) were organized in order to circumvent such bans.[45]

None of the six countries has an outright ban on anonymous donations; all instead set maximum amounts for legally anonymous contributions. This is the practical approach to encouraging smaller donations while ensuring transparency around larger donations; put differently, this type of regulation does not limit the *amount* that can be contributed, only the amount that can be contributed *anonymously*.

Three of the maximums for anonymous donations are rather low: 20 Canadian dollars (CAD) (I$20) in Canada, 20 US dollars (USD)[46] in the USA and 100 euros (EUR) (I$130) in Ireland. Three cut-off points are considerably higher: 500 pounds sterling (GBP) (I$820) in the UK, NZD 1,500 (I$1,000) in New Zealand and as much as 12,100 Australian dollars (AUD) (I$9,350) in Australia.[47] This raises the question of whether such high thresholds contribute to the transparency of political funds.

Figure 8.1. Maximum amounts for legally anonymous contributions in anglophone countries (in I$)

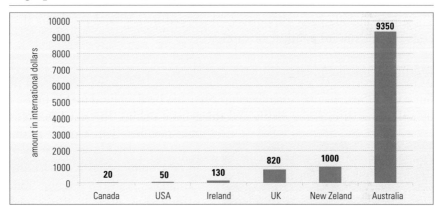

Source: International IDEA Political Finance Database. See http://www.idea.int/political-finance/question.cfm?field=259&region=-1

Contribution limits

Australia, New Zealand and the UK do not limit contributions to either parties or candidates, either during specific time periods or for election campaign purposes. The USA has implemented different contribution limits, depending on whether the donation is to a PAC, a party's Executive Committee or a candidate. Together these limits are the most generous among the anglophone democracies, and this increased further through the April 2014 decision by the US Supreme Court to overturn the existing aggregate donation limits through the *McCutcheon vs Federal Election Commission* case.[48] The annual limits in Ireland are EUR 2,500 (I$2,800) per party and EUR 1,000 (I$1,100) per parliamentary candidate, while the Canadian limits are the strictest in our sample; individual citizens and permanent residents can give no more than CAD 1,100 (I\$980) annually to a political party (party headquarters), plus the same amount to local party associations, constituency candidates or nomination contestants. Because there are separate limits for contributions to non-party candidates and leadership contestants, the maximum amount an individual can legally donate to politics in any calendar year is CAD 4,400 (I\$3,900). In Canada and the USA, limits are automatically adjusted for inflation.[49]

In general, if the law does not specify that these are maximum donations per donor and per year, this results in a legal loophole by which a donor can make many anonymous donations (each of which is close to the legal maximum) in a single year. However, all the countries examined here have closed this potential loophole.

Sources of private funding

This section discusses types of political income from a variety of sources. These may include party supporters, 'interested money' and payments that cross the line toward political corruption.

Membership dues

Since the 1950s, the mass-membership party has been an ideal highly praised by political scientists, the media and the general public. This concept holds that members join a party at the grass-roots level and participate in developing policy and selecting candidates, and the revenue from membership dues is distributed between local, regional and central party organizations. There is no doubt that many party members contribute much of their time to voluntary party activities, among them canvassing voters, discussing party politics and recruiting party representatives. The loss of volunteers as a result of decreasing numbers of party members is probably more significant than the loss of grass-roots funding.[50] The decline in 'free campaigning' by UK party member volunteers is a telling example.[51]

> The loss of volunteers as a result of decreasing numbers of party members is probably more significant than the loss of grass-roots funding.

Unfortunately, there is little information about party revenue and the split of membership dues between local and national parties that fits this ideal of membership-based parties.[52] It is fairly safe to assume that no political party in the countries studied here has ever collected a significant part of its national headquarters' revenue from individual membership dues,[53] for a variety of reasons.

The UK Conservative Party is the only party in our sample that has had a considerable bottom-up contribution toward headquarters' revenue. Such 'constituency quotas' peaked in the late 1960s, and by 1990 they amounted to no more than 5 per cent of total income.[54]

In North America, only some state or provincial branches of the traditional political parties have been active in recruiting party members. Among the labour parties of the four other countries, collective affiliation by trade unions has always yielded more funds for party headquarters than individual membership. Parties that are based on individual members have comparatively small annual dues (less than I$30 per year),[55] and it is unlikely that much of these funds ends up at national headquarters. The member-to-voter ratio in these four countries is low (1–2 per cent) and the number of party members is declining (as it is in all established democracies). In sum, what share of this (declining) revenue is expected to pay for the rising expenses of party headquarters?

Small (individual) donations

Some parties in the anglophone countries have a tradition of soliciting small donations from among their local supporters without a formal commitment from the donor to contribute again in the future. Annual fundraising drives, local yard sales and fundraising events (with low ticket prices) provide funds for local campaigns and the local organization.

However, modern technology has enabled party and campaign headquarters to contact individuals on a large scale to request donations (no matter how small the amount). Telethons in the USA came first,[56] followed by direct mailings by US Republicans, which were successfully copied by the Canadian Progressive Conservative Party.[57] Internet appeals today are state-of-the-art.

Building on the expertise developed by its predecessor parties (the Progressive Conservative Party and the Reform Party), the Conservative Party of Canada (CPC) developed a persistent fundraising advantage over its competitors (Liberals, New Democratic Party, Bloc Qébécois [BQ]) between 2006 and 2009.[58] Taking advantage of the opportunities created by the current regulation (contribution bans and limits, tax credits), the CPC can now engage in fundraising before the start of the official campaign period.[59]

Whereas Obama's two US presidential campaigns demonstrated the possibilities of advanced fundraising techniques, Brian Mulroney's (Progressive Conservative Party in Canada) last years in office revealed their hazards, in particular that all voluntary giving from party supporters depends on acceptance and popularity, both of which go through cycles of boom and bust. If the public is emotionally attached to a party or candidate, it may freely contribute funds; but if policies or politicians do not inspire voters for whatever reason, their funding will be in jeopardy. A decline in popularity tends to trigger a decline in political revenue. Success in fundraising is a bellwether of victory at the polls, while meagre fundraising signals electoral disaster. Just like the bulk of opinion polling, effective fundraising strategies may increase the volatility of politics. As a political system, democracy has to sustain such cycles—possibly with a change of government. For this reason, financial floors to maintain reasonable competition and a level playing field are as important as ceilings.

Unfortunately, all mass solicitations include the risk of 'bundling'. Any organization with a vast number of members (or employees) can assume an intermediate position between individual donors and fundraising politicians. Collecting small cheques and delivering them in a bundle will have a similar impact to a large donation, since the recipient will still know who is doing a favour for him or her. This technique has been applied by US PACs run by efficiently organized lobby groups, such as ALIGNPAC (a life insurance group) and EMILY's list (a group supporting Democratic, pro-choice female candidates).[60]

Moreover, lack of effort (motivation) by the parties and lack of considerable middle-class incomes (in most new democracies) are major obstacles to applying this concept in other countries. Whereas direct mail solicitation and Internet fundraising drives have collected millions of dollars in the USA and Canada, these techniques have not caught on in the other democracies in this sample.

> ...financial floors to maintain reasonable competition and a level playing field are as important as ceilings.

Large donations from individuals, corporations and trade unions

Political donors are frequently classified according to the amount they contribute to a party or candidate. Those who make small donations are assumed to be driven by community-oriented goals or policies in general. Those who give considerably more may do so for ideological or pragmatic/ practical considerations. If the donation cannot be subsumed under either category, the donor is expected to be pursuing some sort of personal gain (a specific policy, a personal favour or simply access to someone in power).[61]

The goal of individuals or groups that make large donations is generally to gain access to argue or explain a particular issue or case, often in the hope that they will receive special treatment. Therefore, large donations may jeopardize democratic politics, which is the main motivation for requiring the disclosure of donors' identities. Such disclosure allows citizens' groups and the media to ask questions about the donor and publicly debate their motive; corporations often expect tangible returns on such investments.[62]

Yet not all donors are corrupt, and not all donations are made as a quid pro quo. Even business and union donors have a legitimate interest in supporting parties with policies they favour. Problems for democracy arise if parties become dependent on large donors, their contributions are clandestine and/or they result in a massive financial imbalance between competitors. Measures of political finance regulation are intended to address all of these situations.

When businesses contribute to political parties, their incentive can be partly ideological or pragmatic—or both. Whereas ideological considerations tend to favour parties with business-friendly policies, pragmatic reasons are more likely to induce donations to the party in power. 'Australian business combines a pragmatic reaction to changing political circumstances with a massive ideological bias towards the more conservative parties.'[63] Only when it is in power (or leading in public opinion polls) can the Australian Labor Party expect to share business donations equally with its Liberal and National competitors.

While the combination of contribution bans and public subsidies has effectively removed such hazards in Canada, in the USA (and to some extent Australia), Supreme/High Court rulings have counteracted all previous attempts to limit the influence of big money on elections.[64] Since Australian parties are allowed to accept large anonymous donations, it is not surprising that the source of about half of the major parties' revenue is unknown; Australian parties probably rely heavily on large donations.[65]

The UK has achieved more transparency, but has not yet gone beyond the traditional funding sources of the three major parties: trade unions, the corporate world and very rich individuals. Trade unions and rich donors are major sources of UK Labour Party funds, while the Conservatives and Liberal Democrats relied on public funds, rich individuals and corporate donors during their time in opposition.[66] The Electoral Commission found that between 2001 and 2010, the 50 largest donors provided 44 per cent of the total reported donations, with almost all this money going to the three largest parties.[67]

A specific problem in UK party funding arose when rich people privately provided loans to Labour and the Conservatives (totaling some GBP 15 million [I$24.5 million] to each); some of the creditors were later nominated for a peerage.[68] Loans have since come under the control of the Electoral Administration Act of 2006.

> Problems for democracy arise if parties become dependent on large donors, their contributions are clandestine and/or they result in a massive financial imbalance between competitors.

During the late 1980s, corporate donors in Canada provided about half the total election-year revenue for the Liberals and the Progressive Conservative Party (PC), and in non-election years about 40 per cent for the PC and 60 per cent for the Liberals. In election years trade union affiliation fees still covered one-quarter of the New Democratic Party's election-related income.[69] Today, federal political finance legislation has completely banned funding from such sources for all Canadian parties.

Fundraising events (dinners and lunches)

In Canada, the United States and Australia, fundraising events, especially dinners, are an old staple of political finance. In its traditional form, such an event 'combines food and wine with a chance for the party faithful and others to meet in a social situation'.[70] Political dignitaries usually meet a large and receptive audience; participants pay for an 'overpriced' ticket and the opportunity to access decision makers.[71]

In recent decades, tables at (sometimes lavish) fundraising dinners have been paid for by corporations, which send their executives to attend and meet with the politicians in order to exchange views. In Australia, a former state premier indicated that parties 'openly call for donations that provide access at rates of [AUD] 10,000 [I$7,700] to the prime minister ... It costs less to get to see a minister'.[72] It has been reported that business leaders have to pay AUD 1,400 (I$1,100) to get near a federal minister.[73]

Income from elected officials

In the established democracies of continental Western Europe the assessment of office holders (a 'party tax' levied on the political income of ministers, members of parliament [MPs], municipal councillors, and managers of government departments or state-owned enterprises) has long been an important source of party revenue. Of the six anglophone countries, such levies are mainly collected in Australia, where such revenue helps to fill state party coffers and does not contribute to the budgets of federal parties.[74]

In the USA it has been, and in some states still is, common practice for incumbent parties to collect deductions from the salaries of public employees ('macing'). However, there is no indication that such funds are still a significant part of political revenue; they are certainly not an important source of federal revenue.

Foreign funding

There are many reasons for individuals or organizations to donate money to foreign political parties. The most recent motivation is to support democratic institution building in new or fledgling democracies. Scandals in some countries have revealed that foreign donations were used as a means to disguise domestic or illegal sources (e.g., business donations or drug trafficking). No such cases can be reported for these six nations recently.

Although Australia does not have bans on foreign donations (and New Zealand and the UK allow them up to a certain limit), such contributions do not pose any major threats to this sample of countries. In the UK, Lakshmi Mittal (an Indian steel maker) and Bearwood Corporate Services (which was closely associated with Lord Ashcroft) made donations to the Labour and Conservative parties, respectively. These and other cases were frequently debated in the media and led to strict limits on donations from foreign sources.[75]

Public funding

Public subsidies (sometimes called 'government funding' or 'state aid' in anglophone countries) can provide an additional (or in some cases alternative) source of funding; depending on the national situation, they can help level the playing field. State aid can be given in cash or in kind. In both cases, the rules for access and allocation are important to ensure the fair treatment of political competitors.

Government funding can be distributed in various ways. Flat grants for many competitors are the most frequent way to support party activity. Other methods include reimbursements of specified expenses (which tie public support to successful fundraising by parties and/or candidates) and tax benefits or matching grants (which provide incentives for donors or fundraisers).

Indirect public funding

In most modern democracies, access to electronic media is important for delivering campaign messages. When stipulating access to these channels for political contesters, Australia refers to 'reasonable access' while the USA uses the term 'equal opportunities' for all participating parties. Neither of the two countries guarantees free or subsidized airtime with any broadcaster.

Canada differentiates between political parties that can afford to pay for advertising and those (most likely new and small) that cannot. Such minority parties can claim two minutes of free advertising with all broadcasters. The other parties are allocated time according to party strength (but have to pay for it).

Ireland, New Zealand and the UK provide free broadcasting time for all parties that have nominated a minimum number of candidates. In the UK, free airtime has to be provided not only by the network in public ownership (the BBC) but also by commercial broadcasters. The allocation formula seeks a fair opportunity for each party, taking into account share of seats and votes, number of candidates or 'any other indication of public support' (e.g., public opinion polls and number of party members) (as in New Zealand). The different indicators of strength ensure the fair treatment of government and opposition, major and minor parties, established and new parties. Whereas none of the six countries has any provision for free or subsidized media time for parliamentary candidates, Ireland grants independent candidates 'some coverage in the news'.[76] The UK supports each parliamentary candidate by delivering one free mailing to all constituents and providing the free use of public meeting rooms for election rallies.

Only two of the anglophone countries offer tax benefits to individual taxpayers for political donations to parties or candidates. Australia offers a tax deduction of up to AUD 1,500 (I$1,200) from taxable income and Canada offers an income tax credit (against tax liability) of up to CAD 500 ($440) for a donation of CAD 1,155 (I$1,000) (or more). In Ireland, New Zealand, the UK and the USA, there are no tax benefits for political donations of any kind or amount.[77]

Direct public funding

All six anglophone democracies offer direct public subsidies to political parties. However, the total amounts and kinds of subsidies are completely different for each country. In Australia parties receive election funding payments, but they do not have to account for their spending. Irish parties are paid two different annual allocations, a Party Leaders Allowance and Exchequer Funding under the Electoral Acts, but there is a statutory ban on using the funds for election campaigns. The USA offers three different kinds of subsidy, all of which are election-related; only the grant to support party nominating conventions is still operational. New Zealand pays a regular entitlement for parliamentary purposes (including general party activities, but expressly excluding electioneering) plus a campaign-oriented broadcasting allocation to be spent only on election advertising. The UK, which by continental European standards offers a very low level of public subsidies, provides allowances for the parliamentary work of the opposition parties (only) in both chambers of parliament, plus a GBP 2 million (I$3.3 million) policy development grant.[78] Subsidies to 'the opposition only' are unique among all subsidies provided, and are meant to counterbalance the advantages associated with control of the government apparatus.[79]

Canada has thus far been a most generous subsidy provider. There are campaign expense reimbursements for candidates (50 per cent of the legal spending limit) and for parties (60 per cent of the legal spending limit). A quarterly allowance is also currently available to five registered parties (including the BQ and the Greens). However, this allowance is being phased out with an end date of 1 April 2015.[80] To sum up this variety, there are:

- subsidies for electioneering in four countries (Australia, Canada, New Zealand, the USA);
- subsidies for current party operations in three countries (Canada, Ireland, New Zealand); and

- subsidies earmarked for specific purposes: (1) parliamentary business, travel costs, and running the office of the opposition leader and policy development (UK), and (2) nominating conventions (the USA).

Access to public funding in all of the countries depends on receiving a minimum number of votes.[81] It is quite easy for minor parties in Canada, Ireland and the UK to access public funds, but a little harder in Australia, New Zealand and the USA. Distribution of subsidies is either according to share of votes or in equal amounts. Ireland pays a base amount to all parties and allocates the rest of the subsidy by number of votes. In a system considered defunct after the 2012 election, government subsidies would match small donations solicited by presidential contenders in US primaries.

In order to compare levels of public subsidies, Table 8.1. lists the annual averages for individual allocations, their total amount per year and the annual country totals per eligible voter (all in I$).[82] As names and purposes of public subsidies differ in the six countries, the various subsidies that are provided have been termed 'subsidy A, B, C'.

Table 8.1. Subsidy levels in anglophone democracies

Country	Subsidy A	Subsidy B	Subsidy C	Total subsidies	Annual subsidy per capita (I$)
	Million I$ per year				
Australia[83]	40.07	None	None	40.07	2.47
Canada[84]	21.45	29.5	22.41	73.36	2.68
Ireland[85]	8.5	6.18	None	14.68	4.17
New Zealand[86]	11.16	2.27	None	13.47	4.13
UK[87]	9.86	0.49	2.34	12.69	0.26
USA[88]	1.04	36.57	42.05	79.66	0.33

Source: Data from the websites of the Australian Electoral Commission, Elections Canada, the Irish Standards in Public Office Commission, the UK Electoral Commission and the US Federal Election Commission.

The data show that a country's size significantly affects the cross-national comparison. On a per voter basis, it is not medium-sized Canada but the much smaller Ireland and New Zealand that are more generous to their parties.

Public subsidies' share of revenue

The highest share of public versus private funding among the six anglophone countries is found in Canada. While two studies found that in 2006 and 2008, the four major parties received on average between 55 per cent and 70 per cent, respectively, of their income from public funds, these calculations do not take into account the net value of tax credits; the overall level is likely to be significantly higher.[89] Public funding is also high in Ireland, and political parties rely 'heavily' on public funding (reportedly around 70 per cent of their total income).[90]

Published data for New Zealand go back to 1996, when about 18 per cent of political parties' total expenditure was covered by the 'broadcasting allowance' to allow parties to take out paid advertising.[91] Due to the recently introduced entitlement for parliamentary parties, the public share of party income should be much higher now.[92]

As noted above, direct public funding in Australia is related to election campaigns. This most probably explains the variation in relative dependency there, as in 1996 and 1998 (both of which were election years) it was 35 per cent, while the average share of major party income from public sources in 2002–03 (non-election years) was estimated at 17 per cent (including tax deductions).[93] In 2007, the proportion of public funding to total party revenue was about 25 per cent.[94]

In the UK, adding up the 'Short Money', the 'Cranborne Money' and the Policy Development Grant shows that public funds amount to 28 per cent of the private donations received by all political parties during 2012.[95] The UK system is structured differently to most others; while the public funding received by the largest government party (the Conservatives) was a negligible percentage of its total income from 2012, it was a significant source of income for its coalition partner (the Liberal Democrats), while the largest opposition party, Labour, received public funds amounting to almost half of its private donations (GBP 7,378,958 [I$12,050,000] compared to GBP 12,036,055 [I$19,660,000]).[96]

In the USA, public funding is negligible. Federal Election Commission (FEC) data show that the total private funding raised in 2012 by political parties and presidential and Congressional candidates and Political Action Committees was around USD 5.8 billion. Public funding was only provided for the major parties' nominating conventions. This amounted to USD 36 million, only 0.6 per cent of the total amount raised for the year.[97]

Gender implications

While the countries discussed in this chapter are all advanced democracies, they are no shining examples in terms of gender equality in political participation. Only New Zealand meets the short-term target set by the UN Economic and Social Council in 1990 that countries should have at least 30 per cent female representation in parliament. Ireland and the USA are even below the world average.

In five of the six countries, there are no public incentives to *promote gender equality* among candidates, or financial incentives to generally encourage gender equality within the parties. Only Ireland has a legal prescription that parties will face a 50 per cent cut of their public subsidy unless at least 30 per cent of the candidates are women and at least 30 per cent are men.[98]

As no general elections have been held in Ireland since this regulation came into force, its impact has yet to be tested.

Moreover, Irish parties must apply public subsidies to a variety of specified purposes, which include (among more general items) promoting youth and female political participation.[99] The reports filed by the three major parties for 2011 show that Fianna Fail spent EUR 7,500 (I$8,500) for the purpose, but Fine Gael no more than EUR 152 (I$170). The Labour Party seems to differ considerably, because it spent EUR 61,107 (I$69,000) to promote female participation (although almost three-quarters of this total was spent on 'salaries and pensions').[100]

Spending by political parties and candidates

Electing public officials in modern democracies requires parties and/or their candidates to run election campaigns. Sometimes there are expensive nomination procedures to select party candidates (especially in North America) and leaders (especially in Canada). The costs of operating party headquarters and local party organizations cannot be ignored, because funding a permanent field organization with full-time party agents at the centre and grass-roots levels has become a financial burden in many countries. However, in the public eye political parties are (more or less) confined to organizing campaign activities. Overall, political spending levels and trends have become an issue of public discourse, which has led to the introduction of spending limits.

Spending limits

Australia does not have spending limits for parties or candidates. The same is true for the USA as far as statutory limits are concerned. Following the 1976 *Buckley v. Valeo* US Supreme Court ruling, there has been a voluntary spending limit for presidential candidates who apply for public subsidies. No presidential candidate has applied for the public subsidies since 2008, and this rule is considered by many to no longer have any practical impact. Ireland limits campaign spending by candidates only. The limit per candidate depends on the size of the constituency: three, four or five seats may be at stake. There is no limit on additional campaign spending by political parties. The other three countries operate limits for party and candidate campaigns.[101] In Canada and Ireland[102] limits are automatically adjusted for inflation. As countries and constituencies differ in size, the legal limits have to be translated into comparable information (see Table 8.2.).

Table 8.2. Spending limits for parties and candidates (in I$)[103]

	Party	Candidate	Party	Candidate
	(maximum)	(average)	(average per voter on list)	(average per voter on list)
USA	no limit	no limit	no limit	no limit
Australia	no limit	no limit	no limit	no limit
Ireland	no limit	39,000	no limit	0.53
Canada	15,000,000	66,400	0.62	0.84
New Zealand	1,930,000	17,000	0.63	0.39
UK	31,850,000	18,540	0.70	0.26

This comparison does not take into account that the spending limits in New Zealand do not include certain costs as election expenses (e.g. opinion polling, travel, consultant fees, etc.).[104] While party spending limits in Canada, New Zealand and the UK are fairly similar, the constituency limits differ considerably; the UK marks the low end and Canada the high end. This may be due to the fact that population density is much higher in the UK than in Canada (on average, as well as with respect to the size of rural constituencies).

Actual spending

Traditionally, the political cultures of North America are campaign-oriented, and this is generally also true for Australia, New Zealand, Ireland and the UK. As a consequence, parties are much more publicly active during campaign periods, and the term *political finance* is frequently substituted by *campaign funds*—that is, money spent to influence the outcome of an election. Does this imply that most of the money political parties spend is used to pay for campaigns?

Types of spending

In the US presidential system, political parties are almost exclusively campaign machines, whereas in the five other countries—due to their parliamentary system of government—parties have other significant roles, for example in determining party policy. US campaigns are run predominantly by candidates and their specific committees, who rely heavily on paid media advertising to reach the voting public. In the 2012 presidential elections, it has been estimated that over 55 per cent of total campaign spending went to media activities.[105] In Australia, commercial TV advertising is also a heavy strain on political budgets.

In the four other countries, spending on commercial advertising is much lower due to free or subsidized airtime (in the UK, paid TV and radio advertising by parties or candidates is banned). The use of different media differs over time: newspapers and radio are losing importance and TV is stagnating, while the Internet is on the rise.[106]

In all six countries, political parties run permanent federal/national headquarters. The split between routine and campaign spending does not always coincide with the public impression. Only in the USA do campaigns dominate political spending totals; and they are also comparatively high in Australia. In the UK, routine spending by central offices, which also sustain a permanent organization in most years, surpasses their campaign outlay. In Canada, Ireland and New Zealand, party headquarters have stepped up their routine activities in recent decades and shifted their budgets accordingly.[107] The costs of running the institutional structures have become a heavy burden on party coffers that can no longer be covered by leftover campaign funds, and parties in all three countries now receive public funds for routine spending.

In Canada and Ireland, salaries, wages and benefits comprise about one-third of party headquarters' annual budget; in the UK they make up between one-half and two-thirds.[108] Permanent organizations also spend considerable amounts on offices: rent and energy, machinery and equipment, stationery and communication charges (mail, telephone). While the local staff is temporary in the USA (and in decline in the UK), parties all over the anglophone democracies have increased the staffing of their party headquarters.[109] Compared to the items mentioned so far, spending on research (polling and focus groups) and professional expertise (lawyers, auditors and consultants) is lower. Yet increasingly advanced regulatory regimes and campaign technology will probably cause such expenses to rise.

Spending levels

Fascinated by rising amounts and the millions (and more recently even billions) of dollars spent on politics, many US observers have felt that political spending in their country is rising extraordinarily fast.[110] Yet if increases in the voting age population, consumer prices and average incomes over the last 60 years[111] are taken into account, the rise in political spending is significantly more modest than observers have assumed.

For the US presidential election years 1972, 1980, 1988 and 1992 (GDP-adjusted)[112] total per capita spending for all federal candidates (i.e., president, House and Senate) was USD 3.23–3.28.[113] Table 8.3. details spending in the last four presidential elections. It shows that GDP-adjusted spending per capita went up by nearly one-third from 2000 to 2012. However, spending in these last four elections, taking into account changes in population size and GDP, was not much higher in 2012 than it was in 1972.

Table 8.3. Campaign spending in US federal elections since 2000

Year	Total spending on behalf of all federal candidates	Voting age population	Nominal spending per capita (USD/I$)	GDP-adjusted spending per capita (USD/I$)
2000	3.812 billion	214.0 million	17.81	2.64
2004	4.273 billion	222.0 million	19.25	2.81
2008	4.869 billion	213.4 million	22.82	3.33
2012	5.765 billion	240.9 million	23.93	3.49

Source: US Federal Election Commission (FEC) data.

In 1972, Canadian federal parties spent CAD 1.01 (I$0.90) per citizen; the leading expert on political finance in Canada at the time contended that this 'may well have been the most expensive ... election in history'.[114] However, in 1984 the same competitors spent CAD 2.36 (I$2.09) per citizen.[115] A different set of contenders in the same country (now including the Reform Party and the BQ) spent CAD 1.84 (I$1.63) per capita in 1993 and CAD 1.71 (I$1.52) in 1997.

The central offices of the three major parties in the UK spent GBP 0.34 (I$0.56) per citizen in 1974 (a year with two general elections) as well as in 1983 and 1992 (which had just one general election each). However, for the 1997 election year the per capita outlay was GBP 0.44 (I$0.72).[116] The developments in recent elections are even more interesting. In nominal terms, spending by all parties increased from around GBP 25 million (I$41 million) in 2001 to over GBP 40 million (I$65 million) in 2005, only to drop to around GBP 30 million (I$49 million) in 2010.[117]

What conclusions can be drawn from the selective data reported above? There may be a spending spree with parties and/or candidates. However, empirical assessment supports two major points: there is no linear rising trend, and the hazard loses much of its alarming character if economic growth indicators are taken into account.

It is also worth considering whether parties and candidates would spend as much if the funds were not forthcoming. Thus political party revenue may be at the heart of the problem rather than the political spending that attracts so much public attention. In order to stop the spending spree that notoriously stimulates political finance (an 'arms race'), reformers may have to aim to control the flow of money into the campaign coffers.

A recent study concluded that Ireland and Canada were slightly ahead of the USA in terms of spending, with Australia and the UK at a much lower level.[118] However, the six anglophone democracies all ranged in the bottom half of the 18 nations studied, and were definitely surpassed in political spending by France, Germany, Sweden, Japan, Mexico and Israel.[119]

Enforcement of political finance regulation

All regulatory systems of the established anglophone democracies require some transparency of political funds (reporting by parties and candidates plus disclosure of specific donors). They also stipulate a variety of bans and limits, and prescribe sanctions for non-compliance. The enforcement of political finance rules is the jurisdiction of the monitoring agency and various other public institutions.

Monitoring agency

In three of the six countries, the body that organizes elections is also charged with collecting and monitoring financial reports: the Australian Electoral Commission (AEC), the Chief Electoral Officer in Canada (Elections Canada) and the Electoral Commission in New Zealand (ECNZ). In the three other countries a separate institution has jurisdiction over party (and candidate) financing, but it is not charged with organizing elections: the Standards in Public Office Commission in Ireland, the Electoral Commission in the UK (ECUK) and the FEC in the United States.[120]

The agencies in charge of collecting financial reports usually have limited jurisdiction to conduct in-depth investigations and issue sanctions related to violating the finance laws (although the mandate of the ECUK has been expanded significantly since 2009). In all countries studied here, they can inspect, review, investigate, ask questions and demand further information, explanation and documentation. Some of them can even prescribe forms and render advisory opinions (that detail specific rules). However, when the agency in charge of financial reports suspects that a (criminal) violation of a regulation has occurred, the case and supporting evidence must be handed over to the police or referred to prosecuting officers or the attorney general (Department of Justice). This is the case in Canada and the USA, for example, where the commissioner of Elections Canada or the FEC has exclusive jurisdiction over civil enforcement, and in Ireland and the UK, where supervisory and auditing powers are detailed.

Regarding their mandates to investigate, enforce and sanction political finance laws, a tentative rank order of the real impact of the monitoring agencies would put Canada far on top, the USA next, Australia and the UK in the middle, and Ireland and New Zealand at the bottom. After the 2005 election in New Zealand, the ECNZ reported 17 potential offences (including campaign finance offences) to the police, which did not prosecute any of the cases.[121] At the other end of the continuum, Elections Canada is described as being overly powerful and a 'juggernaut' compared to the political parties. This has led some to ask of Elections Canada the age-old question: 'who will guard the guardians?'.[122]

Reporting requirements

The basic idea of financial transparency is quite simple: political parties and candidates submit regular reports to a public authority, and public access to such reports informs all voters about the funding of the political competition. In practice, the rules are quite diverse and the world of *reporting units* varies among the anglophone countries. A review of political finance regulation does not easily identify which groups or individuals are required to file financial reports (called reporting units in this section), which creates challenges in terms of oversight.

Legislation in Ireland refers simply to parties and candidates. The Canada Elections Act mentions (registered) political parties, constituency associations, parliamentary candidates, nomination contestants and leadership candidates. In Australia, federal and state parties, associated entities, and donors to parties and candidates are subject to reporting requirements. However, the 'definition of associated entities is not wide enough to encompass all activities and organisations that effectively fund party political competition'.[123] In addition, third parties that incur political expenditures are required to file financial reports with the appropriate monitoring agency in Australia, Canada, New Zealand and the UK. In the USA, while third parties have to register as PACs, there is now a confusing array of PAC types that all have different reporting requirements and responsible oversight institutions.[124]

In all six countries, parties and candidates are obliged to provide financial reports. In Australia there are no specific campaign finance reporting formats, while during US election years, monthly reports are required. Annual reports by political parties in Ireland and New Zealand ('donation statements') do not cover expenses, only revenue; thus routine spending by political parties is not open to public scrutiny. Only British law explicitly requires reporting about loans acquired by parties or candidates, while none of the other five countries requires parties or candidates to file annual balances of debts and assets.[125] Financial reports in all the countries analysed in this chapter are permanently available on the websites of the oversight institutions.[126]

Disclosure requirements

Disclosure reduces the potential for clandestine exchanges between economic interests and politicians.[127] All six countries require the disclosure of political donors to the public via a Donors' Statement that is to be filed with the monitoring agency regularly, after an election or (in some cases) within a certain time frame after receipt.

> ... all six (anglophone) countries have reporting thresholds to protect the privacy of small donors and reduce the administrative burden on those required to report.

However, all six countries have reporting thresholds to protect the privacy of small donors and reduce the administrative burden on those required to report. Three countries (Ireland, New Zealand, UK) have low thresholds for the disclosure of donations to *candidates* and higher thresholds for donations to *parties.* Australia, Canada and the USA do not make this distinction. The highest thresholds (and thus the lowest level of transparency) apply to *parties* in New Zealand (NZD 15,000, I$10,000), Australia (AUD 11,900, I$9,200) and the UK (GBP 5,000, I$8,200). The lowest thresholds are in Canada (CAD 200, I$180) and the USA (USD 200). The threshold for party donations in Ireland—EUR 5,079 (I$5,800)—is somewhere in between, but nonetheless much higher than in North America.

As Australian law allows parties to operate front organizations that collect donations, disclosure is not effective.[128] The timing of disclosure is also a problem. Political parties disclose only annually, and then reports are published seven months after the end of the relevant financial year; candidates and third parties report only after each election.[129] Transparency is also lacking in Ireland, as the amounts and numbers of declared donors do not explain current levels of party revenue.[130] In New Zealand, a donor's true identity can be concealed in several ways (conduit organizations, 'straw' or 'faceless' donors). Moreover, the average reported amount of anonymous donations trebled between 1996 and 2002.[131] In the USA, due to bundling, corporate donors and SuperPACs, neither the original donor nor the final impact of political donations can be assessed without further investigation by the media or civil society groups. Among the established anglophone democracies, only Canada seems to enjoy a reliable disclosure of political funding, while the UK is approaching that threshold.

Scrutiny and enforcement

On their websites, the AEC, the ECUK and the FEC provide detailed information on cases after investigations have been completed, while the monitoring agency in Canada offers no information about its investigations. The Irish Standards in Public Office Commission reveals that investigations on which they report concern incidents with town and county councils, and no case related to national politics has been investigated there.[132] The Electoral Commission in New Zealand does not carry out investigations—it passes cases to the police and would only report if the case went to court.

In all six countries, larger monetary fines and imprisonment are determined by a court decision, which in turn has to be demanded by the prosecution agencies that bring the case to court. US legislation requires that the defendant acts *'wilfully and knowingly'*, which implies that the prosecutor has to prove both aspects in court. Enforcement actions in Canada have reportedly increased after amendments were made to existing legislation in 2003 and 2006.[133]

Summing up the investigative situation, in Australia and New Zealand, enforcement does not significantly affect the real flow of funds due to rules ridden with loopholes. In 2005 in New Zealand, both major parties exceeded the statutory spending limits without being sanctioned.[134] The USA does not require more than formal enforcement of rules that are restricted by the 'freedom of expression'. In Ireland, the monitoring body has displayed respectful neglect of all 'big fish' donations.[135] This leaves Canada and the UK to produce any impact on real-life political funding. The ECUK has recently taken on this mandate and is still searching for its role model, while some claim that Elections Canada has continuously extended (and possibly even overstepped) its monitoring task and oversight mandate.[136]

While at first glance the legislation in the anglophone countries provides 'a broad and flexible range of sanctions',[137] these sanctions are not always proportional and effective. In some cases, the fines are extremely low (AUD 1,000 [I$760] for some violations in Australia) or exceptionally high (up to NZD 100,000 [I$69,000] in New Zealand). Although all anglophone democracies in one way or another provide direct public funding, nowhere has withholding the grant (or some part of it) been instituted as a sanction that could be applied by the monitoring agency.[138] Thus there is no practical way to threaten offenders into complying with the rules.

Information from two countries indicates that, in practice, the agencies deal with infringements in other ways. In addition to fixed and variable monetary penalties, the ECUK can issue compliance, restoration or stop notices to ensure compliance with the law. The Commission may also conclude an enforcement undertaking with the offender.[139] In the USA, the latter procedure is called a 'conciliation agreement'. In the case of the 'young' ECUK, this may be a productive instrument to help improve compliance. In the USA, even complete compliance with insufficient rules will not improve the questionable role of money in politics.

> While at first glance the legislation in the anglophone countries provides 'a broad and flexible range of sanctions', these sanctions are not always proportional and effective.

The role of civil society and the media

All political finance regulations have been framed by interaction between the media, legislators and law courts. The media report on various scandals that involve money in politics and demand legislative action to end such abuses (e.g., expense reimbursements for UK MPs). Legislators respond—sometimes reluctantly, sometimes with symbolic legislation. The more hard-hitting the new rules are, the more likely they are to be challenged in court. The less demanding the new rules, the more likely it is that there will be another scandal in the near future. Either way, rules have to be adapted to court rulings on the one hand and to counteract the most recent scandal, on the other. Real improvement of the situation will require (1) that politicians modify their conduct and (2) the strict, yet subtle, enforcement of the legal framework. Party treasurers, official agents and big donors are not always likely to follow moral appeals. Instead they are more liable to act as law-abiding citizens, and where there are loopholes, history has shown that they are often tempted to use them.

The major demand for substantial legal regulation of political finance comes from civil society (the democratic public) and its agents, activist groups and the media. The fight against corruption starts at home; one potential arena is the funding of politics. The call to all who want to defend their democracy is: observe developments in this field and transform media outcries into policy proposals that aim to increase the transparency of funding first, and to enhance regulations as required. Media stories that focus on the misbehaviour of individuals will temporarily relieve political pressure, but will not influence future behaviour as long as the rules are not improved. Without improved rules, the media may be satisfied by resignations whenever they have been able to 'catch' cases of (moral or legal) misbehaviour, but new politicians will try to get away with the tried and tested methods of malpractice. Cooperation between the media, civil society and legislators is needed to transform the momentum created by scandal into better rules to bring about progress toward an improved set of rules for money in politics.

Conclusions

Common features

Although the established anglophone democracies have different regulatory systems, some common features can be identified. First, each has a single *independent agency* with the responsibility to collect, file, review, verify and publish all financial reports produced by participants in the campaign process. In half of the countries this monitoring agency is the electoral management body (EMB), while the others have assigned jurisdiction over political finance to a different body. Second, each country has a *multitude of reporting units* that are expected to publicize funds raised and/or spent in order to influence the outcome of elections. In five of the six countries, reporting duties extend to parties, candidates and various other groups that get involved in elections. Just one country (Ireland) restricts this obligation to parties and candidates. Third, legislation (more or less) aims at *transparency of political funds* spent in campaigns or for other party purposes. However, there are different thresholds for *disclosing* a donor's identity and the total amount of his or her *donations*.

Issues for further consideration

Third-party advertising

The general challenge of *third-party advertising* has been resolved in three different ways. First, Australia and the USA have opted for transparency, which relies on monitoring by the media and civil society actors. Yet the information open to public scrutiny may downplay the problem of undue influence on the political process. Second, Canada, New Zealand and the UK have legislated statutory limits and reporting duties for third-party activities. The monitoring agency therefore has to ensure that the legal limits are adhered to. It is important to study trends in third-party activity to assess whether they require legislative action. Third, Ireland has spending limits for candidates but neglects party spending and third-party advertising, which has created two regulatory loopholes. Legislators (and the media) should watch for any shift of advertising activity from candidates to parties or from political actors to moneyed interests during campaign periods.

Bans and limits

Only Canada and the USA *ban* all 'hazardous' *contributions*. However, US lawyers have devised ways to circumvent such general restrictions. Ireland and the UK are more liberal in terms of who can donate. Australia and New Zealand seem to be the most laissez faire. Whereas Canada, the USA and Ireland tolerate only anonymous contributions of small amounts, the UK and New Zealand are more tolerant and have higher thresholds. The very high threshold for anonymous donations in Australia is almost lackadaisical in this respect.

The USA and Australia do not have compulsory *spending limits*. Among the countries that limit political spending, two loopholes stand out. First, Ireland limits spending by candidates only (not spending by parties or 'third parties'). Second, Australia, Ireland, New Zealand and the UK have not taken into account the likelihood that expenses incurred by contenders for nomination as a party candidate may be a relevant element of political spending. Such expenses require at least reporting to the monitoring agency, and possibly specific spending limits.

Private funding

Among the sources of *private funding* to parties, most anglophone democracies, with the exception of Canada, demonstrate a rather traditional pattern. Most parties still rely on major donors. Only a few parties have been able to solicit financial support from the grass roots. Although membership dues are frequently seen as an important source of funding for political parties, membership dues do not represent a significant portion of political revenue in any of the anglophone democracies. Small donations from individual supporters provide considerable amounts of political income only in the USA and Canada. In the other four countries, parties (and candidates) rely heavily on large donations by trade unions, by business donors and wealthy individuals, and (more rarely) from foreign sources.

Public funding

In one way or another, all six countries offer *public subsidies* to political parties. Almost half of the subsidies (six of 13) are available for electioneering, and three of 13 are intended to support the ongoing operations of political parties. The rest is earmarked for specific purposes. Only Ireland requires subsidized parties to promote gender equality. In general, access to such funds and their distribution are fair. Calculated per registered voter, annual averages of subsidy totals are quite low in the USA and UK. Ireland's subsidies are exceptionally generous, while the rest of the countries' subsidies fall in between.

The USA stands out as the only democracy that stipulates the fair access of all competitors to radio and TV, but offers neither *free* nor subsidized *airtime* to parties or candidates. The other five countries have tried to improve access to the electronic media either by allocating free or subsidized time. Only half of the countries studied have *matching provisions and tax benefits* to provide incentives for fundraisers or donors to increase the financial involvement of individual citizens in the electoral process. Such programmes encourage parties to raise revenue from different sources,[140] which is an important supplement to bans and limits.

The extent and volume of these tax benefit incentives are not comparable, which highlights the major differences between the two North American systems. In Canada, *public incentives* for individual political contributions are quite significant. In the USA they are only of minor importance (and only apply to candidates in presidential primaries). The same is true for *direct public subsidies*, though the difference between the two countries will decline somewhat as the quarterly allowance for Canadian parties is phased out.

Political spending

Campaigns are a major source of party expenditures. However, only in the USA (and possibly Australia) is such spending still dominant. In the four other democracies, routine spending for a permanent party headquarters (and occasionally party offices) has been increasing over time; staff and office expenses comprise at least half of many parties' annual budget. Therefore, the emphasis on limiting campaign spending (which is more visible to regulators concerned about rising political expenses) does not address their most important category of political spending. A cross-check with spending levels worldwide supports this. The anglophone democracies spend moderately on party and candidate politics compared to many other nations.

Monitoring processes

All monitoring agencies have limited jurisdiction to impose sanctions for non-compliance with political finance rules. For serious violations, the case and supporting evidence has to be referred to prosecuting officers. In all the anglophone democracies, transparency of political funds (reporting by parties and candidates plus disclosure of specific donors) is limited: Canada and the USA lack consolidated reports and disclose even minor amounts, thus burying relevant information in the bulk of details. Australia, Ireland and New Zealand report no details about spending, and the disclosure of donors is incomplete. The UK reports on national and local parties separately, and on loans only after gross abuse has been revealed. None of these countries requires systematic reporting on political parties' debts and assets, which would substantiate external cross-checks. Where disclosure is enforced effectively (Canada, USA, UK), external scrutiny by media and civil society groups requires considerable additional effort. In the other three countries, such efforts do not seem promising due to imperfect legislation. The overall impression is that rules need to be improved before it is worthwhile to discuss the efficiency of implementation.

Recommendations

The opportunities for significant reform of the regulatory systems in *North America* are limited. The *Canadian* political finance regime already covers all theoretically available aspects: practical bans, realistic spending and contribution limits, public subsidies to substitute for hazardous sources of political funds, and tax incentives to entice citizens to donate a small portion of their (above average) personal income to run a democracy. Finally, an independent agency is charged with (and empowered to) implement and monitor the (financial and other) rules of the electoral process.

The US case is similar in some respects but demonstrates important practical loopholes and constitutional restrictions. Given the political and legal framework for electioneering reform in the USA, reforms are unlikely to have much impact. Since the 1970s, the reform process in this country has run in cycles: academics, the media and public opinion identify major problems related to money in politics, most of all the hundreds of millions (by now billions) of dollars spent for campaign purposes. Some politicians demand reform, while others develop legislative proposals. In due course, a piece of reform legislation passes through the cumbersome legislative process and is eventually enacted, for example the Federal Elections Campaign Act or the Bipartisan Campaign Reform. Immediately after the new law has entered into force, groups or individuals that represent moneyed interests initiate litigation, and finally the Supreme Court strikes down parts of the new law and upholds others, as in *Buckley v. Valeo, Citizens United v. FEC and McCutcheon v. FEC.* Practitioners of political finance find ways to continue their specific flow of money into the electoral process, and their opponents catch up on the new practice, as has happened with PACs, soft money, 501(c) groups, 527 groups, independent expenditures and SuperPACs.[141] Very soon academics, the media and the general public feel that their original intention to clean up the political process and stop the increase of political spending has not been served properly, which starts off a new cycle of legislation, litigation and loopholes.

A foreign observer can hardly resist the impression that procedures have been modified and new names have entered the process, but the flow of interested money has not changed significantly. The well-intentioned reform advocate may be surprised that the flow of funds into the coffers of parties, candidates and 'third parties' is continually approaching new peaks, and that politicians and lobby groups do not hesitate to put this money to work. US legislators should consider that full transparency of political funding requires all politically relevant spending (including spending by so-called 527 committees or 'charities') is concentrated in the same agency, the FEC.

The potential for true reform is stifled by two main factors. First, the separation of powers in the USA sets political parties apart from their presidential and congressional candidates (a political heritage of the 'founding fathers'). Second, the Supreme Court has recently extended the protection of free expression under the First Amendment to include corporations and money, not only people and words. Two moderate reform proposals would include (1) tightened disclosure rules for (politically active) 501/527 groups and SuperPACs and (2) measures to 'keep free speech fair' by taking the 'fiction' out of 'independent expenditures'.[142]

The regulatory situation is quite different in *Western Europe* and *Oceania*. In *Australia* there is 'a widespread and multi-partisan feeling that … political finance needs significant reform'.[143] If the country cannot move to more bans or spending limits, it should consider improving the transparency of political donations and spending.[144] One analyst has encouraged Australian legislators 'to craft sensible limits and justify them by balancing values such as integrity and political equality with liberty and the need for meaningfully-resourced campaigns'.[145] Disclosure of donors' identity—and consolidated reporting of revenue and expenses by all parties that receive public subsidies[146]—would be a small price to pay for autonomy of spending and public support for the high costs of campaign advertising. These recommendations are supported by the 2008 Green Paper,[147] which criticized the fact that 'associated entities are not properly defined' and the ease with which donations may be 'hidden' via 'funds, trusts, associated entities or other third parties'.[148]

The major problem in *New Zealand* seems to be the lack of transparency of political funds. Lower cut-off points for anonymous donations, and for disclosing donors' identities, would be important improvements. Moreover a tax incentive for small donations might shift the balance between large and small contributions and ensure that parties are grass-roots oriented.

In *Western Europe*, recent improvements by the 2009 Political Parties and Elections Act (PPEA) leave less to elaborate in the UK than the imperfect steps taken in *Ireland*. In 2011, a total of 14 Irish parties disclosed donations that totalled EUR 30,997 (I\$35,000) while all MPs, senators and members of the European Parliament together disclosed donations of EUR 378,920 (I\$429,000)—which is among the lowest amounts since records have been kept—suggesting that many donations were not disclosed.[149] Two further areas for improvement stand out. First, as long as campaign spending is limited to candidates, there are two major outlets for unlimited expenses: party campaign spending and advertising by third parties. Therefore, closing either of these loopholes would prove legislators' intention to be serious about limits. Second, although parties furnish evidence of how they spent the public subsidy, the rest of their expenses (which are funded by private contributions) are kept private. Transparency (of expenses, not to mention revenue) would require more comprehensive information.

The most pressing political finance issue that has come up in the *UK* recently is the use of loans as a front for large donations.[150] This problem was addressed by the Electoral Administration Act of 2006.[151] A possible improvement would be to consolidate reporting by national parties and their local associations, that is, to make central offices responsible for all the reports that are filed by local associations operating under the same party label (this is currently required for donation and loan reports, but not for the annual party accounts).[152] Moreover, the moderate level of public subsidies indicates that reformers have not given proper consideration to the question of funding alternatives.[153] Simply stipulating expense limits and requiring disclosure ignores the need to provide sufficient funds for party activities. Under the current set of rules the next crisis is bound to erupt in the near future.[154] Hopefully it can be resolved as fast as the 'loans crisis' was. The effectiveness of the ECUK, which was given enhanced powers through PPEA in 2009, remains to be seen.

Legislators (and civil society actors) should examine existing loopholes and decide whether legislative action may be advisable. If so, civil society actors should prepare their demands and proposals well ahead of the next political finance scandal, which will offer them an opportunity to improve the rules.

All over the democratic universe, ill-constructed (or badly implemented) rules of democratic competition create intended or unforeseen loopholes, through which interested money can override the principle of 'one person, one vote' and thus obstruct a level playing field and undermine the fairness of elections.

After decades of experience with political finance regulation, two academics, who were also practitioners in their countries, Khayyam Z. Paltiel of Canada and Colin A. Hughes of Australia, made the following points about the fundamental components of effective regulation:

' ... a system of public financing, full disclosure and an enforcing agency backed by legal sanctions are essential to the success of a reform program. Public funding may be by way of allocations from the consolidated revenue fund, tax credits or matching funds or a combination of these. Disclosure requires systematic reporting, auditing, public access to records and publicity, all this buttressed by a proviso that corporations, trade unions and other groups be required to publicize in their annual reports to shareholders and members the amounts contributed to parties, candidates and other political purposes. Enforcement demands a strong Commissioner, Registrar or Commission endowed with sufficient legal powers to supervise, verify, investigate and if necessary institute legal proceedings. *Anything less is a formula for failure*'.[155]

'The essential components for an election finance system without which the system must be suspect are, first, machinery to enforce, monitor and recommend, and second, continuous, comprehensive and total disclosure of both income and outgo. *All else is bells and whistles*'.[156]

References

Age, The (2006) 'Are Our Politicians for Sale?', available at http://www.theage.com. au/news/in-depth/are-our-politicians-for-sale/2006/05/23/1148150251862.html

Alexander, Herbert E. (1992) *Financing Politics*, 4th ed., Washington, D.C: CQ Press.

Alexander, Herbert E. (1999) 'Spending in the 1996 Elections', in John C. Green (ed.), *Financing the 1996 Election*, pp. 11–36. Armonk, NY and London: M. E. Sharpe.

Alexander, Herbert E. and Corrado, Anthony (1995) *Financing the 1992 Election*. Armonk, NY: M. E. Sharpe.

Austin, Reginald and Tjernström, Maja (eds) (2003) *Funding of Political Parties and Election Campaigns*. Stockholm: International IDEA.

Beange, Pauline E. (2012) *Canadian Campaign Finance Reform in Comparative Perspective 2000–2011. An Exhausted Paradigm or Just a Cautionary Tale?* PhD Thesis, University of Toronto, available at https://tspace.library.utoronto. ca/bitstream/1807/32664/3/Beange_Pauline_E_201206_PhD_thesis.pdf

Biezen, Ingrid van (2004) 'Political Parties as Public Utilities', in: *Party Politics*, 10 (2004) 6, pp. 701-22.

Bloom, Arnold (1956) 'Tax Results of Political Contributions', *Boston University Law Review*, 36, pp. 170–89.

Brändle, Michael (2002) *Strategien der Förderung politischer Parteien: Eine vergleichende Untersuchung der Parteienförderung in der Schweiz, Großbritannien und den Niederlanden*, [Strategies of promotion of political parties: A comparative study of party funding in Switzerland, the UK and the Netherlands]. Bern: Paul Haupt.

Cabinet Office of the UK (2010) *General Election Guidance*. Cabinet Office, 6 April.

Cain, John (2006) 'The Politics of Greed', *The Age*, 18 October, available at http://www.theage.com.au/news/opinion/the-politics-of-greed/2006/10/17/1160850927192.html?page=fullpage#contentSwap1

Carty, R. Kenneth (2002) 'Canada's Nineteenth-century Cadre Parties at the Millennium', in Paul Webb, David Farrell and Ian Holliday (eds), *Political Parties in Advanced Industrial Democracies*, pp. 345–78. Oxford: Oxford University Press.

Chaples, Ernest A. (1994) 'Developments in Australian Election Finance', in Herbert E. Alexander and Rei Shiratori (eds), *Comparative Political Finance Among the Democracies*, pp. 29–40. Boulder, CO: Westview.

Coletto, David (2007) 'Party Finance in Canada Since 2001', *Innovations*, 7, pp. 41–6.

Committee on Standards in Public Life (1998) *The Funding of Political Parties. Issues and Questions* (the Neill Report).

Crotty, William J. (1977) *Political Reform and the American Experiment*. New York: Thomas Y. Crowell Company.

Edwards, Bryce (2008) 'Political Finance and Inequality in New Zealand', *New Zealand Sociology*, 23(2), pp. 4–17.

Ellis, Andrew (2010) 'The "Richmond Case": The United Kingdom', in Jesús Orozco-Henríquez, Ayman Ayoub and Andrew Ellis (eds), *Electoral Justice: The International IDEA Handbook*. Stockholm: International IDEA.

Ellwood, John W. / Spitzer, Robert J. (1979): Democratic National Telethons: Their Successes and Failure, in: *The Journal of Politics*, vol. 41 (1979) 3, pp. 828-64.

Epstein, Leon D. (1986) *Political Parties in the American Mold*. Madison, WI: University of Wisconsin.

Ewing, Keith D. (2007) *The Cost of Democracy: Party Funding in British Politics*. Oxford and Portland, OR: Hart.

Ewing, Keith (2012) 'The Trade Union Question in British Political Funding', in Keith Ewing, Jacob Rowbottom and Joo-Cheong Tham (eds), *The Funding of Political Parties: Where Now?*, pp. 54–74. Abingdon: Routledge.

Ewing, Keith and Rowbottom, Jacob (2012) 'The Role of Spending Controls', in Keith Ewing, Jacob Rowbottom and Joo-Cheong Tham (eds), *The Funding of Political Parties: Where Now?*, pp. 77–91. Abingdon: Routledge.

Feasby, Colin (2010) 'Contemporary Issues in Canadian Political Finance Regulation', *Policy Quarterly*, 6(3), pp. 14–20.

Fisher, Justin (2007) *Party Funding: Back to Square One (and a Half) or Every Cloud Has a Silver Lining*, available at http://bura.brunel.ac.uk/bitstream/2438/3566/1/Fulltextt.pdf

Fisher, Justin (2012) 'Legal Regulation and Political Activity at the Local Level in Britain', in Keith Ewing, Jacob Rowbottom and Joo-Cheong Tham (eds), *The Funding of Political Parties: Where Now?*, pp. 110–25. Abingdon: Routledge.

Geddis, Andrew (2007) 'Rethinking the Funding of New Zealand's Election Campaigns', *Policy Quarterly*, 3(1), pp. 3–10.

Geddis, Andrew (2010) 'The Electoral (Finance Reform and Advance Voting) Amendment Bill', *Policy Quarterly*, 6(3), pp. 3–7.

Godwin, Kenneth R. (1988) *One Billion Dollars of Influence: The Direct Marketing of Politics*. Chatham, NJ: Chatham House.

Group of States against Corruption (GRECO) (2008) *Evaluation Report on the United Kingdom Transparency of Party Funding (Theme II)*.

Group of States against Corruption (GRECO) (2009) *Evaluation Report on Ireland, Transparency of Party Funding (Theme II)*.

Heard, Alexander (1960) *The Costs of Democracy*. Chapel Hill, NC: University of North Carolina.

Hughes, Colin A. (2001) Election Finance Controls: Is There an End Game? In: Nassmacher, Karl-Heinz (ed.), *Foundations to Democracy – Approaches to Comparative Political Finance*, Baden-Baden: Nomos Verlag, pp. 206-21.

Huntington, Samuel P. (1991) *The Third Wave*. Norman, OK: University of Oklahoma.

International IDEA, Political Finance Database, available at http://www.idea.int/political-finance

Jansen, Harold J, Tomas, Melanee & Young, Lisa (2012): Who Donates to Canada's Political Parties?, available at http://www.cpsa-acsp.ca/papers-2012/Jansen-Thomas-Young.pdf

Katz, Richard S. (1996) 'Party Organizations and Finance', in Lawrence LeDuc, Richard G. Niemi and Pippa Norris (eds), *Camparing Democracies: Elections and Voting in Global Perspective*, pp. 107–33. Thousand Oaks, CA: Sage.

Krouwel, Andrae (1999) *The Catch-all Party in Western Europe 1945–1990: A Study in Arrested Development*. Dissertation, Vrije Universiteit, Amsterdam.

Kulick, Manuela S. and Nassmacher, Karl-Heinz (2012) 'Do Parties Spend Too Much?', in Jonathan Mendilow (ed.), *Money, Corruption, and Political Competition in Established and Emerging Democracies*, pp. 17–39. Lanham, MD: Lexington Books.

Leong, Shane, Cummings, Lorne and Hazelton, James (2011) *Accountability and the Australian Federal Political Donation and Expenditure Regime*. Paper presented at a CSEAR conference in Launceston, 7 December, available at http://www.utas.edu.au/__data/assets/pdf_file/0007/188548/Leong_Cummings_Hazelton_18.pdf

McAllister, Ion (2002) 'Political Parties in Australia: Party Stability in a Utilitarian Society', in Paul Webb, David Farrell and Ian Holliday (eds), *Political Parties in Advanced Industrial Democracies*, pp. 379–408. Oxford: Oxford University Press.

McMenamin, Iain (2008) *Business, Politics and Money in Australia: Testing Economic, Political and Ideological Explanations*. Working Papers in International Studies No. 4, Dublin City University, available at http://www.dcu.ie/~cis/PDF/publications/2008-Biz&Pol_Aus.pdf

McMenamin, Iain (2011) *Business Financing of Politics in Ireland: Theory, Evidence and Reform*. Working Papers in International Studies No. 12/2011. Centre for International Studies, Dublin City University.

Murphy, Ronan J. and Farrell, David M. (2002) 'Party Politics in Ireland: Regularizing a Volatile System', in Paul Webb, David Farrell and Ian Holliday (eds), *Political Parties in Advanced Industrial Democracies*, pp. 217–47. Oxford: Oxford University Press.

Nassmacher, Karl-Heinz (1994) 'Citizens' Cash in Canada and the United States', in Herbert E. Alexander and Rei Shiratori (eds), *Comparative Political Finance Among the Democracies*, pp. 145–57. Boulder, CO: Westview.

Nassmacher, Karl-Heinz (2003) 'Introduction: Political Parties, Funding and Democracy', in Reginald Austin and Maja Tjernström (eds), *Funding of Political Parties and Election Campaigns*, pp. 1–19. Stockholm: International IDEA.

Nassmacher, Karl-Heinz (2006) 'Regulation of Party Finance', in Richard S. Katz and William Crotty (eds), *Handbook of Party Politics*, pp. 446–55. Thousand Oaks, CA: Sage.

Nassmacher, Karl-Heinz (2009) *The Funding of Party Competition: Political Finance in 25 Democracies*. Baden-Baden: Nomos.

Ohman, Magnus and Zainulbhai, Hani (2009) *Political Finance Regulation: The Global Experience*. Washington, D.C.: International Foundation for Electoral Systems.

OpenSecrets (2012a) '2012 Presidential Race', available at http://www.opensecrets.org/pres12/index.php?ql3

OpenSecrets (2012b) 'Expenditures', available at http://www.opensecrets.org/pres12/expenditures.php

Orr, Graeme (2010a) 'Public Money and Electioneering – A View from Across the Tasman', *Policy Quarterly*, 6(3), pp. 21–5.

Orr, Graeme (2010b) *The Law of Politics: Elections, Parties and Money in Australia*. Sydney: Federation Press.

Paltiel, Khayyam Z. (1974) 'Party and Candidate Expenditures in the Canadian General Election of 1972', *Canadian Journal of Political Science*, 3(2), pp. 341–52.

Paltiel, Khayyam Z. (1976) *Party, Candidate and Election Finance: A Background Report*. Ottawa: Royal Commission on Corporate Concentration.

Paltiel, Khayyam Z. (1981) 'Campaign Finance: Contrasting Practices and Reform', in David Butler, Howard Rae Penniman and Austin Ranney (eds), *Democracy at the Polls: A Comparative Study of Competitive National Elections*, pp. 138–72. Washington, D.C.: American Enterprise Institute.

Pinto-Duschinsky, Michael (1981) *British Political Finance, 1830–1980*. Washington, D.C.: American Enterprise Institute.

Pinto-Duschinsky, Michael (2001) *Political Financing in the Commonwealth*. London: Commonwealth Secretariat.

Pinto-Duschinsky, Michael (2002) 'Financing Politics: A Global View', *Journal of Democracy*, 13(4), pp. 69–86.

Rose, Richard (1984) *Do Parties Make a Difference?* 2nd ed. London: Macmillan.

Rowbottom, Jacob (2012) 'Institutional Donations to Political Parties' Funding', in Keith Ewing, Jacob Rowbottom and Joo-Cheong Tham (eds), *The Funding of Political Parties: Where Now?*, pp. 11–35. Abingdon: Routledge.

Scarrow, Susan E. (2007) 'Political Finance in Comparative Perspective', *Annual Review of Political Science*, 10, pp. 193–210.

Sorauf, Frank J. (1988) *Money in American Elections*. Glenview, IL: Scott, Foresman and Co.

Stanbury, W. T. (1991) *Money in Politics: Financing Federal Parties and Candidates in Canada*. Toronto: Dundurn Press.

Supreme Court of Canada (2004) *Harper v. Canada (Attorney General)*.

Tham, Joo-Cheong (2010) 'Regulating Political Contributions: Another View from Across the Tasman', *Policy Quarterly*, 6(3), pp. 26–30.

Tham, Joo-Cheong (2012) 'Contribution Limits: A Case for Exempting Trade Union Affiliation Fees', in Keith Ewing, Jacob Rowbottom and Joo-Cheong Tham (eds), *The Funding of Political Parties: Where Now?*, pp. 35–54. Abingdon: Routledge.

Tjernström, Maja (2003) 'Matrix on Political Finance Laws and Regulations', in Reginald Austin and Maja Tjernström (eds), *Funding of Political Parties and Election Campaigns*, pp 184–223. Stockholm: International IDEA.

UK Electoral Commission (2010a) *Party Funding: The Electoral Commission's Submission to the Committee on Standards in Public Life*, October, available at http://www.electoralcommission.org.uk

UK Electoral Commission (2010b) *Enforcement Policy*, available at http://www.electoralcommission.org.uk

UK Electoral Commission (2012), 'Summary of Political Parties' Donations and Borrowing for Quarter 4 2012 (October to December)', available at http://download5.org/download.php?id=12354

US Supreme Court (1976) *Buckley v. Valeo.*

US Supreme Court (2010) *Citizens United v. Federal Election Commission.*

Vowles, Jack (2002) 'Parties and Society in New Zealand', in Paul Webb, David Farrell and Ian Holliday (eds), *Political Parties in Advanced Industrial Democracies*, pp. 409–37. Oxford: Oxford University Press.

Walecki, Marcin (2005) *Money and Politics in Poland*. Warsaw: Institute of Public Affairs.

Webb, Paul, Farrell, David and Holliday, Ian (eds) (2002) *Political Parties in Advanced Industrial Democracies*. Oxford: University of Oxford Press.

Wilson, John F. (2004) *Donations to Political Parties: Disclosure Regimes*, available at http://www.parliament.nz/resource/0000001047

Young, Sally and Tham, Joo-Cheong (2006) *Political Finance in Australia: A Skewed and Secret System*. Canberra: Australian National University.

Notes

1   Huntington (1991, p. 15) classed five of these countries as 'first wave' democracies. Ireland was grouped as a 'second wave' democracy, although it participated in the development of democratic institutions as a part of the UK.

2   Despite its bilingual character, Canada has been included in this study because of its public law tradition. Cf. Austin and Tjernström 2003, p. 51, note 1. While Gaelic is the national and first official language of Ireland, English is its second official language.

3   Orr (2010a, p. 24) calls them 'common law cousins'.

4   Cf. Orr 2010a, p. 22. In practice, this means that a total of more than 70 (potentially) different sets of political finance rules can be discussed. However, this chapter will consider only the federal regulations.

5   The UK has a separate parliament in Scotland, and national assemblies in Northern Ireland and Wales, but party finance rules are generally set by the Westminster parliament.

6   Ireland uses a single transferable vote system and New Zealand uses a mixed-member proportional system.

7   Pinto-Duschinsky 2001, p. 20.

8   US Civil Service Reform Act; UK Illegal Practices (Prevention) Act.

9   Paltiel 1981, p. 138; Geddis 2007, pp. 4, 9.

10 US Supreme Court 1976, 2010.

11 Chaples 1994, pp. 33–4.

12 Through its ruling in the 1992 *Australian Capital Television Pty Ltd. v Commonwealth*, the High Court recognized an implied freedom of political communication in the Australian constitution.

13 Supreme Court of Canada 2004.

14 The main points leading to the court's ruling are outlined in Feasby 2010, p. 16.

15 Paltiel 1981, pp. 151–2.

16 Walecki 2005, pp. 152–6.

17 Cabinet Office 2010, pp. 1–2.

18 Orr 2010a, p. 252.

19 Ibid. By strong convention, such advertising must end before any formal election campaign.

20 Edwards 2008, p. 9. The number of staff may be exaggerated, but the problem of demarcation is real.

21 Murphy and Farrell 2002, p. 231. Until the recent legislation was passed, the situation for the Canadian New Democratic Party was similar; see Carty 2002, p. 360.

22 McAllister 2002, p. 392; Vowles 2002, p. 419; McMenamin 2008, p. 6.

23 Pinto-Duschinsky 1981, pp. 137, 153, 162. See also Alexander 1992, p. 24 and Ewing 2007, p. 231. In the same vein (although argued with more sophistication) see Orr 2010a, p. 261. Much less convincing is the one-sided/ principle-based reasoning by Rowbottom 2012, pp. 19, 25; Tham 2012, pp. 40–6; and Ewing 2012, pp. 71–2. The underlying problems are more expressly presented in Fisher 2007, pp. 2–5. The case of Ireland may be different because for decades Fianna Fail (like the Liberal Party of Canada) was close to business not because of its policy profile but as 'the natural party of government'. Businesses that wanted to stay in touch contributed to party coffers, which happened to be those of a 'bourgeois' party. Cf. McMenamin 2011, p. 5.

24 Cf. Geddis 2007, pp. 6–7.

25 In the USA, voluntary limits on presidential candidates who accept public funding and party spending on behalf of their presidential candidates are the (minor) exception to this general statement.

26 OpenSecrets 2012a.

27 Feasby 2010, pp. 16–17.

28 Electoral (Finance Reform and Advance Voting) Amendment Act 2010, sec. 206U; House of Representatives (New Zealand), Parliamentary Debates (Hansard), 15 December 2010, pp. 16457–8.

29 Political Parties, Elections and Referendums Act 2000, ch. 41, sec. 94.

30 Feasby 2010, pp. 16–7.

31 Ewing and Rowbottom 2012, pp. 78, 80.

32 Nassmacher (2003, pp. 10–13) presents four models of regulation. Brändle (2002, pp. 41–8) identifies four different models of political finance based on two essential categories: public subsidies and public regulation.

33 For comparisons of political finance regulations, see Pinto-Duschinsky 2002, pp. 74–80; Tjernström 2003, pp. 181–223; and Nassmacher 2006, pp. 446–55.

34 Epstein 1986, pp. 7, 155–7; see also Biezen 2004, pp. 702, 716. As an alternative to Epstein's 'public utilities' Geddis (2010, p. 6) offers the less vivid term 'quasi-public organizations'.

35 Epstein 1986, p. 161 (quotes in reverse order).

36 The only exception may be the Honours (Prevention of Abuses) Act of 1925; cf. Ewing 2007, p. 138.

37 Rose 1984, pp. xxxii.

38 Australia has not introduced any changes since an amendment introduced by the Labor government in 1991 was struck down by the High Court in 1992.

39 Geddis (2007, p. 4) contrasts 'supply-side controls' and 'demand-side controls'.

40 Ibid.

41 McMenamin 2008, pp. 12, 18.

42 Throughout this handbook, international dollars (I$) are presented alongside amounts in national currencies. The international dollar is a hypothetical currency that takes into account purchasing power parity and is therefore suitable for comparisons between countries. For countries in which the purchasing power parity varies significantly from the United States (which is used as the baseline for the comparison), the I$ exchange rate may be considerably different from the nominal exchange rate. No conversions are given for US dollars (as this is by default the same amount as the I$) or for those instances where the original currency is unknown and a secondary currency such as the euro has been cited instead. For further information, see Annex V.

43 Foreign interests cannot provide funds above GBP 500 (I$820) to either political parties or candidates in the UK, with the exception of reasonable amounts for international travel, accommodation or subsistence for party officers or staff.

44 Rules on third-party advertising and SuperPACs offer considerable leeway for interest groups to spend money on 'issue' advertising during election campaigns.

45 Wilson 2004, p. 21.

46 For all practical purposes, the cut-off point is higher because below USD 100 the donor does not have to be recorded and below USD 200 his or her identity does not have to be disclosed to the EMB.

47 The conclusion to be drawn from this regulation is that Australian legislators did not intend to require the disclosure of a donor's identity.

48 See also the discussion about SuperPACs in this chapter.

49 For details, see the International IDEA Political Finance Database, nos 13 to 18.

50 Edwards (2008, p. 11) emphasized the dual character of party membership (potential of volunteers and reliable funding).

51 See Fisher 2012, pp. 112–13.

52 New Zealand may be a good example. When in 1980 National boasted 250,000 members and Labour had 100,000 members (Vowles 2002, p. 416), how much cash revenue did they put into party coffers? And how was this revenue divided up between local and national organizations?

53 Data cited by Krouwel (1999, p. 76) indicate that in Ireland and the UK, one-third of party revenue came from this source. However, it was impossible to cross-check whether these data refer to individual membership dues or came from collective membership and/ or constituency quotas.

54 Pinto-Duschinsky 1981, p. 138; Committee on Standards in Public Life 1998, p. 31.

55 E.g., Vowles 2002, p. 418.

56 Ellwood and Spitzer 1979, pp. 828–64.

57 For details, see Godwin 1988.

58 Feasby 2010, pp. 18–20.

59 Feasby 2010, p. 18. Also note that the duration of a 'campaign period' may be extremely short (e.g., 36 days in Canada) or much longer (e.g., 365 days in the US).

60 Alexander 1992, p. 57. Another PAC, called the WISH List, was founded in 1992 to support female pro-choice Republican candidates.

61 Heard 1960, pp. 71–2.

62 'The Nexus of Business, Money, and Politics', *The Economist*, 27 January 2010.

63 McMenamin 2008, p. 14.

64 US Supreme Court 2010.

65 Tham 2010, pp. 27, 28.

66 Ewing 2007, pp. 124–5, 128–32.

67 UK Electoral Commission 2010a, p. 22.

68 Ewing 2007, pp. 133–8.

69 Stanbury 1991, pp. 74, 464, 469.

70 Ibid., p. 276.

71 Wilson 2004, p. 12.

72 Cain 2006.

73 *The Age* 2006.

74 Young and Tham 2006, pp. 43–4.

75 See Ewing 2007, pp. 118, 125–6, 166–7.

76 In this context it may be important to note that 'Irish politicians cannot buy time on the broadcast media' (McMenamin 2011, p. 9).

77 Other regulations can, of course, indirectly support political parties. The compulsory voting system in Australia, for example, means that political parties do not need to spend significant amounts on 'get out the vote' initiatives.

78 British and Irish political parties that participate in so-called Parties at European Level are also eligible to receive EU funding for their European activities. See http://www. europarl.europa.eu/aboutparliament/en/00264f77f5/Grants-to-political-parties-and-foundations.html

79 Ohman and Zainulbhai 2009, p. 68. For the current distribution, see http://www. electoralcommission.org.uk/_data/assets/pdf_file/0010/153982/Summary-of-Q4-2012-donations-and-loans.pdf

80 Jansen, Thomas and Young 2012. See also para. 435.01(2) of the Canada Elections Act as amended by 1 April 2012.

81 Political parties in New Zealand can, however, receive funding for campaign broadcasting even if they have not participated in any elections.

82 Data from the websites of the Australian Electoral Commission, Elections Canada, the Irish Standards in Public Office Commission, the UK Electoral Commission and the US Federal Election Commission.

83 A = Election Funding Entitlement (data from 2010).

84 A = quarterly allowance, B = federal party reimbursement, C = reimbursement to federal candidates (data from 2008–12).

85 A = Party Leader's Allowance, B = funding under the Electoral Acts (data from 2011).

86 A = Entitlement for Parliamentary Purposes, B = Broadcasting Allocation (data from 2011–12).

87 A = Short money, B = Cranborne money, C = Policy Development Grant (data from 2011–12).

88 A = the matching grant for contenders in presidential primaries, B = the national party convention grant, C = the grant to presidential candidates in the general election (averaged for 2008 and 2012 since no candidate accepted such funding in the 2012 elections) (data from 2008–12).

89 Calculated from Coletto 2007, Table 1, p. 42 and Beange 2012, Table 7.1, p. 270. Including tax credits, it is likely that Canadian political parties rely around 80 per cent on public funds.

90 GRECO 2009, p. 23. Due to the limited reporting available on Ireland, we have no data to either prove or reject this estimate.

91 Vowles 2002, p. 422.

92 This is definitely assumed by Edwards (2008, pp. 9–11). However, the author most probably overestimates the share of public funds.

93 McAllister 2002, p. 393, Young and Tham 2006, p. 13.

94 Orr 2010a, pp. 238, 249.

95 Calculated from UK Electoral Commission 2012, Table 1. The Short money is provided to political parties in the House of Commons, while Cranborne money is similar assistance related to the House of Lords—they are named after the leaders of each house at the time the funding was introduced.

96 Calculated from ibid., tables 10 and 11.

97 Data from the FEC Campaign Finance Disclosure database, available at http://fec.gov/pindex.shtml

98 Subsection (4B)(a) of section 17 of the Electoral Act of 1997 as inserted by no. 42 of the Electoral (Amendment) (Political Funding) Act 2012.

99 GRECO 2009, p. 8. Because further clarification is not provided, this may simply refer to operating separate women's and youth groups, which is a traditional feature of many parties in Europe and elsewhere.

100 See http://www.sipo.gov.ie/en/Reports/AnnualDisclosure

101 For details, see the International IDEA Political Finance Database, nos 31 to 34.

102 McMenamin 2011, p. 10.

103 Calculated from the International IDEA Political Finance Database.

104 Geddis 2007, p. 7; Geddis 2010, p. 6.

105 OpenSecrets 2012b. Note that nearly half of the media spending was used for media consultants.

106 Nassmacher 2009, p. 76.

107 Ibid., pp. 77–8, 80–2.

108 Ibid., pp. 62–3.

109 E.g. Webb, Farrell and Holliday 2002, p. 27.

110 Bloom 1956, p. 170; Crotty 1977, pp. 103–5; Sorauf 1988, p. 29; Alexander and Corrado 1995, p. 178; Katz 1996, pp. 129, 132; Alexander 1999, p. 15; Scarrow 2007, p. 206.

[111] For example, on 12 January 2013 *The Economist* reported that US GDP per person increased from USD/I\$10,000 to USD/I\$30,000 during that period.

[112] 1980 = 100.

[113] Data from Nassmacher 2009, p. 188. An even more striking trend for 1912 to 2000 is shown in ibid., p. 185. See also Kulick and Nassmacher 2012, pp. 17–39.

[114] Paltiel 1974, p. 342.

[115] As an active observer of Canadian politics at the time, this author must have missed the outcry.

[116] Nassmacher 2009, p. 188.

[117] See http://www.electoralcommission.org.uk/party-finance/party-finance-analysis/campaign-expenditure/uk-parliamentary-general-election-campaign-expenditure

[118] Comparable data for New Zealand were not included and are still not available. Without giving data, Geddis (2007, p. 4) mentions 'relatively low-cost electioneering' in New Zealand.

[119] Nassmacher 2009, pp. 115, 118.

[120] For constituency candidate reports in the UK, the local returning officer continues to be in charge.

[121] Geddis 2007, p. 8.

[122] Beange 2012, p. 225.

[123] McMenamin 2008, p. 8.

[124] A PAC is a committee that raises and spends money to support or defeat a candidate. PACs date back to the 1940s, but the first main regulation of their work came through the Federal Election Campaign Act of 1974. A 'SuperPAC' (technically an 'independent expenditure only political committee') is not allowed to make contributions to candidates or political parties, but may engage in unlimited spending, as long as the activities are carried out independently of any particular campaign.

[125] The GRECO report on Ireland (2009, pp. 23–4, 27–8) indicates that consolidated reporting of income, expenditure, assets and debts for parties and their local branches is highly advisable.

[126] See http://www.aec.gov.au/, http://www.elections.ca, http://www.sipo.gov.ie, http://www.elections.org.nz, http://www.electoralcommission.org.uk, http://www.fec.gov

[127] McMenamin 2011, p. 9.

[128] Tham 2010, p. 27.

[129] Orr 2010b, p. 245.

[130] According to the 2009 report by the Group of States against Corruption (GRECO), '… according to the figures gathered by the Standards Commission in its 2008 report, of the EUR 10,100,000 [I\$11,440,000] spent by parties and candidates in the 2007 general elections, only EUR 1,300,000 [I\$1,470,000] were disclosed (no information was therefore available as to the origin of income sources of the remaining EUR 8,800,000 [I\$9,960,000]'. GRECO 2009, p. 22.

[131] Wilson 2004, pp. 4, 19–20; Geddis 2007, p. 5.

[132] See http://www.sipo.gov.ie/en/Reports/AnnualDisclosure

[133] Feasby 2010, p. 20.

[134] Geddis 2007, pp. 3, 7; Geddis 2010, p. 3.

[135] Without furnishing evidence for its views, the GRECO report on Ireland (2009, p. 25) assigns a much more positive evaluation to 'the proactive advisory role played by the Standards Commission to promote transparency of party funding' in that country.

[136] Beange 2012, p. 192.

[137] GRECO 2009, p. 26.

[138] For Australia, this has been proposed by Young and Tham 2006, p. xi (R. 16). In the UK this would contribute towards a recommendation by GRECO (2008, pp. 27, 28) to introduce 'more flexible sanctions'.

[139] A compliance notice sets out actions that the recipient must take so that the violation does not continue or recur. A restoration notice describes what must be done to restore the position to what it would have been if no violation had occurred. A stop notice requires the recipient not to begin (or to stop) an activity that may damage public confidence in the Political Parties, Elections and Referendums Act (PPERA) of 2000. See further UK Electoral Commission 2010b. Election expenses can also be the subject of electoral dispute proceedings. See Ellis 2010, pp. 124ff.

[140] Nassmacher 1994, pp. 149–54.

[141] 501(c) groups are in some cases allowed to engage in political activities (it depends on the type of group). 527 groups are allowed to raise money for certain political activities. More information about the different types of groups can be found at http://www.opensecrets.org/527s/types.php

[142] 'Naming Names', *The Economist*, 24 November 2012, p. 18.

[143] Orr 2010a, p. 21.

[144] Young and Tham 2006, pp. ix–xii.

[145] Orr 2010b, p. 258.

[146] Ibid., R. 1 and 2, 15 and 16, 22; Young and Tham 2006.

[147] See http://www.dpmc.gov.au/conultation/elect_reform/docs/electoral_reform_green_paper.pdf

[148] Leong, Cummings and Hazelton 2011, Section 7.

[149] 'Disclosed Party Donations Lowest since Records Began', *Irish Times*, 30 May 2012, and 'Ireland's Politicians Disclose €378,920 Donations for 2011', *The Journal*, 3 April 2012.

[150] Ewing 2007, pp. 136–7.

[151] Ibid., p. 140.

[152] This is in line with recommendations by GRECO (2008, pp. 24, 25, 28) to make the presentation of accounts 'coherent, meaningful and comparable to the greatest extent possible' and to include the local level.

[153] As explained by Geddis 2007, pp. 7–8 and Orr 2010a, p. 24.

[154] GRECO (2008) p. 22 reports that between 2002 and 2005, the Labour Party on average overspent by some 4 million EUR and the Conservative Party by some 6 million EUR annually. Such behaviour is not sustainable and is bound to cause problems in the future.

[155] Paltiel 1976, pp. 108–09 (emphasis added by the author).

[156] Hughes 2001, p. 221 (emphasis added by the author).

CHAPTER 9

CHAPTER 9

Women in Politics: Financing for Gender Equality

Julie Ballington and Muriel Kahane*

Introduction

Funding plays an essential role in politics, and the high cost of election campaigning means that politics often does not afford equal opportunities for all to compete. Those who have financial means, moneyed networks, patrons and party support are disproportionately advantaged over those who do not, making the former more likely to compete for—and win—political office. This is all too apparent when considering the effects of political finance on women candidates and elections.

> 'Money is one of the essential elements that facilitates the election of women and increases their participation in politics. In Liberia, this is key, and one must have sufficient money to transport potential voters to rallies, feed them, print t-shirts, fliers and, on top of that, give them money to buy their time. The candidates also need to pay their campaign team and keep them motivated. Our whole electoral process has been commercialized, and the people with the cash carry the highest votes.'
>
> Cerue Konah Garlo, executive director, Women NGOs Secretariat of Liberia

In 2013, women held 21 per cent of parliamentary seats worldwide, up from 15 per cent a decade ago when International IDEA's *Political Finance Handbook* was first published. Eight women served as elected heads of state and 13 served as heads of government. While there is no global baseline measurement of women's participation in local government, estimates place the proportion of women office holders well below that of parliaments. Systemic and legal barriers persist at all levels and take different forms, including cultural and

---

* Julie Ballington is policy advisor on political participation and Muriel Kahane is programme analyst in the Leadership and Governance Section of UN Women. Research assistance was provided by intern Caitlin Hopping.

patriarchal, prescribed gender roles, unfavourable electoral systems and lack of support from political parties; chief among these barriers is the challenge of political financing.[1]

This chapter analyses the competitive world of political finance through a gender lens. It outlines how political finance poses a particular challenge to women candidates, and provides an overview of legislated and non-legislated measures that can help level the playing field. It describes some of the new practices that are emerging in the field of political financing, and attempts to stimulate more systematic research into the issue. With the exception of a handful of developed democracies, there is very limited empirical data on women's fundraising and spending compared with men. Disaggregating and reporting financial disclosure by sex, for example, would help fill this gap. Likewise, the effects of legislation in this area are still new, and the impacts are not fully assessed. The development of internationally agreed indicators on women and political finance—informed by the vast international normative framework on women's political participation—would strengthen future analysis on this topic.

Normative framework on political participation

The normative framework on women's political participation is derived from a number of human and political rights declarations, conventions and resolutions. Chief among them is the Convention on the Elimination of All Forms of Discrimination against Women (CEDAW), which articulates that women's equal right to participation in public and political life includes eligibility for election to all publicly elected bodies and participation in the formulation and implementation of policy.[2] The Convention commits state parties to take all appropriate measures to eliminate discrimination against women in the political and public life of the country, including through temporary special measures.

The meaning and scope of temporary special measures are further outlined in general recommendation No. 25 (2004) of the CEDAW Committee, and are broadly defined to include legislative, executive, administrative or other regulatory instruments, policies and practices, including the allocation of resources, preferential treatment, targeted recruitment and promotion, and numerical goals connected with time frames and quota systems. 'Under certain circumstances, non-identical treatment of women and men will be required in order to address such differences. Pursuit of the goal of substantive equality also calls for an effective strategy aimed at overcoming underrepresentation of women and a redistribution of resources and power between men and women.'

The most widely legislated temporary special measures are gender electoral quotas, which set specific targets for increasing the proportion of women candidates for election or reserve seats in a legislature for women members.

One-third of all countries, 64 in total, have legislated quotas. However, an increasing trend is the adoption of legislation that provides for the differential allocation of public funding according to gender-equality criteria, which is discussed further below. CEDAW recommendation 25 provides a legal basis for these measures, which promote equal opportunity in political competition.

Other declarations and conventions provide additional incentives, including the Beijing Declaration and Platform of Action (1995) and UN General Assembly Resolution 66/130 (2011) on Women and Political Participation, which call on governments to implement measures to substantially increase the number of women in elective and appointive public offices and functions at all levels. States that are parties to these international conventions share the responsibility to uphold and implement these obligations across a range of institutions, including within political parties, electoral management bodies (EMBs) and other institutions involved in monitoring and overseeing political finance regulation.

Political finance: key issues

Despite recent initiatives in this area, political finance for women candidates remains one of the greatest barriers to women's entry into politics. A 2009 Inter-Parliamentary Union survey of 300 parliamentarians found that one of the strongest deterrents to women entering politics was the lack of finances to contest electoral campaigns.[3] This was confirmed by research conducted by UN Women in 2013; over 80 per cent of respondents identified the lack of access to funding as one of the biggest challenges for women's entry into politics.[4] The research also noted that fundraising was hampered by the gendered division of labour and negative stereotypes of women in politics. While the difficulty of political finance also applies to men, women often face greater challenges for several interrelated reasons, including systemic barriers and type of electoral campaign.

Systemic barriers

Factors influencing women's political participation vary with levels of socio-economic development, culture, education, geography and type of political system.[5] Women vying for or holding political office also have major differences based on class, caste, race, ethnicity and economic and social standing, all of which may be determining factors for pursuing a political career. In addition, the type of electoral system used in a country, and whether it is candidate- or party-centred, will also affect candidates' fundraising requirements.

Socio-economic status

A country's socio-economic environment affects the participation of women in political life in both developed and developing democracies. There is a correlation between women's political participation and the proportion of women working outside the home. In developed democracies, women's increased labour force participation and attitudinal shifts regarding their role in society have enhanced their political opportunities.[6] Women's increased presence in labour unions and professional organizations gives them the opportunity to build skills and develop the networks needed to consider a political career. In all countries, though, significant gender gaps in economic status remain and are reflected in salaries, recruitment, promotion and the feminization of poverty.[7]

Women's lower economic status, especially in developing countries, can be reflected by several measures, such as the number of women living in poverty, low rates of land ownership and the high proportion of unpaid work. Women do a disproportionate share of care and domestic work, spending at least twice as much time as men on unpaid domestic work.[8] The care economy is on the whole unpaid, meaning that women have fewer resources than men. Women are also concentrated in the informal sector, which is often unregulated, vulnerable and low paid. In 2011, it was estimated that more than 80 per cent of working women in Sub-Saharan Africa, Oceania and South Asia held vulnerable jobs.[9]

Women's lower socio-economic positions in most countries mean that they may lack the economic independence to pursue a political career. Gender socialization roles, which position men as the 'breadwinners', mean that men are more accustomed to raising funds for their own use, while women have been traditionally relegated to the private sphere. Women may fear the repercussions of political finance costs on family budgets or, when they do raise funds on their own behalf, they may be accustomed to spend them on immediate family needs. In developing countries in particular, the inability to pay even modest candidate registration fees can exclude women from the election process.

New parties or those not represented in parliament usually feel the challenge of political finance most acutely, as they usually do not qualify for public funding (in countries that offer it). In these instances, women candidates have to finance themselves, and the costs of transport, campaign materials and other needs can be particularly problematic, especially in rural areas where the cost of transport to reach voters is very high.[10]

'Pacific women traditionally have a lower economic status than men. This has two consequences for women's political leadership: (1) women are less able to save the required amount of money to pay their nomination fees and (2) they lack the professional and business networks that generate the financial support needed for the campaign.'[11]

Lisa Baker, Chair, Commonwealth Women Parliamentarians

Electoral systems

Electoral systems are perhaps the most important political and institutional consideration in any country, affecting the broader issues of governance, the political party system and the inclusiveness of elected legislatures. In candidate-centred systems, like majority or plurality systems, candidates often have to raise funds for their own campaigns. This can be particularly costly, as campaigns typically involve high costs for materials and media exposure. In contrast, proportional systems may reduce the costs for individual candidates where political parties assume primary responsibility for campaigning, and are therefore considered more favourable to women candidates. For example, in Tanzania, women with few financial resources have opted to seek election in the reserved seats (which are filled through proportional lists) rather than run for the far more costly constituency seats.[12] Other considerations, such as the length of the campaign period, or holding two rounds of competition, can also place disproportionate financial burdens on women.

Type of campaign

The funding required will fluctuate over the course of an election cycle. There are two key stages in which money has a direct bearing on women's ability to run as candidates: funding to win the party primary or nomination (including early money) and funding for the electoral campaign.

Winning the party primary or nomination

Access to political office depends on being selected or nominated as a candidate by the party. Depending on the political system, candidates are nominated by the party either by winning a party primary election (usually in candidate-centred systems) or by being selected by the party leadership or elections committee (or other equivalent structure) within the party. Criteria for the 'handpicking' of candidates may include rank and standing within the party, name recognition and profile, financial resources and networks.

Party primary elections can be incredibly expensive, as aspiring candidates raise increasing amounts to beat their competitors. One woman parliamentarian in Malawi noted that 'primary elections are more expensive than national elections because that is where you win your place. That is the greatest challenge that remains'.[13] The costs are even greater for higher levels of political office. In the United States in 2008, the two main Democrat presidential primary nominees spent nearly 1 billion US dollars (USD) between them.[14] The high cost of primary elections has led to recommendations that limits be placed on the amount of funds that can be spent in nomination campaigns.

The initial selection of candidates can also be a major obstacle for women seeking elected office, in part due to the importance of early money in winning the party nomination. Early money is the initial funding required to launch a campaign for candidature, and includes gaining exposure and building name recognition, travelling and organizing a campaign team.[15] Much of a campaign's early money will often come from the candidate him/herself; this self-financing is often a major obstacle for many women, given their lower economic status. After winning the nomination, party support may increase and greater visibility may attract additional sources of funding.[16]

Funding the campaign

Having won the party nomination, candidates may need to finance a second campaign in the same election cycle. The election campaign will vary greatly depending on the type of electoral system, the political finance regulations in place, whether public funding is provided and parties' internal rules. In party-centred systems (those based on candidate lists), the party may take the lead in the campaign, so the pressure to raise additional finance may be less than for candidates competing in candidate-centred (majoritarian) systems. In many countries, winning an open seat is often associated with raising more funds than opponents. This is well documented in the United States, where campaign costs can reach into millions of dollars per candidate.[17]

Some situations that may necessitate particularly high expenditures are:[18]

- when winning the election depends on reaching a large number of voters;
- when the electoral system is majoritarian, or in contexts where there is a strong tradition of personality politics;
- when there are open or free lists, with intra-list competition taking place;
- when the political party has limited financial means for the campaign; or
- when clientelism—an informal political practice that requires building and maintaining large, localized networks to help distribute services, goods and money in exchange for political support—is a key method of competition.[19]

Campaign spending varies widely around the world. In India, election expenditure in Uttar Pradesh in 2012 was estimated at USD 3–5 billion. Candidates in Brazil's 2010 election spent an estimated USD 2 billion, while Japan's 2009 campaign cost an estimated USD 780 million. Lower spenders include the United Kingdom, where the 2010 general election cost USD 91 million, and Russia, where the 2011 election is said to have cost USD 70 million.[20] No information is available, however, for fundraising and expenditure disaggregated by sex, which makes it difficult to compare the expenditures of women candidates with men.

Barriers to fundraising

The difficulties that women face in raising the funds needed to win the party nomination and compete in the electoral campaign have been well documented, and include the lack of access to moneyed networks and credit, and political clientelism. Long campaigning periods may dissuade women from running, given their family responsibilities and the costs associated with childcare. In some cases, extra costs might be incurred by the lack of security for candidates to campaign, as candidates have to provide their own security, particularly in post-conflict states or violence-prone elections.

Campaign spending and accessing funds

Women may encounter problems accessing funding, both within political parties and private funding. According to Bryan and Baer, 'A female member of Parliament in one southern African country had heard that male candidates for her party received three times as much as she did'.[21] In many cases, public funding is only available to parties that already have seats. Where public funding exists, consideration should be given to how it is distributed, and whether women are sidelined in the allocations. In post-conflict countries, women's participation might be considered a second-order priority, after establishing political systems and holding the first round of elections. If resources are scarce, women will need to finance the campaign costs themselves, through private and personal funding. These costs can also be particularly high in countries with weak transport infrastructures and large rural constituencies.

Accessing private funding might also be more problematic for women given their limited access to the public sphere, and gender perceptions that call into question their qualifications or suitability as serious political candidates. Women may internalize these negative stereotypes, believing they will not be able to raise the funds necessary for their campaign.[22] In Morocco's 2011 election, women gained 17 per cent of seats, but only seven of them (less than 2 per cent) won in open seat contests and not through the party list quota.[23] In the United States, there is a bias towards male candidates who tend to attract higher average individual and corporate donations.[24] Given women's limited access to moneyed networks, their campaign contributions tend to be smaller, which means they need to campaign harder to reach a broader base of donors to achieve funding parity with male colleagues.

Networks

One of the reasons why women may struggle to raise funds relative to men is that they are less likely to be linked to business and professional networks which can provide financial resources and expertise. The network argument extends to the 'all-boys network' within the party, as most party leaderships today remain male-dominated.[25] Women's absence from these networks means that they might not have access to funding channels that are available to male candidates. As a parliamentarian from Ireland notes: 'Men, male candidates, are involved in various organizations that facilitate their entry into politics: sporting organizations, farmers' associations, and other male-dominated areas'.[26] The absence of women from these networks hampers their ability to raise sufficient funds to campaign effectively—particularly when running against entrenched male incumbents. The exceptions to this are often the spouses, daughters and sisters of well-known politicians who, by virtue of their relationships, have access to family capital and connections.[27] The cultivation of networks is important not only for fundraising, but also for gaining political leverage by building contacts and expertise and using common interests for canvassing purposes.

Incumbency

It is often difficult to unseat an incumbent since they are known to the public, and thus parties may perceive them as a safer bet. Incumbents' campaign expenditure tends to be lower overall, since they are recognized and their political platforms are well established. Less than one in four parliamentarians is a woman, meaning that in most cases incumbents are men. The added costs associated with unseating an incumbent can dissuade women from entering political races.

Measures to level the field

When all these factors coincide, it can be particularly challenging for women to raise political financing. In the past few years, countries have started to adopt political finance reforms to level the playing field for women and other under-represented groups, although regulations vary in their target and effectiveness. Legislated and non-legislated measures can be and have been used to address the issue:

1. *Legislated measures* relate to the political and electoral frameworks and allocations to political parties and candidates through public funding. They may be:
   - *gender-neutral* in their design, but with gendered implications in practice; or
   - *gender-targeted* in their design and application and/or explicitly promote women's political participation through public funding.
2. *Non-legislated measures* are adopted by stakeholders on a voluntary basis. They may include:
   - *political party* measures, which are voluntary and apply only to the party in question; or
   - *civil society measures* and other initiatives aimed at channelling funds directly to women candidates.

More often than not, these initiatives relate to the national election campaigns rather than party primary elections. States may use a combination of measures, depending on their national contexts and the general level of political party regulation. Most of these measures have been adopted recently, and the results and practice are not widely documented. Nevertheless, the remainder of this chapter outlines their actual (or potential) impact on women political aspirants.

Political finance legislation

Legislation on political finance aims to increase the transparency and fairness of the political funding process and level the playing field for all candidates. Regulations may focus on limiting the undue influence of outside or external actors, such as legislation that bans donations from foreign or anonymous sources or sets limits on donations that parties or candidates can receive.[28] Other measures aim to level the playing field, for example by ensuring that incumbents do not have an unfair advantage over other candidates. Legislated measures exist in most countries in the world.[29]

Regulations on spending, such as how much parties and candidates can spend, can contribute to ensuring that candidates with lesser resources can run campaigns without being unfairly disadvantaged. Regulations may include reporting on finances and disclosure requirements, which require parties and candidates to provide information on expenditures. Other measures focus on enforcement. Oversight is usually the responsibility of national electoral bodies, government departments, regulatory bodies created specifically for this purpose or other departments.[30]

Most legislation on political finance is designed in a 'gender-neutral' way. That is, the legislation does not seek to address gender inequalities explicitly, although there may be gender-differentiated outcomes in practice. Some states have recently adopted 'gender-targeted' laws, such as innovative practices to channel more funds to women candidates for election. Overall, 27 states make the allocation of public funding dependent on fulfilling certain gender-equality requirements, including recent reforms in Bosnia and Herzegovina, Croatia, Ireland and Mexico that link political finance allocation to promoting women's participation in decision making.[31] Legislation can also be targeted at other innovative practices, such as earmarking funds for gender-equality initiatives within political parties such as capacity building or supporting the women's wing. The different ways in which finance regulations may have a gender impact, either directly or indirectly, are outlined in Table 9.1. and will be further elaborated below.

Table 9.1. Political funding regulations and gender considerations

Legislation targeting the campaign period (gender-neutral)	Public funding for enforcement of quota provisions and candidate incentives	Legislation targeting gender equality initiatives
• Spending bans and limits for political parties and/or candidates • Contribution bans and limits for political parties and/or candidates • Media access • Time limit on length of campaign period • Disclosure and oversight of political parties and candidates	• Public funding reduced for parties that fail to nominate a certain number of women according to quota laws • Funding withdrawn from parties that fail to elect a certain number of women • Additional funding distributed to parties that nominate a certain number of women • Additional funding distributed to parties that get a certain number of women elected	• Funds earmarked for training and promotion of gender equality • Women's wing or caucus funding • In-kind costs and incentives, such as use of campaign funds for childcare

Source: International IDEA Political Finance Database. See http://www.idea.int/political-finance

Legislation targeting the campaign period (gender-neutral)

While only limited data are available, some of the gendered impacts of gender-neutral designed campaign legislation are outlined below.

Spending bans or limits for parties and candidates

Bans and spending limits for political parties and candidates are designed to regulate the cost of campaigns and ensure that candidates and parties with more access to resources are not unfairly advantaged. Spending bans are typically used to ensure that there can be no vote buying, with 90 per cent of countries having legislation to this effect.[32] Despite the widespread nature of these measures, their effectiveness depends on implementation, which can be difficult given that the execution requires the collaboration of the parliamentary majority, which is the group the legislation targets.[33]

Limits on spending are designed to counteract the unfair advantage that candidates with more resources might have in running a campaign, and to curb the trend of increased campaign expenditure. According to the International IDEA Database on Political Finance (Political Finance Database), nearly one-third of countries for which data are available have limits on political party spending, and over 40 per cent regulate how much candidates may spend.[34] Finance provides a massive advantage to some candidates, particularly in countries where money is associated with speech and visibility. Capping the amount that candidates can spend is therefore posited to have a direct effect on women's ability to run successful campaigns. While quantitative evidence of this is limited, research from the United States and Canada shows that when women are able to raise as much as (or more than) their male opponents, they are equally likely to win the election.[35]

'I think we see that, across the globe, in different societies and cultures, women do not have as much access to campaign financing as men do, for one reason or another. I think it is important for countries and election commissions in those countries to formulate stringent rules on what you can spend on your election campaign—and they need to enforce those rules. If it is an amount that is manageable then the playing field is levelled, but if it is an astronomical amount, then invariably (as most of the world is composed of developing countries) it is the men who have access to that money and not the women. Instead of looking for ways we can increase women's access to that much money, I think we need to decrease everyone's expenditure and make it more manageable.'

Dr Donya Aziz, member of the National Assembly, Pakistan

In many countries, one of the most pervasive obstacles is the power of incumbency, and the majority of incumbent candidates globally are men.[36] Three-quarters of countries have legislated measures that target incumbents, including limitations on the use of state resources and spending limits. One strategy for addressing the incumbency advantage is to allow higher spending limits for challengers. In the state of Minnesota in the United States, for example, legislation allows first-time candidates to have higher spending limits than incumbents, in order to counteract the unfair advantage incumbents may enjoy.[37] As such, setting achievable (and potentially differentiated) spending limits may have a positive, if indirect, effect on a woman's run for election—and on new male challengers, too.

Party spending limits may determine how much money can be spent on a campaign, including on publicity, media, campaign materials and rallies. Political parties decide how funds are allocated within the party, and an important consideration is which candidates receive funds. Internal disbursement of party funds tends to sideline women candidates when they are not high in the party structure or are deemed to have insufficient name recognition.[38]

While limits on campaign spending may have a positive effect on women's decision to run for elections, they do not address the main challenge faced by women, that of raising funds. In some instances, limits may be counterproductive in countries with strong fundraising mechanisms that channel large sums to women candidates, such as in the United States. Further research into the effect of spending limits and bans on women's election rates is needed in other regions.

Contribution bans and limits

An alternative or complementary measure to setting spending limits is to establish a limit on the contributions that a political party or candidate can receive. Contribution limits or bans aim to reduce the influence of wealthy donors. Where limits are high, it is possible for wealthy donors to gain undue influence in the campaign, which can potentially hurt women and challengers, who are less likely to benefit from moneyed networks. Less than half of all countries have adopted regulations setting a ceiling for contributions.

Since individual donations to women tend to be smaller than those to men, on average, women need to attract larger numbers of individual contributions to reach the level of donations reached by their male counterparts.[39] Lower contribution limits might help to level the playing field for women candidates by ensuring that all candidates cultivate a broad base of support rather than rely on a few large donors.

Given the potential for detrimental effects on political parties and candidates, some sources of income are banned altogether.[40] Contribution bans aim to prevent the influence of particular categories of donors, such as foreign donors or those engaged in industries that might request that their interests be given particular consideration. The most common ban relates to the allocation of state resources to parties and candidates. Other bans relate to corporate donations (with over 20 per cent of countries having regulations to this effect), as well as foreign sources, and donations from corporations with government contracts, trade unions and anonymous sources.

Bans on the use of state resources are important. Using government resources other than those earmarked for public funding (such as the use of government vehicles and facilities for campaigning) can unfairly benefit incumbents. Furthermore, bans on the use of state resources can also target corruption, as was the case in 2010 in Brazil, where nearly 30 per cent of members of Congress were facing criminal charges for non-compliance with campaign financing laws or corruption in the form of embezzlement of public funds for campaign purposes.[41] At the time, women held only 45 of the 513 seats (8.8 per cent) in the Brazilian lower house of parliament, meaning that the beneficiaries of these illicit funds were overwhelmingly men.[42]

Donation bans are also important in relation to illicit sources of funding. In some countries, illicit funding has a huge influence on elections, as regulations are notoriously difficult to enforce. Banning illicit funds may directly benefit women candidates who are less likely to receive and use illicit funding. Women tend to be under-represented in the activities where the illicit funds come from, such as drug cartels, warring groups, rebel groups and trafficking groups. In a workshop in Belize, for instance, a number of civil society activists noted that the use of illicit funds to finance campaigns disadvantages women, who are overall less involved in these money-making industries and are far less likely to receive illicit sources of funding.[43] Despite difficulties in enforcing bans on illicit funding, adopting and enforcing legislation contributes to levelling the field for all candidates, and may have a marked effect on women's chances of being elected.

Media access

Legislated media access is an indirect (i.e. non-monetary) form of public funding. Parties and candidates need media access to make their political platforms known to the electorate and to increase their name recognition and support. Three-quarters of countries have regulations on free or subsidized media access for candidates, political parties or both. Media time is allocated either equally among parties, or by share of seats in parliament, by the number of candidates, by share of votes in the preceding election or through other means, such as by criteria decided by the EMB.

Women often face challenges in making their platforms and messages known to the electorate because of limited access to the media.[44] They are either less able to pay for costly media time or are not afforded equal media access by their party. Subsidized media coverage is an important means for women to gain name recognition. In the 2001 East Timorese elections, additional television advertising time was given to women candidates and parties that placed women in 'winnable' positions on their candidate lists.[45] In Brazil, a 2009 reform provided 10 per cent additional media time to political parties, to be used by women candidates.[46] Legislation on media access could stipulate equal access to male and female candidates, or act as an incentive for parties to nominate more women (and for winnable positions). In Afghanistan, while the law does not stipulate how media time is to be allocated,[47] evidence shows that 76 per cent of female candidates took advantage of the subsidized media measure in the 2005 election, compared to 55 per cent of male candidates.

Media exposure is vital to winning a campaign, and can contribute to challenging the widespread stereotypes that preclude women from being seen as capable politicians.[48] Voters have been found to have high standards for what they consider to be a 'qualified' woman candidate, which in turn affects her likeability: the more qualified, the more likeable she is.[49]

Campaign time limits

There is limited information on the number of countries with provisions limiting the length of the campaign period and the potential effects of such provisions. Limiting the duration of the campaign could potentially contribute to levelling the field for women candidates, given that prolonged campaign periods can incur high costs in the form of travel, accommodation and additional campaign materials. The postponement of Malawi's 2010 local elections is reported to have disproportionately affected women candidates, who could not afford the costs of the delay.[50] Long campaigns can be particularly problematic for women when they involve long hours and extended periods away from home. This could deter women who might otherwise consider becoming a candidate, or could affect their ability to campaign because of caring and family responsibilities (particularly if partners or spouses are absent or unwilling to support the candidacy, or to assume household and care duties).

Yet short campaign periods or lead-in times to elections may also negatively affect women candidates. Short campaigns may benefit incumbents, the majority of whom are men. In Libya's 2012 elections for the transitional legislature, the short registration and campaigning period is believed to have adversely affected women's ability to mobilize the funds and people required to mount an effective campaign[51]. As with the other measures listed above, additional research is needed on the potential impact of establishing campaign time limits and possible positive and/or negative effects on women's campaigns.

Disclosure regulations and enforcement

Disclosure regulations may require candidates and parties to disclose the identity of donors, the amounts given and the funds spent during campaigns. These mechanisms are crucial in order to ascertain whether financing regulations are being respected. Disclosure regulations also promote accountability, and may help to prevent corrupt channels through which candidates might be acquiring resources, vote buying or engaging in clientelistic practices. They can contribute to ensuring that leaders and powerful factions within the party (often men) do not abuse their power to gain access to more resources than other candidates in the party.

> 'A lack of transparency within internal parties' campaigns, as well as in external campaigns, affects women in a negative way. When resources are managed by powerful groups within parties, they are destined [for] the members of these groups—who most frequently happen to be men.'
>
> Ms Lilian Soto, former minister, Paraguay[52]

According to the International IDEA Political Finance Database, over 80 per cent of countries have reporting regulations. However, not all countries require that reports be submitted by both political parties and candidates. As noted in the introductory chapter of this handbook, this is worrisome, as it can create a loophole through which illicit funds can be channelled. Disclosure and monitoring mechanisms are necessary to assess whether measures that target gender equality—such as electoral quota enforcement and earmarked funds for female candidates—are being adequately implemented. In Latin America, for instance, Brazil, Mexico and Panama earmark public funding for training and promoting women's participation (2–50 per cent of public funds), but have no mechanisms to ensure that these funds are correctly allocated, leaving it up to the political parties.[53] Without monitoring, it is impossible to ascertain the effects of these measures on women's participation.

Enforceable disclosure can positively contribute to women's participation by increasing the transparency of the electoral process and discouraging the use of illicit funding mechanisms and vote buying—which indirectly disadvantage women. The design of disclosure mechanisms can also be important to track the effect of financing regulations on women's participation in electoral contests. There is no information on whether disclosure regulations require returns and expenditures of candidates to be disaggregated by sex. Such data would be invaluable for determining how women's fundraising and spending compare to those of men, and whether funds allocated within the party are equally distributed among women and men candidates. Disaggregated data may also lead to increased transparency of the process, and enable more effective civil society monitoring. Furthermore, disclosure may help assess the effectiveness of particular legislation on women's successful campaigns and design new practices that can be tested.

The success of political funding regulations depends on enforcement, which varies widely. Fines are the most common penalty, and are used in 73 per cent of countries. Other penalties include incarceration, loss of public funding, party deregistration, loss of nomination of candidates and/or elected office, and suspension of the party.[54] Enforcement is particularly important for women's political participation because it ensures that existing regulations, in particular those that target women's participation, are put into effect. Enforcement of regulations may also have a positive spin-off effect by giving women increased confidence in the system and helping them use the rules to their own advantage. For example, if spending limits are enforced, women may feel more confident in challenging male incumbents. Enforced financing regulations designed to promote inclusiveness can contribute to changing deeply held perceptions about who can participate (and who can win).

Table 9.2. Gendered impacts of finance legislation

Type of intervention	Country usage	Considerations
Spending bans and limits for political parties and candidates	• Spending bans in 90% of countries • Limits on spending by parties in nearly 30% of countries • Limits on spending by candidates in over 40% of countries	• May help women or non-incumbent challengers, who generally have less access to campaign funds • Might alleviate women's concerns about the high cost of running a campaign and the time commitment necessary to raise funds • Effectiveness depends on implementation and oversight • Additional evidence is needed on whether spending limits help women candidates
Contribution bans and limits for political parties and candidates	• Less than 50% of countries have limits on contributions for parties and candidates • Contribution bans on corporate donations in 70% of countries • Only 30% of countries have limits on contributions to candidates	• Women candidates tend to receive smaller donations from a wider base, and contribution limits would thus help reduce large donations by networks and male donors to male candidates • May mitigate the effect of large illicit funding sources, which typically favour male candidates • Women donors tend to donate time and skills more often than male donors • Might increase time spent campaigning to multiple sources of donations, in order to raise the same amount of funds

Media access regulations	• Subsidized access to media for parties in 66% of countries • Subsidized media access for candidates in 46% of countries	• Could allow equal access of male and female candidates to the media • Could be used as an incentive to increase the number of women candidates • Can help challenge media bias against women candidates through greater presence and messaging
Campaign time limits	• No data available	• May level the field for women candidates by reducing costs and limiting the time spent away from home • May negatively affect candidates' ability to raise funds over a longer period of time
Disclosure and enforcement regulations	• Reporting regulations in nearly 90% of countries	• May help diminish the power of networks and individuals by allowing for greater transparency • Can prevent the use of illicit sources of funding • Can ensure gender-targeted legislation is enforced • Could provide an opportunity for sex-disaggregated data on spending and success rates

Public funding to enforce quota provisions and candidate-nomination incentives

The provision of public funding—available in 117 states—targets parties' ability to run effective campaigns and function as institutions.[55] Public funding is overwhelmingly allocated to political parties rather than candidates,[56] and typically covers campaign expenditures, training, party activities and intra-party institution building.

Public funding can be direct or indirect. Direct public funding provides funds for political parties to improve the way they operate, or to ensure that certain priorities are addressed in their platforms.[57] Indirect public funding may provide resources for campaigns such as transport, venues, free or subsidized media access to public or private TV, radio, newspaper or other media. These measures may contribute to levelling the playing field, ensuring that smaller parties gain recognition and that all political platforms are communicated to voters.

Recently, political finance reforms have been adopted that explicitly aim to address gender inequality. These reforms apply mostly to the pre-electoral phase and target the candidacies of women by political parties, although some are directed at parties in the inter-election period. In all, 27 countries have adopted reforms that directly target gender equality.[58] These reforms are divided into three main categories:

1. public funding that is used as an incentive or penalty for *compliance or non-compliance with legislated electoral quota laws*; a portion of funds is either allocated or reduced in line with the quota law;
2. public funding that is used as an *incentive to increase the number of women candidates or elected women*, but is unrelated to the enforcement of a quota law; and

3. public funding that is *earmarked for specific gender-equality or women's empowerment* activities or interventions within the party.

Figure 9.1. Countries that have adopted political finance reforms that directly target gender equality

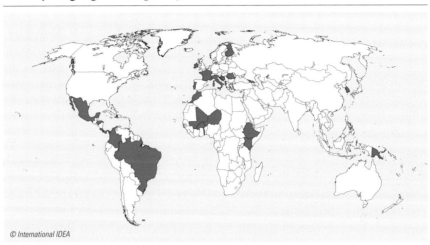

© International IDEA

Over two-thirds of these measures were adopted in the last five years, and so have only applied to one election cycle. The results and practice of the reforms are therefore not widely documented. This section outlines some of the main initiatives and identifies the actual (or potential) impact on women candidates.

Public funding and enforcement of electoral quota laws

Eleven countries tie the allocation of public funding to the enforcement of electoral quotas and the nomination of women as candidates (see Table 9.3.). Public funding gives parties financial incentives to meet the quota target or penalizes them if they fail to meet the agreed proportion of women candidates or elected representatives. These reforms are relatively recent. France led the way by adopting a law on equality between women and men in 1999, which provided for the equal access of women and men to electoral mandates and elective positions. In 2000, an electoral reform set the penalty for non-compliance with the parity rule as a reduction in the public funding provided to parties based on the number of votes they received in the first round of elections.[59] In 2006, Portugal adopted a similar reform. However, the majority of the reforms have only been adopted since 2010. More often than not, newly adopted quota laws include a reduction in public finance as one of the sanctions for non-compliance, as in Albania, Georgia and Ireland.

Incentives and penalties take different forms. Candidate nomination incentives are those measures that allocate additional funding to parties that nominate a certain proportion of women candidates in line with the quota law, as is the case in Croatia and Georgia. In Georgia, for instance, parties that have at least 20 per cent of either sex on candidate lists will receive an additional 10 per cent of public funding. In the 2012 election, however, the financial incentive did not have the intended impact. While several parties complied with the law and received additional funding, the two parties that won seats in parliament did not. Amendments to the law regulating the financial incentives for political parties (Organic Law of Georgia on Political Unions of Citizens) were proposed in July 2013, proposing that parties receive a 30 per cent supplement from the state budget (up from 10 per cent) if the nominated party list includes at least 30 per cent of each gender (up from 20 per cent) for each group of ten candidates.[60] These incentives may have a limited impact on larger and better-funded parties, which can afford to forfeit the additional funds.

Public funding can also be used as a penalty for non-compliance with quota legislation, where the funding a party receives is reduced if a certain proportion of candidates or elected members are not women, as in Albania, France, Ireland and Portugal. The 2012 amendment to the Irish Electoral Act stipulates that parties will lose 50 per cent of their funding if either gender is represented by less than 30 per cent of party candidates. In Kenya, parties may not be eligible for funding if a certain percentage or number of women is not elected. This provision, together with the introduction of reserved seats, resulted in a doubling of the number of women elected in Kenya to 18.6 per cent.

However, these measures may have limited impact on parties with large resources, which may choose to pay the penalty rather than nominate more women candidates, as has been the case in France.[61] There, smaller parties have tended to respect the 50 per cent candidacy requirement, as they are more dependent on public financing than bigger parties, which often choose to field incumbents (who are largely men) in the belief that they are more likely to win.[62] In Albania's June 2013 election, each candidate list had to include at least one male and one female in the top three positions, and in total comprise at least 30 per cent of each gender. To meet the quota, many parties included women at the bottom of the lists in unwinnable positions. As the provision that would have denied registration to non-compliant lists was repealed in 2012, the EMB issued fines instead to the three largest parliamentary parties for failing to meet the gender quota in some districts. In 2012, the fine for non-compliant lists was increased from 30,000 Albanian lek (ALL) (I$520)[63] to ALL 1 million (I$17,000).[64]

In addition to funding incentives or penalties, other quota enforcement mechanisms include rejecting candidate lists that do not meet the target, as in Serbia. While these measures may contribute to increasing the number of women candidates, they do not necessarily tackle the underlying challenge of accessing campaign finance. Indeed, research is needed to ascertain how nominated women candidates who may have benefited from the incentives or penalties were able to fund their campaigns, and how much funding came from the party. In addition, it would be useful to explore how the parties that received additional funding spent the funds, and if the funds were directed to support women candidates. Women may need to be part of the parties' decision-making bodies in order to guarantee that funds are disbursed in a way that benefits all candidates.

Table 9.3. Enforcement of electoral quotas through public funding[65]

Country	Quota type	Political finance provision details	year(s) of reform
Albania	30% of candidates must be women	Failure to comply is punishable with a fine of ALL 1,000,000 (I\$17,000) in the case of elections to the Assembly and ALL 50,000 (I\$860) for elections for local government bodies.	2012
Burkina Faso	30% of candidates must be women	Failure to comply will result in a 50% cut to the party's public funding. If a party reaches or exceeds the 30% quota, it will receive additional funding.	2009
Cape Verde	Balanced representation of both sexes on candidate lists	Subsidies will be awarded to parties or coalitions of parties whose lists (if elected at the national level) contain at least 25% women candidates.	2010
Croatia	Balance between women and men on candidate lists	For each elected deputy who belongs to an under-represented gender, political parties shall be entitled to a bonus of 10% of the amount allocated to each deputy or member of the representative body.	2011
France	No more than 51% of candidates may be of one gender	If the gender difference among candidates is larger than 2%, the public funding is reduced by three-quarters of this difference.	2011 1998
Georgia	20% of candidates must be women	An additional 10% funding will be awarded to parties that have 20% women in every 10 candidates.	2012
Ireland	30% of candidates must be women (40% by 2019)	Parties will be sanctioned with a reduction of up to 50% of public funds if they have less than 30% women candidates.	2012
Kenya	30% reserved seats	Parties will not be eligible for public funding if more than two-thirds of their registered office holders are of the same gender.	2011
Korea, Republic of	50% women candidates for list proportional representation elections	Female candidate nomination subsidies are distributed to parties based on the ratio of the National Assembly seats held and the votes received.	2010
Niger	Reserved seats	The grant funding of parties is set at 30% of annual tax revenues of the state; 10% is distributed in proportion to the number of women elected by the quota at all levels.	2010

| Portugal | 33% of candidates must be women | Public subsidies are reduced by 50% if one sex is represented below 20%. If either sex is represented between 20% and 33.3%, the public subsidy is reduced by 25%. | 2006 |

Note: ALL = Albanian lek.

Public funding incentives to nominate more female candidates

Public funding is also used as an incentive to increase the number of women nominated, and is not necessarily linked to quota law enforcement. Table 9.4. illustrates the eight countries that have adopted these measures, six of which have no legislated electoral quotas. While Bosnia and Herzegovina and Colombia have legislated quotas, the provision of public funding is not linked to their enforcement. In Colombia, Mali and Romania, the amount of public funding a party is entitled to may increase depending on the number of women elected. Only Haiti bases the distribution of additional funds on both nomination and the number of women elected.

Important factors that influence the effectiveness of such measures are the timeline of the distribution of funds (before or after the election), the degree to which political parties rely on public funding, and the amount of the penalty or reward as a percentage of the total funding. The timing of the application of the provision may also be an important consideration. Basing funding penalties or rewards on the number of women elected may lessen the impact of these measures, since they are implemented post-election when there is less media attention and campaign funds are already spent. Efforts must be made to monitor and publicize the outcome of political finance initiatives post-election.

In Bosnia and Herzegovina, the 2009 Law on Party Finance states that 10 per cent of total funds will be distributed to parliamentary groups in proportion to the number of seats held by the less-represented gender. In the 2010 election, there was a small increase of 2 percentage points in the number of women elected over the number in the previous parliament, bringing the total to 16.7 per cent. Overall, parties respected and surpassed the legal requirement of one-third women on the candidate lists, reaching 37.7 per cent. The Organization for Security and Co-operation in Europe noted that, according to the political finance law, 'parties that are not represented in parliament are totally exempt from receiving any kind of public funds'.[66] This raises the important question of eligibility for access to public funds, and whether only parties with seats in parliament are eligible to receive such funds.

Romania's 2006 Law on the Financing of the Activity of Political Parties and Electoral Campaigns stipulates that 'for the political parties that promote women on their electoral lists in eligible positions, the amount allotted from the state budget shall be increased in direct proportion with the number of the mandates obtained during election by the female candidates'.[67] The law has had limited impact thus far, with women winning just 7 per cent of seats in the Senate and 13 per cent in the House in the 2012 elections. In Romania, some political parties rely heavily on public funding, while the larger parties received a significant amount of funding from party members. The degree to which public funding is an effective incentive depends on the political party and its access to other funding sources.

According to a 2009 Ethiopian law, government funding granted is apportioned according to different criteria, including the number of women candidates nominated by the party. However, data from the National Electoral Board show that the proportion of women candidates actually decreased from 15 per cent in the 2005 elections to 12.4 per cent in 2010. Overall there was an increase in the number of women elected in Ethiopia in 2010; however, it is not necessarily a direct consequence of the financing legislation.

Haiti's 2006 Law on Political Parties and 2008 Electoral Law state that political parties that run at least 30 per cent women candidates (and succeed in electing 20 per cent of them) will have double the public funding after the election.[68] The legislation also requires that 50 per cent of these funds be used to support women candidates and political education. Haiti has a new constitutional amendment (adopted in 2012) that requires a minimum 30 per cent quota for women in all elected and appointed positions; it has not yet been enforced as no elections have been held since then.

One of the potential challenges of targeting nomination is that parties might view it as an easy way of accessing funding, without intending to ensure women candidates are elected by placing them in winnable positions. Women might be nominated but fielded in difficult-to-win-seats, or have their names placed far down the list, making their election less likely, as was seen in the case of Albania. The legislation in Haiti seeks to circumvent this by stipulating that the funding initially allocated for the nomination of women candidates will be doubled if at least 20 per cent of those elected are women, to ensure that nomination incentives do not fall short of their intentions.[69] However, legislation needs to be enforced to be effective.

Table 9.4. Public funding disbursement relative to number of women candidates[70]

Country	Political finance provision details	Year of reform
Bosnia and Herzegovina	10% of public funds will be distributed to parliamentary groups in proportion to the number of seats held by the less-represented gender.	2006
Colombia	5% of state funding shall be allocated equally among all parties or movements in proportion to the number of women elected to public bodies.	2011
Ethiopia	Financial support will be apportioned according to the number of female candidates nominated by the party.	2009

Haiti	Parties that have at least 30% female candidates (and succeed in electing 20% of them) will, after the elections for the same functions, double the public funding to which they would have been entitled.	2008
Italy	Neither sex should exceed two-thirds of candidates selected for the party lists. If this provision is not achieved, the public campaign subsidy to the political party is reduced in proportion to the number of candidates exceeding the maximum allowed (up to 50%). The withheld amount will be disbursed as a premium to parties that adhere to the law.	2012
Mali	10% of funds are allocated to political parties in proportion to the number of women elected.	2005
Papua New Guinea	Where a female party candidate obtains at least 10% of the votes, the registered political party shall be entitled to receive from the Central Fund 75% of 10,000.00 kina (I$8,900) payable to a successful candidate, as election campaign expenses on her behalf (or an amount fixed by the Commission).	2003
Romania	The amount allocated from the state budget will be increased in proportion to the number of seats obtained in the election of women candidates.	2006

Earmarking for gender-equality initiatives

Public funding can also be explicitly earmarked for gender-equality initiatives. Thirteen countries have recently adopted these reforms (most within the last five years), including training of women candidates, programmes related to women's empowerment and funds to support the functioning of women's wings.[71]

In Brazil, Colombia and Haiti, public funds are to be used to support empowerment programmes and education, while in Costa Rica, Honduras and Ireland, parties are required to submit reports on their expenses, including compliance with gender-equality provisions.[72] Finland requires that a portion of funds be used to support the functioning of women's wings within parties. In Ireland, funds received by qualified parties must fulfil certain criteria, including the promotion of participation by women and young people in political activity. However, the amount varies widely among political parties.[73] Other examples are provided in Table 9.5.

Like the other reforms discussed, earmarking for gender equality initiatives is a recent development, with most legislation having been enacted in the past five years. Countries that include gender-targeted legislation in their political financing regulations tend to be countries that have already taken measures to address women's under-representation through candidate quotas.

Funds targeting training and other programmes

Nine countries have adopted legislation requiring political parties to earmark funds targeting training activities and other programmes within political parties. Women have historically been under-represented in decision-making bodies, resulting in less political experience. Indeed, women's lesser experience of politics has been used by political parties to justify not nominating women, or relegating them to unelectable posts.[74] Candidates have emphasized the importance of training and capacity building, not just in terms of building skills for effective political engagement, but also training on how to raise campaign funds.

Costa Rica's Law for the Promotion of Political Social Equality requires parties to assign a percentage of state funds for the political development and participation of women, to be equally distributed between male and female candidates.[75] Box 9.1. illustrates how two political parties distribute these funds.

Box 9.1. Costa Rica financing for gender equality

Citizen's Action Party

The party assigns 20 per cent of the total funds received from state allotments to training and organizational efforts, of which 15 per cent is allotted to training women and youth. The funds are directed to male and female candidates in elected positions and within the party, and target awareness-raising activities. The party has created an Office for Gender Equality, under the internal election board, which works to implement all the requirements on gender equality set out in the party's statutes.[76]

National Liberation Party

Article 171 of the party's statutes indicates that at least 10 per cent of the budget shall be devoted to women's political development. Compliance is overseen by a Political Education Secretariat in coordination with the president of the party's Women's Movement. The Women's Movement facilitates training programmes for women candidates and legislators.[77]

Mexico's legislation requires that 2 per cent of public funding be allocated to promoting and training for women's political leadership. The application of the law has faced difficulties in practice, with most parties spending the funds on administration rather than on building the skills of women politicians. This may be because parties are unsure about what strengthening women's participation and capacity building means, or because they would rather pay the low fines established for non-compliance with this measure.[78]

Funds to female candidates

Haiti's new law stipulates that 50 per cent of the public funds received must be used for the political education of party members and to support women's electoral contests, although the provision has not yet been put into practice. This is nevertheless a unique law, containing provisions for the distribution of funds within the party to women's campaigns.

Women's wings

Finland has a unique provision that requires all parties to allocate 12 per cent of their annual party subsidy to support women's wings. This can be an important initiative, as women's wings can contribute to articulating policy on gender equality—including on women's nominations and placement rules, financing mechanisms, building a platform base and support from constituents, advocating for women candidates and acting as mentors to contenders with less experience. Key to the success of women's wings is the clear delineation of their roles and responsibilities, their integration into the party structure and access to funding.[79] Finland is the only country with this initiative; in other Nordic countries (Denmark, Norway and Sweden), funding for women's wings comes from outside public party assistance.

Reduction in nomination fees

Togo's law specifies a reduction in nomination fees for women candidates, thereby facilitating women's registration as candidates for election and reducing the total cost of the campaign to the party. High registration fees have been a challenge reported in a number of countries, including in Myanmar's 2010 elections, where candidates had to pay the Election Commission the equivalent of USD 500 to register. Parties challenged the fee, noting that a schoolteacher's monthly salary was USD 70.[80] High registration fees are a particular concern for women, who typically have access to fewer resources than men. This point was also made by the Sierra Leone Women's Forum, an umbrella organization for women's groups. Ahead of the 2012 local and parliamentary elections, the Forum started a petition urging the National Electoral Commission to revise the increased registration fee, noting that it was keeping women out of the competition, particularly in rural areas.[81]

Childcare and costs for caring for relatives can also be a factor deterring women from running for office. The Canadian Elections Act includes childcare expenses as a legitimate personal expense during a campaign:[82]

> Personal expenses of a candidate are his or her electoral campaign expenses, other than election expenses, that are reasonably incurred in relation to his or her campaign and include (a) travel and living expenses; (b) childcare expenses; (c) expenses relating to the provision of care for a person with a physical or mental incapacity for whom the candidate normally provides such care; and (d) in the case of a candidate who has a disability, additional personal expenses that are related to the disability.

Some states in the United States have similar regulations, including Minnesota, where childcare can be considered a legitimate campaign expense to be covered in total by campaign funds.[83] This could be an important initiative to help level the field for women, as they typically take on most of the caring responsibilities.

Table 9.5. Legislation targeting gender-equality measures and earmarking[84]

Country	Training and gender-equality initiatives	Year(s) of reform
Brazil	The proceeds from the party fund will be used to create and maintain programmes that promote women's political participation; the national party leadership will determine the percentage (minimum of 5% of the total). Ten per cent of media time shall be allocated to promote women's political participation.	2009
Colombia	Proceeds from state funding will fund the activities undertaken to include women, youth and ethnic minorities in the political process.	2011
Costa Rica	Political parties are mandated to assign a percentage of state funds for the political development and participation of women, to be equally distributed between male and female candidates.	1990 2009
Haiti	Parties that receive public funding based on the proportion of women candidates should ensure that 50 per cent of these funds is allocated to the political education of their members and financial support to female candidates to electoral contests.	2008
Honduras	Additional funds equivalent to 10% of the total public funding allocation shall be distributed among parties for women's capacity-building activities.	2012
Ireland	The funds received by qualified parties must fulfil certain purposes, including the promotion of participation of women and young persons in political activities.	2009
Italy	Each political party or movement shall allocate at least 5% of the reimbursements to initiatives aimed at increasing the active participation of women in politics.	1999
Korea, Republic of	Every political party shall use no less than 10% of its subsidy to promote women's political participation.	2010
Mexico	Each party shall allocate annually 2% of regular public funding for training, promotion and development of women's political leadership.	2008
Morocco	A support fund is dedicated to support projects that aim to strengthen women's representation (up to MAD 200,000 (I$34,000) each).	2009
Panama	Activities will be allocated a minimum of 50% of the annual contribution based on votes, of which a minimum of 10% should be used to develop exclusive activities for the empowerment of women.	2006 2012
Compliance		
Costa Rica	Political parties are mandated to assign a percentage of state funds to the political development and participation of women. The parties must ensure that the expenses incurred during non-election periods for training and promotion target both genders, which should be reported with a certification issued by a certified public accountant. If certification is not provided, the Supreme Electoral Tribunal (TSE) will not authorize the payment of any amount for this purpose.	1990 2009
Honduras	Political parties must submit a gender-equity policy, to be monitored by the Supreme Electoral Tribunal, six months prior to primaries. Failure to comply will make parties liable to a penalty of 5% of the political debt.	2009
Funding to women candidates		
Haiti	50% of the incentives obtained through the nomination of female candidates should be assigned to the political education of their members and financial support to female candidates in electoral contests.	2008

Funding to women's wings		
Finland	All parliamentary parties must use 12% of their annual party subsidy to fund women's wings	1975
Reduced candidate nomination fee		
Togo	The nomination fee is 25% less if a party list contains women candidates.	2007

Note: MAD = Moroccan dirham

Non-legislated initiatives

Political parties, civil society and other non-government actors have also created initiatives to support political financing for women. At the party level, these policies seek to increase the number of elected women by lowering entry costs for candidates, implementing gender strategies such as capacity building, and providing additional opportunities for fundraising support. Partisan organizations such as international foundations have also made a significant impact in aiding women candidates in their fundraising efforts.

Non-party affiliated international organizations and civil society organizations also provide assistance to women candidates in the form of funds for training and capacity building, or funding and credit programmes for campaign funds. Voluntary initiatives are generally more difficult to monitor, as these experiences have not been captured at the global level. The tracking of comparative information on voluntary funding initiatives would enable the monitoring of initiatives in order to ascertain good practices and the effects on women's participation in electoral races.

Political party initiatives

As political parties control candidate recruitment and nomination, they are the vital link for achieving equality and the inclusive participation of women. They are also responsible for managing the party's campaigns and controlling its finances, and so have a key role in supporting women's electoral competition. Some political parties in different regions have adopted voluntary initiatives to level the field for women candidates, including reducing or waiving nomination fees and establishing fundraising mechanisms, as outlined below.

Intra-party fundraising mechanisms

Recognizing the challenges that women face in raising funds for campaigns, particularly for challengers and first-time candidates, political parties have begun to adopt mechanisms to fundraise for women candidates. These fundraising mechanisms are internal to the party, which distinguishes them from other partisan fundraising mechanisms such as political action committees (PACs). In the few documented examples, this type of initiative has contributed greatly to increasing the funds available to support women candidates.

In Canada, the Liberal Party established the Judy LaMarsh Fund to raise and spend money in support of women candidates. The party has direct control over how the funds are spent and which women candidates are prioritized to receive funds. The fund works within the finance regulations in Canada and raises funds primarily through fundraising events, direct mailings and the Internet, which have helped women to run election campaigns successfully.[85]

In Ireland, the women's wing of the Labour Party has developed an initiative to address the particular 'five-C' challenges they have identified as disproportionately affecting women: care, culture, cash, confidence and candidate selection. The party provides training courses for women members and organizes outreach activities and fundraises on behalf of female candidates, with an emphasis on supporting new or first-time candidates.[86] In Ghana, a group of political parties expressed commitment to develop a Women's Fund to support women aspirants in elections. A 2011 multiparty meeting resulted in a statement in which several parties proposed to allocate 10 per cent of the funds they receive directly to women political aspirants.[87]

Box 9.2. El Salvador's FMLN

In El Salvador, the Farabundo Martí National Liberation Front (FMLN) established an Electoral Committee to highlight women's participation. The Committee raised funds by contacting companies, supporters and friends inside and outside the country. Additional activities were organized, particularly to cover advertising costs, including dinners and targeted fundraising. The funds raised were spent on media exposure, printing posters and t-shirts with the names of all women candidates, and printing the party's platform to be distributed throughout the country.[88]

Subsidies to women candidates

Some political parties have adopted reforms to provide subsidies or in-kind contributions to women candidates. The provision of caring responsibilities and childcare, which primarily falls on women, can be difficult to combine with long hours of campaigning. Recognizing this challenge, the Liberal Party in Canada provides subsidies to women candidates to be reimbursed up to 500 Canadian dollars (CAD) (I$440) for childcare during the party nomination, and an additional sum for travel costs in geographically large ridings (electoral districts). Other initiatives may involve reimbursing the costs of childcare or providing women with in-kind contributions, as the Sam Rainsy Party in Cambodia does: women candidates are provided with key items they might need during the campaign, such as appropriate clothing or transport for campaigning.[89] In-kind donations in the form of clothes, transport, provision of campaign materials and other items can alleviate the financial burden that campaigns might impose on women candidates.

Registration fees

In order to participate in an election, potential candidates must often pay initial fees, including party membership and candidate registration fees. Party membership fees are one of the most common sources of income for parties, and are used to help fund party activities and keep the party machinery running.[90] In addition, parties may also require that candidates self-fund the costs to register as a candidate, either to the political party or directly to the body charged with registering candidates, usually the EMB. The amount of these fees varies widely, but can be prohibitive for some women candidates.

In an effort to encourage more women to run for office, some political parties have voluntarily reduced or waived fees associated with membership and candidate registration, although there is no way of ascertaining how many have done so worldwide. In Ghana, for instance, women parliamentarians have noted that almost all the political parties allow women to pay 50 per cent of what their male counterparts pay when it comes to filing nominations.[91] The practice is similarly widespread in Nigeria, although in recent years it has become problematic for women nominees as party leaders claim that this is evidence of women not being as committed to the party as men.[92]

The potential backlash of this measure against the legitimacy of women candidates underscores the importance of legitimizing these initiatives through legislation, as Togo has done, and implementing concurrent measures to address patriarchal power structures within political parties. Ultimately, reducing or waiving membership and candidate registration fees may encourage more women to run, but these measures will have limited impact in the absence of additional measures to encourage party support and fundraising assistance throughout the campaign process.

Partisan fundraising networks

Partisan fundraising networks raise funds through member contributions to support or oppose a candidate or issue. The funds are either donated directly to the candidate's campaign or spent independently. In the United States these are PACs, like the Democratic EMILY's List and the Republican WISH List. EMILY's List has had substantial success collecting donations on behalf of women candidates, as Box 9.3. describes. Fundraising organizations such as these can channel large amounts of money to candidates, which is particularly important in candidate-centred systems like that of the USA, where large amounts of money are required to fund both nomination and election campaigns.

EMILY's List

One of the important underpinnings of EMILY's List is the acknowledgement that women need money early in the campaign process in order to gain name recognition, exposure and organize campaign teams, including hiring fundraising staff that can raise more money.[93] The availability of early money is key to improving a candidate's chances of being nominated, particularly when nomination requires unseating an incumbent. EMILY's List's focus has also meant that more attention has been paid to 'seed money', the funds used to attract the early money necessary to secure the party's nomination, which is often self-financed by the candidate.[94]

Box 9.3. EMILY'S List[95]

The United States PAC EMILY's List (an acronym for the political fundraising aphorism Early Money is Like Yeast) was started in 1985 to support Democratic women running for political office. Prior to the mid-1980s, women candidates raised fewer campaign funds than their male counterparts.[96] EMILY's List sought to alleviate these disparities by providing seed money for women's campaigns.

One of the first candidates backed by EMILY's List was Senator Barbara Mikulski in 1986. Senator Mikulski received 20 per cent of her total campaign funding, USD 60,000, in the first quarter of her campaign through EMILY's List.[97] Now the longest-serving woman in Congress and the first woman to chair the powerful Senate Appropriations Committee, Senator Mikulski remarked in 2011 that 'I would not be in the United States Senate if it were not for EMILY and for EMILY coming in at the right time, and giving me the right help to show that I was the right candidate. It was absolutely crucial.'[98]

Since Senator Mikulski's election and the advent of EMILY's List, women candidates have been able to raise equal or greater amounts of money than their male counterparts. However, the cost of a campaign has continued to rise and the prospect of having to raise millions of dollars may discourage women from running for office.[99]

During the 2012 election cycle the cost of a campaign averaged USD 1.7 million for a House of Representatives seat and USD 10.5 million for a Senate seat, with heavily contested elections costing significantly more than the average.[100] To account for these changes, EMILY's List has since grown beyond its original mission of providing seed money to offer a variety of skills-building and training programmes for prospective women candidates and campaign staff, as well as get-out-the-vote programmes. Fundraising throughout the election process remains one of its most important activities, in the form of soliciting and bundling donations to carefully selected pro-choice Democratic women candidates.

This method of collecting donations from EMILY's List members directly for the endorsed candidates has allowed it to facilitate the funding of women's campaigns far beyond the USD 5,000 election-cycle cap for PACs. In 1992, called the Year of the Woman for the record number of women elected to the House of Representatives, EMILY's List contributed an average of USD 100,000 to each endorsed candidate.[101] EMILY's List was the top PAC by funds disbursed from 1992 to 2006 and has remained near the top in every election since.[102] Since its inception in 1985, the organization has helped over 100 women win Congressional campaigns and hundreds more at the local level.[103] It has raised over USD 350 million to support women candidates—making it one of the most successful PACs in the country.

The success of EMILY's List has not gone unnoticed internationally, with organizations such as EMILY's List Australia and the Labour Women's Network in the United Kingdom employing a similar model of donation bundling to support women candidates. Studies have shown that, although women may now be able to raise greater amounts on average than men, 'women not supported by these networks [such as EMILY's List] are significantly worse off compared to other candidates'.[104] These findings suggest that EMILY's List and similar organizations have provided an important alternative to traditional fundraising networks, within which women may still difficulty operating.

The WISH List

The WISH List (Women in the Senate and House) was created in 1992 to raise funds and support pro-choice Republican women candidates. Similar to EMILY's List, the Republican PAC focuses on providing financial help to selected contenders, as well as advice and strategic support on fundraising, campaign management and media techniques. Donors are encouraged to make three annual donations: a general allocation to the PAC and two donations to candidates of their choice. WISH List's efforts have succeeded in raising over USD 3.5 million for Republican women candidates, contributing to quadrupling the number of Republican women in the Senate and maintaining the number of Republican women in the House since its inception.[105]

Despite these successes, research has shown that Democrat PACs such as EMILY's List have been more successful than their Republican counterparts.[106] Furthermore, research also shows that women are better represented amongst Democrat donors (36 per cent) than amongst Republican ones (16 per cent).[107] Republican women's difficulties in raising funds might also explain why they are less represented than their Democrat counterparts in the House of Representatives, and as a proportion of their party's seats.[108]

EMILY's List Australia

Taking note of the success of EMILY's List in the United States, former state Premier Joan Kirner moved to establish a similar organization along the same principles of bundling donations in support of Australian Labor Party (ALP) women. The backdrop for the organization's formation in 1996 was an internal struggle within the party, with the right faction opposing the organization as a tool of the left. EMILY's List Australia backers believed that 'it could never hope to attract financial and other support from women in the community if it were perceived to be under the thumb of the male structures of the party'.[109] EMILY's List Australia was thus formed as an independent organization, and 40 per cent of its members came from outside the ALP.[110] However, it is considered an 'associated entity' of the ALP in terms of political finance disclosure. In 1996, the ALP established its own women's organization, the National Labor Women's Network, which is designed to increase the numbers of women active in the party at all levels.[111]

Civil society and other initiatives

Civil society and international assistance initiatives have also sought to address gender inequality in political finance. In several countries these initiatives take the form of voluntary fundraising networks to support women candidates, regardless of which party they are running for or their stand on particular political issues. Civil society and international organizations can also be important in helping women run successful campaigns. Although not legislated, and entirely dependent on the will and advocacy of particular interest groups, initiatives such as these have had a significant impact in reducing the gender gap in fundraising, as detailed below.

Micro-finance and trust funds

The burden of campaign financing can also be alleviated through innovative micro-financing initiatives that aim to provide much-needed funds to aspiring female candidates. The Country Women's Association of Nigeria (COWAN) provides low- or no-interest loans to women candidates. It works in 32 states in Nigeria to promote traditional saving schemes, giving women access to low-cost loans that enable them to raise the necessary funds to run a campaign, pay statutory election registration fees, print posters and fund door-to-door campaigning. The initiative was deemed successful: 36 out of 48 aspirants supported by COWAN were elected to various offices in the 1999 elections, including the parliament.[112]

It must be noted, however, that women still have to repay such loans, and they do find it harder to raise funds than men do. In Indonesia, funds are channelled to women's campaigns through the Arisan process, a form of rotating savings and credit associations that holds social gatherings in which women contribute to a pot, and each participant can win the pot to fund their campaign.[113] The Arisan process is not a form of credit, as the money is the recipients' once it has been won. This may work to mitigate women's fears about their ability to pay back the money received.[114]

In a recent initiative in Nigeria, the Ministry of Women's Affairs and Development launched the Nigerian Women's Trust Fund in 2011, which aims to provide aspiring women candidates with financial and other resources for their campaigns, regardless of their political affiliation.[115] This initiative was complemented by another fund under the auspices of the Women for Change Initiative, which distributed funds to over 800 women candidates.[116] These initiatives—combined with initiatives by several political parties to exempt women from paying some of the fees associated with participating in elections—supported the campaigns of female candidates.[117]

Support from international and regional organizations

While international and regional organizations are usually barred from directly supporting women candidates through bans on foreign contributions and concerns about partisanship, they have contributed to identifying financing opportunities and helped build women's skills to raise funds during political campaigns. These organizations have addressed campaign financing as part of the holistic approach to women's empowerment, which includes not just participation but also economic empowerment and access to resources.[118] As the National Democratic Institute (NDI) notes, 'Socio-cultural constraints mean that women have difficulties raising funds. The NDI provides training for women candidates. These courses give women the necessary skills to conduct a good campaign. They also provide benefits for women candidates. These benefits are important and allow them to reach their constituents.'[119] The NDI, International IDEA, UN Women, the United

Nations Development Programme and others have carried out numerous trainings for aspiring women candidates, often in partnership with national civil society organizations.

Further to trainings, international organizations have also helped raise the media profile of women candidates, as was the case in Sierra Leone in 2007 through the contributions of the International Foundation for Electoral Systems and the NDI. These in-kind contributions can decrease women candidates' advertising costs, and thus reduce the overall cost of the campaign. Non-legislated media initiatives of this kind may be more widespread than current research suggests, but the lack of data makes it difficult to systematically analyse their effect.

Non-partisan fundraising networks

In 1999 a group of prominent Japanese women established Women in the World, International Network (WIN WIN). All of the women were members of Leadership 111, an organization formed in 1994 to promote women's involvement in policy making in Japan, and had learned of EMILY's List on an educational tour to the United States.[120] The organization hoped the model would transform traditional fundraising methods, which relied on male-dominated politics. Former WIN WIN Vice-president Shinomura Mistsuko stated that 'Elections cost a lot of money, but the method of collecting money humbly from all over the country has the possibility to change conditional giving and pork-barrel politics'.[121]

In contrast to the US and Australian versions of EMILY's List, WIN WIN is not based on particular party affiliations or ideological views. The candidate endorsed by WIN WIN must instead 'promote gender consciousness' in a broad sense and be vetted by the organization's board. While WIN WIN achieved some initial success, it has struggled to raise funds in recent years and suspended its financial support of women candidates in 2005.[122] There are many possible explanations for the decline of WIN WIN, including differences in political funding mechanisms in Japan and cultures of political giving, or its failure to appeal to women donors and candidates alike.

The success of fundraising networks partly depends on the existence of 'highly organized women's interest and campaign groups'.[123] The case of Japan's WIN WIN initiative indicates that fundraising success requires a strong cause to rally both donors and candidates, which is supported by a strong women's movement and gender awareness. In another example, a Women in Politics Appeal was launched in Fiji before the 2006 elections, which raised USD 11,000 and allocated the funds equally among all women candidates, regardless of their party affiliation or whether they were gender-equality proponents.[124]

Conclusion

This chapter has examined political finance from a gender perspective. It acknowledges that one of the most difficult obstacles for women political aspirants and candidates is the substantial sums of money usually required to run a campaign and win an election. Getting elected is closely correlated with the amount of money raised for the campaign and media exposure in many countries. Lack of finances disproportionately affects women candidates, as their lower socio-economic status usually results in less access to moneyed networks and credit, and less time and confidence to raise funds on their own behalf. The chapter has examined recent legislative reforms that were adopted to either close the gender-funding gap between women and men or address the low number of women candidates and elected representatives.

In all, 27 countries have adopted political finance reforms to level the playing field for women, although these regulations vary in their target and effectiveness. Evidence shows an upward trend in countries adopting gender-targeted initiatives through public finance, such as measures that aim to increase the number of women candidates put forward by political parties or the number of women elected. In these instances, public funding is used as an incentive or as a penalty to ensure compliance with existing quota legislation.

The increase in the number of countries using public funding to promote gender equality is also evident in earmarking measures intended to increase women's participation, such as training and capacity-building activities, the allocation of funds to women's wings, or legislation that provides for lower registration fees for women candidates. Although these measures do not directly tackle the challenge of women's difficulty in mobilizing resources, they are part of a range of measures that together can contribute to levelling the playing field and providing strong advocacy messages about the importance of women's participation.

While political finance legislation is typically gender-neutral, it may be able to help level the playing field for women. Regulations on spending bans and spending and contribution limits for parties and candidates can contribute to curbing the influence of clientelistic practices and countering the power of incumbency. Campaigning time limits and contribution limits may ease women's fears about the difficulties involved in raising funds and the impact of campaigning on family life. Public funding that facilitates access to the media can improve the visibility of women candidates. Disclosure and enforcement mechanisms are important, particularly in monitoring and ensuring compliance with gender-targeted measures.

Ultimately, political parties have a key role in addressing the gender-funding gap, as they can either carry out or disregard the legislation. They may also go beyond legislated measures to adopt their own brand of reforms to promote women's participation and raise funds on their behalf. Data on voluntary party measures are limited, which hinders the systematic analysis of how these contribute to improving women's ability to run campaigns. Further research on the issue of gender and political financing should examine these voluntary initiatives, as well as the effects of legislated measures, taking into consideration that political parties are the gatekeepers to women's political participation.

Recommendations

Legislators

1. Financing legislation should follow international conventions and agreements—including, where appropriate, special measures to redress discrimination against women and ensure de facto equality. These may include different financing regulations for women, where appropriate.
2. New political financing regulations must be analysed through a gender lens to ascertain their effectiveness and their impact on women candidates.
3. Gender-neutral legislation should be adequately framed to ensure its effectiveness and remove discriminatory provisions. The gendered impact of spending and contribution limits should be examined. Contribution and spending limits, in particular, should not be so high as to be rendered meaningless.
4. Include in-kind incentives and provisions that may level the field, including childcare, transport, accommodation, security and media time.
5. The provision of public funding should be tied to gender-equality commitments where appropriate. Public funding can be used to incentivize parties to nominate more women candidates.
6. Public funding that is dependent on gender-equality commitments should give consideration to all the stages of the electoral cycle in its enforcement, including nomination, registration, campaign and post-election.
7. Legislation must be adequately enforced. Consideration should be given to disclosure regulations and the need for data on returns and candidate expenditures to be disaggregated by sex. Such data would be invaluable for determining how women's fundraising and spending levels compare to those of men, and whether funds allocated within the party are equally distributed among women and men candidates.

Political finance regulatory bodies

1. Ensure that all finance legislation is complied with, and report sex-disaggregated data where appropriate.
2. Provide reports on political parties' compliance with gender-targeted

legislation, such as quota enforcement and earmarked funds for female candidates.

Political parties

1. Conduct an internal review of the differential effects of raising funds on women and men within the party, and develop a plan for ensuring gender equality in relation to political financing.
2. Implement a dedicated fundraising mechanism to channel funds to women candidates for party primary competitions and to run election campaigns.
3. Adopt mechanisms to ensure the equal allocation of funds and media/air time to male and female candidates for election campaigns.
4. Lower the entry cost for women candidates by reducing or subsidizing membership and/or registration fees. Earmark funds within the party for gender-equality initiatives including financing women candidates' campaigns, training candidates on gender equality and effective campaign mechanisms (including fundraising), and promoting gender equality in party statutes.

Media actors

1. Ensure that there is equal access to (and coverage of) women and men candidates during elections.
2. Ensure that the media present balanced views of women and men candidates where media access is legislated.
3. Cover pertinent topics, including gender equality, civic education messaging and women's economic status, to improve the electorate's knowledge on key issues that affect the population as a whole.

Civil society

1. Support networks to finance women's campaigns, at both the primary and campaigning stages. The networks can also contribute to raising early money, which is key to ensuring support at the nomination stage.
2. Financial institutions and other organizations can set up easily accessible micro-credit loans and trust funds for women candidates to help them raise funds for their campaigns.
3. Monitor compliance with political finance laws and undertake media monitoring.

International actors

1. Understand the gendered implications of political finance and that it poses a particular challenge to women candidates given their lower economic status in most countries.
2. Implement targeted programmes to bolster women's political participation,

in particular by providing skills building and training on fundraising skills and other relevant areas.

References

Alexander, Herbert, and Corrado, Anthony (1995) 'Senate and House Financing and PAC Trends', in *Financing the 1992 Election*. New York: M. E. Sharpe, pp. 17–224.

Baker, Ashley (2006) 'Reexamining the Gender Implications of Campaign Finance Reform: How Higher Ceilings on Individual Donations Disproportionately Impact Female Candidates', in *The Modern Americas*. Washington, D.C.: University of Washington College of Law, pp. 18–23.

Ballington, Julie (2003) 'Gender Equality in Political Party Funding', in Reginald Austin and Maja Tjernström (eds), *Funding of Political Parties and Election Campaigns*. Stockholm: International IDEA.

Ballington, Julie (2008) *Equality in Politics: A Survey of Women and Men in Parliaments*. Geneva: Inter-Parliamentary Union.

Ballington, Julie (2011) *Empowering Women for Stronger Political Parties: A Good Practices Guide to Promote Women's Political Participation*. New York: UN Development Programme and National Democratic Institute.

Ballington, Julie and Karam, Azza (eds) (2005) *Women in Parliament: Beyond Numbers*. Stockholm: International IDEA.

Bangura, Jariatu (2012) 'Sierra Leone: Women Urge NEC to Revisit Nomination Fees', *Concord Free Times*, 9 August, available at http://allafrica.com/stories/201208100119.html

Barbara Lee Family Foundation (2012) *Pitch Perfect: Winning Strategies for Women Candidates*, available at http://www.barbaraleefoundation.org/wp-content/uploads/BLFF-Lake-Pitch-Perfect-Wining-Strategies-for-Women-Candidates-11.08.12.pdf, accessed August 2013.

Bingham, Amy (2012) *Millionaire Political Donors Club: Where Are the Women?*, ABC News, 25 July, available at http://abcnews.go.com/Politics/OTUS/millionaire-donors-club-women/story?id=16849004, accessed August 2013.

Bryan, Shari and Baer, Denise (2005) *Money in Politics: A Study of Party Financing Practices in 22 States*. Washington, D.C.: National Democratic Institute.

Burrell, Barbara (1996) *A Woman's Place Is in the House: Campaigning for Congress in the Feminist Era*. Ann Arbor, MI: University of Michigan Press.

Burrell, Barbara (1998) 'Campaign Finance: Women's Experience in the Modern Era', in Sue Thomas and Clyde Wilcox (eds), *Women and Elective Office: Past, Present and Future.* Oxford: Oxford University Press.

Cardenas Morales, Natividad (2011) *El Financiamiento Público de los Partidos Políticos Nacionales para el Desarrollo del Liderazgo Político de las Mujeres* [Public Financing of National Political Parties for the Development of Women's Political Leadership]. México, D.F.: Cuadernos de Divulgación de la Justicia Electoral.

Carroll, Susan (1994) *Women as Candidates in American Politics.* Bloomington, IN: University of Indiana Press.

Costa, Jay (2013) 'What's the Cost of a Seat in Congress?', available at http://maplight.org/content/73190

Crespin, Michael H. and Deitz, Janna L. (2010) 'If You Can't Join 'Em, Beat 'Em: The Gender Gap in Individual Donations to Congressional Candidates', *Political Research Quarterly*, 63(3), pp. 581–93.

Day, Christine and Hadle, Charles (2005) *Women's PACs, Abortion and Elections.* New Jersey: Prentice Hall.

Dolez, Bernard and Laurent, Annie (2011) *How Did the French Political Parties 'Play' with the Gender Parity Law? The Socialist Party Case.* Paper presented at the 2011 Annual Meeting of the American Political Association, 1–4 September, Seattle, WA.

DPKO, DFS, DPA (Forthcoming). *Joint Guidelines on Enhancing the Role of Women in Electoral Processes in Countries Emerging from Conflict or in Political Transition.* New York: United Nations.

Economist, The (2010) 'Brazil's Congress: Cleaning Up', 8 July.

EMILY's List (2013) 'Women We Helped Elect', available at http://emilyslist.org/who/women_we_helped_elect

Eto, Mikiko (2008) 'Vitalizing Democracy at the Grassroots: A Contribution of Post-war Women's Movements in Japan', *East Asia: An International Quarterly*, 25(2), pp. 115–43.

Ferreira Rubio, Delia (2009) *Financiación Política y Género en América Latina y el Caribe* [Political Financing and Gender in Latin America and the Caribbean]. Paper presented at the UNIFEM, UNDP, AECID Encuentro de Mujeres Parlamentarias de América Latina y el Caribe, Madrid, 15–16 June.

Ferris, Anne (MP, Ireland) (2013) Personal interview, March, New York.

Francia, Peter, Green, John, Hernson, Paul, Powell, Lynda and Wilcox, Claude (2003) *The Financiers of Congressional Elections: Investors, Ideologues, and Intimates (Power, Conflict and Democracy: American Politics Into the 21st Century).* New York: Columbia University Press.

Gaunder, Alisa (2011) 'WIN WIN's Struggles with the Institutional Transfer of the EMILY's List Model to Japan: The Role of Accountability and Policy', *Japanese Journal of Political Science*, 12(1), pp. 75–94.

Government of Brazil (2009) Law No. 12,034.

Huffington Post (2010) 'Myanmar Parties Complain Election Fee Too High', 20 August, available at http://www.huffingtonpost.com/huff-wires/20100830/as-myanmar-election/

Independent Electoral Commission of Afghanistan (IECA) (2010) *Electoral Campaign Period*, available at http://www.iec.org.af/pdf/wsfactsheets/fs_campaign_period.pdf, accessed August 2013.

International IDEA (2013) Political Finance Database, available at http://www.idea.int/political-finance/index.cfm

Inter-Parliamentary Union (IPU) (2010) 'Women in National Parliaments', available at http://www.ipu.org/wmn-e/classif.htm, accessed August 2013.

Jakobsen, Carolyn (2004) *Re-personalizing the Body Politic: EMILY's List and the Australian Labor Party*. Paper presented at the Australasian Political Studies Association Conference, Adelaide University, 29 September–1 October.

Krook, Mona Lena (2013) *Gender and Elections: Temporary Special Measures beyond Quotas*. Commissioned by the Electoral Affairs Division of the United Nations Department of Political Affairs.

Llanos, Beatriz (2011) *Unseeing Eyes: Media Coverage and Gender in Latin American Elections*. Stockholm and New York: International IDEA and UN Women.

Llanos, Beatriz (2012) *Igualdad: ¿Para Cuándo? Género y Elecciones Peruanas 2010–2011* [Equality: When? Gender and the Peruvian Elections 2010-2011]. Stockholm: International IDEA.

Llanos, Beatriz and Sample, Kristen (2008) *From Words to Action: Best Practices for Women's Participation in Latin American Political Parties*. Stockholm: International IDEA.

Manning, Jennifer and Shogan, Colleen (2012) *Women in the United States Congress: 1917–2012*. Washington, D.C.: Congressional Research Service.

McCollom, Susanna, Haffert, Kristin and Kozma, Alyson (2008) *Assessing Women's Political Party Programs: Best Practices and Recommendations*. Washington, D.C.: National Democratic Institute.

McLean, J. E. (2003) 'Campaign Strategy', in S. Carroll (ed.), *Women and American Politics: New Questions, New Directions*. Oxford: Oxford University Press.

Mikulski, Barbara (2011) 'Mikulski Remarks on Women in Leadership with EMILY's List', available at http://www.mikulski.senate.gov/media/speeches/5-12-2011.cfm

Minnesota Campaign Finance and Public Disclosure Board (MCFPDB) (2005) *Campaign Expenditure and Non-Campaign Disbursement Issues*, available at http://www.cfboard.state.mn.us/issues/expend_disburse.pdf

Ngozo, Claire (2010) 'Malawi: Women Candidates Hard Hit by Election Postponement', Inter Press Service, 26 August.

Nwanko, Oby (2011) 'Women & 2011 Elections in Nigeria', Heinrich Böll Stiftung, 13 April, available at http://www.ng.boell.org/web/gender-231.html

Ohman, Magnus (2013) *Political Finance Regulations Around the World*. Stockholm: International IDEA.

Ohman, Magnus and Zainulbhai, Hani (2009) *Political Finance Regulation: The Global Experience*. Washington, D.C.: International Foundation for Electoral Systems.

Organization for Security and Co-operation in Europe and Office for Democratic Institutions and Human Rights (OSCE/ODIHR) (2011) *Comments on the Law on Political Party Financing of Bosnia and Herzegovina*.

Organization for Security and Co-operation in Europe and Office for Democratic Institutions and Human Rights (OSCE/ODIHR) (2013) *International Election Observation Report: Albania*.

Partido Acción Ciudadana (2010) *Estatuto del Partido Acción Ciudadana* [Statute of the Citizen's Action Party], available at http://www.tse.go.cr/pdf/normativa/estatutos/accionciudadana.pdf

Pires, Milena (2002) 'East Timor and the Debate on Quotas', in *The Implementation of Quotas: Asian Experiences*. Stockholm: International IDEA, pp. 36–9.

Sawer, Marian (2004) *When Women Support Women: EMILY's List and the Substantive Representation of Women in Australia*. Paper presented at the Australasian Political Studies Association Conference, Adelaide University, 29 September–1 October 2004.

Shvedova, Nadezhda (2005) 'Obstacles to Women's Participation in Parliament', in Julie Ballington and Azza Karam (eds), *Women in Parliament: Beyond Numbers*. Stockholm: International IDEA.

Standards in Public Office Commission (SIPO) (2012) 'Exchequer Funding Received by Political Parties for 2012,' available at http://www.sipo.gov.ie/en/reports/state-financing/expenditure-of-state-funding/2012-exchequer-funding-received-by-political-parties/, accessed August 2013.

Thompson, Nick (2012) 'International Campaign Finance: How Do Countries Compare?', CNN, available at http://www.cnn.com/2012/01/24/world/global-campaign-finance/, accessed November 2013.

Trent, Judith, Friedenberg, Robert and Denton, Robert Jr (2011) *Political Campaign Communication: Principles and Practices*. Lanham, MD: Rowman & Littlefield.

United Nations (UN) (1979) Convention on the Elimination of All Forms of Discrimination Against Women.

United Nations (2013) *Joint Guidelines on Enhancing the Role of Women in Electoral Processes in Countries Emerging from Conflict or in Political Transition*.

UN Development Programme (UNDP) and UN Women (2013) BRIDGE Gender and Elections Workshop, Session on Political Finance, 13 February, Belize City.

WISH List (2013) 'FAQs about the WISH List', available at http://www.thewishlist.org/FAQs.htm

Women's Environment and Development Organization (WEDO) (2007) *Women Candidates and Campaign Finance*. New York: WEDO, available at http://www.wedo.org/library/women-candidates-and-campaign-finance-december-2007

Notes

1   Ballington and Karam 2005.
2   UN 1979, article 7.
3   Ballington 2008.
4   UN Women undertook an assessment of parliamentarians and activists during the 57th Session of the Commission on the Status of Women in New York in March 2013, and with members of the iKNOW Politics network, http://www.iknowpolitics.org. A total of 70 respondents provided their views on the issue of political financing.
5   Shvedova 2005, p. 33.
6   Ibid., p. 40.
7   Ibid., p. 42.
8   See http://unstats.un.org/unsd/demographic/products/Worldswomen/Executive%20summary.htm
9   See http://www.un.org/millenniumgoals/poverty.shtml, accessed August 2013.
10   Ballington 2011, p. 27.
11   See http://iknowpolitics.org/en/comment/7709#comment-7709, accessed August 2013.
12   Ballington 2003, p. 164.
13   Personal interview with Ms Cecilia Chazama, Malawi, iKNOW Politics.
14   See http://www.opensecrets.org/pres08/summary.php?cid=N00000019&cycle=2008, accessed August 2013.
15   Ballington 2011, p. 27.
16   Ibid.
17   Ballington 2003, p. 160.
18   Ferreira Rubio 2009.
19   Ibid.
20   Thompson 2012.

21 Bryan and Baer 2005.

22 Carroll 1994.

23 IPU 2010.

24 Day and Hadle 2005.

25 Ballington 2011, p. 27.

26 Personal interview with Anne Ferris, 6 March 2013, New York.

27 Ballington 2011, p. 27.

28 Ohman 2013, p. 20.

29 Ibid., p. 11.

30 Ohman and Zainulbhai 2009, pp. 88–9.

31 Albania, Bosnia and Herzegovina, Brazil, Burkina Faso, Cape Verde, Colombia, Costa Rica, Croatia, Ethiopia, Finland, France, Georgia, Haiti, Honduras, Ireland, Italy, Kenya, Republic of Korea, Mali, Mexico, Morocco, Niger, Panama, Papua New Guinea, Portugal, Romania and Togo.

32 Ohman 2013, p. 33.

33 Ibid., p. 34.

34 See also Ohman 2013, p. 36.

35 Burrell 1996, 1998.

36 Ballington 2003, p. 164.

37 Minnesota Campaign and Public Disclosure Board 2005.

38 See http://iknowpolitics.org/es/comment/7448#comment-7448

39 Baker 2006, pp. 18–23.

40 Ohman 2013, p. 17.

41 *The Economist* 2010.

42 IPU 2010.

43 UNDP and UN Women 2013.

44 Llanos 2011.

45 Pires 2002, p. 36.

46 Government of Brazil 2009, Article 2.

47 IECA 2010.

48 Krook 2013, pp. 9–10.

49 Barbara Lee Family Foundation 2012.

50 Ngozo 2010.

51 DPKO, DFS, DPA (Forthcoming).

52 WEDO 2007.

53 See http://iknowpolitics.org/es/comment/7688#comment-7688

54 Ohman 2013, p. 4.

55 Ibid., p. 24.

56 Ibid., p. 23.

57 Ohman 2013, p. 24.

58 Albania, Bosnia and Herzegovina, Brazil, Burkina Faso, Cape Verde, Colombia, Costa Rica, Croatia, Ethiopia, Finland, France, Georgia, Haiti, Honduras, Ireland, Italy, Kenya, Korea (Republic of), Mali, Mexico, Morocco, Niger, Panama, Papua New Guinea, Portugal, Romania and Togo.

59 See http://www.quotaproject.org

60 Email correspondence with Zurab Kharatishvili, chair, Central Election Commission of Georgia, July 2013.

61 Ohman 2013.

62 Dolez and Laurent 2011.

63 Throughout this handbook, international dollars (I$) are presented alongside amounts in national currencies. The international dollar is a hypothetical currency that takes into account purchasing power parity and is therefore suitable for comparisons between countries. For countries in which the power purchasing power parity varies significantly from the United States (which is used as the baseline for the comparison), the I$ exchange rate may be considerably different from the nominal exchange rate. No conversions are given for US dollars (as this is by default the same amount as the I$) or for those instances where the original currency is unknown and a secondary currency such as the euro has been cited instead. For further information, see Annex V.

64 OSCE/ODIHR 2013.

65 International IDEA Political Finance Database.

66 OSCE/ODIHR 2011.

67 Romanian Parliament, Law No. 334/2006 (2006).

68 Haiti, Electoral Law, Article 129.

69 Haiti, Electoral Law, Article 129.

70 International IDEA Political Finance Database.

71 Brazil, Colombia, Costa Rica, Finland, Haiti, Honduras, Ireland, Italy, Korea (Republic of, South Korea), Mexico, Morocco, Panama, Togo.

72 See Chapter 8 on the established anglophone democracies for details on implementation.

73 SIPO 2012.

74 Ballington 2011, p. 30.

75 Law No. 8765, Article 52p.

76 Partido Accion Ciudadana 2010 .

77 Llanos and Sample 2008, p. 41.

78 Cardenas Morales 2011.

79 Ballington 2011, p. 17.

80 *Huffington Post* 2010.

81 Bangura 2012.

82 Ballington 2003, p. 163.

83 MCFPDB 2005.

84 International IDEA Political Finance Database.

85 Ballington 2011, p. 28.

86 Ferris 2013.

87 Ballington 2011, p. 29.

88 Llanos and Sample 2008.

89 Ibid.

90 Bryan and Baer 2005, p. 10.

91 See http://iknowpolitics.org/en/comment/7432#comment-7432, accessed August 2013.

92 Nwanko 2011.

93 Ballington 2003, p. 161.

94 Ibid.

95 Text box information provided by Caitlin Hopping.

96 Burrell 1998.

97 Burrell 1996, p. 124.

98 Mikulski 2011.

99 McLean 2003.

100 Costa 2013.

101 Alexander and Corrado 1995, p. 212.

102 Trent, Friedenberg and Denton 2001, p. 11. See also http://www.fec.gov/press/
    summaries/2012/PAC/6mnth/4pactop50disburse6mos11.pdf for 2012 list.

103 EMILY's List 2013.

104 Crespin and Deitz 2010.

105 WISH List 2013.

106 Crespin and Deitz 2010.

107 Francia et al. 2003, p. 38.

108 Manning and Shogan 2012.

109 Sawer 2004.

110 Jakobsen 2004, p. 10.

111 See http://trove.nla.gov.au/people/734078?c=people, accessed August 2013.

112 See http://www.wedo.org/library/chief-bisi-ogunleye-the-country-women per centE2 per
    cent80 per cent99s-association-of-nigeria-cowan, accessed August 2013.

113 McCollom, Haffert and Kozma 2008.

114 See http://iknowpolitics.org/es/comment/7878#comment-7878, accessed August 2013.

115 Krook 2013.

116 Ibid.

117 Ibid.

118 McCollom, Haffert and Kozma 2008.

119 See http://iknowpolitics.org/fr/comment/7670#comment-7670, accessed August 2013.

120 Eto 2008.

121 Gaunder 2011.

122 Ibid.

123 Ballington 2003, p. 165.

124 Krook 2013, p. 22.

CHAPTER 10

CHAPTER 10

Conclusions

Elin Falguera

The introductory chapters discussed the importance of money in politics and gave an overview of political finance regulations and their enforcement, as well as some guidelines for how to design and implement such regulations. It was argued that any efforts to control money in politics must be based on an understanding of the particular context and challenges in each country. The regional chapters then assessed the similarities and differences in the challenges faced and solutions sought in different parts of the world. Chapter 9, 'Women in Politics: Financing for Gender Equality', examined the challenges faced by women trying to raise enough funds to run for office effectively, and how women around the world have addressed these challenges.

This chapter draws together the conclusions from the preceding chapters and analyses the overall experiences, similarities and differences from around the world. In particular, it addresses the challenges of the role of money in politics and international trends in political finance regulations. Recommendations for different stakeholders are also provided, as well as overall lessons learned.

Money and politics: a contextual overview

Money and politics are closely intertwined; the way that parties and candidates access their funding greatly affects how the political system functions and how democratic politics is conducted. As reiterated throughout this volume, money is necessary for a democracy to function well, and helps strengthen the core components of democracy, establish sustainable party organizations and provide the opportunity to compete on (more) equal terms. Yet it also poses serious challenges and threats to the political process—for example, the pernicious influence of drug money in Latin America, the huge corporate influence over politics in Asia, the clientelistic networks in Africa or the abuse of state resources in Europe. Therefore money in politics must be monitored and controlled. The challenge for policy makers and politicians is to strike the right balance: limiting negative effects while encouraging democratic consolidation through pluralistic competition. In this effort, it is important to view both the use and control of money in politics as the means to an end, rather than the end itself.

Today there is a growing perception of corruption in political life, which besmirches the public image of parties and politicians. Findings from Transparency International's 2013 Global Barometer reveal that political parties are perceived to be the most corrupt institution of those surveyed, ahead, for example, of the police, public officials, parliament and the judiciary.[1] Regional surveys such as the Latino- and Afrobarometers reveal a similarly bleak picture, with low levels of trust in political parties.[2] Such distrust can be explained at least in part by the exposure of financial misconduct of parties and politicians in a wide range of countries.

For parties to win voters' trust and support, they need to be transparent and accountable in relation to their finances. If parties fail to meet citizen demands for clean politics, voters will continually question their integrity and become apathetic and disillusioned with the democratic process; they may create protest movements and circumvent the traditional bodies of political representation. Although each country examined in this volume has its own unique challenges related to money and politics, there are a number of challenges that span virtually all the regions.

Global challenges

High costs

The involvement of vast amounts of 'big money' in politics is an increasing concern among voters around the world. The high costs of campaigning in different regions are usually attributed to the increased professionalization of politics, in which parties and candidates spend more money on opinion polls, political advisors and media advertisement. In Western Europe, campaign spending rivals the traditional primary expense of running large and bureaucratic party structures, while in the United States, 5.8 billion US dollars (USD) was spent in the 2012 presidential and parliamentary elections.

The high costs of campaigning lead parties and candidates to seek funds from a wide variety of sources. In many cases, parties become dependent on either large private contributions or state funding, which raises the risk that individuals who donate large amounts have more influence over the political process than others.

Lack of grass-roots support

Despite the high costs of politics, political parties receive little financial support from their members, even in the European countries where this type of funding was once a relevant source of income.[3] Elsewhere, donations from members have never been a significant source of income. This lack of support means that parties rely on corporate donations or other organized interests, public funds or illicit finances (or, in some countries, money from individual party leaders or candidates).

In some parts of Africa, Latin America and Asia, the financial contributions between politicians and grass-roots supporters actually run in the opposite direction, with clientelistic or patronage relationships between the parties and their supporters, in which voters expect gifts or perks in exchange for their support or votes.

Illicit funding and criminal sources

The illicit funding of parties and candidates presents a particularly challenging problem in many of the regions discussed in this volume. Even though it is difficult to know exactly how influential illicit donations are, given their obscure nature, various cases that have been uncovered suggest that illicit funding represents a significant source of income for political actors.[4]

The issue becomes particularly serious when funding comes from organized crime, which involves an agenda to influence politicians and their policy decisions to advance the interests of criminal networks.

As shown in the regional chapters, there are different types of relationships between politics and organized crime. In its most basic form, the criminal actors remain outside the political process but try to influence it, for example via campaign donations or bribes. There are also more systematic relationships between politics and criminal networks in which the latter penetrate much deeper into the political sphere; criminal elements infiltrate and take over (or 'capture') the political institutions, including the political parties.

Countries located in drug-trafficking corridors are especially vulnerable to this type of influence. Drug trading routes can be found in virtually every region. In Latin America they stretch from the Andean region to Mexico,[5] while in Africa countries such as Guinea-Bissau and Mali[6] have been exposed to the destabilizing effect of the drugs that are making their way from Latin America to Europe via the western shores of Africa.

Politicians and legislators are sometimes unwilling or unable, at times out of fear, to put in place measures such as strong enforcement agencies that can prevent this type of money flowing into politics. The financial benefits for politicians, or the threat posed by the donor, may be seen to exceed the potential consequences of exposure and punishment.

As pointed out in Chapter 5 on Latin America, illegal money channelled into the political process cannot be addressed in isolation from the broader problem of organized crime.[7] It is therefore crucial that the organizations that are tasked with overseeing party and candidate finances cooperate closely with other law enforcement and judicial institutions working on this issue. To be able to do so, oversight bodies need the mandate, tools and protection (as well as sufficient flexibility) to carry out their monitoring role and cooperate with other relevant actors.

Business and politics

The influence of money over politics opens the political arena to private companies to realize their interests through politics by providing financial support to politicians. Although some businesses support political parties out of ideological conviction, many others want or expect something in return that will benefit their enterprise. Donations that are seen as an investment by corporate interests have been reported from virtually all of the regions. In some cases, large donations are sometimes given to parties across the political spectrum, which can be a way to ensure government favours regardless of who ends up in power.[8]

A more intricate and direct relationship between business interests and the state has also become apparent. Although not exclusive to Asia, the phenomenon of very wealthy businesspeople starting their own parties or taking seats in parliament (and even running for president) is widespread across that continent, from Thailand to the Republic of Korea. The danger in such situations is that the political party revolves around the interests of the individual businessman or corporation and is entirely dependent on its finances for organizational survival.

Unequal access to funds

Another problem related to political finance is when parties or candidates have unequal opportunities to access funds. Although the popularity of a party or politician will always produce varying levels of financial support, there should not be structural obstacles to equal opportunities for fundraising. If individuals or corporations can (through large donations) pay to get politicians to listen to them, this may severely undermine the core principles of democracy, in which each person has one vote. Likewise, if there are no (or very high) limits on the amount that can be raised and spent by parties and candidates, this can lead to unequal competition.

This issue is also connected to the relationship between business and politics discussed in the previous section. Government parties are often more likely to attract business donations than opposition parties. This is hardly surprising, given the governing parties' ability to influence public contracts and set policies on issues that may affect the commercial success of the business donors.

The gender imbalance in access to funds should be a central part of any discussion of the unequal distribution of money in politics. Chapter 9, 'Women in Politics: Financing for Gender Equality', includes numerous examples of the fundraising difficulties that female candidates face, which is a main cause of the continued gender inequality in political representation.

Abuse of state resources

A different aspect of unequal access to funds is when government parties use public resources for their own partisan purposes. Abuse of state resources is a problem across the globe, and almost all countries have legal bans against it. As discussed in Chapter 8 on the established anglophone democracies, it is almost unavoidable that office holders have access to a certain number of privileges and powers that other contestants do not—such as more media exposure for their party leader and more focus on their policies—but there are limits on what should be considered unavoidable. Using public resources for political purposes weakens democracy and can damage political plurality.

Abuse is even harder to control where the government does not spend money in favour of a political party but instead abuses other resources at its disposal, such as biased media coverage in the ruling party's favour, or engaging civil servants in campaign activities during working hours. In several regions (e.g. Africa, Asia, and Eastern Europe and Central Asia), especially where one party has long dominated the political scene, there is a distinct blurring of the line between the state and the government party's resources. State premises, state vehicles and public servants are used in electoral campaigns and other party activities.

The government party may also set and use the country's legal framework to its own advantage or to persecute the opposition. Where the ruling party dominates the state institutions as well as the legislature, it may design the rules in order to entrench its hold on power. Thresholds for accessing public funding, for example, may be set so high as to deprive new actors of the chance to enter the political arena. In Latin America, the temptation to use state resources to enhance the chances of re-wining elections is greater in those countries that used to have one-term limits but which now permit immediate presidential re-election.

Lack of enforcement

All regions have a large gap between the established political finance regulations and their implementation. One of the reasons why regulations are so poorly implemented is that the agencies tasked with overseeing the parties' and candidates' finances lack the mandates and capacities they would need to effectively carry out their role. Many such agencies only have procedural roles (e.g. receiving financial reports from parties) but lack the investigative powers needed to follow up inaccuracies or to dig deeper into sources of income or levels of expenditure. The responsibility of controlling party and candidate finance is often spread across several different institutions, making holistic oversight difficult.[9]

Part of this incapability can be attributed to a lack of resources or staff. Underlying these weaknesses is politicians' reluctance to strengthen regulation of their behaviour. This lack of political will often translates into weak enforcement agencies.

Closely related to this is the fact that in many countries the enforcement agencies are not sufficiently independent of the government to exercise the necessary control. In Western Europe, control of political finance is often exercised by parliamentary commissions or by the executive branch, either directly or through institutions or special commissions that are accountable to them. The result is that few countries in the region have fully independent institutions responsible for the enforcement of the political finance legislation—which for the most part is not cause for public concern, as there is sufficient trust in the enforcement body's integrity. Many Asian countries also lack independent enforcement agencies: in Malaysia, for example, the Election Commission is government controlled and thus less willing to check closely the finances of parties and candidates.[10]

Another problem is that few violators are punished. This culture of impunity seems to be widespread in all the regions surveyed in this volume. The number of sanctions issued does not necessarily indicate a system's effectiveness. As pointed out in the introductory chapter, prevention is better than penalties; in many cases, the goal of the enforcement institution should be more focused on enhancing compliance than on implementing sanctions. However, compliance is unlikely if there is no credible threat of sanctions against even blatant violations. Sanctions also need to be proportional to the offence in order to be effective.[11] In France, fines have been imposed that were lower than the amount of unpermitted funding accepted; such sanctions are unlikely to have a deterrent effect.

Selective enforcement of the rules is another area of concern, especially in several of the highly regulated countries of Eastern Europe and Central Asia, where this tactic has been used to suppress the opposition. In Georgia, for example, political finance regulations were allegedly used to target the main opposition candidate in the 2012 elections.[12] In Latin America, the application of political finance sanctions in Argentina has been accused of being rooted in political bias; the electoral judges who issue sanctions are seen as political players.[13]

In some countries, a conflicting mandate renders the enforcement body ineffective. Where an agency is mandated both to organize elections and to monitor political finance, its tasks may become too convoluted. For example, electoral management bodies often consider the administrative tasks of organizing elections as their main purpose, and shy away from more politically sensitive issues such as how election campaigns are funded. Where the agency is in charge of both distributing public funding and punishing parties, it might sometimes choose to ignore one task in order to be effective in the other.

Another common explanation of why politicians and parties continue to break the law is that the violations simply never enter the monitoring system. Compared to the number of violations that are revealed continuously by the media or civil society groups, relatively few cases are officially reported to the monitoring authorities, and even fewer are sanctioned. In the African context, there are very few reports of sanctions being imposed in relation to political finance violations.[14]

In order for enforcement to be effective, the enforcing agencies cannot work alone. They need to form broad coalitions with other state institutions, as well as with civil society initiatives that are working to combat the negative influence of money in politics. This may be especially relevant in countries where criminal elements exercise a significant influence over politics.[15]

More focus should also be given to the underlying reasons why agencies cannot fulfil their roles. In some cases, the enforcement agencies may be unwilling to risk taking on powerful politicians or criminal networks that have infiltrated politics.

Self-regulation of parties and politicians

As previously mentioned, there is a potential conflict of interest when elected representatives of political parties are in control of designing the rules that will govern their own behaviour. Politicians have the responsibility to create long-term sustainable policies that are appropriate for the country's context and to shape the playing field for future generations of politicians.

To be successful, reform work should also address the potential weaknesses of the self-regulatory role of parties. Although political parties are ultimately responsible for adopting political finance laws, the creation of rules governing money in politics should be agreed upon through wide consultation involving a broad section of stakeholders. This includes not only the government, parliament and political parties, but also the enforcement agencies, the judiciary and civil society.

Although the main focus of this volume has not been on political parties' internal accountability measures, this is an important element of regulating political finance. There will be little chance of meaningful change on political finance issues unless parties themselves also display the commitment, internal capacity and organization to adhere to their legal responsibilities. Based on the view that party matters should be left alone, internal party conduct is seldom included in national party laws, and several countries do not require parties to create the necessary institutional arrangements to be able to meet the regulatory demands. There are exceptions. Some countries in Latin America formally require political parties to set up specialized internal bodies or treasurers to manage party funds.[16] This measure puts the onus on the parties to demonstrate their commitment to transparency by institutionalizing the necessary mechanisms. Yet many parties around the world are weak, and need to strengthen their internal capacity before such financial mechanisms can be institutionalized.

Global regulatory trends

This publication has shown that political finance and its associated challenges are dealt with in a wide variety of ways around the world. A country's political system, level of economic development and degree of democratic consolidation are important factors to help determine the most suitable political finance regulations (as discussed in Chapter 2, 'Getting the Political Finance System Right'). However, a number of developments can be identified in most regions, which form the basis for identifying some global trends.

Growing (and more specific) legislation

Since the early 1990s, there has been a movement toward increasing levels of regulation (but not necessarily increased enforcement) in most of the regions examined in this publication. This development has gone hand in hand with increased levels of overall democratization and legislation to shape and regulate new democratic systems. As will be discussed further below, this might also relate to the changing public perception of political parties, which are increasingly seen as being closer to bodies of government[17] than the older style mass-membership citizen groups that aim to mobilize scores of citizens on a voluntary basis in political decision-making processes.

It is important that this view does not lead to regulations on political parties and their financial transactions that restrict their crucial role in the democratic process. Political finance policies have been said to:

> ... often reflect a reform ideology that is reflexively anti-political—a 'civic vision' of politics as the pursuit of the public interest and of government as existing to provide technically sound administration ... Parties, in many instances, come to be seen as something akin to public utilities rather than as ways in which people and groups seek to influence politics and government—a view that drains the vitality out of democratic politics.[18]

Even so, as recipients of public subsidies, financial transparency among political parties is a legitimate demand; the public requires increased accountability in the usage of funds. In addition to more regulations overall, additional areas of political finance (such as who is entitled to public funding and on what basis) have become subject to legal regulation. In Africa the appearance, or reappearance, of multiparty democratic systems in the early 1990s induced countries to issue regulations on political finance. In Latin America—with the exception of a few countries, such as Uruguay and Costa Rica, which had already introduced state subsidies for parties—it was not until the 1980s (when widespread democratic changes, including the consolidation of political institutions, swept across the continent) that the issue of regulating money in politics gained prominence.

In Eastern and Central Europe, the anti-corruption agenda and its demands for 'clean politics' have been a driving force behind the increased focus on political finance regulations since the fall of communism in the 1990s. In this region, where accusations of corruption have been used to discredit political opponents, political finance regulations have on occasion been used to suppress political opponents by making it more difficult for them to receive funding or by using transparency requirements to find out who their supporters are.

There also seems to be a global trend toward the creation of more specific legislation on political party and campaign finance. Whereas in some countries political finance regulation was previously spread across several legal instruments—such as the electoral act, the constitution or even criminal codes—there is now a movement to establish comprehensive legislative acts governing political finance. Newer democracies that had little legislation in place at the beginning are, partly due to influence from the international community, jumping straight to creating such political finance acts. South Sudan is a case in point.

Public funding

There is a global increase in the funding of political parties through public subsidies. Today, around two-thirds of the world's countries provide direct public funding. Public funding can make up for the shortage of income from the grass roots and help to level the political playing field. Such support also corresponds to the perception of parties as essential pillars of democracy that need to be invested in to allow the system to function.

However, the legal provision of public funding says nothing of its levels or the extent of its implementation. Although the state provides monetary support to political parties in 69 per cent of African countries, levels are often far from sufficient to cover parties' basic needs, which means they still need to raise almost all of their funds from private sources; this negates the purpose of introducing public funding to level the playing field. This is especially the case in countries where the party funding constitutes a percentage of the state budget if the overall state budget is low. There are also cases, for example in Peru, where the executive can cite budgetary reasons for not paying any public funding.[19]

As the regional chapters show, public funding for political parties is less widespread in Asia overall than in other regions. There are a number of countries in South Asia, such as Afghanistan, Nepal and Pakistan, which do not provide public funding at all. These countries' rationale for choosing not to do so requires further analysis. The most generous public financing schemes in Asia are found in North-east Asia. In a number of Latin American countries, state funds account for around 35 per cent of the parties' reported income.

A combination of public and private funding is preferable, as recommended for example by the Council of Europe.[20] However, many European countries display a worrying trend related to public funding. Political parties in this region have become extremely dependent on this revenue—up to an average of two-thirds of their total income, and in some countries above 80 per cent. The gradual increase in the amounts of public subsidies that parties have effectively granted themselves through legislation could be interpreted by some as self-interest. To counteract this high dependence, innovative mechanisms to find a better balance should be encouraged. In this regard, Germany provides an interesting case. It has worked to encourage party fundraising through a 'matching grants' mechanism in which public subsidies can never be higher than the amount raised by the party itself.[21] Where state dependency is high, innovative efforts should be promoted. There is no formulaic ratio for ideal levels of public and private political funding; the suitable balance should be determined by context. If used, public funding should, however, provide for at least the basic needs of any party that has passed a certain threshold of public support so that it can perform its core functions of citizen participation and representation.

Another aspect related to the provision of public finance is the conditions that countries across all regions place on receiving these funds.[22] For example, parties have to use the money for particular activities (normally related to campaigning or ongoing party activities, and sometimes related to internal party democracy such as gender balance) or abide by certain reporting rules. Yet in most countries the parties can decide how to use the funds. The very few attempts to influence internal party affairs using public funding are especially notable in Western Europe, where levels of state support are very high.[23]

Gender and public funding

Today there is a small but growing group of countries that link the provision of public funding to increased gender equality within parties and among candidates either by earmarking public funding for activities relating to gender equality or by increasing (or decreasing) public funding to parties that fulfil (or do not fulfil) legislated quotas of female candidates. Such initiatives are important, as they aim to address the shortage of funds for women, which is often seen as one of the main obstacles for women entering politics. However, most countries have not linked public funding of political parties to gender equality.

Since these reforms are quite recent, it is hard to establish their impact thus far. Yet it is fair to assume that, in order for these measures to be effective, the party should incur a substantial financial penalty for non-compliance. Linking public funding to nominating the under-represented sex is, however, often not substantive enough to have this effect. As long as parties feel that it may be more worthwhile to field a male candidate despite the financial sanctions, this type of reform initiative is likely to serve only as window dressing. It also follows that regulations of this kind will be more effective in countries where parties are highly dependent on public funding.

Recommendations

As stated in Chapter 2, 'Getting the Political Finance System Right', political finance regulations must be based on an understanding of each country's overall political context and challenges. The regional chapters in this publication have confirmed this assertion and shown that simply increasing the scope of regulation does not solve any problems by itself. Neither unduly strict nor overly lax regulatory frameworks are desirable. On the one hand, creating a very dense and detailed legal framework may well be counterproductive, especially if there is no institution capable of monitoring and enforcing it. Yet, on the other hand, the legal framework must be comprehensive enough to articulate the boundaries of acceptable political finance.

The challenge of finding the right solution is that recommendations often target political institutions and actors, yet this focus is too narrow. Simply changing the rules related to political finance will not, for example, tackle a large informal illicit sector or alter an authoritarian rule. Such outcomes require much broader and deeper reforms that include changing the power balance in a country or addressing issues that affect entire societies. For example, vote buying is difficult to eradicate in an impoverished society, and as long as organized crime plays a powerful role in a country, efforts to insulate the political sector from its influence will face significant challenges.

The political sector cannot be separated from other sectors in society, and cooperation—across institutions and between various societal actors—is required if the challenges of political finance are to be successfully addressed. This could, for example, take the form of information sharing between political finance enforcement agencies and law enforcement agencies to tackle illicit finance.

Although the recommendations in each chapter were developed to meet the challenges of that particular region, there are commonalities. This section brings together the main messages for various political stakeholders on how they could improve their work and approach political finance reforms, and forms the basis for a number of global recommendations in the final section.

Policy makers[24]

Recommendations to policy makers are clearly defined by their responsibility to put in place the rules and institutions that govern political finance. In this capacity they have the important task of providing the best possible foundations for a healthy relationship between money and politics.

The starting point is to create an effective legal framework to achieve the identified political goals. Recommendations from the regions in this regard urge policy makers to design coherent, country-specific rules that cover both parties and candidates—as stipulated in the United Nations Convention against Corruption (UNCAC)[25]—and third parties, where applicable. Even more importantly, they need to be implementable; overly ambitious rules are of no use without an institution with the capacity to make sure they are enforced. Policy makers are also urged to prioritize the most important rules to address contextual needs, and not to try to move too quickly from an unregulated to a highly regulated system.

Low levels of financial support from party members and dependency on private donations can be mitigated by introducing a public funding system. When administered and distributed appropriately, public funding can act as a good counterbalance to private donations and give a variety of political actors access to funds, and hence help level the playing field. Public funding can also increase transparency and give parties incentives to invest in female candidates. Yet there is a danger that political parties will become overly dependent on public funding; this reliance should be monitored carefully.

Recognizing the importance of the media, and the financial pressure on parties and candidates to purchase media advertising, policy makers are advised to prioritize free or subsidized media access as part of their public funding programmes and place controls on privately funded media access. In countries that are struggling with their state budgets, indirect funding can be used as a cheaper and more easily controlled complement to direct public funding.

In an effort to further level the playing field, policy makers are also encouraged to consider regulations to limit the amount of money spent during election campaigns. Unrestricted spending (and, consequently, expensive campaigns) elevates the importance and impact of money in politics, and increases the likelihood that large donors will have a disproportionate influence over the political process, which endangers democratic equality.

Regulations that can facilitate a healthy relationship between political parties and the business sector should also be considered. Contacts between political parties and the business sector can help inform policy decisions and provide much-needed funding, but the risk of undue influence must be carefully weighed. Some countries ban corporate donations outright. In some countries such a ban might leave political parties without sufficient funding to carry out their activities, while in others it would simply be ignored. Increased transparency may in some cases be a better approach—ensuring that financial connections between business interests and political parties (and individual candidates) are made public. Bans on donations from corporations with public contracts can also help reduce the risk of quid pro quo contributions.

Policy makers are encouraged to find innovative ways to help parties diversify their sources of income so they are less tempted to turn to illicit money or violate political finance regulations; this especially so in contexts where parties generally are underfunded. For example, in countries with a broad enough tax base, tax reduction for donations may encourage more people to contribute to parties; this practice is mainly found in Europe. Another approach could be the provision of public funds to match, and thereby encourage, small donations. Lowering costs can be another way forward, for example through indirect public funding such as access to the media, free or subsidized access to public venues for campaign events, or party offices.

In line with the UNCAC, policy makers are recommended to ensure that regulations cover both parties and candidates. This has to do with the fluid relationship between the two whereby only controlling one actor may result in funds being channelled through the other.

In Western Europe, parties have long been granted state support with few demands on their internal behaviour. While it is important to protect the independence of political parties from the state, the provision of taxpayer money means that certain demands on parties are reasonable. It is therefore recommended that public funding should be contingent upon compliance with requirements such as filing reports by appropriate deadlines, disclosing finances and (where suitable) having institutionalized financial management. Connecting the provision of public funding to responsiveness to gender equality should also be considered.

Since policy makers have the power to institutionalize the organizations that exercise control over politicians and political parties, they also have a great responsibility to ensure that there are adequate control mechanisms in place to help monitor compliance and take action when the rules are not followed. Since financial control must not stifle political competition, policy makers should establish a strong institution that is independent from any political powers, as recommended in the UNCAC.[26]

Monitoring and enforcement agencies

Each regional chapter has noted that monitoring and enforcement agencies have a key task in controlling the flow of money in and out of politics. Yet these agencies are often criticized for not performing their job well. Our recommendations reflect the dire need for these agencies to improve their effectiveness. The regional chapters have emphasized their responsibility to apply and enforce the rules impartially. Otherwise they may be accused of political bias and selectively enforcing the rules, as in Cambodia and Georgia.

The starting point for any agency embarking on an improvement agenda is to identify and understand its core structural problems: is it unenforceable rules, a flawed institutional design, lack of resources or technical capacity, an inadequate mandate, compromised neutrality or lack of powers that prevents it from effectively carrying out its role?

A single independent monitoring and enforcement agency is recommended, which has overall control of the parties' and candidates' financial management. Inter-institutional coordination with other control authorities (or in some cases the private sector, such as the banking system) can help track funds and expenditures and tackle illicit funding. Creating networks with civil society groups will also help improve monitoring agencies' effectiveness.

Agencies are also encouraged to focus more on preventive measures, for example by working with parties and politicians to help them comply with the rules. The development of longer-term plans, starting with building capacity and awareness within parties and gradually increasing their focus on sanctioning violations, could be one aspect of this.

Virtually all the regional chapters in this volume stressed that transparency—making information available and accessible for public scrutiny, including parties' financial statements—is among the core tasks of these agencies. A prerequisite for the latter is that information is presented in a standardized format so the public can easily make comparisons. Chapter 5 on Latin America showed that only a handful of agencies had established electronic portals where the public could easily access and analyse financial reports in a standardized format. Working toward more transparent procedures, agencies are also urged to communicate openly about their own work and keep parties up to date about changes in regulations and reporting requirements. Where appropriate, it is recommended that monitoring agencies report sex-disaggregated data and compliance with gender-targeted legislation, in order to clearly compare men and women's fundraising and spending. The privacy of small donors can be protected by setting a threshold for reporting or publication (so that only the identity of those donating more than a given amount over a specific time period is made known), which balances the protection of privacy and the public right to know who funds the political system.

Monitoring and enforcement agencies' control and analysis of information could also be improved. Too often, infringements of the rules are simply never detected. Agencies therefore need to focus on developing investigative methods, including random monitoring of candidates and parties, and conduct risk mapping to help target their efforts.

Agencies are also recommended to issue proportional sanctions when infringements have been detected. In some instances, this might involve issuing only minor sanctions. As discussed above, there is a general sense that impunity prevails, which gradually undermines the credibility of the monitoring institutions and the underpinning rules.

To improve their work procedures and advocate better regulations or stronger mandates, it is advised that agencies join (or help form) international networks that help them share experiences and learn from each other. One such network is the Association of World Election Bodies, an initiative of the South Korean election management body, which brought together monitoring agencies from around the world for its inaugural assembly in 2013. Such collaboration can be useful, since many monitoring and enforcement agencies around the world are struggling with the same kinds of challenges.

Political parties and politicians

As noted at the beginning of this chapter, political parties in many parts of the world suffer from low levels of public confidence. They are often seen as elitist institutions that do not necessarily act in the interest of average citizens. Addressing this lack of popular support is a complicated issue that requires action in many areas. In many cases, an important step is increased transparency in how parties raise and spend money.

Political parties are encouraged to include political finance policy stances in their manifestos. This would make parties more accountable to citizens and demonstrate the political will that is crucial to help level the playing field for parties and candidates, tackle illicit funding and ensure that citizens are at the centre of politics. Political will is the starting point for meaningful reform and change: it affects every aspect, including law-making and the creation of institutions to control implementation.

Political parties are called upon to take responsibility for their finances and show good practice by institutionalizing self-regulatory mechanisms even where formal regulations may not exist. Parties are urged to set up transparency in intra-party procedures and pay particular attention to accounting and communicating to the public that they are actively responsible for these matters. A very important part of this is demonstrating how they are preventing illicit funding.

It is also recommended that parties be subject to independent external auditing and make their financial reports available to the public in a user-friendly way, as suggested by the UNCAC, which calls for effective public access to information.[27] This would go some way to rebuilding public trust in political parties.

Female candidates can be given financial support through measures such as reduced nomination fees and subsidized media coverage. Parties are also encouraged to consider having an internal party fund earmarked for female candidates. Attracting women to a political party will increase the pool of talented people available to it.

All political parties can act as watchdogs of other parties, doing their best to ensure that all adhere to political finance regulations. To maintain integrity and avoid mud-slinging, however, it is good practice that any exposure of wrongdoing by others is evidence-based. Opposition parties can distinguish themselves from the government by showing how they can 'do it better', for example by complying with political finance regulations.

Media actors

The media (especially investigative journalists) have an important role in monitoring money in politics and exposing violations of political finance regulations, where there is sufficient evidence to do so (e.g., corruption, abuse of state resources, the undue influence of business on politics); they may often do more to uncover violations than formal enforcement institutions. The regional chapters all urge the media to safeguard their independence and to stay independent of undue political influence.

The regional chapters also show that the media can play an important role in educating the public. In this regard, the media are encouraged not only to report on individual scandals, but to go further and make issues relating to money in politics an editorial priority and focus on in-depth journalism. This could include, for example, mapping the finances of parties and politicians, including who are the main donors, and explaining the damaging effects of the abuse of state resources.

Civil society

Civil society groups working in the area of democracy should note that money is often essential to the functioning of the democratic process, including the quality of elections. These groups are recommended to direct their energies primarily within two areas: awareness raising and monitoring. To raise awareness, they can educate citizens about how money matters within politics, the negative effects that violations of rules may have on their everyday lives, and how the abuse of state resources wastes money that belongs to the people. They could also try to discourage citizen participation in vote-buying practices. This may admittedly be a difficult task where the exchange of gifts or perks for political support may be the only (or most reliable) method of distributing welfare.

Civil society organizations also have a crucial role in monitoring the conduct and finances of parties and candidates. It is recommended that ways be found to systematically document and analyse parties' and candidates' finances and present the information to the public in a way that is understandable to the average citizen. If possible, civil society organizations are encouraged to develop and share monitoring methodologies so that comparisons can be made over time and between countries or sub-national regions. Financial monitoring of parties and candidates is also recommended to be an integral part of domestic election observation.

Having a monitoring role does not, however, mean that such organizations automatically need to place themselves in 'opposition' to the political parties. They are also recommended to find ways to help the parties become more accountable and transparent.

International actors

Although local stakeholders should be the key drivers of any reform, international actors can play a supporting role. Weak and poorly institutionalized political parties are more prone to corrupt practices. The international community would therefore benefit from combining efforts to prevent corruption with the strengthening and capacity building of political parties. Exchanging best practices between political parties in different countries can be an important part of such activities.

While there have been improvements in recent years, regional intergovernmental organizations such as the European Union and the Organization of American States that carry out election observation can do more to include political finance matters in their long-term election observation missions, and define and coordinate a common, comparative methodology for monitoring party and candidate financing. Financial information should be made available to observers as soon as possible so that it can be included in election observation reports. Such a methodology would mean that observers need to analyse how money is distributed between political actors, the shape of the legal framework and issues related to its implementation. In doing this, increased cooperation with domestic civil society organizations and observers will often prove helpful.

International and regional organizations are also urged to help monitoring and enforcement agencies improve their work on political finance. As discussed above, these agencies are challenged in the way they carry out their work in this field. International and regional organizations could help them gather and present information, for example, by developing, better procedures and standards for systematizing information.[28] Any assistance should be equally focused on advancing the agencies' preventive measures, which in the long run is more sustainable than only focusing on detecting and sanctioning existing problems.

International actors, especially aid donors, must also increase their efforts to prevent the abuse of state resources as a consequence of their aid programmes. Experiences from Africa have shown that government parties have sometimes used aid money to stay in power.[29] Initiatives to counteract the abuse of state resources are important not only to improve the democratic process in the partner country, but also to protect against the misuse of tax money given as international assistance.

Main recommendations

A few lessons learned can summarize the current state of affairs in the area of political finance. These lessons are drawn from this publication and from International IDEA's activities relating to political finance around the world. While not exhaustive, it is hoped that these main findings will help inform the debate on political finance and prompt reform.

1. *Context is key.* Political finance regulations that are tailor-made to a given country's context stand a better chance of successful implementation and compliance. A country's political system and culture—in particular how its people view politics and the role of political parties—should shape its political finance regulatory framework and how it addresses its challenges. This is not to say that no general lessons can be drawn about the advantages and disadvantages of various elements of political finance regulation, or that countries cannot learn from each other's experiences, but context should always be taken into consideration.

2. *Laws matter, but accomplish little on their own.* The legal framework is the starting point for the role that money ought to have in political life. However, formal rules alone cannot have a significant impact. Far too often, rules are circumvented or even used as a tool for political oppression. Factors such as a reasonably democratic environment with overall respect for the rule of law greatly affect the possibility of controlling finance, more so than the legal provisions themselves. Developing or reforming finance rules can therefore not be delinked from the overall political settings in which they are supposed to function, which is discussed in more detail in Chapter 2, 'Getting the Political Finance System Right'.

3. *Enforcement is the weakest link.* During the last decade, the lack of enforcement has repeatedly been identified as the weakest link in the control of political finance; this trend continues to date. Although there is much knowledge today about the various problems related to money in politics, and a large majority of countries have legal frameworks in place, the system of ensuring compliance is often weak. The starting point for improvement should be a thorough analysis of the specific needs per agency—identifying whether there is a lack of political will expressed as a lack of force and mandate for the agency, a lack of technical know-how, or a lack of independence from the parties and candidates they are supposed to monitor. Policy makers must give agencies the political power they need to enforce effectively in order to demonstrate a serious commitment to create political finance transparency and increase public trust in the political sector.

4. *The gender funding gap needs to be addressed.* Women face more obstacles to raising or accessing funds than men. Since there are many reasons for these structural obstacles, any solution should be multifaceted. Political finance legislation needs to address these inequalities, and public funding can provide incentives and support for female candidates. Political parties have a key role to play in addressing this gender funding gap; in addition to adhering to political finance regulations, they can (and should) show initiative by introducing voluntary internal reforms to promote women's participation and raise funds on their behalf.

5. *Peer networks are an effective way to encourage reform.* There is a general dearth of regional initiatives through which countries develop joint standards for political finance and monitor overall compliance.[30] Establishing such regional initiatives would help countries identify weaknesses in national political finance policies and pressure each other to undergo necessary legislative and institutional reforms. Creating regional peer networks would hopefully have a positive effect on the quality as well as the enforcement of the laws.

6. *Broader involvement in the development of political finance regulations is needed.* Better laws, stronger enforcement and improved financial management within the parties are all measures that have been promoted to improve control over money in politics. Yet politicians themselves design the rules they are supposed to obey. Thus regulation continues to include loopholes, enforcement agencies are not sufficiently empowered and parties do not adequately account for their finances. In a democratic system, decisions are to be taken by elected politicians; this situation is partly an inescapable dilemma of democracy. However, one way to ensure that political finance regulations do not exclusively serve the short-term interests of politicians is to involve a wide range of stakeholders in their development. In doing so, care should be taken to avoid regulatory frameworks that are so restrictive that they weaken the vitality and dynamism of party politics.

7. *Party and candidate finance information needs to be clear and accessible.* For the last decade there have been lively discussions on how and from where parties and candidates should get their money, and what they should be allowed to spend it on. As the result of the media uncovering political finance scandals, including corruption and bribes, laws and regulations have been instigated or revised over and over again. In spite of this, there is surprisingly little systematic documentation about the income and expenditures of political parties and candidates (not to mention third parties) around the world. Very few monitoring agencies can provide comprehensive records, few civil society organizations have a well-developed monitoring methodology and perhaps even fewer political parties have thorough bookkeeping available to the public. Until very basic information about party and candidate finances is provided in a systematic and easily accessible way, true transparency regarding money in politics will be difficult to achieve.

References

Afrobarometer (2008) 'The Quality of Democracy and Governance in Africa: New Results from Afrobarometer Round 4, A Compendium of Public Opinion Findings from 19 African Countries', available at http://www.afrobarometer.org/files/documents/working_papers/AfropaperNo108.pdf, accessed 19 February 2014.

Council of Europe (2003) Recommendation 2003/4 of the Committee of Ministers to Member States on Common Rules against Corruption in the Funding of Political Parties and Electoral Campaigns.

International IDEA, Political Finance Database, available at http://www.idea.int/political-finance

Johnston, Michael (2005) *Political Parties and Democracy in Theoretical and Practical Perspectives: Political Finance Policy, Parties, and Democratic Development*. Washington, D.C.: National Democratic Institute.

Latinobarometro (2010) *Annual Report 2010*, available at http://www.latinobarometro.org/latContents.jsp, accessed 19 February 2014.

Ohman, Magnus (2011) *Global Trends in the Regulation of Political Finance*. IPSA-ECPR Conference in Sao Paulo, 16–19 February 2011.

Transparency International (2013) *Global Corruption Barometer 2013*, available at http://www.transparency.org/whatwedo/pub/global_corruption_barometer_2013, accessed 20 November 2013.

United Nations (UN) (2004) United Nations Convention against Corruption, available at https://www.unodc.org/unodc/en/treaties/CAC/, accessed 10 February 2014.

Notes

[1] Respondents reported that political parties were the most corrupt institutions in 51 of 107 surveyed countries. See Transparency International 2013.

[2] Afrobarometer (2008) found that an average of 58 per cent of respondents had little or no trust in opposition parties and 42 per cent had little or no trust in the ruling party. In Latin America, trust in political parties is 23 per cent (Latinobarometro 2010), which (while low) represents an increase from its nadir in 2003 (11 per cent) but a decrease from its highest point of 28 per cent (in 1997) since the surveys began in 1996.

[3] See the section 'Private funding of political parties' in Chapter 7, 'Political Finance in Northern, Western and Southern Europe', in this volume.

[4] A distinction needs to be made between different types of illegal funding. All donations that fall outside legal limits are per se illegal, including those that are slightly over the limit and those that are from legitimate businesses in a country where such donations are forbidden. Such donations are not necessarily morally questionable, and the money may not have been made through illegal activity.

[5] See the section on 'Infiltration of illicit financing' in Chapter 5, 'Latin America', in this volume.

6   See the section on 'Illicit funding' in Chapter 3, 'Africa', in this volume.

7   See the section on 'Private sources of income' in Chapter 5, 'Latin America', in this volume.

8   See Chapter 5, 'Latin America', in this volume.

9   See the section on 'Enforcing political finance regulations' in Chapter 2, 'Getting the Political Finance System Right', in this volume.

10 See the section on 'Ineffective implementation and unintended consequences' in Chapter 4, 'Asia', in this volume.

11 See the section on 'Enforcement' in Chapter 1, 'Introduction to Political Finance', in this volume.

12 See the section on 'Enforcement of political finance regulations' in Chapter 6, 'Eastern, Central and South-east Europe and Central Asia', in this volume.

13 See the section on 'Sanctions' in Chapter 5, 'Latin America', in this volume.

14 See the section on 'Sanctions' in Chapter 3, 'Africa', in this volume.

15 See the section on 'Problems of political finance' in Chapter 5, 'Latin America', in this volume.

16 See the section on 'Oversight and compliance' in Chapter 5, 'Latin America', in this volume.

17 It is worth emphasizing that, although political parties are increasingly perceived as bodies of government, they differ from state institutions. They are political entities, and still, for example, shape state policy and in many countries have the power to remove governments.

18 Johnston 2005, p. 3.

19 See the section on 'Direct public financing' in Chapter 5, 'Latin America', in this volume.

20 Council of Europe (2003, Article 1) recommends that state support must be limited to 'reasonable contributions' and must not 'interfere with the independence of political parties'.

21 See the 'Public funding of political parties' section in the 'Political Finance in Northern, Western and Southern Europe' chapter in this volume.

22 For detailed information about the regulation of public funding in different countries, see the International IDEA Political Finance Database.

23 A possible counter-trend has also appeared in which a small number of countries that used to have public funding have abolished it. Venezuela did so after 26 years, and countries that have recently done the same are Bolivia (2008), Azerbaijan and Nigeria (2010) (Ohman 2011). Given that public funding is assumed to help prevent undue influence and create a more equal playing field, this trend requires close attention.

24 Policy makers here include those involved in drafting, amending and adopting political finance policies, either from the executive or from the legislative branch of government. The focus is on their role rather than a particular institution.

25 United Nations Convention against Corruption (2004) Article 30(7) and Article 26(1).

26 Ibid., Article 5(1).

27 United Nations Convention against Corruption, 2004, Article 13(1).

28 One example is the Inter-regional Dialogue on Democracy, a platform for regional organizations working on democracy issues.

29 See the section on 'Abuse of state resources' in Chapter 3, 'Africa', in this volume.

30 The main exception to this is the Group of States against Corruption (GRECO), which has 49 member states (48 European and the United States).

Annexes

Annex I: Comparative tables

The International IDEA Political Finance Database includes information about the regulations of political party and candidate finance in 180 countries around the world. The database includes 43 questions. The following tables show the data in table form. To save space, some questions have been combined. Also, some questions including more detailed information have not been included here. For example, the database includes information about the level of contributions and spending limits, regulations against vote buying and available sanctions against political finance violations.

The Political Finance Database also includes further comments about the different regulations, as well as quotes from legislation and other sources, which often provide additional details. Those interested in knowing more about the regulations are recommended to visit the database at http://www.idea.int/political-finance.*

---

* The collection of data for the Political Finance Database included input from many individual experts and researchers and was mainly carried out during 2012. International IDEA tries to ensure that the database is continuously updated as regulations change, but it cannot guarantee that all the answers are correct.

Where the coding shows that a certain regulation exists, for example a ban on foreign donations to candidates, or a spending limit for political parties, this indicates that such a regulation applies in at least certain conditions. The regulation does not necessarily apply in all cases (for example, foreign donations may be banned to some types of candidates but not others, and parties may be limited by a spending limit in relation to election campaigns but not otherwise).

Country	Ban on foreign donations to parties/candidates	Ban on corporate donations to parties/candidates	Ban on donations from corporations with government contracts or partial gov't. ownership to parties/candidates	Ban on trade union donations to parties/candidates	Ban on anonymous donations to parties/candidates	Ban on state resources being given to or received by political parties or candidates	Limit on the amount a donor can contribute to a political party over a time period	Limit on the amount a donor can contribute to a political party in relation to an election	Limit on the amount a donor can contribute to a candidate	Provisions for direct public funding to political parties	public funding
Afghanistan	Yes/Yes	Yes/Yes	Yes/Yes	Yes/Yes	No/Yes	Yes	Yes	Regular limit applies	Yes	No	Not applicable
Albania	Yes/Yes	No/No	Yes/Yes	No/No	Yes/Yes	Yes	No	Yes	Yes	•Yes, regularly provided funding •Yes, in relation to campaigns	•Representation in elect body •Share of votes in previo election •Share of seats in previo election •Registration as a politic party
Algeria	Yes/Yes	Yes/No	No/ No data	No/No	Yes/No	No data	Yes	Regular limit applies	No	Yes, regularly provided funding	Representation in electe body
Andorra	No/Yes	No/No	No/Yes	No/No	No/Yes	Yes	No	Yes	Yes	No	Not applicable
Angola	Yes/Yes	No/No	Yes/Yes	No/No	No/No	Yes	No	No	No	Yes, in relation to campaigns	Participation in election
Antigua and Barbuda	No/No	No/No	No/No	No/No	No, but specific limit/ No	No	No	No	No	No	Not applicable
Argentina	Yes/No	No/No	Yes/No	Yes/No	Yes/Yes	Yes	Yes	Regular limit applies	No	•Yes, regularly provided funding •Yes, in relation to campaigns	Participation in election
Armenia	Yes/Yes	No/Yes	Yes/Yes	No/Yes	Yes/No	Yes	No	Yes	Yes	Yes, regularly provided funding	Share of votes in previou election
Australia	No/No	No/No	No/No	No/No	No, but specific limit/No, but specific limit	No data	No	No	No	Yes, in relation to campaigns	Share of votes in previou election
Austria	No/No	No/No	Yes/No	No/No	No, but specific limit/ No	No	No	No	No	Yes, regularly provided funding	•Representation in electe body •Share of votes in previc election •Share of seats in previc election
Azerbaijan	Yes/Yes	Yes/No	Yes/Yes	No/No	Yes/Yes	Yes	No	Yes	Yes	Yes, regularly provided funding	•Representation in electe body •Share of votes in previc election
Bahamas	No/No	No/No	No/No	No/No	No/No	No data	No	No	No	No	Not applicable
Bahrain	Yes/No	No/No	No/No	No/No	Yes/No data	Yes	No	No	No	Yes, regularly provided funding	No data
Bangladesh	Yes/No	No/No	No/No	No/No	No, but specific limit/ Yes	No	Yes	Regular limit applies	No	No	Not applicable
Barbados	No/No	No/No	No data/ No	No data	No data/Yes	No data	No	No	No	Yes, regularly provided funding	Representation in electe body
Belarus	Yes/Yes	No/No	No/No	No/No	Yes/Yes	Yes	No	Yes	Yes	No	Not applicable
Belgium	No/No	Yes/Yes	Yes/Yes	Yes/Yes	No, but specific limit/No, but specific limit	Yes	Yes	Regular limit applies	Yes	Yes, regularly provided funding	Representation in electe body

Allocation calculation for direct public funding	Earmarking for direct public funding	Free or subsidized access to media for political parties/candidates	Provision of direct public funding to political parties related to gender equality among candidates	Provisions for other financial advantages to encourage gender equality in political parties	Limits on the amount a political party/candidate can spend	Political parties have to report on their finances regularly/for election campaigns	Candidates have to report on their campaign finance	Information in financial reports is to be made public/must include identity of donor	Institution mandated to receive financial reports	Institution responsible for examining financial reports and/or investigating violations
applicable	Not applicable	No/Yes	Not applicable	• Yes, reduced nomination fee • No	No/No	Yes/No	Yes	Yes/Sometimes	EMB	Yes, EMB
...qual ...oportional to ...ts received	No	Yes/No	No	No	Yes/Yes	Yes/Yes	Yes	Yes/Yes	EMB	•Yes, EMB •Yes, auditing agency •Yes, other
...portional to ...ts received	No	No/Yes	No	No data	No/Yes	Yes/No data	Yes	Yes/Yes	•Ministry •Other	No data
applicable	Not applicable	No/Yes	Not applicable	No	No/No	No/Yes	Yes	Yes/No	•EMB •Auditing agency	Yes, court
...al	Campaign spending	Yes/Yes	No	No	No/No	No/Yes	Yes	Yes/Sometimes	EMB	Yes, EMB
applicable	Not applicable	Yes/Yes	Not applicable	No	No/No	No/Yes	No	No/Sometimes	EMB	No
...ual ...oportional to ...es received	•Campaign spending •Ongoing party activities •Printing of ballots	Yes/No	No	No	Yes/No	Yes/Yes	No	Yes/Yes	Court	Yes, other
...portional to ...es received	No	Yes/No	No	No	Yes/Yes	Yes/Yes	Yes	Yes/No	•EMB •Other	Yes, EMB
...rate by votes ...eived	No	No/No	No	No	No/No	Yes/No	Yes	Yes/Sometimes	EMB	Yes, EMB
...qual ...oportional to ...es received ...at rate by votes ...eived	No	No/No	No	No	Yes/Yes	Yes/No	No	Yes/Sometimes	Auditing agency	Yes, auditing agency
...ual ...oportional to ...es received	No	Yes/Yes	No	No	Yes/Yes	Yes/Yes	Yes	Yes/Yes	EMB	•Yes, EMB •Yes, other
applicable	Not applicable	No/No	Not applicable	No	No/No	No/No	No	Not applicable/ Not applicable	Not applicable	No data
...data	No data	No data/No data	No	No data	No/No data	Yes/No	No	No/Yes	Ministry	Yes, other
applicable	Not applicable	Yes/No	Not applicable	No	Yes/Yes	Yes/Yes	Yes	Yes/Sometimes	EMB	Yes, EMB
...data	No data	Yes/No	No	No	No/Yes	No/No	Yes	No/No	Other	No data
applicable	Not applicable	Yes/Yes	Not applicable	No	No/Yes	No/No	Yes	No/Sometimes	EMB	•Yes, ministry •Yes, other
...ual ...oportional to ...es received	No	Yes/No	No	No	Yes/Yes	Yes/Yes	Yes	Yes/Sometimes	•Ministry •Other	Yes, other

Country	Ban on foreign donations to parties/candidates	Ban on corporate donations to parties/candidates	Ban on donations from corporations with government contracts or partial gov't, ownership to parties/candidates	Ban on trade union donations to parties/candidates	Ban on anonymous donations to parties/candidates	Ban on state resources being given to or received by political parties or candidates	Limit on the amount a donor can contribute to a political party over a time period	Limit on the amount a donor can contribute to a political party in relation to an election	Limit on the amount a donor can contribute to a candidate	Provisions for direct public funding to political parties	public funding
Belize	No/No data	No/No data	No/No data	No/No data	No/No data	No data	No	No	No	No	Not applicable
Benin	No/No	No/No	No/No data	No/No	Yes/No data	Yes	Yes	Regular limit applies	No	•Yes, regularly provided funding •Yes, in relation to campaigns	•Representation in elect body •Share of votes in next election
Bhutan	Yes/Yes	Yes/Yes	Yes/Yes	Yes/Yes	Yes/Yes	Yes	Yes	Yes	Yes	Yes, in relation to campaigns	•Share of votes in previo election •Number of candidates
Bolivia	Yes/No data	No/No	No/No data	No/No data	Yes/Yes	Yes	Yes	Regular limit applies	No	No	Share of votes in previou election
Bosnia and Herzegovina	Yes/Yes	No/No	Yes/Yes	Yes/Yes	Yes/Yes	Yes	Yes	Regular limit applies	No	•Yes, regularly provided funding •Yes, in relation to campaigns	Representation in electe body
Botswana	No/No	No/No	No/No	No/No data	No/No	No data	No	No	No	No	Not applicable
Brazil	Yes/Yes	No/No	Yes/Yes	Yes/Yes	Yes/Yes	Yes	No	Yes	Yes	Yes, regularly provided funding	Registration as a politica party
Bulgaria	Yes/Yes	Yes/Yes	Yes/Yes	Yes/No	Yes/Yes	Yes	Yes	Yes	Yes	Yes, regularly provided funding	•Representation in elect body •Share of votes in previo election
Burkina Faso	No/No	No/No	No/No	No/No	No/No data	No data	No	No	No	•Yes, regularly provided funding •Yes, in relation to campaigns	•Share of votes in previo election •Must operate regularly and be up-to-date with th statutory obligations
Burundi	Yes/Yes	No/No	Yes/No	No/No	No/No	No data	No	No	No	Yes, in relation to campaigns	All parties
Cambodia	Yes/No	No/No	No/No	Yes/No	No/No	Yes	No	No	No	No	Not applicable
Cameroon	Yes/No	No/No	No/No	No/No	No/No	No data	Yes	Regular limit applies	No	•Yes, regularly provided funding •Yes, in relation to campaigns	•Representation in elect body •Share of votes in previc election
Canada	Yes/Yes	Yes/Yes	Yes/Yes	Yes/Yes	No, but specific limit/No, but specific limit	Yes	Yes	Regular limit applies	Yes	•Yes, regularly provided funding •Yes, in relation to campaigns	Share of votes in previou election
Cape Verde	Yes/Yes	No/No	Yes/Yes	No/No	Yes/Yes	Yes	No	No	No	Yes, in relation to campaigns	Participation in election
Central African Republic	No/No	No/No	No/No	No/No	No/No	No data	No	No	No	No	Not applicable
Chad	No/No	No/No	No/No	No/No	No/No	No data	No	No	No	Yes, in relation to campaigns	Share of votes in next election
Chile	Yes/Yes	No/No	Yes/Yes	Yes/Yes	No, but specific limit/No, but specific limit	Yes	No	Yes	Yes	Yes, in relation to campaigns	Participation in election

Allocation calculation for direct public funding	Earmarking for direct public funding	Free or subsidized access to media for political parties/candidates	Provision of direct public funding to political parties related to gender equality among candidates	Provisions for other financial advantages to encourage gender equality in political parties	Limits on the amount a political party/candidate can spend	Political parties have to report on their finances regularly/for election campaigns	Candidates have to report on their campaign finance	Information in financial reports is to be made public/must include identity of donor	Institution mandated to receive financial reports	Institution responsible for examining financial reports and/or investigating violations
applicable	Not applicable	No/No	Not applicable	No	No/No	No/No	No	Not applicable/ Not applicable	Not applicable	No data
qual oportional to ts received	Campaign spending	Yes/Yes	No	No	Yes/Yes	Yes/Yes	Yes	Yes/ Sometimes	•Ministry •Court	Yes, court
al	Campaign spending	Yes/Yes	No	No	Yes/Yes	Yes/Yes	Yes	Yes/Yes	•EMB •Auditing agency	Yes, EMB
oportional to es received	No	Yes/No	Yes	No	No/No	Yes/Yes	No	No/Yes	EMB	•Yes, ministry •Yes, auditing agency
qual oportional to ts received	No	Yes/Yes	Yes	No	Yes/Yes	Yes/Yes	Yes	Yes/Yes	EMB	Yes, EMB
applicable	Not applicable	No/No	No	No	Yes/Yes	No/Yes	Yes	Yes/ Sometimes	EMB	Yes, court
qual oportional to es received	•Campaign spending •Ongoing party activities •Intra-party institution	Yes/No	No	Yes, funds earmarked for gender activities	No/No	Yes/Yes	Yes	Yes/Yes	EMB	Yes, EMB
oortional to es received	•Campaign spending •Ongoing party activities	Yes/Yes	No	No	Yes/Yes	Yes/Yes	Yes	Yes/Yes	Auditing agency	•Yes, auditing agency •Yes, other
qual oportional to es received oportional to didates fielded	No	Yes/No	Yes	No	No/No	Yes/Yes	Yes	No/No	Court	Yes, court
al	No	Yes/Yes	No	No	No/No	Yes/No	No	No/Yes	Ministry	Yes, court
applicable	Not applicable	Yes/No	Not applicable	No	No/No	Yes/No	No	No/No	Ministry	•Yes, EMB •Yes, ministry
oortional to ts received oportional to didates fielded	•Campaign spending •Ongoing party activities	Yes/No	No	No	No/No	Yes/No	No data	No/No	Special institution	Yes, institution for this purpose
at rate by votes eived are of enses hbursed	No	Yes/No	No	No	Yes/Yes	Yes/Yes	Yes	Yes/ Sometimes	EMB	Yes, EMB
oortional to es received	No	Yes/Yes	Yes	No	Yes/Yes	No data/Yes	Yes	Yes/Yes	EMB	Yes, EMB
applicable	Not applicable	Yes/Yes	Not applicable	No	No/No	No/No	Yes	Yes/No	Court	No
re of expenses hbursed	Campaign spending	Yes/Yes	No	No	No/No	No data/ No data	No data	No data/ No data	No data	No
rate by votes eived	No	Yes/Yes	No	No	Yes/Yes	Yes/Yes	Yes	Yes/ Sometimes	EMB	Yes, EMB

Country	Ban on foreign donations to parties/candidates	Ban on corporate donations to parties/candidates	Ban on donations from corporations with government contracts or partial gov't. ownership to parties/candidates	Ban on trade union donations to parties/candidates	Ban on anonymous donations to parties/candidates	Ban on state resources being given to or received by political parties or candidates	Limit on the amount a donor can contribute to a political party over a time period	Limit on the amount a donor can contribute to a political party in relation to an election	Limit on the amount a donor can contribute to a candidate	Provisions for direct public funding to political parties	public funding
Colombia	Yes/Yes	No/Yes	No/Yes	No/Yes	Yes/Yes	Yes	No	Yes	Yes	•Yes, regularly provided funding •Yes, in relation to campaigns	•Representation in elect[ed] body •Share of votes in next election •Share of seats in next election •Participation in election[s] •Having women and you[th] in elected/leading positio[ns]
Comoros	No data/No data	No data/No data	No data/No data	No data/No data	No data/No data	No data	No data	No data	No data	No	Not applicable
Congo, Democratic Republic of	Yes/No	No/No	Yes/No	No/No	Yes/No	No	No	No	No	Yes, regularly provided funding	Representation in elected body
Costa Rica	Yes/Yes	Yes/Yes	Yes/Yes	Yes/Yes	Yes/Yes	No data	No	No	Yes	•Yes, regularly provided funding •Yes, in relation to campaigns	•Representation in elect[ed] body •Share of votes in next election •Expenses must be repor[ted] to the EMB
Croatia	Yes/Yes	No/Yes	Yes/Yes	Yes/Yes	Yes/Yes	Yes	Yes	Regular limit applies	Yes	•Yes, regularly provided funding •Yes, in relation to campaigns	•Representation in elect[ed] body •Share of votes in next election •Participation in election[s]
Cyprus	Yes/No	No/No	Yes/No	No/No	No/No	Yes	Yes	Regular limit applies	No	•Yes, regularly provided funding •Yes, in relation to campaigns	•Number of candidates •Registration as a politic[al] party
Czech Republic	Yes/No	No/No	Yes/No	No/No	Yes/No	Yes	No	No	No	•Yes, regularly provided funding •Yes, in relation to campaigns	•Representation in elect[ed] body •Share of votes in previous election
Côte d'Ivoire	Yes/Yes	No/No	Yes/No	No/No	Yes/No	Yes	No	No	No	Yes, regularly provided funding	•Representation in elect[ed] body •Share of votes in previo[us] election
Denmark	No/No	No/No	No/No	No/No	No/No	No	No	No	No	Yes, regularly provided funding	Share of votes in previous election
Djibouti	No data/No	No data/No	No data/No	No data/No	No data/No	No data	No data	No	No	Yes, regularly provided funding	Representation in elected body
Dominica	No/No	No/No	No/No	No/No	No/No	No data	No	No	No	No	Not applicable
Dominican Republic	Yes/Yes	No/No	No/No	No/No	No/No	Yes	No	No	No	Yes, regularly provided funding	•Share of votes in previo[us] election •Participation in election[s]
East Timor	Yes/No	Yes/No	Yes/No	Yes/No	Yes/No	Yes	No	No	No	Yes, regularly provided funding	Representation in elected body
Ecuador	Yes/Yes	No/Yes	Yes/Yes	No/Yes	Yes/Yes	Yes	Yes	Yes	Yes	•Yes, regularly provided funding •Yes, in relation to campaigns	•Share of votes in previo[us] election •Share of seats in previo[us] election

Allocation calculation for direct public funding	Earmarking for direct public funding	Free or subsidized access to media for political parties/candidates	Provision of direct public funding to political parties related to gender equality among candidates	Provisions for other financial advantages to encourage gender equality in political parties	Limits on the amount a political party/candidate can spend	Political parties have to report on their finances regularly/for election campaigns	Candidates have to report on their campaign finance	Information in financial reports is to be made public/must include identity of donor	Institution mandated to receive financial reports	Institution responsible for examining financial reports and/or investigating violations
qual at rate by votes eived roportional to ts received ongoing istance, 90% istributed portionally in ordance with eral criteria.	•Ongoing party activities •Intra-party institution	Yes/Yes	Yes	Yes, funds earmarked for gender activities	Yes/Yes	Yes/Yes	No	Yes/Sometimes	EMB	Yes, EMB
applicable	Not applicable	No data/Yes	Not applicable	No data	No data/No data	No data/No data	No data	No data/No data	No data	No data
portional to ts received	No	Yes/Yes	No	No	No/No	Yes/No	No	No/Yes	Ministry	Yes, ministry
portional to es received	No	No/No	No	Yes, other	No/No	Yes/Yes	No	Yes/Yes	EMB	Yes, EMB
qual roportional to ts received	Fulfilling the goals defined in the programme and statute of the political party	Yes/Yes	Yes	No	No/Yes	Yes/Yes	Yes	Yes/Yes	•Ministry •Auditing agency	•Yes, ministry •Yes, auditing agency
qual roportional to es received etermined	No	Yes/Yes	No	No	No/Yes	Yes/Yes	Yes	Yes/No	•Ministry •Auditing agency	•Yes, ministry •Yes, auditing agency
qual roportional to es received at rate by votes eived oportional to ts received	No	Yes/No	No	No	No/Yes	Yes/No	No	Yes/Yes	Other	Yes, other
oportional to es received oportional to ts received umber of mbers	•Campaign spending •Ongoing party activities	Yes/Yes	No	No	No/No	Yes/No	No	Yes/Yes	Court	Yes, court
rate by votes eived	No	Yes/No	No	No	No/No	Yes/No	Yes	Yes/Sometimes	•Ministry •Other	No
data	No	No/No	Not applicable	No	No/No	No data/No	No	No/No data	No data	No data
applicable	Not applicable	No/No	Not applicable	No	No/No	No/No	No	Not applicable/Not applicable	Not applicable	No
qual oportional to es received	No	Yes/No	No	No	No/No	No data/Yes	No	No/No	EMB	No
qual oportional to ts received	No	No/No	No	No	No/No	Yes/No	No	Yes/No	EMB	•Yes, EMB •Yes, other
qual oportional to es received	•Campaign spending •Ongoing party activities	Yes/Yes	No	No	Yes/Yes	Yes/Yes	Yes	Yes/Yes	EMB	•Yes, EMB •Yes, other

373

Country	Ban on foreign donations to parties/candidates	Ban on corporate donations to parties/candidates	Ban on donations from corporations with government contracts or partial govt. ownership to parties/candidates	Ban on trade union donations to parties/candidates	Ban on anonymous donations to parties/candidates	Ban on state resources being given to or received by political parties or candidates	Limit on the amount a donor can contribute to a political party over a time period	Limit on the amount a donor can contribute to a political party in relation to an election	Limit on the amount a donor can contribute to a candidate	Provisions for direct public funding to political parties	
Egypt	Yes/Yes	Yes/Yes	Yes/Yes	Yes/Yes	No data/Yes	Yes	No	No	Yes	No	Not applicable
El Salvador	No/No	No/No	No/No	No/No	No/No	No	No	No	No	Yes, in relation to campaigns	•Participation in election •Registration as a politic party
Equatorial Guinea	No data/ No data	No data/ No data	No data/ No data	No data/ No data	No data/ No data	No data	No data	No data	No data	Yes, in relation to campaigns	No data
Estonia	No/No	Yes/No	Yes/No	Yes/No	Yes/Yes	Yes	No	No	No	Yes, regularly provided funding	•Representation in elect body •Share of votes in previo election
Ethiopia	Yes/No	No/No	Yes/No	Yes/No	Yes/No	Yes	No	No	No	Yes, regularly provided funding	Representation in elected body
Fiji	Yes/Yes	Yes/Yes	Yes/Yes	Yes/Yes	Yes/Yes	Yes	Yes	Regular limit applies	Yes	No	Not applicable
Finland	Yes/Yes	No/No	Yes/Yes	No/No	Yes/Yes	Yes	Yes	Regular limit applies	Yes	Yes, regularly provided funding	Representation in elected body
France	Yes/Yes	Yes/Yes	Yes/Yes	Yes/Yes	Yes/Yes	Yes	Yes	Regular limit applies	Yes	•Yes, regularly provided funding •Yes, in relation to campaigns	Share of votes in previous election
Gabon	Yes/No	No/No	No/No	No/No	No/No	No data	No	No	No	•Yes, regularly provided funding •Yes, in relation to campaigns	•Share of seats in previo election •Number of candidates
Gambia	No/No	No/No	No/No	No/No	No/No data	No data	No	No	No	No	Not applicable
Georgia	Yes/Yes	Yes/Yes	Yes/Yes	Yes/Yes	Yes/Yes	Yes	Yes	Yes	Yes	Yes, regularly provided funding	Share of votes in previous election
Germany	No/No	No/No	Yes/No	No/No	No, but specific limit/ No	Yes	No	No	No	Yes, regularly provided funding	Share of votes in previous election
Ghana	Yes/No	No/No	Yes/No	No/No	Yes/No	Yes	No	No	No	No	Not applicable
Greece	Yes/Yes	Yes/Yes	Yes/Yes	Yes/Yes	Yes/Yes	Yes	Yes	Regular limit applies	Yes	•Yes, regularly provided funding •Yes, in relation to campaigns	•Representation in elect body •Share of votes in previo election •Number of candidates

Allocation calculation for direct public funding	Earmarking for direct public funding	Free or subsidized access to media for political parties/candidates	Provision of direct public funding to political parties related to gender equality among candidates	Provisions for other financial advantages to encourage gender equality in political parties	Limits on the amount a political party/candidate can spend	Political parties have to report on their finances regularly/for election campaigns	Candidates have to report on their campaign finance	Information in financial reports is to be made public/must include identity of donor	Institution mandated to receive financial reports	Institution responsible for examining financial reports and/or investigating violations
t applicable	Not applicable	No/No data	Not applicable	No	No/Yes	Yes/Yes	Yes	No/Sometimes	EMB	Yes, auditing agency
t rate by votes eived	No	Yes/No	No	No	No/No	No/No	No	Not applicable/Not applicable	Not applicable	No
data	No data	Yes/No data	No data	No data	No data/No data	No data/No data	No data	No data/No data	No data	No data
qual roportional to es received roportional to ats received	No	No/No	No	No	No/No	Yes/Yes	Yes	Yes/Yes	•Special institution •Other	Yes, other
portional to ats received	•Campaign spending •Ongoing party activities	Yes/Yes	Yes	No	No/No	Yes/Yes	No	No/Yes	EMB	Yes, auditing agency
t applicable	Not applicable	No/No	Not applicable	No	No/No	Yes/Yes	Yes	Yes/Yes	EMB	Yes, EMB
portional to ats received	No	No/No	No	Yes, funding to women's wings	No/No	Yes/Yes	Yes	Yes/Sometimes	•Ministry •Auditing agency	•Yes, ministry •Yes, auditing agency
roportional to es received roportional to ats received	No	Yes/Yes	Yes	No	No/Yes	Yes/No	Yes	Yes/Yes	Special institution	•Yes, court •Yes, institution for this purpose
termined by ulation	No	Yes/Yes	No	No	No/No	Yes/No	No	No/No	Ministry	No
t applicable	Not applicable	Yes/Yes	No	No	No/No	No/No	No	Not applicable/Not applicable	Not applicable	No data
qual roportional to es received	•Ongoing party activities •For the purpose of facilitating creation of healthy, competitive political system	Yes/Yes	Yes	No	No/No	Yes/Yes	Yes	Yes/Yes	•EMB •Other	•Yes, EMB •Yes, other
lat rate by votes eived hare of penses mbursed unding can not higher than private funds sed by the party	No	Yes/No	No	No	No/No	Yes/No	No	Yes/Sometimes	Other	Yes, other
t applicable	Not applicable	Yes/Yes	Not applicable	No	No/No	Yes/Yes	Yes	Yes/Yes	EMB	Yes, EMB
qual roportional to es received	•Campaign spending •Ongoing party activities •Research and study centres	Yes/No	No	No	Yes/Yes	Yes/Yes	Yes	Yes/Sometimes	•Ministry •Special institution •Other	•Yes, other •Yes, institution for this purpose

375

Country	Ban on foreign donations to parties/candidates	Ban on corporate donations to parties/candidates	Ban on donations from corporations with government contracts or partial gov't. ownership to parties/candidates	Ban on trade union donations to parties/candidates	Ban on anonymous donations to parties/candidates	Ban on state resources being given to or received by political parties or candidates	Limit on the amount a donor can contribute to a political party over a time period	Limit on the amount a donor can contribute to a political party in relation to an election	Limit on the amount a donor can contribute to a candidate	Provisions for direct public funding to political parties	public funding
Grenada	No data/No	No data/No data	No data/No data	No data/No data	No data/No data	No data	No	No	No	No	Not applicable
Guatemala	Yes/Yes	No/Yes	No/Yes	No/Yes	Yes/Yes	Yes	Yes	Regular limit applies	Yes	Yes, regularly provided funding	•Representation in elected body •Share of votes in previous election
Guinea	Yes/No	No/No	No/No	No/No	Yes/No data	No data	No	No	No	No	Not applicable
Guinea-Bissau	Yes/Yes	No/Yes	No/Yes	No/Yes	No/No	Yes	No	No	No	No	Not applicable
Guyana	No data/No data	No data/No data	No data/No data	No data/No data	No data/No data	No data	No	No	No	No	Not applicable
Haiti	No data/No data	No data/No data	No data/No data	No data/No data	No, but specific limit/No, but specific limit	No data	No data	Yes	Yes	Yes, in relation to campaigns	Signatures of 40,000 citizens
Honduras	Yes/Yes	Yes/Yes	Yes/Yes	No/No	Yes/Yes	No	No	No	No	Yes, in relation to campaigns	Participation in election
Hungary	Yes/No	No/No	Yes/No	No/No	Yes/No	Yes	No	No	No	•Yes, regularly provided funding •Yes, in relation to campaigns	•Representation in elected body •Share of votes in previous election •Participation in election
Iceland	Yes/Yes	No/No	Yes/Yes	No/No	Yes/Yes	Yes	Yes	Regular limit applies	Yes	Yes, regularly provided funding	•Representation in elected body •Share of votes in previous election
India	Yes/Yes	No/No	Yes/Yes	No/No	Yes/No	Yes	No	No	No	No	Not applicable
Indonesia	Yes/Yes	No/No	No/No	Yes/No	Yes/Yes	Yes	Yes	Yes	No	Yes, regularly provided funding	Representation in elected body
Iran, Islamic Republic of	Yes/No data	No/No data	No/No data	No/No data	Yes/No data	Yes	No	No	No data	No	Not applicable
Iraq	No/Yes	No/No	No/No	No/No	No/No	No data	No	No	No	No	Not applicable
Ireland	Yes/Yes	No/No	No/No	No/No	No, but specific limit/No, but specific limit	Yes	Yes	Regular limit applies	Yes	Yes, regularly provided funding	Share of votes in previous election
Israel	Yes/Yes	Yes/Yes	Yes/Yes	Yes/Yes	Yes/Yes	Yes	Yes	Yes	Yes	•Yes, regularly provided funding •Yes, in relation to campaigns	Representation in elected body
Italy	No/No	No/No	Yes/Yes	No/No	No, but specific limit/No, but specific limit	Yes	No	No	No	•Yes, regularly provided funding •Yes, in relation to campaigns	Representation in elected body
Jamaica	No/No	No/No	No/No	No/No	No/No	No	No	No	No	No	Not applicable

376

Allocation calculation for direct public funding	Earmarking for direct public funding	Free or subsidized access to media for political parties/candidates	Provision of direct public funding to political parties related to gender equality among candidates	Provisions for other financial advantages to encourage gender equality in political parties	Limits on the amount a political party/candidate can spend	Political parties have to report on their finances regularly/for election campaigns	Candidates have to report on their campaign finance	Information in financial reports is to be made public/must include identity of donor	Institution mandated to receive financial reports	Institution responsible for examining financial reports and/or investigating violations
ot applicable	Not applicable	No/No	Not applicable	No	No/Yes	No/No	No	Not applicable/Not applicable	Not applicable	Yes, EMB
at rate by votes ceived	No	Yes/No	No	No	Yes/No data	Yes/No	No	Yes/Yes	EMB	No
ot applicable	Not applicable	Yes/Yes	Not applicable	No	Yes/Yes	Yes/Yes	Yes	Yes/Yes	Court	•Yes, ministry •Yes, court
ot applicable	Not applicable	Yes/Yes	Not applicable	No	No/No	Yes/Yes	Yes	Yes/No	EMB	Yes, EMB
ot applicable	Not applicable	No/No	Not applicable	No	No data/Yes	No data/Yes	Yes	Yes/Yes	EMB	No data
oportional to ndidates fielded	•Campaign spending •Political education	No/Yes	Yes	No	No/No	No/Yes	Yes	No data/Sometimes	•EMB •Ministry	Yes, EMB
oportional to ats received	No	No/No	No	Yes, other	No/No	Yes/No	Yes	Yes/No	EMB	No
qual roportional to tes received roportional to ndidates fielded	Campaign spending	Yes/Yes	No	No	Yes/Yes	Yes/Yes	Yes	Yes/Sometimes	Auditing agency	Yes, auditing agency
qual roportional to tes received	No	Yes/No	No	No	No/Yes	Yes/Yes	Yes	Yes/Sometimes	Auditing agency	Yes, auditing agency
ot applicable	Not applicable	Yes/No	Not applicable	No	No/Yes	Yes/No	Yes	Yes/Sometimes	•EMB •Other	Yes, EMB
oportional to tes received	Political education of members and citizens	No/No	No	No	No/No	Yes/Yes	Yes	Yes/Yes	•EMB •Auditing agency	•Yes, auditing agency •Yes, other
ot applicable	Not applicable	No/Yes	Not applicable	No	No/No data	Yes/No	No data	No data/No data	Special institution	No
ot applicable	Not applicable	No/No	Not applicable	No	No/No	No/No	No	Not applicable/Not applicable	Not applicable	No
oportional to tes received	•Ongoing party activities •Promotion of women and young persons participation.	Yes/Yes	Yes	Yes, other	No/Yes	Yes/Yes	Yes	Yes/Sometimes	Other	Yes, other
qual lat rate by votes ceived	No	Yes/No	No	No	Yes/Yes	Yes/Yes	Yes	Yes/Yes	Auditing agency	Yes, auditing agency
roportional to tes received 0% of the funds e distributed cording to the rties' self-ancing capacity e comments for re information)	Campaign spending	Yes/Yes	Yes	Yes, funds earmarked for gender activities	Yes/Yes	Yes/Yes	Yes	Yes/Sometimes	•Special institution •Other	Yes, institution for this purpose
t applicable	Not applicable	No/No	Not applicable	No	No/Yes	No/No	Yes	Yes/No	EMB	No

Country	Ban on foreign donations to parties/candidates	Ban on corporate donations to parties/candidates	Ban on donations from corporations with government contracts or partial gov't ownership to parties/candidates	Ban on trade union donations to parties/candidates	Ban on anonymous donations to parties/candidates	Ban on state resources being given to or received by political parties or candidates	Limit on the amount a donor can contribute to a political party over a time period	Limit on the amount a donor can contribute to a political party in relation to an election	Limit on the amount a donor can contribute to a candidate	Provisions for direct public funding to political parties	public funding
Japan	Yes/Yes	No/Yes	Yes/Yes	No/Yes	No, but specific limit/Yes	Yes	Yes	Regular limit applies	Yes	Yes, regularly provided funding	•Representation in electe body •Share of votes in previou election •Share of seats in previou election
Jordan	Yes/Yes	Yes/No	Yes/No	Yes/No	Yes/No	Yes	Yes	Regular limit applies	No	Yes, regularly provided funding	Commitment of the politica party to "the law and the system"
Kazakhstan	Yes/Yes	No/No	No/No	No/No	Yes/Yes	Yes	No	No	No	Yes, regularly provided funding	Representation in elected body
Kenya	Yes/No	No/No	Yes/Yes	No/No	Yes/Yes	Yes	Yes	Yes	Yes	Yes, regularly provided funding	•Share of votes in previou election •More than two-thirds of registered office bearers a not of the same gender
Kiribati	No data/No data	No/No data	No/No data	No/No data	No/No data	No data	No	No	No data	No	Not applicable
Korea, Republic of	Yes/Yes	Yes/Yes	Yes/Yes	Yes/Yes	Yes/No, but specific limit	Yes	No	No	Yes	•Yes, regularly provided funding •Yes, in relation to campaigns	•Representation in electe body •Share of votes in previou election •Share of seats in previou election
Kyrgyzstan	Yes/Yes	No/No	Yes/Yes	No/No	Yes/Yes	Yes	No	Yes	Yes	No	Not applicable
Latvia	Yes/Yes	Yes/Yes	Yes/Yes	Yes/Yes	Yes/Yes	Yes	Yes	Regular limit applies	Yes	Yes, regularly provided funding	Share of votes in previous election
Lebanon	No/Yes	No/No	No/No	No/No	No/Yes	Yes	Yes	Regular limit applies	No	No	Not applicable
Lesotho	No/No	No/No	No/No	No/No	No, but specific limit/No data	No data	No	No	No	Yes, in relation to campaigns	•Number of members •Participation in election
Liberia	Yes/Yes	Yes/Yes	Yes/Yes	Yes/Yes	Yes/Yes	Yes	No	No	No	No	Not applicable
Libya	Yes/Yes	No/No	No/No	No/No	Yes/Yes	Yes	No	No	No	No	Not applicable
Liechtenstein	No/No	No/No	No/No	No/No	No/No	No data	No	No	No	Yes, regularly provided funding	•Representation in electe body •Share of votes in previou election
Lithuania	Yes/Yes	Yes/No	Yes/Yes	No/No	Yes/Yes	Yes	Yes	Yes	Yes	•Yes, regularly provided funding •Yes, in relation to campaigns	•Share of votes in previou election •Share of votes in next election
Luxembourg	No/No	Yes/Yes	Yes/Yes	Yes/Yes	Yes/Yes	Yes	No	No	No	•Yes, regularly provided funding •Yes, in relation to campaigns	•Share of votes in previou election •Number of candidates
Macedonia, former Yugoslav Republic (1993-)	Yes/Yes	No/No	Yes/No	No/No	Yes/Yes	Yes	Yes	Yes	Yes	Yes, regularly provided funding	•Representation in electe body •Share of votes in previou election
Madagascar	Yes/No	No/No	No/No	Yes/No	No/No	Yes	No	No	No	Yes, regularly provided funding	Registration as a political party

Allocation calculation for direct public funding	Earmarking for direct public funding	Free or subsidized access to media for political parties/candidates	Provision of direct public funding to political parties related to gender equality among candidates	Provisions for other financial advantages to encourage gender equality in political parties	Limits on the amount a political party/candidate can spend	Political parties have to report on their finances regularly/for election campaigns	Candidates have to report on their campaign finance	Information in financial reports is to be made public/must include identity of donor	Institution mandated to receive financial reports	Institution responsible for examining financial reports and/or investigating violations
oportional to es received oportional to ts received	No	Yes/Yes	No	No	No/Yes	Yes/No	Yes	Yes/ Sometimes	•EMB •Ministry	•Yes, EMB •Yes, ministry •Yes, other
al	Ongoing party activities	Yes/No	No	No	No/No	Yes/No	No	No/Yes	Ministry	No
portional to es received	No	No/Yes	No	No	No/No	Yes/Yes	Yes	Yes/Yes	•EMB •Other	•Yes, EMB •Yes, other
portional to es received	•Campaign spending •Ongoing party activities •Civic education and related activities	Yes/No	Yes	No	Yes/Yes	Yes/Yes	Yes	Yes/ Sometimes	•Yes, auditing agency •Yes, EMB	•Yes, auditing agency •Yes, institution for this purpose
applicable	Not applicable	No data/ No data	Not applicable	No	No/No data	No/No	No data	No/No	No data	Yes, court
qual oportional to es received hare of enses mbursed	•Campaign spending •Ongoing party activities •Intra-party institution	Yes/Yes	Yes	• Yes, funds earmarked for gender activities • Yes, other	Yes/Yes	Yes/Yes	Yes	Yes/ Sometimes	EMB	Yes, EMB
applicable	Not applicable	Yes/Yes	Not applicable	No	Yes/Yes	Yes/Yes	Yes	Yes/Yes	• EMB • Ministry	Yes, EMB
rate by votes eived	•Campaign spending •Ongoing party activities	Yes/Yes	No	No	Yes/Yes	Yes/Yes	No	Yes/Yes	• Auditing agency • Other	Yes, other
applicable	Not applicable	No/No	Not applicable	No	No/Yes	No/No	Yes	No/Yes	EMB	Yes, institution for this purpose
qual oportional to es received	Campaign spending	Yes/No	No	No	No/No	No/Yes	No	Yes/Yes	EMB	No
applicable	Not applicable	No/No	Not applicable	No	Yes/Yes	Yes/Yes	Yes	Yes/ Sometimes	EMB	Yes, EMB
applicable	Not applicable	No/Yes	Not applicable	No	Yes/Yes	No/Yes	Yes	Yes/Yes	EMB	Yes, EMB
qual oportional to es received	Ongoing party activities	No/No	No	No	No/No	Yes/No	No	Yes/No	Other	No
portional to es received	Campaign spending	Yes/Yes	No	No	Yes/Yes	Yes/Yes	Yes	Yes/Yes	• EMB • Other	•Yes, EMB •Yes, court •Yes, other
qual oportional to es received	•Campaign spending •Ongoing party activities	No/No	No	No	No/No	Yes/No	No	Yes/Yes	• Court • Other	Yes, court
qual oportional to es received	No	Yes/Yes	No	No	Yes/Yes	Yes/Yes	Yes	Yes/Yes	• EMB • Auditing agency • Other	•Yes, auditing agency •Yes, other
portional to es received	No	Yes/Yes	No	No	No/No	Yes/No	No	No/No	Other	No

Country	Ban on foreign donations to parties/candidates	Ban on corporate donations to parties/candidates	Ban on donations from corporations with government contracts or partial gov't. ownership to parties/candidates	Ban on trade union donations to parties/candidates	Ban on anonymous donations to parties/candidates	Ban on state resources being given to or received by political parties or candidates	Limit on the amount a donor can contribute to a political party over a time period	Limit on the amount a donor can contribute to a political party in relation to an election	Limit on the amount a donor can contribute to a candidate	Provisions for direct public funding to political parties	public funding
Malawi	No/No	No/No	No/No	No/No	No/No data	Yes	No	No	No	Yes, regularly provided funding	Share of votes in previous election
Malaysia	No/No	No/No	No/No	No/No	No data/No	No data	No	No	No	No	Not applicable
Maldives	Yes/Yes	Yes/Yes	Yes/Yes	No/No	Yes/Yes	Yes	No	No	Yes	Yes, regularly provided funding	Registration as a political party
Mali	No/No	Yes/No	No/No	No/No	No/No data	No data	No	No	No	Yes, regularly provided funding	•Representation in electe body •Share of votes in previo election •Participation in election •Having women Deputies and Counsellors
Malta	Yes/Yes	No/No	No/No	No/No	No/No	No	No	No	No	No	Not applicable
Marshall Islands	No/No	No/No	No/No	No/No	No/No	No data	No	No	No	No	Not applicable
Mauritania	Yes/Yes	No/No	No/Yes	No/No	Yes/Yes	No data	No	Yes	Yes	No	No data
Mauritius	No/No	No/No	No/No	No/No	No/No data	No data	No	No	No	No	Not applicable
Mexico	Yes/Yes	Yes/Yes	Yes/Yes	No/Yes	Yes/Yes	Yes	No	No	Yes	•Yes, regularly provided funding •Yes, in relation to campaigns	•Share of votes in previo election •Registration as a politica party
Micronesia, Federated States of	No/No	No/No	No/No	No/No	No/No	No data	No	No	No	No	Not applicable
Moldova, Republic of	Yes/Yes	No/No	Yes/Yes	Yes/No	Yes/Yes	Yes	Yes	Regular limit applies	No	No	Not applicable
Monaco	No/No	No/No	No/No	No/No	No/No	No data	No	No	No	Yes, in relation to campaigns	Share of votes in previous election
Mongolia	Yes/Yes	No/No	Yes/Yes	No/Yes	Yes/Yes	Yes	Yes	Yes	Yes	Yes, regularly provided funding	Representation in elected body
Montenegro	Yes/Yes	No/No	Yes/Yes	Yes/Yes	Yes/Yes	Yes	Yes	Yes	No	•Yes, regularly provided funding •Yes, in relation to campaigns	•Representation in electe body •Participation in election
Morocco	Yes/No data	No/No	Yes/No	No/No	Nn/No data	No data	Yes	Regular limit applies	No	Yes, regularly provided funding	Share of votes in previous election
Mozambique	Yes/Yes	Yes/No	No/No	No/No	No data/No data	Yes	No	No	No	Yes, in relation to campaigns	•Representation in electe body •Participation in election
Myanmar	Yes/No	No/No	No/No	No/No	No data/No data	Yes	No	No	No	No	Not applicable

Allocation calculation for direct public funding	Earmarking for direct public funding	Free or subsidized access to media for political parties/candidates	Provision of direct public funding to political parties related to gender equality among candidates	Provisions for other financial advantages to encourage gender equality in political parties	Limits on the amount a political party/candidate can spend	Political parties have to report on their finances regularly/for election campaigns	Candidates have to report on their campaign finance	Information in financial reports is to be made public/must include identity of donor	Institution mandated to receive financial reports	Institution responsible for examining financial reports and/or investigating violations
…data	No	Yes/No	No	No	No/No	No/No	No	Not applicable/ Not applicable	Not applicable	No
…applicable	Not applicable	No/No	Not applicable	No data	No/Yes	No/No	Yes	No/Yes	EMB	No
…qual …umber of …mbers	No	No/Yes	No	No	No/Yes	Yes/No	Yes	Yes/Yes	• EMB • Ministry	Yes, EMB
…qual …roportional to …ts received …proportion …women …uties (5%) and …nsellors (5%)	No	Yes/Yes	Yes	No	No/No	Yes/No	No	No/No	• Ministry • Court	Yes, court
…applicable	Not applicable	Yes/Yes	Not applicable	No	No/No	No/No	Yes	No/No	EMB	No
…applicable	Not applicable	No/Yes	Not applicable	No	No/No	No/No	No	Not applicable/ Not applicable	Not applicable	No
…applicable	Not applicable	No/No	No	No	No/Yes	Yes/No data	Yes	No/No data	Ministry	No
…applicable	Not applicable	Yes/No	Not applicable	No	No/Yes	No/Yes	Yes	No/Yes	EMB	No
…qual …roportional to …es received	•Campaign spending •Ongoing party activities •Intra-party institution	Yes/No	No	Yes, funds earmarked for gender activities	Yes/Yes	Yes/Yes	No	Yes/Yes	EMB	Yes, EMB
…applicable	Not applicable	No/No	Not applicable	No	No/No	No/No	No	Not applicable/ Not applicable	Not applicable	Yes, EMB
…applicable	Not applicable	Yes/Yes	Not applicable	No	Yes/Yes	Yes/Yes	Yes	Yes/ Sometimes	• EMB • Ministry • Auditing agency	•Yes, EMB •Yes, ministry •Yes, auditing agency
…are of expenses …nbursed	Campaign spending	No/No	No	No	No/No	No/Yes	No	No/No	Ministry	Yes, other
…portional to …es received	Half the ongoing support should go to "parliamentary election unit areas"	Yes/Yes	No	No	Yes/Yes	Yes/Yes	Yes	Yes/Yes	• EMB • Other	•Yes, EMB •Yes, auditing agency
…qual …roportional to …ts received	•Campaign spending •Ongoing party activities •Party offices	Yes/No	No	No	No/No	Yes/Yes	Yes	Yes/Yes	• EMB • Court	•Yes, EMB •Yes, auditing agency
…data	No	Yes/No	No	• Yes, funds earmarked for gender activities • Yes, other	No/Yes	Yes/No	Yes	Yes/No	Special institution	Yes, institution for this purpose
…roportional to …ts received …roportional to …didates fielded	Ongoing party activities	Yes/Yes	No	No	No/No	No/Yes	Yes	Yes/No data	EMB	Yes, EMB
…applicable	Not applicable	No/No	Not applicable	No	No/Yes	Yes/No	Yes	No data/ No data	EMB	Yes, EMB

Country	Ban on foreign donations to parties/candidates	Ban on corporate donations to parties/candidates	Ban on donations from corporations with government contracts or partial gov't. ownership to parties/candidates	Ban on trade union donations to parties/candidates	Ban on anonymous donations to parties/candidates	Ban on state resources being given to or received by political parties or candidates	Limit on the amount a donor can contribute to a political party over a time period	Limit on the amount a donor can contribute to a political party in relation to an election	Limit on the amount a donor can contribute to a candidate	Provisions for direct public funding to political parties	public funding
Namibia	No/No	No/No	No/No	No/No	No/No data	No	No	No	No	Yes, regularly provided funding	Representation in elected body
Nauru	No/No	No/No	No/No	No/No	No/No	No data	No	No	No	No	Not applicable
Nepal	Yes/Yes	No/No	Yes/Yes	No/No	No, but specific limit/No data	No data	No	No	No	No	Not applicable
Netherlands	No/No	No/No	No/No	No/No	No/No, but specific limit	No data	No	No	No	Yes, regularly provided funding	•Representation in elected body •Number of members
New Zealand	No/No	No/No	No/No	No/No	No, but specific limit/No, but specific limit	Yes	No	No	No	•Yes, regularly provided funding •Yes, in relation to campaigns	•Representation in elected body •Registration as a political party •Party must give notice
Nicaragua	No/No	No/No	No/No	No/No	Yes/No data	Yes	No	No	No	Yes, in relation to campaigns	Share of votes in next election
Niger	Yes/No	No/No	No/No data	No/No	Yes/No data	Yes	No	No	No	Yes, regularly provided funding	•Representation in elected body •Participation in election •Having women candidate elected
Nigeria	Yes/No	No/No	No/No	No/No	Yes/No	No data	No	No	Yes	No	Not applicable
Norway	Yes/No	No/No	No/No	No/No	Yes/No	Yes	No	No	No	Yes, regularly provided funding	•Representation in elected body •Share of votes in previous election •For part of the funding there is no threshold
Pakistan	Yes/No	Yes/No	Yes/No	Yes/No	Yes/Yes	No data	No	No	No	No	Not applicable
Palau	No/Yes	No/No	No/No	No/No	No/No, but specific limit	No data	No	No	No	No	Not applicable
Panama	Yes/Yes	No/No	Yes/Yes	No/No	Yes/Yes	No data	No	No	No	•Yes, regularly provided funding •Yes, in relation to campaigns	•Participation in election •Registration as a political party
Papua New Guinea	Yes/No	No/No	No/No	No/No	Yes/Yes	No data	Yes	Regular limit applies	Yes	Yes, regularly provided funding	•Representation in elected body •Filing of a financial return
Paraguay	Yes/Yes	Yes/Yes	Yes/Yes	Yes/Yes	Yes/Yes	Yes	No	Yes	No	•Yes, regularly provided funding •Yes, in relation to campaigns	Registration
Peru	Yes/Yes	No/Yes	Yes/Yes	No/Yes	No, but specific limit/Yes	No data	Yes	Regular limit applies	Yes	Yes, regularly provided funding	Representation in elected body
Philippines	Yes/Yes	Yes/Yes	Yes/Yes	No/No	Yes/Yes	Yes	No	No	No	No	Not applicable

Allocation calculation for direct public funding	Earmarking for direct public funding	Free or subsidized access to media for political parties/candidates	Provision of direct public funding to political parties related to gender equality among candidates	Provisions for other financial advantages to encourage gender equality in political parties	Limits on the amount a political party/candidate can spend	Political parties have to report on their finances regularly/for election campaigns	Candidates have to report on their campaign finance	Information in financial reports is to be made public/must include identity of donor	Institution mandated to receive financial reports	Institution responsible for examining financial reports and/or investigating violations
…portional to …es received	No	Yes/No	No	No	No/No	No/No	No	Not applicable/ Not applicable	Not applicable	No
…t applicable	Not applicable	No/No	Not applicable	No	No/No	No/No	No	Not applicable/ Not applicable	Not applicable	No
…t applicable	Not applicable	Yes/No	Not applicable	No	Yes/Yes	Yes/Yes	Yes	Yes/ Sometimes	EMB	•Yes, EMB •Yes, other
…qual …roportional to …ats received	•Campaign spending •Ongoing party activities •Intra-party institution	Yes/No	No	No	No/No	Yes/No	No	Yes/ Sometimes	Ministry	Yes, ministry
…roportional to …es received …roportional to …ats received	•Campaign spending •Ongoing party activities	Yes/No	No	No	Yes/Yes	Yes/Yes	Yes	Yes/ Sometimes	EMB	•Yes, EMB •Yes, other
…portional to …es received	No	Yes/No	No	No	No/No	Yes/No	No	Yes/No	• EMB • Ministry • Auditing agency	No
…qual …roportional to …ats received …/omen	No	Yes/Yes	Yes	No	No/No	Yes/No	No	Yes/Yes	Court	Yes, court
…t applicable	Not applicable	Yes/Yes	Not applicable	No	No/Yes	Yes/Yes	No	Yes/Yes	EMB	Yes, EMB
…portional to …es received	No	No/No	No	No	No/No	Yes/Yes	No	Yes/ Sometimes	Other	•Yes, institution for this purpose
…t applicable	Not applicable	No/No	Not applicable	No	No/Yes	Yes/No	Yes	Yes/Yes	EMB	No
…t applicable	Not applicable	No/No	Not applicable	No	No/No	No/No	Yes	Yes/ Sometimes	Other	•Yes, EMB •Yes, other
…qual …roportional to …es received	•Campaign spending •Ongoing party activities •Civic and political education and women training	Yes/No	No	Yes, funds earmarked for gender activities	No/No	Yes/Yes	Yes	No/Yes	EMB	Yes, EMB
…roportional to …ats received …/omen	No	No/No	Yes	No	No/No	Yes/Yes	Yes	No/Yes	Special institution	Yes, other
…lat rate by votes …eived …roportional to …ats received	Campaign spending	Yes/No	No	No	No/No	Yes/Yes	Yes	No/Yes	EMB	Yes, EMB
…qual …roportional to …es received	Ongoing party activities	Yes/No	No	No	No/No	Yes/Yes	Yes	Yes/Yes	EMB	Yes, EMB
…t applicable	Not applicable	No/Yes	Not applicable	No	Yes/Yes	No/Yes	Yes	No/Yes	EMB	Yes, EMB

Country	Ban on foreign donations to parties/candidates	Ban on corporate donations to parties/candidates	Ban on donations from corporations with government contracts or partial gov't. ownership to parties/candidates	Ban on trade union donations to parties/candidates	Ban on anonymous donations to parties/candidates	Ban on state resources being given to or received by political parties or candidates	Limit on the amount a donor can contribute to a political party over a time period	Limit on the amount a donor can contribute to a political party in relation to an election	Limit on the amount a donor can contribute to a candidate	Provisions for direct public funding to political parties	public funding
Poland	Yes/Yes	Yes/Yes	Yes/Yes	Yes/Yes	Yes/No, but specific limit	Yes	Yes	Yes	Yes	Yes, regularly provided funding	Share of votes in previous election
Portugal	Yes/Yes	Yes/Yes	Yes/Yes	Yes/Yes	Yes/Yes	Yes	Yes	Yes	Yes	•Yes, regularly provided funding •Yes, in relation to campaigns	•Representation in elected body •Share of votes in previous election •Number of candidates •Participation in election
Republic of The Congo (Brazzaville)	Yes/No data	Yes/No data	No/No	No/No	Yes/No data	No data	Yes	Regular limit applies	No data	Yes, regularly provided funding	•Representation in elected body •Share of votes in previous election
Romania	Yes/Yes	No/Yes	Yes/Yes	Yes/Yes	No, but specific limit/No	Yes	Yes	Yes	No	Yes, regularly provided funding	•Representation in elected body •Share of seats in previous election
Russian Federation	Yes/Yes	Yes/No	Yes/Yes	No/No	Yes/Yes	Yes	Yes	Yes	Yes	Yes, regularly provided funding	Share of votes in previous election
Rwanda	Yes/No	No/No	No/No	No/No	Yes/No data	Yes	No	No	No	•Yes, regularly provided funding •Yes, in relation to campaigns	Share of votes in previous election
Saint Kitts and Nevis	No/No	No/No	No/No	No/No	No/No	No data	No	No	No	No	Not applicable
Saint Lucia	No/No	No/No	No/No	No/No	No/No	No data	No	No	No	No	Not applicable
Saint Vincent and The Grenadines	No data/No data	No data/No data	No data/No data	No data/No data	No data/No data	No data	No	No	No	Yes, regularly provided funding	Representation in elected body
Samoa	No data/No data	No data/No data	No data/No data	No data/No data	No data/No data	No data	No data	No data	No data	No data	No data
San Marino	No/No data	No data/No data	No data/No data	No data/No data	Yes/No data	No data	No data	No data	No data	Yes, regularly provided funding	Representation in elected body
Sao Tome and Principe	Yes/Yes	Yes/Yes	Yes/Yes	No data/Yes	Yes/No data	No data	Yes	No data	Yes	•Yes, regularly provided funding •Yes, in relation to campaigns	•Representation in elected body •Share of votes in previous election •Number of candidates
Senegal	Yes/No	No/No	No/No	No/No	No data/No data	No data	No	No	No	No	Not applicable

Allocation calculation for direct public funding	Earmarking for direct public funding	Free or subsidized access to media for political parties/candidates	Provision of direct public funding to political parties related to gender equality among candidates	Provisions for other financial advantages to encourage gender equality in political parties	Limits on the amount a political party/candidate can spend	Political parties have to report on their finances regularly/for election campaigns	Candidates have to report on their campaign finance	Information in financial reports is to be made public/must include identity of donor	Institution mandated to receive financial reports	Institution responsible for examining financial reports and/or investigating violations
portional to es received	•Campaign spending •Activities in line with the party constitution and charity	Yes/Yes	No	No	Yes/Yes	Yes/Yes	Yes	Yes/Sometimes	EMB	Yes, EMB
qual roportional to es received	No	Yes/Yes	Yes	No	Yes/Yes	Yes/Yes	Yes	Yes/Yes	• EMB • Court	•Yes, EMB •Yes, court •Yes, institution for this purpose
known	No	Yes/Yes	No	No	No/No	Yes/No	No	No/Yes	Ministry	No
portional to es received	•Campaign spending •Ongoing party activities	Yes/Yes	Yes	No	Yes/Yes	Yes/Yes	Yes	Yes/Sometimes	EMB	•Yes, EMB •Yes, court
t rate by votes eived	Realize the objectives and to attain the goals provided in the charter and program of a political party	Yes/Yes	No	No	Yes/Yes	Yes/Yes	Yes	Yes/Yes	EMB	•Yes, EMB •Yes, other
ual	•Campaign spending •Ongoing party activities	Yes/Yes	No	No	No/No	Yes/No	No	No/Yes	• Ministry • Special institution	Yes, institution for this purpose
t applicable	Not applicable	No/No	Not applicable	No	No/No	No/No	No	Not applicable/ Not applicable	Not applicable	No
t applicable	Not applicable	Yes/Yes	Not applicable	No	No/No	No/No	No	Not applicable/ Not applicable	Not applicable	No
data	No data	No/No	No data	No data	No/No	No/No	No	Not applicable/ Not applicable	Not applicable	No data
data	No data	No data/ No data	No data	No data	No data/ No data	No/No	No	Not applicable/ Not applicable	Not applicable	No data
portional to ats received	No data	Yes/Yes	No data	No data	Yes/Yes	Yes/Yes	No	Yes/ Sometimes	• EMB • Auditing agency	No data
qual roportional to es received	No	No data/ No data	No	No	Yes/No	Yes/Yes	No data	Yes/No data	Court	Yes, court
t applicable	Not applicable	Yes/Yes	Not applicable	No	No/No	Yes/No	No	No/No	Ministry	No

385

Country	Ban on foreign donations to parties/candidates	Ban on corporate donations to parties/candidates	Ban on donations from corporations with government contracts or partial gov't. ownership to parties/candidates	Ban on trade union donations to parties/candidates	Ban on anonymous donations to parties/candidates	Ban on state resources being given to or received by political parties or candidates	Limit on the amount a donor can contribute to a political party over a time period	Limit on the amount a donor can contribute to a political party in relation to an election	Limit on the amount a donor can contribute to a candidate	Provisions for direct public funding to political parties	public funding
Serbia	Yes/Yes	No/No	Yes/Yes	Yes/Yes	Yes/Yes	Yes	Yes	Yes	Yes	•Yes, regularly provided funding •Yes, in relation to campaigns	•Representation in electe body •Share of votes in previou election •Participation in election
Seychelles	No/No	No/No	No/No	No/No	No/No	No data	No	No	No	Yes, regularly provided funding	•Number of candidates •Registration as a politica party
Sierra Leone	Yes/No	Yes/No	Yes/No	Yes/No	Yes/Yes	Yes	No	No	No	No	Not applicable
Singapore	Yes/Yes	No/No	No/No	Yes/Yes	Yes/No, but specific limit	No data	No	No	No	No	Not applicable
Slovakia	Yes/Yes	No/No	Yes/No	Yes/No	Yes/No, but specific limit	Yes	No	No	No	• Yes, regularly provided funding • Yes, in relation to campaigns	•Representation in electe body •Share of votes in previou election
Slovenia	Yes/Yes	No/No	Yes/Yes	No/No	No, but specific limit/No, but specific limit	No data	Yes	Regular limit applies	Yes	Yes, regularly provided funding	Share of votes in previous election
Solomon Islands	No/No	No/No	No/No	No/No	No/No	No data	No	No	No	No	Not applicable
South Africa	No/No	No/No	No/No	No/No	No/No data	No	No	No	No	Yes, regularly provided funding	Representation in elected body
Spain	Yes/No	No/No	Yes/No	No/No	No/No	Yes	Yes	Yes	No	•Yes, regularly provided funding •Yes, in relation to campaigns	•Representation in electe body • Not having anyone in leading position who has been found guilty of serio offence
Sri Lanka	No/No	No/No	No/No	No/No	No/No	No	No	No	No	Yes, in relation to campaigns	•Share of votes in previou election •Application

Allocation calculation for direct public funding	Earmarking for direct public funding	Free or subsidized access to media for political parties/candidates	Provision of direct public funding to political parties related to gender equality among candidates	Provisions for other financial advantages to encourage gender equality in political parties	Limits on the amount a political party/candidate can spend	Political parties have to report on their finances regularly/for election campaigns	Candidates have to report on their campaign finance	Information in financial reports is to be made public/must include identity of donor	Institution mandated to receive financial reports	Institution responsible for examining financial reports and/or investigating violations
portional to es received	•Ongoing party activities •Professional upgrading and training, acquiring practical skills, international cooperation and work with membership	Yes/Yes	Yes	No	No/No	Yes/Yes	Yes	Yes/Yes	Special institution	•Yes, auditing agency •Yes, institution for this purpose
portional to es received	No	Yes/Yes	No	No	No/No	No/Yes	Yes	No/No	EMB	Yes, institution for this purpose
applicable	Not applicable	Yes/Yes	Not applicable	No	No/No	Yes/Yes	Yes	Yes/Yes	Special institution	Yes, institution for this purpose
applicable	Not applicable	No/No	Not applicable	No	No/Yes	Yes/No data	Yes	Yes/Sometimes	• Special institution • Other	No
roportional to es received roportional to ats received	Must not be used for loans, settling fines, donations or to support Presidential election campaigns	Yes/Yes	No	No	Yes/Yes	Yes/Yes	Yes	Yes/Sometimes	• Ministry • Other	•Yes, ministry •Yes, other
qual roportional to es received	No	Yes/Yes	No	No	Yes/Yes	Yes/Yes	Yes	Yes/Sometimes	• Auditing agency • Other	•Yes, auditing agency •Yes, other
applicable	Not applicable	No data/No data	Not applicable	No	No/Yes	No/No	Yes	No/No	EMB	Yes, EMB
qual roportional to ats received	•Campaign spending •Ongoing party activities •Intra-party institution	No/No	No	No	No/No	Yes/No	No	Yes/No	EMB	Yes, auditing agency
roportional to es received roportional to ats received	•Campaign spending •Ongoing party activities •Extraordinary subsidies for advertising purposes & security expenses, direct public funding from the budget of local communities, extraordinary funds for referendum purposes	Yes/No	No	No	Yes/No	Yes/Yes	No	No/Yes	Auditing agency	Yes, auditing agency
rate by votes eived	No	Yes/Yes	No	No	No/No	Yes/No	No data	No data/Not applicable	EMB	No data

Country	Ban on foreign donations to parties/candidates	Ban on corporate donations to parties/candidates	Ban on donations from corporations with government contracts or partial gov't. ownership to parties/candidates	Ban on trade union donations to parties/candidates	Ban on anonymous donations to parties/candidates	Ban on state resources being given to or received by political parties or candidates	Limit on the amount a donor can contribute to a political party over a time period	Limit on the amount a donor can contribute to a political party in relation to an election	Limit on the amount a donor can contribute to a candidate	Provisions for direct public funding to political parties	public funding
Sudan	Yes/Yes	No/No	No/No	No/No	Yes/Yes	Yes	No	No	No	No	Not applicable
Suriname	No data/No data	No data/No data	No data/No data	No data/No data	No data/No data	No data	No	No	No	No	Not applicable
Swaziland	No/No	No/No	No/No	No/No	No/No data	No	No	No	No	No	Not applicable
Sweden	Yes/Yes	No/No	No/No	No/No	No/No	Yes	No	No	No	Yes, regularly provided funding	•Representation in electe[d] body •Share of votes in previou[s] election •Not having accepted anonymous donations
Switzerland	No/No	No/No	No/No	No/No	No/No	No data	No	No	No	No	Not applicable
Syrian Arab Republic	Yes/No	No/No	No/No	No/No	Yes/No data	No data	Yes	Regular limit applies	No	Yes, regularly provided funding	•Representation in electe[d] body •Share of votes in previou[s] election
Taiwan	Yes/Yes	No/No	Yes/No	No/No	Yes/Yes	Yes	Yes	Regular limit applies	Yes	Yes, regularly provided funding	•Share of votes in previou[s] election •Showing receipts to the Central Election Commission.
Tajikistan	Yes/Yes	No/No	Yes/No	No/No	Yes/Yes	Yes	No	Yes	Yes	Yes, in relation to campaigns	Registration as a political party
Tanzania, United Republic of	No/Yes	No/No	No/No	No/No	Yes/Yes	No data	No	No	No	Yes, regularly provided funding	Representation in elected body
Thailand	Yes/No	No/No	Yes/No	No/No	No, but specific limit/No data	Yes	No	No	No	Yes, regularly provided funding	•Share of votes in previou[s] election •Matching funds availabl[e] to all parties receiving certain type of small priva[te] donations.
Togo	No/No	No/No	No/No	No/No	No data/No data	No data	No	No	No	Yes, regularly provided funding	•Representation in electe[d] body •Share of votes in previou[s] election
Tonga	No/No	No/No	No/No	No/No	No/No	No	No	No	No	No data	No data
Trinidad and Tobago	No data/No data	No/No data	No data/No data	No data/No data	No data/Yes	No data	No	No	Yes	No	Not applicable
Tunisia	Yes/Yes	Yes/Yes	Yes/Yes	Yes/Yes	Yes/Yes	Yes	Yes	Regular limit applies	Yes	Yes, in relation to campaigns	Participation in election
Turkey	Yes/Yes	No/No	Yes/No	No/No	Yes/No	Yes	Yes	Regular limit applies	No	•Yes, regularly provided funding •Yes, in relation to campaigns	Share of votes in previous election

388

Allocation calculation for direct public funding	Earmarking for direct public funding	Free or subsidised access to media for political parties/candidates	Provision of direct public funding to political parties related to gender equality among candidates	Provisions for other financial advantages to encourage gender equality in political parties	Limits on the amount a political party/candidate can spend	Political parties have to report on their finances regularly/for election campaigns	Candidates have to report on their campaign finance	Information in financial reports is to be made public/must include identity of donor	Institution mandated to receive financial reports	Institution responsible for examining financial reports and/or investigating violations
t applicable	Not applicable	Yes/No	Not applicable	No	No/Yes	Yes/Yes	Yes	Yes/Yes	• EMB • Special institution	No
t applicable	Not applicable	Yes/No data	Not applicable	No	No/No	Yes/Yes	Yes	Yes/No data	Other	No
t applicable	Not applicable	No/No	Not applicable	No	No/No	No/No	No	Not applicable/ Not applicable	Not applicable	No
qual roportional to es received roportional to ats received	No	No/No	No	No	No/No	Yes/No	No	Yes/ Sometimes	Other	Yes, other
t applicable	Not applicable	Yes/No	Not applicable	No	No/No	No/No	No	Not applicable/ Not applicable	Not applicable	No
roportional to es received roportional to ats received	No	Yes/No	No	No	No/No	Yes/No	No	No/Yes	No data	Yes, institution for this purpose
t rate by votes eived	Campaign spending	Yes/Yes	No	No	No/Yes	Yes/No	Yes	No/Yes	Other	Yes, other
ual	No	Yes/Yes	No	No	No/Yes	Yes/Yes	Yes	Yes/Yes	EMB	Yes, EMB
roportional to es received roportional to ats received	No	Yes/Yes	No	No	Yes/Yes	Yes/Yes	No	No/Yes	Special institution	Yes, auditing agency
roportional to es received umber of mbers umber of party nches and tching funds of donations exceeding baht, not eeding 50% of al allocation of lic funds)	No	Yes/No	No	No	Yes/Yes	Yes/Yes	Yes	Yes/ Sometimes	EMB	Yes, EMB
roportional to es received roportional to ats received umber of men elected	No	Yes/Yes	Yes	Yes, reduced nomination fee	Yes/Yes	Yes/Yes	Yes	Yes/Yes	• Court • Other	Yes, court
data	No data	No data/ No data	No data	No data	No/Yes	No/No	Yes	No/No	Other	No
t applicable	Not applicable	Yes/No data	Not applicable	No data	No/Yes	No/No	Yes	Yes/Yes	EMB	No data
ual	No	Yes/No	No	No	Yes/Yes	Yes/Yes	Yes	Yes/Yes	Auditing agency	•Yes, EMB •Yes, auditing agency
portional to es received	No	Yes/No	No	No	No/No	Yes/No	No	No/Yes	• Court • Other	Yes, court

Country	Ban on foreign donations to parties/candidates	Ban on corporate donations to parties/candidates	Ban on donations from corporations with government contracts or partial gov't. ownership to parties/candidates	Ban on trade union donations to parties/candidates	Ban on anonymous donations to parties/candidates	Ban on state resources being given to or received by political parties or candidates	Limit on the amount a donor can contribute to a political party over a time period	Limit on the amount a donor can contribute to a political party in relation to an election	Limit on the amount a donor can contribute to a candidate	Provisions for direct public funding to political parties	public funding
Turkmenistan	Yes/No	No/No	No/No	No/No	Yes/No	Yes	No	No	No	No	Not applicable
Tuvalu	No/No data	No/No data	No/No data	No/No data	No/No data	No data	No	No	No data	No data	No data
Uganda	No/Yes	No/No	No/No	No/No	Yes/Yes	Yes	Yes	Regular limit applies	No	•Yes, regularly provided funding •Yes, in relation to campaigns	Representation in elected body
Ukraine	Yes/Yes	No/Yes	Yes/Yes	No/Yes	Yes/Yes	Yes	No	Yes	Yes	No	Not applicable
United Kingdom	Yes/Yes	No/No	No/No	No/No	No, but specific limit/No, but specific limit	Yes	No	No	No	Yes, regularly provided funding	•Representation in elected body •Share of votes in previous election •Share of seats in next election
United States	Yes/Yes	Yes/Yes	Yes/Yes	Yes/Yes	No, but specific limit/No, but specific limit	Yes	Yes	Regular limit applies	Yes	Yes, in relation to campaigns	•Share of votes in previous election •Share of votes in next election •Limit campaign expenses and private contributions; providing closed captioning in tv commercials for hearing impaired individuals
Uruguay	Yes/Yes	No/No	Yes/Yes	Yes/Yes	No, but specific limit/No, but specific limit	No	Yes	Regular limit applies	Yes	•Yes, regularly provided funding •Yes, in relation to campaigns	Registration as a political party
Uzbekistan	Yes/Yes	No/Yes	No/Yes	No/Yes	Yes/Yes	No data	Yes	Yes	Yes	•Yes, regularly provided funding •Yes, in relation to campaigns	•Share of seats in previous election •Participation in election
Vanuatu	No/No	No/No	No/No	No/No	No/No	No data	No	No	No	No	Not applicable
Venezuela	Yes/Yes	No/No	Yes/Yes	No/No	Yes/Yes	Yes	No	No	No	No	Not applicable
Yemen	Yes/Yes	No/Yes	No/Yes	No/No	Yes/No	Yes	No	No	No	Yes, regularly provided funding	•Representation in elected body •Share of votes in previous election
Zambia	No/No	No/No	No/No	No/No	No/No	Yes	No	No	No	No	Not applicable
Zimbabwe	Yes/Yes	No/No	No/No	No/No	No/No	No	No	No	No	Yes, regularly provided funding	Share of votes in previous election

Allocation calculation for direct public funding	Earmarking for direct public funding	Free or subsidized access to media for political parties/candidates	Provision of direct public funding to political parties related to gender equality among candidates	Provisions for other financial advantages to encourage gender equality in political parties	Limits on the amount a political party/candidate can spend	Political parties have to report on their finances regularly/for election campaigns	Candidates have to report on their campaign finance	Information in financial reports is to be made public/must include identity of donor	Institution mandated to receive financial reports	Institution responsible for examining financial reports and/or investigating violations
applicable	Not applicable	Yes/Yes	Not applicable	No	No/No	No/No	No	Not applicable/ Not applicable	Not applicable	Yes, EMB
data	No data	No data/ No data	No data	No data	No/No data	No data/ No data	No data	No data/ No data	No data	No data
qual oportional to ts received	No	No/Yes	No	No	No/No	Yes/Yes	Yes	Yes/Yes	EMB	Yes, EMB
applicable	Not applicable	Yes/Yes	Not applicable	No	No/No	Yes/Yes	Yes	Yes/ Sometimes	EMB	•Yes, EMB •Yes, other
oportional to es received oportional to ts received nding related he House of ds is determined he House of ds	Public funds are earmarked for the purpose to which they are allocated	Yes/No	No	No	Yes/Yes	Yes/Yes	Yes	Yes/ Sometimes	• Special institution • Other	•Yes, other •Yes, institution for this purpose
al	Nominating convention	No/No	No	No	Yes/No	Yes/Yes	Yes	Yes/ Sometimes	EMB	•Yes, EMB •Yes, ministry
rate by votes eived	No	Yes/Yes	No	No	No/No	Yes/Yes	Yes	Yes/Yes	EMB	Yes, EMB
oportional to ts received etermined	•Campaign spending •Ongoing party activities	Yes/Yes	No	No	No/No	Yes/No	No	Yes/Yes	• Ministry • Auditing agency • Other	•Yes, auditing agency •Yes, other
applicable	Not applicable	No data/ No data	Not applicable	No	No/No	No/No	No	Not applicable/ No	Not applicable	No
applicable	Not applicable	No/Yes	Not applicable	No	No/No	No/Yes	Yes	No/Yes	EMB	Yes, EMB
qual oportional to es received	Goals and activities established by party by-laws	Yes/Yes	No	No	No/No	Yes/No	No	No/ Sometimes	Special institution	Yes, institution for this purpose
applicable	Not applicable	Yes/Yes	Not applicable	No	No/No	No/No	No	Not applicable/ No	Not applicable	No
portional to es received	No	Yes/Yes	No	No	No/No	No/No	No	Not applicable/ Not applicable	Not applicable	No

Annex II: Glossary

Abuse of state resources: The use of state and public sector powers and resources by (normally) incumbent politicians or political parties to further their own prospects of election, in violation of legal and/or other norms and responsibilities governing the exercise of public office.

Allocation criteria for public funding: The rules regarding how public funding should be divided among eligible political parties or candidates. (See also *Eligibility criteria for public funding*)

Campaign finance: Financial transactions related to an electoral campaign that could include formal, financial, or in-kind donations or expenditures.

Campaign finance account: Special bank account for party or candidate campaign finance. In many cases, parties/candidates are required to report information about their accounts to the enforcing institution, and all donations and spending must go through their accounts.

Cartel parties: Parties that are closely connected to the state apparatus and rely on state resources to maintain their position in the political system.

Clientelism: The relationship between politicians/political parties and the voters who exchange their political support in return for various favours.

Commercialization of politics: The trend of overall rising costs for campaigning.

Contribution (or donation) limit: The maximum amount of money that an individual, organization or political party may contribute to a candidate's campaign or to a political party annually or per election period.

Corporate donations: Support for or donations to political parties and/or candidates from entities such as corporations, companies and/or business enterprises.

Direct public funding: Government money provided to political parties or candidates during election campaigns or for regular party financing.

Disclosure: The obligation that political parties and candidates must provide certain financial information, submit reports or make financial statements regularly or in relation to an election campaign. Reports should be submitted to the relevant body or be made public directly by the political party or candidate. The disclosure sometimes includes a requirement to reveal the identity of the donors.

Earmarking of public funding: A provision that public funding provided to political parties or candidates must only be used for certain purposes, such as election campaigns or ongoing party activities, or by particular institutions within the parties.

Electoral district: One of the geographic areas into which a country or region may be divided for electoral purposes.

Electoral management bodies: Organizations that are legally responsible for managing one or more of the elements necessary for conducting elections and direct democracy instruments (e.g., referendums) if they are part of the legal framework.

Eligibility criteria for public funding: Conditions that a political party or candidate must meet in order to access public funding (often a threshold of popular support such as winning a certain share of the vote in an election or a number of seats in an elected body).

Enforcement agencies: Actors that receive and/or investigate financial reports from political parties and/or candidates and can, in certain cases, issue sanctions on parties and/or candidates. Enforcement agencies can be part of different institutions, such as electoral management bodies, courts, auditing institutions or ministries.

Foreign interests: In order to limit influence over national politics to forces within the country, it is common to ban foreign interests from making donations to political parties. Entities that are generally prohibited from contributing directly or indirectly include governments, corporations, organizations or individuals who are not citizens; who do not reside in the country; or which have a large share of foreign ownership.

Illegal funding: Funding that violates political finance regulations.

Illicit funding: Funding that has been earned through activity which is forbidden by law, rules, ethical norms or custom, such as organized crime or the drugs trade. Often called black money or dirty money.

Independent expenditure: Payment in support of a political campaign that explicitly advocates the election or defeat of a candidate, which is made independently of the candidate's campaign (i.e., without the cooperation or consent of or a request from the candidate's campaign). (See also *Third-party campaigning*)

Indirect public funding: The provision of state resources other than money to political parties or candidates (e.g., subsidized or free access to public media, tax relief, advertising).

In-kind donations: Donations of goods and services, as opposed to financial donations.

International dollars: See Annex V for an explanation of international dollars.

Macing: The practice of requiring public servants to make contributions to the party in power in order to keep their jobs or promote their careers.

Monitoring agencies: See *Enforcement agencies*

Party taxes: When parties oblige their elected representatives and/or other office holders to turn over a portion of their income earned in office to the party.

Political finance: All financial flows to and from political parties, candidates and third parties (including formal and informal income and expenditure, and financial and in-kind contributions). These transactions are not limited to a certain time period.

Political party finance: The income and expenditure of political parties, both regularly and in relation to political party election campaigns.

Private donations: Financial contributions from individuals or non-state legal persons that fund the activities of political parties, candidates and electoral campaigns.

Professionalization of politics: The expanded use of marketing and research in the political process, in which parties employ a range of strategies to gauge and influence voters. It often involves the use of public relations firms, social media strategists, polls and focus groups.

Public funding: Assistance provided by the government to qualified political parties or candidates for their campaigns or regular party activities. (See also *Direct public funding* and *Indirect public funding*)

Quid pro quo donations: Contributions made in expectation of a personal or institutional gain in return.

Sanctions: Penalties imposed to punish the financial misconduct of a party or candidate that has violated a regulation. Common sanctions include warnings, fines, prison terms, loss of public funding and forfeiture.

Spending limits: The maximum amount that a political party or a candidate can spend during the electoral campaign period or during a defined period of time (e.g., per constituency or per voter).

Third-party campaigning: Electoral campaigning undertaken by individuals and/or organizations other than political parties or candidates. These third parties may campaign for or against specific parties, candidates or issues.

Vote buying: A form of electoral fraud that is intended to increase the number of votes a particular candidate or political party receives in an election by promising or providing money or other benefits to constituents in exchange for their vote.

Westminster model: A democratic parliamentary system of government modelled after that of the United Kingdom, where the government is formed from the legislature.

Annex III: About the authors

Julie Ballington is the policy advisor on Political Participation in the Leadership and Governance Section at UN Women. She oversees the section's work on women's political participation, including in electoral assistance, parliamentary strengthening, political party support and governance at the local level. She previously served as the UN Development Programme's gender advisor in the Global Programme on Elections within the Division for Democratic Governance. Prior to joining the UN, Julie was the programme specialist in the Gender Partnership Programme at the Inter-Parliamentary Union, where she worked on enhancing women's participation in parliaments, in electoral processes and within political parties. She also led the project on Gender-Sensitive Parliaments. From 2001 to 2005 she was responsible for the Women in Politics Programme at International IDEA, where she initiated the global project on Electoral Quotas for Women. She also previously worked at the Electoral Institute of Southern Africa, managing its work on gender-related aspects of electoral participation and administration in Southern Africa. She has also participated in several electoral observation missions in Africa and the Middle East. Julie holds a Master's degree in Political Science from the University of Witwatersrand in Johannesburg, South Africa, and a Bachelor's degree in Political Science and Philosophy from Auckland University, New Zealand.

Elin Falguera works as a programme officer in International IDEA's Political Parties team and is the project manager of the Institute's global project on political finance. In addition to researching and writing about the impact of money on politics, she has provided legislative advice in the area of political finance law and was co-creator of the 2012 International IDEA Political Finance Database. Before joining International IDEA, she worked as an independent researcher. She holds a Master's degree in Public Administration from the University of Gothenburg, Sweden.

Dr Muriel Kahane joined UN Women in 2011 as a policy analyst on Political Participation and Constitutional Reform in the Leadership and Governance Section. She also serves as the policy focal point on Youth. Muriel supports UN Women's work on electoral assistance, parliamentary support, constitutional reform and local-level governance. She was previously a researcher for the UK Parliament, focusing on gender issues, human trafficking and European affairs. Between 2003 and 2010 she was a founding member and European research director of Transform, a Berlin-based NGO focused on conflict transformation and civil society engagement. Muriel has taught political science and theory at the London School of Economics and Political Science (LSE) and the Open University in the United Kingdom. She holds a Bachelor's degree in Sociology, a Master's degree in Political Theory and a PhD in Gender and Government, all from the LSE.

Juan Fernando Londoño served as Vice-Minister of the Interior in Colombia from 2011 to 2012 and has worked on political financing issues as a policy maker. In 2002, he promoted the creation of the Inter-American Forum of Political Parties in the Organization of American States (OAS) and contributed to a report on political financing in the region (*From Norms to Good Practices: The Challenges of Political Finance in the Americas*), which was jointly published by International IDEA and the OAS, under the coordination of Daniel Zovatto and Steve Griner. In 2004, he advised the Colombian Senate on the drafting of Law No. 996 of 2005, known in Colombia as the Electoral Guarantees Law. He subsequently coordinated the Project for Strengthening Democracy, sponsored by the UN Development Programme and International IDEA from 2007 to 2009, which contributed significantly to the approval of the constitutional reform of 2009. In 2010, he advised the Ministry of the Interior on the formulation and discussion of the Political Parties Law, which became Law No. 1475 of 2011. He now works as a political consultant.

Professor Karl-Heinz Nassmacher is professor emeritus of Political Science at the Institute of Social Sciences at Carl von Ossietzky University in Oldenburg, Germany. His books include *Bürger finanzieren Wahlkämpfe* [Citizens Financing Election Campaigns] (1992), *Foundations for Democracy: Approaches to Comparative Political Finance* (2001) and *The Funding of Party Competition* (2009). He has also contributed to *Comparative Political Finance in the 1980s* (1989), *Campaign and Party Finance in North America and Western Europe* (1993), *Political Finance Among the Democracies* (1994), *Handbook of Party Politics* (2006), *Money, Corruption, and Political Competition in Established and Emerging Democracies* (2012) and International IDEA's Handbook on Funding of Political Parties and Election Campaigns (2003). Between 1995 and 1999 he was a member of the Presidential Committee of Experts on Party Funding in Germany, and between 1986 and 2006 he served on the board of the Research Committee on Political Finance and Political Corruption of the International Political Science Association.

Dr Magnus Ohman has worked with the issue of political finance since the 1990s, and has conducted both country analyses and reviews of global trends, which have been translated into 11 languages. He has also assisted legislators, regulatory institutions, civil society groups, media and political parties in the area of political finance in over 25 countries. Dr Ohman serves as the senior political finance advisor at the International Foundation for Electoral Systems (IFES), and has worked with institutions such as the Carter Center, the Danish Institute for Parties and Democracy (DIPD), Electoral Reform International Services (ERIS), the European Commission, International IDEA, the Organization for Security and Co-operation in Europe/Office for Democratic Institutions and Human Rights, the Swedish International Development Cooperation Agency (Sida) and the UN Development Programme. He was lead writer for the BRIDGE (Building Resources in Democracy, Governance and Elections) module on political finance, the IFES *Political Finance Oversight Handbook* and the International IDEA Political Finance Database. He is a board member of the Research Committee on Political Finance and Political Corruption of the International Political Science Association. Dr Ohman holds a PhD in Political Science from Uppsala University, Sweden.

Dr Daniela R. Piccio holds a PhD in Political Science from the European University Institute of Florence. She has worked on the role of political parties as channels of political representation, and on their linkages with society and social movements. Since 2010 she has been a member of the European Research Council-funded research project Re-conceptualizing Party Democracy at Leiden University, which has involved conducting research and writing extensively on party regulation and comparative political finance in Europe. Her work has been published with Cambridge University Press and is forthcoming at ECPR Press and Leiden University Press. Additionally, she has provided political finance policy assessments, and has assisted International IDEA in the development of the Political Finance Database.

Dr Fredrik M. Sjöberg is a political scientist and a governance expert with extensive experience from the developing world. He regularly works for the World Bank, EU, UNDP and OSCE on governance and election-related issues, specializing in advanced empirical methods, including experimental methods, fraud forensics and data visualization. Dr Sjöberg was awarded his PhD from Uppsala University's Department of Government. He also has an MPhil degree from the LSE and a BA from Helsinki University. In 2008–09 he was a Fulbright Scholar at Harvard University. Dr Sjöberg has held post-doctoral appointments at Columbia University and New York University.

Dr Daniel Smilov is a comparative constitutional lawyer and political scientist. He is currently programme director at the Centre for Liberal Strategies (Sofia), assistant professor of Political Science at the University of Sofia and recurrent visiting professor in the Legal Studies Department of the

Central European University (Budapest). He has previously been a senior legal consultant at COLPI and the Open Society Institute in Budapest, and a research fellow at the Centre for Policy Studies at the Central European University. Dr Smilov holds doctorates from the Central European University (1999) and the University of Oxford (2003) and is a member of the Bulgarian European Community Studies Association as well as the Research Committee on Political Finance and Political Corruption of the International Political Science Association.

Professor Andreas Ufen is a senior research fellow at the German Institute of Global and Area Studies in Hamburg, Germany and professor of Political Science in Erlangen-Nuremberg, Germany. He is also co-editor of the *Journal of Current Southeast Asian Affairs*. Among his publications are books on politics in Malaysia and Indonesia, edited volumes on *Democratization in Post-Suharto Indonesia and Party Politics in Southeast Asia, Clientelism and Electoral Competition in Indonesia, Thailand and the Philippines*, and articles in journals such as *Pacific Review, Southeast Asia Research, Democratization* and *Asian Survey*.

Dr Daniel Zovatto has been International IDEA's regional director for Latin America and the Caribbean since 1997. He has a PhD in International Law from the Universidad Complutense de Madrid, and a PhD in Government and Public Administration from the Instituto Universitario de Investigación Ortega y Gassett of Spain. He has an MA in Public Management from the John F. Kennedy School of Government at Harvard University, as well as an MA in International Studies from the Escuela Diplomática del Ministerio de Relaciones Exteriores of Spain. He holds a law degree from the Universidad Nacional de Córdoba, and has a licentiate degree in Political Sciences and International Relations from the Universidad Católica de Córdoba. He is a political analyst for CNN en Español, and for various Ibero-American media outlets. He is an international speaker and visiting professor in several Latin American, European and North American universities, and an advisor to several Latin American governments. He is a member of the Latinobarómetro international advisory board, as well as of the international advisory board for the Latin American Program of the Woodrow Wilson International Center for Scholars (United States), the African Governance Programme of the Mo Ibrahim Foundation (UK), the Council of Arab Relations with Latin America and the Caribbean (CARLAC), the editorial board of Foreign Affairs Latinoamérica, and the external advisory board of the Political Studies Department at the Salvadoran Foundation for Economic and Social Development (FUSADES), and is a non-resident senior fellow with *Foreign Policy*'s Latin American Initiative at the Brookings Institution. He is the author of over 20 books and 100 articles on law, democracy, elections, political parties and governability in Latin America.

Annex IV: International dollars (I$)

The international dollar (I$) is a hypothetical currency that has the same purchasing power for goods and services in all countries. In the International IDEA Database on Political Finance (Political Finance Database), in order to make the monetary amounts included in this Database more readily comparable and consistent over relative price and income levels in various countries, currency conversions to international dollars have been made, based on data provided by the University of Pennsylvania's world table.

The Penn World Table provides purchasing power parity (PPP)-based conversion rates for 189 countries/territories for some or all of the years 1950–2010. This handbook uses the 2010 conversion rates. The conversion rates use the price levels in the United States as the baseline, which means that one US dollar equals one international dollar (although the I$ rate is different in other countries using the US dollar as currency due to differences in PPP).

The international dollar value can be obtained by dividing the given amount in the national currency by the PPP rate.

For example, 500,000 Icelandic Krona (ISK)

500,000/124.09 (the PPP conversion rate for Iceland) = 4029.33

= I$ 4029.33

In order to maintain consistency, amounts up to I$1,000 have been rounded to the nearest I$10 and amounts up to I$10,000 to the nearest I$100. Amounts between I$10,000 and I$999,999 have been rounded to the nearest I$1,000. All amounts over I$1,000,000 have been rounded to the nearest I$10,000.

This handbook throughout lists the international dollar value along with the amount in the national currency, except for US dollar values (as these are by default the same amount as the I$). No conversions are given in those instances where the original currency is unknown and a secondary currency such as the euro has been cited instead.

For further information on the Penn World Table, see http://pwt.econ.upenn. edu/php_site/pwt_index.php

Annex V:
About International IDEA

What is International IDEA?

The International Institute for Democracy and Electoral Assistance (International IDEA) is an intergovernmental organization with a mission to support sustainable democracy worldwide.

The objectives of the Institute are to support stronger democratic institutions and processes, and more sustainable, effective and legitimate democracy.

What does International IDEA do?

The Institute's work is organized at global, regional and country level, focusing on the citizen as the driver of change.

International IDEA produces comparative knowledge in its key areas of expertise: electoral processes, constitution building, political participation and representation, and democracy and development, as well as on democracy as it relates to gender, diversity, and conflict and security.

IDEA brings this knowledge to national and local actors who are working for democratic reform, and facilitates dialogue in support of democratic change.

In its work, IDEA aims for:

- increased capacity, legitimacy and credibility of democracy;
- more inclusive participation and accountable representation; and
- more effective and legitimate democracy cooperation.

Where does International IDEA work?

International IDEA works worldwide. Based in Stockholm, Sweden, the Institute has offices in the Africa, Asia and the Pacific, Latin America and the Caribbean, and West Asia and North Africa regions.

Index

A

E

F

Gutierrez, Lucio (President of Ecuador), 132

H

Haiti, 320-2, 325, 376
    gender equality, financing for, 321-2, 325
    political finance regulation in, 376
    public funding in, 320
Hasina, Sheik, 85
Honduras, 140-3, 322, 325, 376
    gender equality, financing for, 142, 322, 325
    political finance regulation in, 376
    public funding in, 140-1, 143
Hungary, 180-1, 183, 187, 189, 376
    political finance regulation in, 187, 376
    public funding in, 180-3, 189

I

Iceland, 220-1, 229, 235, 376, 400
    political finance regulation in, 220-1, 229, 235, 376
    public funding in, 220-1
    sanctions, use of in, 235
IDASA (Institute for Democracy in Africa), 63
IFES (International Foundation for Electoral Systems), 189, 332, 398
iKNOW-Politics, 157
illicit funding, 8, 20, 40, 42, 48, 80, 87, 176, 180, 182-3, 237, 312-5, 347, 358-9
India, 85-7, 92-3, 98-9, 102-3, 104-5,108, 110, 269, 306, 376
    clan politics in, 85
    corporate donation in, 93, 110
    financial reporting in, 104-5
    illicit funding in, 87
    political finance regulation in, 86-7, 92-3, 102, 104-5, 110, 376
    political party membership in, 92-3
    public funding in, 98-9
Indian Association for Democratic Reforms, 108-9
Indian National Congress, 92, 121
Indonesia, 8, 83, 86-7, 89-98, 101, 103-5, 107, 331, 376, 399
    financial reporting in, 104
    gender equality, financing for, 331
    illicit funding in, 87
    media access in, 102-3
    political finance regulation in, 89-96, 101, 104-5, 376
    public funding in, 96-98
    sanctions, use of in, 107
Indonesia Corruption Watch, 105, 117

monitoring, electoral, 4, 19, 32, 62, 65, 67, 89, 100, 106-8, 112, 130, 132, 149-50, 155-7, 158, 177-8, 184, 190, 193, 196, 209, 231, 233-4, 237-9, 256, 259, 277-82, 284, 303, 314-5, 333, 335, 348, 351, 355, 357-63, 394

Montenegro, 186-7, 380

  media access in, 186-7

  political finance regulation in, 380

Morales, Evo (President of Bolivia), 135

Morocco, 44, 50-2, 307, 325, 380

  financial reporting in, 44

  gender equality, financing for, 52, 307, 325

  political finance regulation in, 44, 50-2, 307, 325

  public funding in, 50-1

Movement for Democratic Change (MDC - Zimbabwe), 52

Movimiento Al Socialismo Bolivia (MAS), 146

Mozambique, 45, 47, 50-1, 54, 60-1, 69, 380

  abuse of state resources in, 54

  corporate donation in, 45

  financial reporting in, 60-1

  political finance regulation in, 47, 50-1, 60-1, 380

  public funding in, 50-1

MPLA (Popular Movement for the Liberation of Angola), 55

Musambayi, Katumanga, 44

Muttahida Qaumi Movement (Pakistan), 95

Myanmar, 83, 90, 95, 109, 324, 380

  gender equality, financing for, 324

  political finance regulation in, 90, 380

  political parties in, 109

N

Namibia, 48, 50-1, 60, 382

  financial reporting in, 60

  foreign funding in, 48

  political finance regulation in, 48, 50-1, 382

  public funding in, 50-1

Nasdem party (Indonesia), 93, 98

National Action Party (PAN - Mexico),

National Congress for Timorese Reconstruction (Conselho Nacional de Reconstrucao de Timor, CNRT), 95, 100

National Democratic Institute (NDI), 133, 178, 331ff

National Election Commission (South Korea), 96-7, 101, 106

National Election Commission (Timor-Leste), 89

National Election Observation Committee of Nepal, 88

National Election Watch, 87

National Electoral Council (Colombia), 150

S

T

V